TOURISM
MARKETING

MANJULA CHAUDHARY

Professor
Department of Tourism and Hotel Management
Kurukshetra University

OXFORD
UNIVERSITY PRESS

OXFORD
UNIVERSITY PRESS

Oxford University Press is a department of the University of Oxford.
It furthers the University's objective of excellence in research, scholarship,
and education by publishing worldwide. Oxford is a registered trademark of
Oxford University Press in the UK and in certain other countries

Published in India by
Oxford University Press
22 Workspace, 2nd Floor, 1/22 Asaf Ali Road, New Delhi 110 002

© Oxford University Press 2010

The moral rights of the author have been asserted

First published 2010
Sixth impression 2020

ISBN-13: 978-0-19-806630-9
ISBN-10: 0-19-806630-9

Typeset in Palatino
by Spectrum Media
Printed in India by Repro books Limited, Thane

For product information and current price, please visit www.india.oup.com

Third-Party website addresses mentioned in this book are
provided by Oxford University Press in good faith and for information only.
Oxford University Press disclaims any responsibility for the material contained therein.

Preface

The subject of tourism marketing has matured with the growth of tourism and tourism economies around the world. Essentially an offshoot of marketing and service marketing, it has now come of age with its own set of concepts and frameworks. It has borrowed heavily from multiple disciplines, such as history, culture, and geography, which form the backbone of all tourism products. The focus of tourism marketing lies on the product having a legacy, an aura, and an authenticity that satisfy the tourists' needs. For example, attractive tourist destinations such as the Taj Mahal, the Ajanta Caves, Corbett National Park, and beaches in Goa. The creation of a memorable experience is the essence of tourism marketing.

Exploration is the first nature of mankind that makes people travel across the globe to reach a particular destination. However, it is restrained due to the complexities involved. Tourism marketing offers varied solutions in the form of packaged and customized tours. A product that best suits one's likings is chosen, with necessary customization. Relationship building among tourists and marketers is the key to achieving success of tourism marketing.

About the Book

Tourism Marketing is a comprehensive textbook designed for students of hotel management, tourism management, and tourism marketing. It is a unique and informative textbook covering all the concepts of tourism marketing—right from an introduction of tourism marketing to its process, promotion, pricing, environment and marketing mix, technological changes and the challenges involved therein. All the concepts are well supported by examples, illustrations, and cases.

Each chapter of the book deals with topics in detail and has the following reader-friendly features.

Learning objectives briefly explain what to expect when going through the text. They give an initial framework for reading. Introduction sets the conceptual framework for the main concepts in the chapter. The text explains the chapter theme lucidly and comprehensively with the help of flow charts, tables, and figures. Attempt has been made to quote a large number of examples from the Indian tourism marketing industry. Summary briefly explains the main text and will help readers to place ideas in a format. Key terms are the important words used in the main text and are defined for building necessary clarity. References quote sources of the text referred to and can be used to search more material on specific aspects. Review questions deal with concepts covered in the text and help the reader to review his or her level of knowledge.

Practice exercises are questions to test the learning of application of concepts. Projects consist of exercises that can be performed by field work or desk studies. Their basic aim is to bridge the gap between theory and practice and help readers in better learning of the subject. Case studies have been included in each chapter to help readers in further understanding the subject.

Following are the key features of this book:

- Provides numerous tables and figures to explain the processes, making learning more interesting
- Includes comprehensive case studies at the end of the book, illustrating real-life strategies related to tourism marketing
- Discusses marketing management information system (MMIS) and the various methods of demand forecasting

Besides students of tourism and hotel management, the book would also be useful to professionals in understanding the theory as well as practical applications of the subject.

Coverage and Structure

Divided into sixteen chapters, the book brings out the principle concepts of tourism marketing in a lucid and simple manner.

Chapter 1, *Introduction to Tourism Marketing*, draws a parallel between the evolution of tourism marketing and the different phases of growth of tourism. It also discusses the application of the principles of service marketing in tourism.

Chapter 2, *Challenges of Tourism Marketing*, explores the service–product continuum that tourism offers and the marketing strategies adopted therein.

Chapter 3, *Tourism Marketing Environment and Marketing Mix*, covers the different parts of environment and their impact on marketing, followed by marketing mix to deal with external contingencies.

Chapter 4, *Marketing Management Information System and Demand Forecasting*, talks about analysis of marketing environment and use of a system for dissemination of information to the managers for intelligent decision-making. The important managerial decision of estimation of the demand through forecasting techniques is also covered in this chapter.

Understanding of demand requires insight in the psyche of buyers and that forms the basis of Chapter 5, *Tourism Markets and Tourist Behaviour*. It includes different types of tourism markets, dynamics of tourist buying, and tourist decision-making models.

The insights of marketplace are followed by marketers' response strategies to reach there and Chapter 6, *Market Segmentation, Targeting, and Positioning*, discusses them.

Marketing strategies revolve around marketing mix and this book adopts the Seven Ps framework of Bitner suggested for services. Chapters 7 to 13 deal with these seven elements: *Tourism Product, Tourism Distribution, Tourism Pricing, Tourism Promotion, People in Tourism, Process in Tourism Marketing,* and *Physical Evidence.* All concepts and their respective strategies are covered in detail.

Chapter 14, *Market Competition and Competitive Tourism Marketing Strategies,* talks about the role of competition in marketing strategies. The nature of competition and the generic marketing strategies are discussed in the context of tourism.

Chapter 15, *Technology in Tourism Marketing*, highlights the role of technology in every aspect of tourism marketing, ranging from product design to delivery through e-travel.

Chapter 16, *Tourism Marketing and Development*, explores how tourism can be pro development if marketed suitably.

The book concludes with case studies of various renowned companies relevant to the field of tourism marketing.

Acknowledgements

This book would not have been possible without the support of a number of people.

I acknowledge the contribution of my teachers, students, and colleagues, whose queries and discussions helped me crystallize my thoughts on marketing. The understanding, reading, and research over the past 25 years have gone in the composition of this book.

The support of the Ministry of Tourism (Government of India), IN-TACH, Kuoni Academy (New Delhi), Cox and Kings (New Delhi), Oriental Journeys and Vacations (New Delhi), yatra.com, Sri Krishna Museum (Kurukshetra), and photojournalist Poras Chaudhary is acknowledged for providing the necessary case studies and advertisement copies. I would also like to thank my students working in tourism organizations who arranged the case studies needed for the book.

My son, Swapan, has been a constant source of help with his advice, proofreading, conceptual inputs, and constructive criticism. I also express my gratitude towards my husband, who showed tremendous support during my long hours of work.

The constant encouragement and continuous support of my parents and friends also helped me in bringing this long process of writing to an end.

Thank you all for your help in shaping my efforts.

Manjula Chaudhary

Brief Contents

Detailed Contents

CHAPTER 1

Introduction to Tourism Marketing

LEARNING OBJECTIVES

The focus of this chapter is to develop a framework for tourism marketing. In this chapter, we will explore the following basic issues of tourism and tourism marketing.

- How important is tourism for our economy?
- What are the major changes occurring in the tourism sector and how are these affecting the market and shaping the tourism industry?
- What is tourism marketing?
- How did tourism marketing evolve?
- What are the marketers' approaches towards tourism marketing?
- How do tourism marketing approaches relate to generic approaches of marketing?
- How is tourism marketing related to service marketing and product marketing?

The World Tourism Organization (WTO) defines tourism as activities of people who 'travel to and stay in places outside their usual environment for not more than one consecutive year for leisure, business and other purposes'. This definition recognizes tourism as comprising a broad range of activities, and goes beyond the common perception of tourism as being limited to holiday activity only.

INTRODUCTION

Tourism is a business activity connected with providing accommodation, services, and entertainment for people who are visiting a place for pleasure, recreation, leisure, business, and so on. It has become an integral part of today's lifestyle. Tourism activity has been taken up by mankind for very long in one form or the other. However, lately its effects are being increasingly felt at an individual level and on the society as a whole. Due to its widening and increasing impact on society and the consequent need to study and understand it, it is imperative to define what tourism is. It is also particularly important from the statistical point of view as what is being measured should be clear.

Tourism is referred to as an 'industry' and industries are traditionally defined in supply-side terms. Industries are defined in terms of groups of business enterprises which are engaged in a common type of economic activity. Economic activities are categorized according to some classification system and these categories identify the production or supply of a particular good or service. However, tourism cannot be defined in terms of the supply of particular goods/services. It is not the nature of the good/service which identifies an activity as tourism, but rather the circumstance of the consumer of the good/service. For example, if a person purchases a soft drink from a local store, the transaction is clearly not 'tourism activity'. However, if someone who is visiting that area for a holiday, purchases the same soft drink from the same store, the activity is tourism. The definition of 'tourism', therefore, relies on defining the type of consumer whose activity constitutes tourism, rather than the type of product consumed.

The ultimate objective on which this industry operates is 'positive tourism experience'. Tourism experience is derived from a complex mix of a number of products and services used for travel, stay, and recreation/business. Destination and facilities managers endeavour to make this experience worth remembering. Although experience has become an everyday buzzword, most businesses do not know how to change the core business processes to render customer experiences worthwhile. However, understanding the business logic behind the experience economy brings a significant competitive edge.

Experience management is a unique opportunity to create innovative business models for the benefit of tourism internationally.

For this, managers cultivate a marketing orientation throughout their organizations where customers are the focal point of every effort. This ensures tourist-friendly offers that result in higher satisfaction. In this book you will learn how such an orientation is managed.

TOURISM AND MODERN ECONOMIES

Tourism is emerging as an important activity and industry in modern times. International tourism travel has increased from 100 million in 1964 to 920 million in 2008. There has been continuous uptrend, except for 2009 when the number came down to 880 million because of global recession. In India, a total of 5.28 million foreign tourists visited in 2008, representing a 4 per cent year-on-year increase on 2007, when 5.08 million tourists arrived in the country. Growth was particularly strong between 2003, 2004, 2005, and 2006 when arrivals grew by 14.3 per cent, 26.8 per cent, 13.3 per cent, and 13.5 per cent respectively. This was also positive for foreign exchange earnings, which rose by 14.4 per cent to a total of Rs 50,730 crore in 2008.

Tourism plays an important role within the Indian economy. It is the third-largest generator of foreign exchange earnings. The World Travel and Tourism Council (WTTC) believes that tourism is expected to contribute 8.6 per cent (INR 5,532.5bn or US$ 117.9bn) to the gross domestic product (GDP) in 2010 and 9.0% (INR18,543.8bn or US$ 330.1bn) by 2020. The WTTC also predicted that the total demand for Indian tourism should grow at an annual rate of around 8 per cent a year between 2008 and 2017. However, it is a sector that has not been prioritized in terms of capital investment. Capital investment is estimated by the WTTC at INR 1,628.1bn, US$ 34.7bn, or 7.2%, and INR 6,137.2bn, US$ 109.3bn, or 7.7% of total investment by 2010 and 2020 respectively.

As per the United Nations World Tourism Organization (UNWTO), in 2008, international tourism has generated huge revenues of USD 944 billion at a global level and 11,832 million in India. It accounted for 255 million global jobs (7.8 per cent of global workforce) and 49.8 million jobs (9.24 per cent of workforce—direct and indirect) in India in 2007–2008.

Table 1.1 Tourism and Indian Economy, 2004–2012

Indicators of economy	Years								
	2004	2005e	2006e	2007e	2008f	2009f	2010f	2011f	2012f
Government expenditure (US$ billion)									
Individual	0.19	0.20	0.22	0.23	0.25	0.27	0.28	0.30	0.32
Collective	0.43	0.46	0.50	0.54	0.58	0.61	0.65	0.69	0.74
Capital investment (US$ billion)	10.71	11.98	12.92	13.87	15.00	15.98	16.98	18.08	19.45
Travel and tourism as a percentage of GDP	2.13	2.20	2.10	2.05	2.03	2.02	2.02	2.01	2.01
Employment in tourism sector ('000)	16,279	16,985	16,839	16,876	17,063	17,226	17,442	17,642	18,982
Tourism as a percentage of total employment (direct)	2.48	2.45	2.47	2.62	2.61	2.62	2.64	2.65	2.64

Note: e/f = estimate/forecast

(*Source:* World Travel and Tourism Council)

FACTORS SHAPING THE INDIAN TOURISM SECTOR

Tourism in the country is changing on parameters such as the number and profile of tourists, destination preferences, activities and expenditure on tours, tour party size and composition, etc. The implications of these changes are crucial for marketers and need to be continuously tracked and monitored. A number of factors contribute to the growth of the tourism sector in India. These are discussed as follows.

The Growing Middle Class

According to a McKinsey (2007) report, 'The "Bird of Gold": The Rise of India's Consumer Market,' by the year 2025, India's middle class is expected to swell almost 12-fold from its size of 50 million people to over 583 million—41 per cent of the population by the year 2025. This will trigger explosive growth in the consumer market, taking it to USD 1.5 trillion, making India the world's fifth largest consumer economy by 2025. Moreover, middle-class India's discretionary spending will rise to 70 per cent of all spending by 2025 from 39 per cent (at the time of survey).

This will have significant implications for the tourism industry as it is a well-recognized axiom that travel is the first priority of an income earner after the basic requirements of home, food, and essentials. Thus, as people acquire more disposable income, the demand for travel and tourism will grow exponentially. Also, there will be more such people with disposable incomes as the demographic transition in the country would produce a huge surge in people in the 20–60 years age group. This creates many opportunities for the tourism industry and meeting the needs of the expanding middle class will be the key to it in India.

Young Population

India is a young country with 44 per cent of its population belonging to the under-19 age bracket. This segment coupled with other factors, such as new age jobs, disposable incomes, and mobility, gives a very important base for tourism. A study commissioned by Cartoon Network in 2002 measured the 'pester power'—the influence children have on purchase decisions—of Indian kids as substantial (close to 40 per cent) and growing. Children's power in decision-making also extends to places to eat in, choice of menus, movies to watch, and destinations to travel to. Hong Kong recorded 28.17 million tourist arrivals in 2007, and one of the driving forces of this growth was Disneyland. It is time that the Indian travel industry, too, took notice of this important demographic segment and designed child-friendly facilities and manpower across the tourism spectrum. Entertainment for children

'Buddy Birds' show in Singapore's Jurong Park, the 'Dolphin Show' and 'Underwater World' in Sentosa, and 'Wetland Park' in Hong Kong specifically cater to the young population.

includes a whole gamut of indoor and outdoor activities under trained supervision, apart from the 'popularly conceived' notions of rides and video games. It also varies according to the age and the stage of a child's development. However, some features cut across all age groups such as safe water play areas along the beachfront, and imaginative and educative programs in collaboration with science museums/zoos.

New Industries and New Professionals

The information technology (IT), information technology enabled services (ITES), retail, insurance, and banking sectors are creating new jobs which pay higher salaries. As a result, we have a large number of young people with good income who are in the initial stages of the family life cycle. They also get to travel as part of their job engagements. This exposure makes them take tours whenever they can find time. Researches on international travel have found a link between tourism expenditure and incomes of source countries. This similar income elasticity of tourism expenditure is seen in the country.

Rise of Information Technology

Information technology in day-to-day applications has developed very fast after the year 2000. Various modes of communication, such as the phone and the Internet, have brought the world closer and booking tour packages or tickets is just a click away. This makes people plan and confirm their tour arrangements as per personal convenience. The psychological barrier of moving from agent to agent has been completely removed. Information systems in tourism, such as computer reservation, yield management, and tourism marketing, have been among the pioneers in leading edge technology applications and have driven the dynamics of development in tourism services. Tourism is regarded as one of the most successful applications of electronic commerce.

Government Policies

The government too has adopted a proactive approach towards tourism policy from the tenth five-year plan. It increased its budget to Rs 2,900 crore at 0.43 per cent of total budgetary support from 0.27 per cent (Rs 595 crore) in the ninth plan. In the eleventh five-year plan (2007-2012), the Ministry of Tourism proposes to continue supporting creation of world-class infrastructure in the country so that existing tourism products can be further improved and expanded to meet new market requirements and enhance the competitiveness of India as a tourist destination. In consultation with the state governments and the union territories, the Ministry of Tourism has identified several tourist circuits and destinations for integrated development.

The dynamics of the above forces has created a class of people who have money and want to travel. The challenge for the tour organizers is to tap this market.

WHAT IS TOURISM MARKETING?

A product can be 'ideas, goods, or services'. Since tourism is primarily a service-based industry, the principal products provided by tourism businesses are recreational experiences and hospitality. These are intangible products and much more difficult to market than tangible products. The intangible nature of the services makes quality control difficult but crucial. It also makes it more difficult for potential customers to evaluate and compare service offerings. In addition, instead of moving the product to the customer, the customer must travel to the product (area/ community). Travel forms a significant portion of the time and money spent in association with tourism experiences and is a major factor in people's decisions on whether or not to visit a place.

As an industry, tourism has many components comprising the overall 'travel experience'. Along with transportation, it includes accommodation, food and beverage services, shops, entertainment, aesthetics, and special events. It is rare for one business to provide all the variety of activities or facilities tourists need or desire. This adds to the difficulty of maintaining and controlling the quality of the experience. To overcome this hurdle, tourism-related businesses, agencies, and organizations need to work together to package and promote tourism opportunities and align their efforts to ensure consistency and excellence in product quality. To achieve this objective and keeping in mind the unique nature of this industry, tourism marketing must play a significant role.

Tourism marketing or the marketing in relation to tourism means the process of achieving voluntary exchanges between:

- *tourists* who want to appreciate/experience products and services
- *organizations* which put together and offer the products and services

In terms of tourists, marketing is concerned with:

- understanding their needs and desires (why they might visit, their motivations)
- which products they choose, when, how often, and how much (if they need to pay)

- how they feel after their visit/experience—expectations versus reality

In terms of organizations, marketing focuses on the following.

- What to offer and why?
- What is the appropriate charge for arranging the experience?
- When and to whom to make the offer available?

From the above, it follows that marketing involves a management decision process by organizations on visitor decision process. It also involves decision by visitors regarding the choice of tour and the organization conducting the tour. The two sets of decisions come together in a transaction.

According to Gilbert, 'Marketing within tourism becomes the application of marketing process to the specific characteristics which apply to the tourism industry and its products, (Gilbert 1992).

Marketing is defined by the British Institute of Marketing as, 'the management process responsible for identifying, anticipating and satisfying consumers, profitably'.

Kotler defines it as a social and managerial process by which individuals and groups obtain what they need and want through creating and exchanging products and values with others (Kotler 1995). The American Marketing Association (AMA) defines marketing as, 'an organizational function and a set of processes for creating, communicating and delivering value to customers and for managing customer relationships in ways that benefit the organization and its stakeholders.' The underpinnings of this definition are as follows.

Tourism marketing is the marketing concept applied to tourism. The assumptions of general marketing are good for tourism too.

- Marketing as organizational function and process: Marketing is a continuous activity. From a systems perspective, marketing consists of a set of organizational processes closely linked with other functions.
- Customer value: The customer shall get value from the goods when they are used. The marketer may put value in its offer but the customer may not perceive it as valuable. Therefore, the involvement of both is essential. For example, a package tour offers value in terms of cost saving but tourists may not appreciate it if they want flexibility.
- Managing customer relationship: Customer relationship is maintained through a process of creating, communicating, and delivering value to customers. The techniques of relationship marketing may be used to maintain the relations.

- Benefit to the organization and stakeholders: Both the creation of customer value and maintenance of customer relationship shall be beneficial to the organization and its stakeholders. A true marketing organization is one that provides consumer centricity and process efficiency. It is an organization that makes every facet of marketing work brilliantly in service of the business' overarching goals.

The above definitions of marketing have the following important propositions which are entirely relevant to tourism marketing.

- It is a managerial process.
- It emphasizes customer needs and wants as the starting point.
- Customer satisfaction is the final objective.

The WTO defines tourism marketing as a 'management philosophy that in the light of tourism demand makes it possible through research, forecasting and selection to place tourism products on the market most in line with the organization's purpose for the greatest benefit'.

In addition to this, tourism marketing is often explained as a type of service marketing because of the importance of service component in the overall tour experience.

Tourism marketing is a process through which both tourists and marketers enter into an exchange for certain benefits. Both parties evaluate the benefits beforehand. The marketer's evaluation as a corporate tends to be logical and organized and the same can be the case with group purchases by travel agents or business houses, but individual tourists can be emotional. Marketers attempt to make this exchange meaningful through proper management.

As a managerial process, tourism marketing involves planning, organizing, directing, and controlling of marketing activities. Planning entails deciding goals for the market (market position, market share, etc.), deciding action path (strategies, plans, policies, etc.) to achieve the set goals. Organizing is putting resources in terms of budgetary support, manpower, and facilities (market segmentation, marketing mix) for the realization of goals. Directing ensures that efforts are made in the right direction through internal marketing. Control checks ensure achievement of goals and help in correcting the managerial process for future.

This iterative process improves marketing through continuous feedback and learning. For example, ecotourism was offered as an alternative to the harmful effects of other industries, such as mining, but soon it became clear that it had its own drawbacks. That led to the emergence of marketing of sustainable tourism, community-based tourism, eco-certified ecotourism, etc.

NATURE OF TOURISM MARKETING

Marketing is defined from different perspectives that provide an understanding of the nature of marketing and tourism marketing.

Marketing is an activity

Marketing is explained as an activity that is carried by a marketer to give its offers to customers. For example, marketing of a tour package involves assembling the package, promoting it, and arranging it for sales. The focus in this perspective is to make the activity cost-effective and efficient.

Marketing is an economic process

Marketing generates revenues directly through transactions and indirectly through its multiplier effect and employment generation. Here efforts are made to maximize the economic benefits. Tourism marketing in its initial phase focused on economic benefits.

Marketing is a social process

Marketing as a social process involves interaction and relationship between participants coming from different walks of life and society. Social processes make host–guest relationship an important part of tourism marketing. Right to travel and pro-poor tourism have developed in response to different social processes.

Marketing is a managerial process

Marketing is considered to be a business function that undertakes all managerial functions of planning, organizing, directing, and controlling to carry out different activities.

Overall, marketing can be combined together. It can be economic, social, managerial process and activity at the same time. However, its different natures may dominate at different times.

PROCESS OF TOURISM MARKETING

Tourism marketing is a cyclic process that begins with the understanding of drives, needs, wants, and demands of tourists who are satisfied through suitable offers by entering into an exchange process with marketers. The feedback of exchange is used by both the parties for future relations (Fig. 1.1).

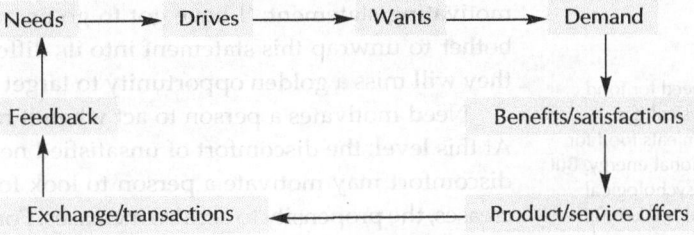

Fig. 1.1 Tourism Marketing Process

The different elements of a cyclic process give an insight into tourism marketing.

Traditional marketing advises to 'find a need and fill it'. Using that approach to create a marketing strategy is too limiting and can even lead to a disastrous plan. To design a well-focused marketing and advertising plan, an advertiser must first understand some basic facts about marketing psychology and buyer behaviour.

Here is the most important fact: People do not want a product or service. They want answers to problems, solutions to needs, pathways to wants, a secret door to their heart's desires, and so on.

Each consumer has slightly different needs and motivations. But groups of consumers share some common motivations. For example, one common motivation of tourists is to get away from their respective places of residence for some time.

The adventurous ones are motivated to have a perfect thrill. Nature lovers are motivated to take tours so that they can spend some time in the midst of natural surroundings. It is these inner psychological motivations, common to target buyers that marketers must ferret out and use.

> Kerela does not sell ayurveda; it sells health. Himachal Pradesh sells romance and not hills. Understanding the real motivations and needs of buyers is the first step in creating a successful marketing strategy.

Understanding Needs, Drives, Wants, and Demands of Tourists

An insight into the why, what, when, where, how, etc., of tourist behaviour helps in delivering desired satisfaction. This begins with the identification of their needs, drives, wants, and demands.

Need

Need is the felt gap between the existing and the desired state. Needs are simply things that we think we must have. If we are hungry, we need some food. If we are sick, we need some medicine. If we must go on a tour, we need a car—but we do not need a Mercedes; any reliable car will satisfy this need. A Mercedes would satisfy a different type of motivation. Buyers often unconsciously wrap up different motivations into one general motivating statement: 'I have got to go on a tour.' If marketers do not bother to unwrap this statement into its different, specific motivations, they will miss a golden opportunity to target customers' needs.

Need motivates a person to act when it reaches the threshold level. At this level, the discomfort of unsatisfied need is very high. The lesser discomfort may motivate a person to look for information but as it increases, the propensity to act also increases. For example, a hungry person can wait for food for some time but not for very long. Needs can be both physical and psychological.

> The need for food is physical if a person eats food for additional energy. But it is psychological if food is taken for socialization and to entertain friends.

Marketers identify the needs of people that direct their tourism behaviours and offer alternatives to satisfy these needs. Maslow's framework can be used to understand these needs. It divides the human needs into five categories of physical, safety, love, esteem, and self-actualization, which are arranged in a hierarchy (Maslow 1943). First, the efforts are to satisfy the lower-level needs and after this, upward progression is made. Physical needs are the basic needs of food, shelter, etc. Tourists need a minimum acceptable level of food and accommodation at a place before travel. Safety need is reflected in the form of tourists' need for law and order. That makes tourists avoid places of war, terrorism, and conflicts. Need for love is the acceptance of tourists in the host society. Tourists prefer open societies than closed ones. Esteem needs are tourists' expectation that the host society would understand their importance and recognize the same. Self-actualization is undertaking trips that have always been dreamt such as travelling to outer space, *Char Dham Yatra*, and hajj pilgrimage.

Marketers can intervene in need recognition of tourists by presenting an impressive picture of a desired state or by creating the dissatisfaction with the existing one. This intervention can trigger the act of tourists. An appreciation of the nature of needs helps marketers in handling needs better. The important features of needs are as follows.

- Needs are never fully satisfied but only partially satisfied.
- New needs emerge if old needs are satisfied.
- Similar needs can be satisfied in many ways.

As a result, people always have unsatisfied needs. Marketers need to discover even the latent needs, as these decide the rest of the buying behaviour.

Drive

Drive is the force created by needs. Unsatisfied needs create tension that drive the consumers to look for solutions. These solutions take the form of specific products. Buyers search for the best solution for their needs. The stimuli present in the environment give direction to drives.

Want

Want is the expression of need in the specific form. Wants are things which you would like, but which are not really necessary. They are things which you can get along without. You may want an ice cream cone or a tour to Switzerland, but you do not need them. You may want a new dress or a tie, but you have a dozen perfectly good dresses or ties in your closet at present. People sometimes convince themselves that they 'need' something, when it is really just a 'want'. Many purchases are made to satisfy this type of motivation. It is important to recognize the difference between a buyer's 'needs' and 'wants' because the resulting psychological stimulators used in advertising are different.

The need for hunger can be expressed in wanting Indian, Continental, or any other food. The need for recreation can be fulfilled through participating in sports, going on tours, watching movies and plays, socializing, etc. Marketers fit into the want framework either by redesigning offers or by assisting buyers in learning about new forms of products. The case of McDonald's illustrates this point. It has introduced *aloo-tikki* burger in the Indian market. The *aloo-tikki* fits into the traditional eating styles and new learning is about the burger. Most local adaptations of products and services centre on wants.

Demand

Demand is want accompanied by the purchasing power. It decides if the buyer has enough money to purchase. Demand changes with prices, substitutes, marketing efforts, inflation levels, income, etc. Demand can be created by building the purchasing power. Price reductions and credit facilities assist in it. For example, demand for air travel has gone up in India with the entry of budget airlines and reduced fares. Outbound tourism has grown because of the reduced prices of foreign tours and financing options available through banks.

Benefits and satisfactions

The needs and wants of tourists can be satisfied by offering desired benefits. For example, the need for recreation can be met through leisure tours within the country or abroad at a number of destinations. Marketers find the benefits tourists are looking for and build these in their offers. The key to a successful marketing plan lies in matching up the buyer's strongest needs, wants, desires, and fears with the product's strongest attributes that can satisfy those motivations. Advertising and other marketing media should stimulate those motivations in the buyer's mind, then promise that the product or service will satisfy them, no matter how little or loosely related to the product they may seem.

No tour can be sold in a terrorism-affected area, as the need for safety is more important than the need to get away from routine. Marketing which sells satisfaction instead of the product will pull customers in like a magnet.

Tourism Product–Service Offer

Suitable offers are made to satisfy needs, wants, and demands of tourists. Usually, these are in the form of packages that combine a number of individual offers into a ready-made or tailor-made bundle.

Packaging gives a choice of different permutations and combinations to tourists. A suitable combination as per the needs of tourists is designed that may combine many tangible and intangible benefits. These can range from budget tours, hotels, and airlines on one hand, to luxury tours, hotels, and airlines on the other. Overall, packaging is an innovative task of deciding components and combining these for maximizing profits.

Exchange and Transaction

Transaction is defined as exchanging values. The tourists and marketers exchange values with each other. The marketers offer products–services or packages and the tourists pay in return. This exchange depends upon perception of value by each party. Tourists will not purchase a package if they feel that it is not giving value for money or marketers too will not sell if they fail to get the right price.

Feedback

After the exchange process, both parties will gain experience for future exchanges. This experience is a feedback for the marketer to know if tourists are satisfied and for the tourists to decide about further exchanges. Marketers use the feedback to achieve their marketing goals.

GROWTH OF TOURISM MARKETING

Tourism marketing evolved with the growth of tourism. The concept of tourism is very old, but its modern organized form started in the late eighteenth century. Earlier, travel was undertaken for business and religious purposes. Some people also travelled for recreation. Tourism as a full-fledged business did not exist. Its marketing started with the first organized tours offered by Thomas Cook in 1841.

Acceptance of marketing in tourism industry has been slow. Roger March observes 'Given the importance of tourism, it is ironic that the management discipline of marketing should be underutilized and even misunderstood by government policy makers and private tourism practitioners, (March 1994). The slowness of the tourism industry in embracing rich managerial and strategic insights that marketing offers is potentially damaging, because it inhibits both the growth prospects of tourism industry as a whole and the commercial viability of its individual participants.'

But later, when tourism marketing was adopted its orientations changed over time.

Evolution of Tourism Marketing

Tourism marketing and its orientation has changed with the growth of tourism. As tourism passed through different phases, so did marketing. Internationally, tourism came of age in 1950 and since then has seen a continuous change in the approach towards its development. Tourism marketing too followed a similar line.

The stages of tourism development and the corresponding marketing approaches are discussed below.

Boosterism approach in the 1950s

It was the beginning of modern tourism and the emphasis was on boosting the tourism activity. This approach was based on the following assumptions towards tourism.

- Tourism is inherently good and should be developed.
- Cultural and natural resources should be exploited for tourism development.

The focus was on giving boost to tourism through proper facilitation and overcoming the obstacles. The following issues were the focus areas.

- How can more tourists be attracted and accommodated?
- How can the obstacles to the growth of tourism be overcome?
- How can hosts be convinced to be receptive to tourists?

The marketing strategy at this time was destination centric and all efforts were made to develop destinations and the related infrastructure.

This is very similar to production and product orientations of marketing that assume that available, affordable durable, and quality products sell.

Economic planning approach in the 1960s

As a result of the efforts of the earlier phases, the economic potential of tourism was well understood and new assumptions towards tourism were as follows.

- Tourism is like any other industry.
- Tourism can be used to create jobs, earn foreign exchange, and improve terms of trade, encourage regional development, and overcome economic disparities.

The focus shifted to developing tourism as a vehicle of growth for providing economic value through maximization of income and as an employment multiplier.

The marketing orientation at this phase continued to remain destination/attraction oriented for its economic benefits. However, an additional dimension of selling the destination highlighting its benefits was adopted.

Physical and spatial approach in the 1970s and the 1980s

The earlier approaches resulted in the massive growth of tourism. Mass tourism was not without consequences and its negative impacts on environment became visible and well known. This changed the earlier assumption of it being inherently good and harmless and new assumptions were formed. These were as follows.

- Tourism is a resource user. It exploits and destroys the natural resources used as tourist attractions.
- There has to be an ecological basis for its development to preserve the natural resources and tourist attractions.
- Tourism development can be geographically distributed to reduce the impacts.

The approach adopted for tourism development at this stage included the following.

- Understanding the physical carrying capacity of a destination.
- Manipulating travel patterns and visitor flow through visitor management to keep tourism within limits.
- Dispersal of tourist traffic according to the environmental sensitivity of natural environments.

Marketing orientation now was environment focused and destinations were marketed for their ability to maintain the environments and pass these to the next progeny.

Burkart and Medlik (1981) identified that marketing assumed a new significance in the 1970s that was linked to overproduction within the airlines and hotel industry and also the rapid growth of inclusive tours in Europe. By the 1980s, companies discovered the proper role of marketing and customer orientation was adopted. Calatone and Mazanae (1991) observed that tourism is one of the last industries to experience the change from seller's to buyer's market.

Community approach in the 1990s

As tourism continued to develop, its social impacts were noticed. Particularly the local communities felt alienated. They were inconvenienced by the growth of mass tourism and were not in a position to decide on tourism development. As a result, tourism was opposed. It led to the focus on the following assumptions.

- Local community control on tourism development in the area is needed.

- Need for balanced development of tourism and search for alternatives to 'mass' tourism.
- Social impacts of tourism on a community and their attitudes towards tourism should be understood.

Marketing orientation at this time became societal, where active role was given to society as tourism exchange no longer remained confined to tourists and marketers.

Sustainable approach in the 1990s

Large-scale tourism development forced tourism planners to think of tourism development in a more holistic manner where the economic, environmental, and sociocultural issues could be balanced. The concept of sustainable tourism was adopted for this purpose.

The assumption for this approach is that a suitable balance must be established between environmental, economic, and sociocultural dimensions of tourism development to ensure its long-term sustainability. Marketing orientation too became socio-environmental to balance the interests of tourists, marketers, and the environment.

TOURISM MARKETING ORIENTATIONS AND MARKETING MANAGEMENT ORIENTATIONS

A brief discussion on orientations of marketing will help in understanding their relevance to tourism as well. Tourism marketing has also witnessed similar approaches, though it developed later and faster.

Marketing orientations and approaches to marketing have developed over time in response to the changing environments. The following stages or phases are identified with it.

Production Approach

The basic assumption of this approach is that buyers will buy the products that are available and affordable. This puts the focus on production efficiencies to mass produce goods. This approach was very useful in the initial stages of industrialization, when factory production replaced cottage industries and goods were produced on a large scale. Scientific management practices developed to assist in increasing production. This approach worked well at that time because buyers were getting better products at lesser prices. But this did not satisfy buyers for very long as after some time buyers wanted something more. This led to the transition of marketers to the next stage.

Product Approach

This approach rests on the assumption that buyers will purchase products for quality, features, and durability. As a result, the focus shifted to product innovation. This phase was marked by the development of new feature-packed products. This approach too worked well for some time but later it was observed that buyers were no longer purchasing for this reason alone. This forced marketers to change their approach and a new approach of sales was identified.

Sales Approach

This approach assumed that buyers will not buy unless backed by proper selling efforts. At this time, all efforts were made to develop selling techniques. These techniques helped in selling goods to the markets. But this too was criticized after some time for its seller centrism and so marketers made a shift towards buyer centrism.

Marketing Approach

For the first time, the buyer was placed at the centre point and the purpose was to find out his/her needs and wants and to develop products accordingly. All the earlier approaches helped in selling what was produced. This approach began with the identification of buyers' needs and offered satisfaction in the form of suitable products. It considered marketing to be an activity between buyers and sellers. But soon the impacts of marketing on ecology and society became visible and it was felt that these issues need to be an integral part of marketing. Consequently, societal orientation developed.

Marketing Management Approach/Societal Approach

This approach tries to balance the interests of the buyers, the marketers, and the society. This not only begins with the assessment of the needs of buyers and delivers satisfaction but also takes into account the society. Marketing activities are carried out in a socially acceptable manner.

Societal marketing is much more relevant in tourism. Chris Ryan (1991) says that it needs to pay attention to the following.

- Enhancement of visitor satisfaction which may involve the recognition that social carrying capacities are less than the physical carrying capacities.
- Acceptance that growth in visitor number is inconsistent with the objectives of maintaining environments and tourist satisfaction.

- More careful marketing of an attraction in the sense of matching tourist zones with types of tourists and their needs.
- The establishment of alternative criteria of success so that more number of tourists are not seen as the goal of tourism marketing, but rather the achievement of high rates of satisfaction.
- The residents as well as tourists are consumers of tourism. The interests of residents need a wider, difficult sociological and socio-psychological definition of interest than a simple economic one.

The discussion on approaches to marketing must have set you thinking about the most suitable approach. As a matter of fact, all the approaches are suitable under different conditions. But as the market develops, marketing management becomes acceptable. Marketing management is not acceptable in undeveloped areas where buyers are not aware about the issues of ecology and do not want to pay higher prices for environment-friendly products.

As a result, all the different approaches are practised in different parts of the world. A company may follow different approaches for different markets. For example, a company may follow varied environmental norms of the host countries than its own benchmarks.

In different approaches, the focus and the roles of marketers and consumers is different as shown in Table 1.2.

Tourism marketing also uses similar approaches though the shift from production to societal has been quick.

Table 1.3 presents a comparison between the orientations of marketing and tourism marketing. It shows that boosterism focuses on production and product, while economic planning focuses on sales by highlighting the benefits of tourism. Spatial planning, community-based, and sustainable approaches towards tourism development take into account the

Table 1.2 Marketing Approaches and Roles of Marketers and Consumers

		Production Approach	Product Approach	Sales Approach	Marketing Approach	Marketing Management
Focus		Available and affordable product	Features of the product	Selling to buyers	Offering products after need identification	Offers that balance interests of buyers, sellers, and society
Role	Sellers	Active	Active	Active	Active	Active
	Buyers	Passive	Passive	Passive	Active	Active

Table 1.3 Orientations of Marketing and Tourism Marketing

Marketing	Tourism Marketing
Production	Boosterism
Product	Boosterism
Sales	Economic planning
Marketing	Economic planning
Marketing management	Spatial planning, community-based, sustainable approaches

environmental aspects of tourism. In tourism, the impacts of boosting were soon realized because of the nature of impacts, and transition to more responsible approaches was faster. But in many developing countries boosterism is still followed for quick gains.

SERVICES AND THEIR MARKETING

Tourism as an offer is a mix of goods and services. But it is often categorized under services because of their dominance in most tourism offers. It has borrowed a lot from services marketing. An understanding of services and their marketing will help in learning about tourism marketing.

What are Services?

Services are defined as, 'activities, benefits and satisfactions, which are offered for sale or are provided in connection with the sale of goods' (American Marketing Association, 1960). Quinn, Baruch, and Paquette (1987) comment that 'Services include all economic activities whose output is not a physical product or construction, is generally consumed at the time it is produced, and provides added value in forms (such as convenience, amusement, timeliness, comfort or health) that are essentially intangible concerns of its first purchaser'. According to Grönroos (1990), services are 'an activity or series of activities of more or less intangible nature that normally, but not necessarily, take place in interactions between the customer and the service employees and/or physical resources or goods and/or systems of the service provider, which are provided as solutions to customers problems'.

To put it simply, services are the benefits that one party offer to another party. Banking, insurance, retail, education, health, tourism, and

Services grow when people have paying capacity to outsource and no time to work themselves. The increasing participation of women in workforce has created babysitting and housekeeping as separate services. Rising number of old people in the population has increased the demand for better health facilities.

hospitality are some of the important services in modern society. The services increase with the development of economies. India has a 55 per cent contribution to GDP from services.

The list of services can be long but a suitable classification system will help in knowing the different types of services.

Types of Services

Services can be classified on the following criteria and the categories can be overlapping.

Types of markets

The markets that are offered services form the basis of this classification.

Consumer services: These are targeted at final users. Tour packages sold and managed for tourists by travel agencies is an example of consumer services. The same packages when sold by the tour operators to travel agents make these business services. While the components of services may be the same, the difference is visible at the time of delivery or execution of services. A travel agent would require an entirely different interaction and relation with tourists than any other buyer.

Business services: These services are offered to institutions and middlemen who may use these or add further value and convert these to consumer services. Tour operators and travel agents get business services from principals such as hotels, airlines, attractions, etc. When the tour operators further assemble these and sell packages to tourists, these services become consumer services.

Degree of labour intensiveness

Depending on the fact that performance of services requires less people or more, services can be categorized like the following.

People based: These services require a high participation of people performers in the delivery of services. For example, large number of service staff is required in sit-down meals.

Equipment based: The services can be performed by machines without the immediate presence of any service provider. Booking online tickets, tele check-in, and check-in in automatic hotels are examples of such services.

Degree of customer contact/involvement

The services can be planned in a way where the customer develops very little contact with the service process and remains at the end of the chain to get the benefit. It is also possible to involve the customer in the process and allow him/her to be a participant beneficiary.

Low contact/involvement: It allows very little role to the tourist/customer. A packaged tour falls in this category as the tourist does not participate with the seller in deciding the itinerary.

High contact/involvement: In customized tours, tourists sit with the agent and both work together on the itinerary. This gives a chance to the tourists to decide places, duration of tour, mode of transport, etc. The tourist also feels empowered in such situations.

Skills of the service provider

Services can be provided by both professionals and non-professionals.

Professionals Professionals are qualified people and accepted as such for the performance of services. Doctors, lawyers, accountants, and so on are some professionals in India who have to take permission/licence from their concerned bodies to deliver the services. Tourism service providers are not yet classified as professionals in India. Also, there exists no professional body to regulate their code of conduct in the interest of the profession. However, travel agencies are registered by the Ministry of Tourism, Government of India and they also get attached to certain associations such as International Air Transporters Association (IATA), Indian Association of Tour Operators (IATO), and Travel Agents Association of India (TAAI). Similarly, hotels are graded into star categories by the Ministry of Tourism. This ensures a degree of professionalism in their services. Lately, tourism organizations are also employing more and more qualified tourism people, thus making these almost professionals.

Non-professionals If services are delivered by people who have neither studied the subject formally nor have undergone any prescribed training, they are called non-professional. It is quite common in tourism, where unregistered travel agencies and non-star hotels are present.

Goals of the services provider

The objectives of the service provider can be the basis of classification. Two common goals can be to make profit or to function on non-profit basis.

Profit goal Most tourism concerns are commercial and operate for profit. Hotels, airlines, tour-operators are some examples.

Non-profit Some organizations working for philanthropic purposes or other social interests may give profit a secondary consideration. Indian

Railways carry large number of tourists every day but the rates are not guided by profits.

Service marketing means identifying the needs of potential buyers and selling need-satisfying solutions in the forms of services in a socially and environmentally acceptable manner. Services and their marketing developed much later but these were identified as part of products package much earlier. In case of marketing of goods, it was observed that if all competitive products are almost equal, then something extra should be offered to attract buyers. Services were found to provide this extra edge. This led to the marketing of products enveloped in services. But with increasing incomes of the consumers, services emerged as complete offers that needed to be marketed. The principles of general marketing were used for the services with modifications to suit the services. Tourism as an offer mixes goods and services both and is sold as such. Its marketing borrowed the understanding of both services and goods marketing. It can be marketed as product dominated or service dominated, depending upon its nature. This makes the study of services and their marketing a prerequisite to understand tourism marketing.

Services are marketed as potential intangible benefits and sold as promises that cannot be verified in advance, but a belief gets attached to the promises based on the image of the marketer. Good medical services, education, effective child care, etc. are all such examples. As a result, marketing strategies revolve around service features with the added effort of highlighting the product component used in services. For example, features such as air-conditioned buildings, good location, etc. are often mentioned.

In the next chapter, you will study the features of services, related marketing challenges and the strategies used.

SUMMARY

Tourism is emerging as an important activity and industry in modern times. International tourism travel had increased from 100 million in 1964 to 920 million in 2008. In India tourism accounted for 255 million global jobs (7.8 per cent of the global workforce) and 49.8 million jobs (9.24 per cent of workforce—direct and indirect) in India in 2007–08. A number of factors, such as the growing middle class, young population, new industries and professionals, information technology, and government policies, have contributed to the growth of tourism in India. The advantages of tourism can be realized with the help of tourism marketing. 'Tourism marketing' is the concept of marketing applied to tourism. 'Marketing' is defined as an organizational function and a set of processes for creating, communicating, and delivering value to the customers and for managing customer relationships in ways that benefit the organization and its stakeholders. Tourism marketing is a management philosophy, which in the light of tourism demand makes it possible through research, forecasting, and selection, to place tourism products in the market most in line with the organization's purpose for the greatest benefit. This is an activity, a managerial process, as well as a social and an economic process. It can be understood as a cyclic process that begins with the needs and wants of tourists that are satisfied through suitable offers by an exchange process. Tourism marketing has developed with the growth of the tourism industry. The different stages in the growth of this industry are boosterism, economic planning, physical and spatial planning, community approach, and sustainable approach. The different stages mark a change of focus from a maximum use of resources to a balanced use. Tourism marketing too changed orientation from the marketer to the tourists and

the society. Marketing has also passed through similar phases of production, product, sales, marketing, and marketing management. Thus, a clear similarity exists between the approaches of marketing and tourism marketing.

Tourism as an offer is a mix of products and services, where the service element dominates and the knowledge of services and their marketing helps in understanding tourism as well. 'Services' are defined as the benefits offered. These are marketed as potential intangible benefits and sold as promises that cannot be verified in advance. However, a belief gets attached to the promises based on the image of the marketer. Tourism marketing sells services as intangibles bundled with products or tangibles.

KEY TERMS

Boosterism approach It is the approach towards tourism development that assumes that tourism is inherently good and cultural and natural resources should be exploited for its development.

Community approach This approach assumes that local communities should play a very important role in tourism development.

Demand Demand is probable sales under specific marketing conditions. It is also explained as want accompanied by purchasing power.

Economic planning approach This tourism development approach assumes that tourism should be developed as a vehicle of growth for providing economic value through maximization of income and as employment multiplier.

Marketing It is the management process responsible for identifying, anticipating, and satisfying consumers profitably.

Marketing approach This approach considers that marketing begins with the identification of the

buyers' needs and offers satisfaction through suitable products.

Marketing management approach This approach tries to balance the interests of the buyers, the marketers, and the society. This approach not only begins with the assessment of the needs of the buyers and delivers satisfaction, but also takes into account the concerns of the society.

Need Need is the felt gap between the existing and the desired state. Need motivates a person to act when it reaches the threshold level.

Physical and spatial planning approach In tourism development, this approach considers tourism as a resource user which should be geographically distributed to reduce its impacts.

Product approach This marketing approach rests on the assumption that buyers will purchase products for their quality, features, and durability.

Production approach This approach towards marketing assumes that buyers will buy the products that are available and affordable.

Services Activities, benefits, and satisfactions, which are offered for sale or are provided in connection with the sale of goods are called services.

Services marketing Services marketing is identifying the needs of the potential buyers and selling need-satisfying service solutions in a socially and environmentally acceptable manner.

Sustainable approach This approach assumes that a suitable balance must be established between environmental, economic, and sociocultural aspects of tourism development to guarantee its long-term sustainability.

Tourism marketing It is a management philosophy, which in the light of tourism demand, makes it possible through research, forecasting, and selection, to place tourism products in the market, most in line with the organization's purpose for the greatest benefit.

Want Want is the expression of need in a specific form.

EXERCISES

REVIEW QUESTIONS

1. What is the importance of tourism in the Indian economy? Explain the factors that have led to its growth?
2. What is marketing, services marketing, and tourism marketing? Distinguish the three.
3. What have been the different phases of the growth of tourism? How did the orientation towards marketing change along these phases?
4. How is the marketing approach of boosterism phase different from the sustainable approach phase?
5. Compare the marketing during the community-based, ecological, and sustainable phases.

PRACTICE EXERCISES

1. Study the National Tourism Policy, 2002 and discuss the type of marketing orientation suggested in the policy.

2. Read the guidelines regarding visitors' behaviour in the national parks in India. How can these be incorporated in the marketing plan?

PROJECTS

1. What type of marketing is used for ecotourism destinations? How is it different from nature tourism? Discuss with the help of the case of the Himalayas.
2. Collect the marketing brochures of different types of destinations. Study these and prepare a comparative table of the marketing orientations.
3. Browse the UNWTO website to study the following focus area, 'Climate Change and Tourism'. What are its implications for marketing?

REFERENCES

Burkart, A. J., S. Medlik 1981, *Tourism, Past, Present and Future*, Heinemann, London.

Calatone, R.J., J. A. Mazanae 1991, 'Marketing Management and Tourism', Annals of Tourism Research, vol.18, no.1, pp.101-119.

Cooper, Chris, et al. 1993, *Tourism Principles and Practice*, Pitman Publishing, London.

Eilat, Yair and Liran Einav 2004, 'Determinants of International Tourism: A Three Dimensional Panel Data Analysis', Applied Economics, vol. 36, no.12, pp.1315-1327.

Gilbert, D.C. 1992, 'Tourism Marketing—Its Emergence and Establishment,' in Cooper, C.P. (ed.), *Progress in Tourism, Recreation and Hospitality Management*, pp. 77-90, CBS Publishers, New Delhi.

Go, Frank M. 1996, 'A Conceptual Framework for Managing Global Tourism and Hospitality Marketing', Tourism Recreation Research, vol.21, no.2, pp.37-43.

Grönroos Christian 2006, 'On Defining Marketing: Finding a New Roadmap for Marketing,' *Marketing Theory,* vol.6, no. 4, pp. 395–417.

Gronroos, C. 1990, *Service Management and Marketing: Managing the Moments of Truth in Service Competition,* Lexington Books.

Gummesson, Evert 2007, 'Exist Services Marketing—Enter Service Marketing', Journal of Customer Behaviour, vol.6, no.2, pp.113-141.

Holloway, J.C., and R.V. Plant 1988, Marketing for Tourism, Pitman, London.

Houston, Franklin S. 1986, 'The Marketing Concept: What it is and What it is Not', Journal of Marketing, vol.50, pp.81-87.

Kotler, Philip 1995, *Marketing Management—Analysis, Planning, Implementation and Control,* Prentice Hall of India, New Delhi.

Kotler, Philip, John Bowen, and James Makens 2004, *Marketing for Hospitality and Tourism,* Pearson Education, Delhi.

Lally, Anne Marie and Brian Fynes 2006, Annual Conference of the Irish Academy of Management, Tourism Track, Competitive Paper.

Lovelock, Christopher and Jochen Wirtz 2004, *Services Marketing—People, Technology, Strategy,* Pearson Education, Delhi.

March, Roger 1994, 'Tourism Marketing Myopia', Tourism Management, vol. 15, no.6, pp. 411-415.

Maslow, A.H. 1943, 'A Theory of Human Motivation,' Psychological Review, 50(4), 370–396.

McKinsey Global Institute 2007, 'The "Bird of Gold": The Rise of India's Consumer Market.'

Middleton, V. T. C. 1988, *Marketing in Travel and Tourism,* Heinemann, Oxford.

National Tourism Policy 2002, Ministry of Tourism, Government of India.

Nordic Innovation Centre 2008, June, Experience Design in City Tourism.

Ryan, Chris 1991, 'Tourism and Marketing—A Symbiotic Relationship', Tourism Management, vol. 12, no. 2, pp. 101-111.

Tosun, Cevat and Carson L. Jenkins 1998, 'The Evolution of Tourism Planning in Third-world Countries: A Critique,' Progress in Tourism and Hospitality Research, vol 4, pp.101–114.

UNWTO World Tourism Barometer 2006, June, vol.4 no.2.

Webster Jr, Fredrick E. 1992, 'The Changing Role of Marketing in the Corporation', Journal of Marketing, vol.56, no.4, pp.1-17.

Witt, Stephen F. and Luiz Moutinho 1989, *Tourism Marketing and Management Handbook,* Prentice Hall International, Hemel Hempstead, UK.

WTO 1995, Technical Manual-Collection of Tourism Expenditure Statistics.

Website References

Tourism Highlights 2009, www.world-tourism.org, accessed on 20 March 2010.

Tourism Statistics at a Glance 2008, Ministry of Tourism, Government of India.

WTTC 2002, 'The Impact of Travel & Tourism on Jobs and the Economy', www.wttc.org, accessed on 10 January 2006.

CASE STUDY

SUSTAINABLE MARKETING—RAGHURAJPUR IN ORISSA

Raghurajpur is a small village in Orissa on the tourist route of Bhubaneshwar, Puri, and a World Heritage Site of Konark. It has 123 households of artisans, craftsmen, and performers, and is renowned for its traditional paintings (*pattachitra*), ancient temple dance form, *Gotipua,* and 15 national and state awardees in various arts forms. But over time, traditional occupations based on mural paintings and crafts skills lost economic viability and many painters turned to agriculture. Most of the village population lived well below the poverty line.

Homes and Studios of Artisans
(*Photo Courtesy:* INTACH)

Indian National Trust for Art and Cultural Heritage (INTACH) took up the village of Raghurajpur in Orissa as part of the Endogenous Tourism Project/Rural Tourism Scheme of the Ministry of Tourism, Government of India, and United Nations Development Programme (UNDP) to develop tourism potential and promote rural India. The focus was on sustainable tourism as a tool for heritage conservation and socioeconomic development of an entire village. It prepared an integrated development plan with the primary objective to generate additional employment opportunities through increasing tourism, strength-

Craft Centre of Raghurajpur Village
(*Photo Courtesy:* INTACH)

ening infrastructure and facilities, and marketing local products.

Tourism facilities, such as the Heritage Interpretation Centre, tourist lodge, and restaurant managed by the local community, street signage, open air theatre, and nature walks, were provided. Besides, locals were trained to work as information officers, guides, and also to work for the tourist lodge.

The marketing strategies adopted included the following.

• Publication and widespread distribution of an attractive brochure
• Encouraging corporate clients, hotels, and private individuals to commission artists for wall painting projects
• Website for Raghurajpur
• Collaboration with researchers, architects, and designers
• Collaboration with art schools
• Marketing to student groups

The results of the project are satisfactory in terms of:

• increased employment opportunities,
• improved living standards,
• preservation and continuation of social and cultural values,
• equitable distribution of socioeconomic benefits among the entire communities,
• economic and social upliftment of women, and
• increased tourism from 6,080 visitors in 2001 to 34,880 in 2005.

The basics elements of this project are as follows.

1. Complete participation of the community at all stages
2. Conservation as a tool to preserve the community's identity, promote social development, and improve the quality of its lives

3. Close partnerships with national and local government bodies as well as with international funding agencies

(*Source:* INTACH)

DISCUSSION QUESTIONS

1. How are the basics of sustainable marketing built in Raghurajpur project? What are the dangers of its slipping into other marketing modes?
2. What factors have favoured sustainable marketing in this project?
3. What are the advantages of sustainable marketing in Raghurajpur?
4. If this project is replicated at other places, would it succeed?

CHAPTER 2

Challenges of Tourism Marketing

LEARNING OBJECTIVES

Tourism marketing is different from the marketing of products or services. Tourism offers are hybrid in nature because of the presence of the features of both goods and services. Its marketing is developed around the combined features, i.e., the product marketing options for the products part and the service marketing for the services part. This gives a unique character to tourism marketing.

In this chapter, you will learn how the marketing of tourism takes into account its basic features. The following are discussed in detail.

• The nature of tourism offers
• Issues and challenges in adopting general marketing practices to tourism
• Tourism marketing strategies

INTRODUCTION

'Tourism' is defined as the movement of people from one place to another for leisure, pleasure, business, etc. This movement is facilitated by three basic components: accommodation, travel/transport, and attraction. Each component further provides a vast array of options. It is very much possible for a tourist to get a ready-made package or a customized offer. Tourism offers can be service or product dominated. Most offers contain a combination of the two and can be placed on a scale between pure services and products (Fig. 2.1).

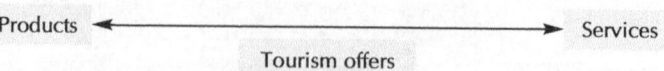

Products ←——————————→ Services

Tourism offers

Fig. 2.1 Tourism Offers

This product–service mix has wide implications for marketing, as to what should be highlighted—products or services? If products are focused, whether it should be core or augmented. Augmentation involves service features. And if services are taken as key benefits, these too are sold and transferred through servicescape or the physical settings and environment. It again involves tangibilization. The dilemma is that products get a competitive edge from services and services from add-on products. What about tourism that already has both services and products?

NATURE AND CHARACTERISTICS OF TOURISM OFFERS

The nature of tourism can be understood with the help of the basic features of products and services. The following features characterize pure products and services.

- Tangibility and intangibility
- Non-perishability and perishability
- Homogeneity and heterogeneity
- Separability and inseparability
- Ownership and non-ownership

Pure products have all the features of products and pure services of services. Most of the products and services fall on the continuum between the two ends. Tourism too shares the characteristics of both, as discussed below.

Tangibility and Intangibility

Tangibility is the materiality of products that make these possible to be touched and seen. Kotler (1995) considers it as a characteristic that makes products to be seen, tasted, felt, heard, and smelt before purchase. The perception about the products is derived from the senses of touch and sight. You see and touch furniture, clothes, shoes, and fixtures before deciding the quality. Other senses are also used for products, such as food, that can be tasted and smelt. The sense of smell is used for cosmetics and toiletries too, while the sense of sound can be used in the perception of items such as toys and automobiles. Sensation–perception help consumers to judge a product before purchase and the use of more senses makes the judgement better. On the other hand, intangibility is associated with services that involve perception based on feelings and experience without any physical sensation. For example, consultancies and teaching services can only be experienced and not physically sensed. Tourism has its

Tourism as a product has the elements of both tangibility and intangibility. A part of it can be physically experienced but not all. For example, a good aircraft can be physically felt but the pleasure of good service can only be experienced.

Fig. 2.2   Selling Intangibles
(*Photo Courtesy:* Poras Chaudhary)

unique intangibility. How do you spread something as unique as peace, meditation, and prayers (Fig 2.2)

Non-perishability and Perishability

Non-perishability is the ability of the product to be stocked for some time without any impact on its use or quality. Different types of products differ in the degree of non-perishability. Consumer durables, such as, cars and refrigerators, can be stocked for quite a long time, but non-durables, such as cosmetics and toiletries, have a comparatively shorter stocking period of six months to one year. Perishables, such as processed food, have a very short shelf life of three to six months. The stocks help a firm to sell products when the demand exceeds the supply. Perishability is the feature of the services that makes storage impossible. As a result, these products are consumed as and when produced. A motor mechanic can do the repair job only when vehicles arrive for servicing, otherwise, he sits idle. He may have the capability of mending 20 vehicles in a day but if all the 20 come at the same time and the owners want the servicing done in one hour, he can take up only a few. The repair services here cannot be stocked for future use. Similar is the case with hotel rooms and air/rail seats that cannot be stored and are, thus, perishable. A 100-room hotel with a 20 per cent occupancy on a day cannot transfer the balance 80 per cent capacity to the next day. The next day again, only 100 rooms will be available. A tourist who reaches the airport late and misses his/her flight cannot get the one booked earlier. This requires simultaneity of production and consumption and a balance between supply and demand.

Homogeneity and Heterogeneity

Products are homogenous in nature and every item has the same quality. The last soap produced in a factory on a day, in a month, or a year, is the same as the first one. The definite and tangible ingredients of a soap, and the quality control between production and sales, make this possible. A bad product cannot be put up for sale. On the other hand, services are heterogeneous, where a high level of human involvement makes it vary every time the consumer consumes it. A doctor will not have a uniform behaviour with every patient or with the same patient at different occasions.

The heterogeneity in tourism experience may also come from the external natural environment. Tourists travelling to far off places for the sun will be disappointed if the place remains clouded. Similarly, a visit to national parks or wildlife areas may be fruitless if the animals do not come out in the open areas.

In tourism, the aspects of the type of hotel room or cab service can be uniform but the service and the facilitation of these will not be the same. The cleanliness of a hotel room may have different standards if the housekeeping supervisor or the room cleaner is changed. This gives a wide range of standards in tourism experience.

Separability and Inseparability

Separability is the separation of production from consumption. A product is manufactured at a different place and time from that of its consumption. After production, it can be stocked to be retrieved later for consumption. It helps in balancing the resources of an organization that keeps the same production levels throughout and uses stocks in high-demand season. On the other hand, inseparability means that production and consumption are simultaneous. A dish is readied in a restaurant only when diners come to eat. It means keeping the staff and facilities ready for production when the demand for consumption arises. It makes resource management a challenging job. You keep the staff ready for the service but the demand may not come. Factors such as bad weather, road blocks, or cancelled trains may dampen demand. It leads to unused capital, human, and other resources during the lean period and shortage of the same during the peak season. Tourism is highly inseparable. For example, a chartered plane will fly only on demand otherwise it will remain grounded. Scheduled flights will fly even if the number of passengers in a flight is very less.

Ownership and Non-ownership

Ownership means that after purchase, buyers become the legal owners. In case of products, the legal title is transferred to the buyers with the purchase. A car or a bottle of soft drink belongs to the buyer, while the non-ownership of services transfers only the right to use the services for a specified time. A train ticket gives the right to travel on a particular day, in a particular train, in a defined compartment and seat. The next day someone else will travel on the same train. Selling services with non-ownership is a challenge. For example, after spending Rs 3 lakh, a person may buy a car that will remain with him for many years to come but the same expenditure on a tour will give only memories, photographs, and souvenirs. Thus, convincing a person about the benefits of non-ownership is difficult.

Table 2.1 gives an overview of the main components of tourism and the product–service elements present therein.

Table 2.1 Product and Service Features in Tourism

Features	Transportation	Accommodation	Attraction
Intangible	Service, cleanliness, ambience, timeliness, value, frequency, connectivity	Service, cleanliness, ambience, reputation, availability, value	Ambience, image, popularity, accessibility
Tangible	Type of coach/craft, comfort of seats (leg space), climate control, price	Type of hotel, types of rooms, room size, phone, conference facility	Hotels, local transport, souvenirs
Perishable	Unsold seats on the journey	Unsold rooms and food	Unutilized capacity
Non-perishable	Physical features (seats, curtains, air conditioner)	Fixtures, furnishings	Attraction as such
Separable	Water bottles, towels, pillows, blankets	Linen, crockery,	Souvenirs
Inseparable	Seats	Rooms and food	Attraction
Homogenous	Type of facilities (seat type, leg space)	Standardization of rooms	Regular staged events for tourists such as Surajkund crafts fair in Haryana or Dilli Haat (Delhi)

Contd

Features	Transportation	Accommodation	Attraction
Heterogeneous	Service (timeliness, behaviour of staff)	Variability in room maintenance and service	Detailed activities in events, different theme for each year
Ownership	Only of right to travel	Right to stay	Right to experience
Non-ownership	Transport vehicle	Accommodation	Attraction

From Table 2.1, it is evident that tourism lies on a continuum between products and services as shown in Fig. 2.3.

A tourism offer can be developed as a distinct mix of the products and services. For example, leisure tours are more service oriented than business tours and fast food outlets are more product oriented than sit-down meals.

The marketing strategies used for tourism depend upon this product–service mix.

ISSUES AND CHALLENGES IN TOURISM MARKETING

The issues and challenges of tourism marketing emerge from the nature of tourism offers. The total offer and its components build the tour experience. For effective marketing, the composition of components and product–service mix is used judiciously. So, product features can be highlighted for tourists who prefer concrete benefits and service features for those who want intangible benefits.

Issue of Tangibility and Intangibility Mix

A buyer's key concern is to gain benefits from a purchase. In tourism, the main benefit or attraction is intangible such as, beauty, serenity,

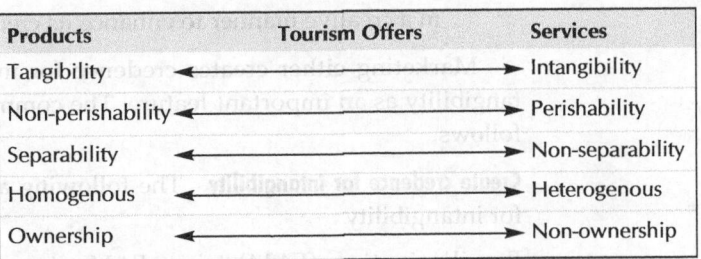

Products	Tourism Offers	Services
Tangibility	◄─────────►	Intangibility
Non-perishability	◄─────────►	Perishability
Separability	◄─────────►	Non-separability
Homogenous	◄─────────►	Heterogenous
Ownership	◄─────────►	Non-ownership

Fig. 2.3 Tourism on Product–Service Continuum

or religiosity of a place, while the other facilitating aspects, such as transport and accommodation, are tangible. Tour purchase is based on the evaluation of key features first, and the other aspects are given secondary consideration. A visit to a place may be planned for its tour value than for the new approach road or the new hotel. Similarly, in choosing a flight, the focus is on the flying experience and not the airlines company. But a bad road, hotel, or airlines may be decisive in the final purchase.

Challenge

How to sell this intangibility? How to convince tourists about its value? This is a big problem when a new offer is to be marketed, as images of intangibles need to be created over a very long period. All the destinations and countries that started tourism development a little late faced this problem. For example, Kashmir valley and Kausani (Uttarakhand) are called 'Switzerland of India'. This analogy helped in building an image and attracting tourists who could not visit Switzerland and wanted an alternative.

The specific problems resulting from intangibility of services are as follows.

- These cannot be stored
- These cannot be patented
- They cannot be displayed or readily communicated
- Their prices are difficult to set

Marketing strategies adopted to overcome the intangibility factor

Intangibility makes tourism highly information sensitive and most of the marketing strategies focus on information. The following understanding is used to plan strategies.

- Tourists may not trust information supplied by the marketers.
- Tourists may believe the words of fellow travellers, independent persons, social leaders, and so on. Therefore, information is used in a creative manner to enhance its credibility.

Marketing either creates credence for intangibility or highlights tangibility as an important feature. The common strategies used are as follows.

Create credence for intangibility The following are important to credence for intangibility.

Familiarization (FAM) trips: FAM trips are complimentary trips organized for people who can shape the opinion of tourists. Tour operators and media personnel are given these tours, who further, pass the information to potential tourists. Their credibility and influence help to overcome the inhibitions of tourists in accepting the intangible features of the tours. The Government of India has included this strategy in the 'India–China action plan for year of friendship to invite 10–12 members of the Chinese media and tour operators with a view to promote the country in China. Similarly, the Turkish Indian Tourism Council (TITC) offered a FAM trip to 40 Indian tour operators to promote Turkey as a potential tourist destination among the Indians. Restaurants use this strategy by inviting food critics to try out various cuisines and comment on them.

Their comments would then act as a stamp of authenticity to the claims of sellers for a lot many buyers.

Net groups: Marketers provide web space to users to discuss and express opinions, and to seek expert advice. Tourists can be given convincing opinions on intangible features by keeping tab on such forums and by inserting appropriate information. Such groups are present on independent sites such as Yahoo and Google, or product review sites such as mouthshut.com, indiamike.com, virtualtourist. com, and so on. Online travel firms also encourage their buyers to post comments and provide space for discussion. Cleartrip.com has tied up with Twitter where their customers can share opinions, and makemytrip.com is linked to oktatabyebye.com for customer review on the tours.

Opinion leaders: Tourists may not believe the marketers but are impressed by other people in society. If these people talk positively about a tour, then information passes on as word of mouth and is easily accepted. The same also applies to opinion sharing on the Web, in user generated groups. The marketers convince these leaders believing that the others will get the information through them. These leaders can be community leaders or work group heads. These leaders are widely travelled and in a position to pass useful information to the opinion receivers.

Testimonials and brand ambassadors: Celebrities, such as film stars and sportspersons, can transfer their personal influence to the brand sponsored. When they talk about tourist destinations, their words carry high reliability and value. The Government of India has chosen actor Aamir Khan as the face of *Atithi Devo Bhava* for showcasing the country's rich heritage and culture. Actress Celina Jaitley is endorsing Egypt in India for outbound tourism.

Building brands: A brand name is worth many words and is associated with intangibles such as quality, service, and trust. It is created after a long and laborious process and helps in selling services that otherwise may not find many takers. Franchising is very common in hotel industry where a stand-alone local property may attach itself to an established brand. It requires alterations in working and processes as per the requirements of the name, and the payment of franchise fees. But the brand name helps in attracting the customers.

Using films: Destinations are often included as locales in films and tele-serials. These destinations become popular with the films and tourists get attracted to these places after seeing them in movies. Countries such as Scotland, New Zealand, Switzerland, Seychelles, and Mauritius have been promoting the use of their locales through movies. These countries offer special facilities and incentives to movie makers. The British Tourist Authority showcased Britain in India through Indian movies like *Lamhe* and *Dilwale Dulhania Le Jayenge*.

Increase tangibility   Intangibility can also be overcome through tangibility. For example, increasing tangibility and highlighting value for money is a good option for budget tours than focusing on intangibles. The strategies for the use of tangibility are as follows.

Building tangibles: Intangibles can be tangibilized too. Ecotourism is intangible but eco-certified eco tours are easy to sell. Telling the tourists that the tour has a green globe or ecotel mark convinces them easily. They can understand that a standard process must have been followed to get the certification. Similarly, hospitals in developing countries are taking up global quality certificates to convince the medical tourists about the standards of medical services.

Highlighting tangibles: Tourism has both the products and services features. Highlighting the products may help in enhancing the overall value to the tourists. *Vaishno Devi* pilgrimage is more attractive now because of the increased facilities and products, though its religious value always stood high.

Add-on tangibles: Small gifts and souvenirs offered to tourists enhance their experience. Hotels offer chocolates and takeaways. These tokens are of little monetary value to the guests compared to the total purchase value but they make the guests feel special. Add-ons, such as, pens, calendars, and clocks, remain with the tourists for a long time and create a post-purchase association with the marketers.

Issue of Perishability and Non-perishability Combination

Tourism supplies have fixed capacities with little flexibility of expansion. A destination has a fixed carrying capacity and the same applies to the hotel or the transport vehicle. Some expansion can be provided by adopting measures such as putting additional beds in rooms or allowing standing travel to the passengers. This fixed capacity does not match the uneven demand pattern. As a result, whenever the demand is less, some of the supplies are not used. The unused capacity of all the components of tourism is a very critical issue. The marketers are always worried about the unsold capacity as it reduces revenue. Even if the demand exceeds the capacity, the additional tourists cannot be accommodated, and so they go back with a poor impression of a lack of facilities.

Challenge

What to do when the facilities do not have enough visitors or when more visitors than the capacity turn up? This situation, first of all, leads to financial loss and secondly, customer dissatisfaction. In both the cases, the loss is of the tourism supplier.

Marketing strategies

A two-pronged marketing approach is adopted. On one hand, capacities are expanded without compromising on the quality of the services and on the other, efforts are made to shift some demand from a high period to a low period.

Capacity management The capacity of tourism supplies is fixed but not rigid and some adjustments can be made, suitable to both the suppliers and the tourists. These adjustments help in stretching the capacity a little in times of demand and altering it for alternate uses when the demand is low. A destination may ask its residents to offer their extra rooms for paying guests in the peak season, and in the off season, business tourism or educational trips can be promoted on reduced rates.

Using satellite destinations: Most of the tourists visit popular destinations, such as, Delhi, Agra, and Jaipur, which often fail to meet the demand due to heavy pressure. To disperse the traffic, nearby places are developed where the tourists can travel and stay. This keeps both the demand and the supply within the carrying capacity.

Use of tourist circuits: A tourist route can be provided and the tourists can travel to a number of places instead of a single place. It keeps the tourists on the move. Delhi–Agra–Jaipur tourist circuit is one such example.

Queuing: If the demand cannot be dispersed, the queuing method can be used and the tourists can be asked to wait for the supply. It is often used in fast food joints, where order numbers are allotted on payment and announcements are made when the food is ready. Restricted areas also follow this approach, and tourists apply for permission to travel to these areas and wait in queue for them. Protected monuments may also limit the number of footfalls on a single day.

Tie-up with other suppliers: A supplier can enter into an agreement with other similar suppliers to share facilities with each other in case of over demand. Hotels often follow this, and in case of excess demand, recommend guests to other hotels.

Additional part-time manpower: The demand pattern of tourism may see a rush during certain hours, week days, and months. By keeping additional part-time manpower, such as trainees, the capacity for functions, such as, food service, bell job, can be increased.

Cross-training of manpower: This is often used in hotels. All the areas or departments may not be under pressure of work and the cross-training of employees helps in shifting them from low-rush to high-rush areas for assistance. This also saves the cost of keeping additional manpower.

Adjustable facilities: With the use of flexi systems, a large hall can be used for a variety of purposes such as meetings, banquets, and conferences. In rooms also, additional cots can be provided as per the guests' needs.

Forecasting and scheduling: A good forecast helps in proper scheduling and the use of facilities as per demand.

Part-time booking: Conference halls and hotel rooms can be rented out for half day for a better use of the capacities.

Demand management   It involves the following strategies.

Price: Reduced prices can be very effectively used to build demand and similarly, prices can be increased to shift demand from the peak season.

Discounts, packages, and happy hours: Sales promotion schemes, such as discounts, packages, and happy hours, are often used to build strong demand. Packages give advantage only if the whole bundled product is purchased. Discounts are usually with a particular amount or time of purchase. Happy hours are used in restaurants when certain items are offered at very low prices during specific hours.

Balanced market: A balanced market in terms of visiting pattern and purposes is a very useful strategy. Most of the destinations focus on business tourism that is insensitive to the general demand pattern of leisure tourists. So, if a place can have all types of tourists, demand fluctuations will lessen.

Events: Sports and cultural events can be held in the lean season to even out the demand. Some tourists from the peak season also might shift to the days when the event is organized.

Varied product attractions: A broad profile attracts more tourists. This is possible through innovative ideas.. Many destinations have invented themselves for shopping tourism, business tourism, and conferences, and so on.

Frequent customer schemes: Additional incentives are given to regular clients for repeat buys. This gives a constant source of supply.

Issue of Separability and Inseparability

Tourism services are produced and consumed simultaneously, and require the presence of both the producers and the tourists at the same time and place. Generally, suppliers get ready and wait for the tourists to prepare services for them. But the suppliers may not be able to satisfy the tourists if they come in large numbers. As a result, either there are empty capacities waiting for the tourists or tourists waiting for the capacities. This creates the problems of lost revenues and customer dissatisfaction.

Challenge
The challenge is to create separation and if it is not possible to do so then prepare a performer or the supplier to meet the demands of more tourists.

Marketing strategies
These are targeted at systems, processes, and people, and help in overcoming some of the problems of inseparability.

Systems focused   The systems used for the delivery of services speed up work, improving productivity of people and transfer the repetitive jobs to machines.

Automation: Automatic operations transfer some of the jobs to the machines and free the performer for other duties. Central reservation networks and property management systems have made the job of reservation easier by using computers for inventory management. Automation in laundry, kitchen, and security are some of the other examples.

People focused   These strategies focus on attitudes and behaviour of people that directly or indirectly influence the tour experience.

Training service staff to work faster: Performance usually improves with training and practice. A proper training programme can be conducted to help the employees work faster and increase supplies.

Involve tourists in service delivery: Tourists are asked to actively participate in a few areas of service production and transfer, thus, easing the task of the supplier. Self service by the tourists is one such example.

Process focussed   These strategies improve work flow of activities used for tour and travel experience.

Simplifying work: Simple and easy procedures improve the efficiency of the employees and make them work faster.

Group delivery: Serving each tourist separately can be very time consuming. Therefore, group service can be used. For instance, scheduled tourist coaches can serve more tourists than cabs. Buffet style in restaurants also serves the same purpose.

Using more service providers: Sometimes, part of the job, if not all, can be done by the other performers without any effect on quality. Besides increasing supplies, it also prepares manpower for the future.

Advance preparation: Proper forecasts give an estimate of demand, and, thus, basic preparation can be done in advance. For example, rooms are kept ready in hotels and food is semi-processed for the diners. A destination can be readied at a short notice by completing all the infrastructure maintenance jobs earlier.

Issue of Heterogeneity

Tourism is a people-intensive industry and tourism experience heavily depends upon the experience of contact between the service personnel and the tourists. Human behaviour cannot be controlled and creates variance in performance. As a result, the tourists feel a wide difference in service experiences. This also makes quality control difficult.

Challenge

How to minimize the variability and create uniformity in delivery?

Marketing strategies

Suitable strategies are used to get standard performance to the maximum possible extent through processes and people. These are discussed below.

Processes The work flows are standardized for ensuring uniformity in the experiences of tourists.

Guidelines: The general instructions to carry out work provide a uniform generic framework and ensure some degree of uniformity. For example, guidelines, such as, 'customer is king,' 'guest is God,' 'do not argue with guest,' and so on, direct employees to be courteous and good.

Standard operating procedures (SOPs): For some activities, step-wise detailing of tasks is possible and every employee is required to follow these. For example, reservation, registration of foreigners, currency exchange, and so on. Standard operating procedures make performance standards uniform.

Certifications: These are control systems that can be output or process based. In both the cases, certifications help in achieving standardization. All eco-friendly destinations and five-star hotels follow certain basic rules that ensure uniformity in performance. Hospitals in India are using international certifications to promote medical tourism. For instance, Apollo and Wockhardt hospital chains have obtained the gold standard certificate from the Joint Commission International. Many other hospitals have taken the ISO 9001: 2000 certification.

Benchmarking: It is continuously upgrading performance against the past standards and this naturally leads to variable but better experience. It enhances customer satisfaction by offering something better.

Automation: Automated operations ensure uniformity of processes. Computerized billing, ticketing, and bookings have solved many problems of the tourism industry.

People Behavioural controls are used to control variability arising out of the differences among people.

Training: It can be used to train employees in standardizing performance. Soft skills training in the tourism industry is very common. This controls interaction between the employees and the tourists.

External uniformity: Some visible aspects also create a sense of quality control and uniform performance. For instance, to develop this impression the use of uniforms is very common in the tourism industry.

Internal marketing: Good human resource (HR) practices encourage and consolidate good service standards. These motivate the employees to deliver quality and uniform services.

Issue of Non-ownership

Tourism is a high-value purchase and involves well thought out decisions. The tourists not only evaluate many tour options, but also, compare the tour and the other non-tour purchases. They need to be convinced that the tours shall give a better value for their money. The marketers find it a little difficult because of the non-ownership feature of the services that allows use but no possession. At the end of the tour what remain are the experiences and the memories.

Challenge

How to convince the tourists for a purchase where nothing is physically possessed and owned?

Marketing strategies

These emphasize benefits of non-ownership or create partial ownership.

Emphasize the benefits of non-ownership The benefits of refreshed and rejuvenated mind, body, and soul carry much more weightage than any physical possession. This view can be reinforced to sell tourism services. Health and medical tourists understand this well, and frequent nature cure centres, spas, hospitals, and so on.

Finance to make purchase easy The decision to purchase without ownership often depends on the disposable income. Easy finance options can persuade tourists to make such purchases. Many travel companies have tied up with banks for funding tourists, who can later refund through easy installments. Banks have also separated travel from personal loans, making decision-making easy for the tourists. 'Synd Yatra' of Syndicate bank, 'Can Travel' of Canara bank, 'Shubh Yatra' of Indian Overseas Bank, 'Star Holidays' of Bank of India, and 'Easy Travel Loan' of State Bank of India are some of the financing options available in the country.

Create ownership Certain options, such as time share, can be used that give some ownership to the tourists. In this, the tourists pay an initial amount and purchase the right to use a particular resort for a fixed period in a year. After this, only the annual maintenance fee is paid. In case, they do not take the tour, it can be used by their friends.

A suitable combination of all the above strategies can be used to overcome the disadvantages of services and products and use the advantages of both.

SUMMARY

Marketing tourism requires different strategies because of the different nature of tourism offers. Tourism offers are a combination of goods and services. They have the qualities of both. Products and services are distinguished through features of tangibility–intangibility, perishability–non-perishability, separability–inseparability, homogeneity–heterogeneity, and ownership–non-ownership. Tourism offers are placed on a product–service continuum and can be either product or service dominated. The marketers mix products and services to develop tour offers. The challenges of tourism marketing arise from here. Certain strategies which are completely different from the products and the services are devised. These are based on overcoming service features that make marketing difficult. Intangibility is overcome by building tangibility. The suggested strategies for this are familiarization trips, using net groups and opinion leaders, testimonials and brand ambassadors, and brands and films. Tangibility can be built, added, or highlighted. Per-

ishability of tourism makes it difficult to balance demand and supply. All strategies aim to get this balance. These are the use of satellite destinations and tourist circuits, queues, part-time manpower, cross-training, adjustable features, forecasting and scheduling, part-time booking, price adjustments, discounts, packages, happy hours, balancing market and product portfolios, and frequent customer schemes. The strategies to overcome inseparability are automation, advance preparation, simple and fast procedures, additional manpower, and involving customers in service production. Heterogeneity is a big issue and cannot be eliminated because of the people-intensive nature of services. But automation, training, guidelines, standard operating procedures, certifications, and benchmarking minimize variation. Ownership is not possible in tourism industry but the benefits of not owning can be highlighted. A suitable combination of all these strategies helps in effective marketing of tourism.

KEY TERMS

Familiarization trips These are complementary trips to familiarize the prospective tourists about the tour. A good experience is transferred as word of mouth to the other tourists.

Frequent customer schemes Schemes to reward frequent customers for loyalty and to encourage more purchases are called frequent customer schemes.

Heterogeneity It is the lack of uniformity in services produced at different times.

Homogeneity It is the uniformity in products produced at different times.

Inseparability A service quality of simultaneous consumption and production is called inseparability.

Intangibility It is used to denote the non-material nature of services. Services can be felt and experienced but cannot be physically sensed by human senses.

Non-ownership A service quality that does not give the title of services to the buyers but only transfers the right to use them for a limited period.

Non-perishability Products do not perish if not consumed and can, thus, be stocked.

Ownership A product quality where the title is legally transferred to the buyers is called ownership.

Perishability Services perish if not consumed. Services cannot be stocked for future use.

Separability It is the product quality that separates the consumption from the production.

Servicescapes The environment in which the service is experienced is called servicescape.

Tangibility It is the material quality of goods that makes their experience possible through human senses.

EXERCISES

REVIEW QUESTIONS

1. What is intangibility of services? What are its implications for marketing? Suggest strategies for marketing intangibles in tourism.
2. 'Heterogeneity in services is the result of intensive use of people.' Suggest methods to overcome problems of heterogeneity.
3. What is ownership in tourism? How can it be marketed? Explain.

PRACTICE EXERCISES

1. Study the guidelines of hotel classification of the Ministry of Tourism, Government of India. Separate product and service features. What differences do you note for the lower and the higher class hotels?
2. Compare the tour packages of the same circuit in different price brackets. Analyse the differences on the basis of product and service features.
3. Conduct a survey of tourists to find out if they are ready to pay more for better services and why?

PROJECTS

1. Collect brochures of different categories of hotels. Prepare a comparative chart of their offers under tangibles and intangibles. Find their link with prices. Why would a customer pay more for one hotel over the other?
2. Conduct a survey of tourists to find their expectations of tour components. Ask them what price they are ready to pay for each. Prepare a report to link prices with tangible and intangible elements.

REFERENCES

Gummesson, Evert 2007, 'Exit services marketing—enter service marketing', *Journal of Customer Behaviour*, vol. 6, no. 2 pp., 113-141.

Holloway, J.C. and Plant, R.V. 1988, *Marketing for Tourism*, Pitman, London.

Houston, Franklin S. 1986, 'The marketing concept: What it is and what it is not', *Journal of Marketing*, vol. 50, pp. 81-87.

Kotler, Philip, Bowen John, and Makens James 2004, *Marketing for Hospitality and Tourism*, Pearson Education, Delhi.

Kotler Philip 1995, *Marketing Management:Analysis, Planning, Implementation and Control*, Prentice Hall of India, New Delhi.

Lovelock, Christopher and Evert Gummesson 2004, 'Whither services marketing?: In search of a new paradigm and fresh perspectives,' *Journal of Service Research*, vol.7, no.1, pp. 20–41.

Lovelock, Christopher and Jochen Wirtz 2004, *Services Marketing:People, Technology, Strategy*, Pearson Education, Delhi.

Middleton, V.T.C. 1988, *Marketing in Travel and Tourism*, Heinemann, Oxford.

Vargo, Stephen L. and Robert F. Lusch 2004, 'The four service marketing myths: remnants of a goods-based,

manufacturing model', *Journal of Service Research*, vol.6, no. 4, pp., 324-335.

Valarie, Zeithaml A., Parsuraman, A., and Bery L. Leonard 1985, 'Problems and strategies in services marketing', *Journal of Marketing*, vol. 49, pp.33-46.

Valarie, Zeithaml A. and Bitner Jo Mary 1996, *Services Marketing*, McGraw-Hill , Singapore.

CASE STUDIES

1. SPIRITUAL TOURISM—SELLING NIRVANA

Spiritual tourism is joining the bandwagon to cash on the economic gains of worldwide growth of tourism. Spiritual tourism as an offer is different from others, as it promises more than food, shelter, and travel. It satisfies the inner needs of human beings than simply arranging transport, accommodation, and visits. It offers a journey of self, though externally, through visit to temples, religious sites, gurus, and so on.

People search for spiritualism to get respite from the pressures of modern and hectic lifestyles. India's religious diversity and mysticism offer plentiful options to satiate such needs. The association of popular personalities, such as Richard Gere and members of The Beatles band, to the Indian gurus has added to the image of India as a spiritual destination. The popularity of Indian gurus, such as Paramhans Yoganand, Sri Sri Ravi Shankar, Osho, Maharshi Mahesh Yogi, and others, cuts across national borders.

This potential of India has prompted the tourism industry to offer spiritual tours to India. The experience of spiritualism is offered through tangibles such as participation in puja, visit to temples, offering *prasad*, staying near religious

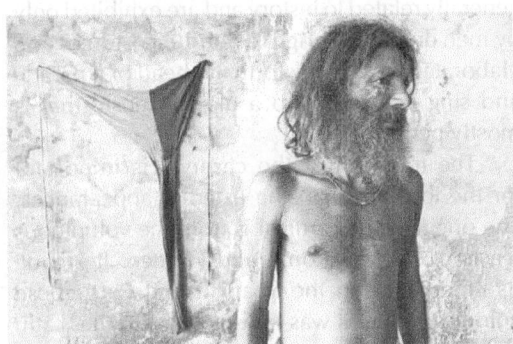

Fig. 2.4 Selling Nirvana
(*Photo Courtesy*: Poras Chaudhary)

sites, and so on (Fig. 2.4). These tours are planned coinciding with days considered auspicious, thus, signifying inseparability and perishability.

DISCUSSION QUESTIONS

1. Identify the five service characteristics in spiritual tours.
2. How are these characteristics used to market spiritual tours?
3. What products and products features are used to sell spiritual tours?

2. GOA CARNIVAL

The Goa carnival is a well-known annual festival held in mid-February and is marked by a four-day celebration. This has been celebrated since the eighteenth century just before the 40 days of Lent, a time of chastity and devotion.

This is one of the popular festivals in the country that draws a large number of foreign and Indian visitors. It is known for its feasting-drinking-merrymaking party when the streets come alive with colour for three days and nights. The people perform street plays, songs, and dances before the audience. The plays are generally related to history and are exhibited only by men dressed in bright colourful costumes and elaborate masks. They form the head of a parade and sing and dance to a playful music that is mostly performed live.

The tradition of the carnival is important for the localites than the external appearances. The origin of the carnival is from the voluptuous feasts of ancient Rome and Greece. It made its emergence in the Spanish and Portuguese colonies, where it was transmuted into the Latin singing-dancing-drinking turns. The carnival is governed by King Momo, who on the opening day orders his subjects to party. The carnival signifies the fun-loving culture that is symbolic of Goa. It was initiated by the erstwhile rulers and has continued with the same spirit.

But over the years, like all festivals, commercialization has started dominating it. Tours for the Goa carnival are packaged and sold in advance to people who consider it no more than merrymaking

DISCUSSION QUESTIONS

1. How is the commercialization of a festival, such as the Goa Carnival, linked to its product and service features?

2. What can be the challenges of the marketers in packaging such festivals as tour offers?

3. How does commercialization change the character of such festivals and associated product-service features?

CHAPTER 3

Tourism Marketing Environment and Marketing Mix

LEARNING OBJECTIVES

Tourism marketing is influenced by a number of forces external to the marketers' control. These forces together constitute the tourism marketing environment. Some of these may have long-term implications such as demography and culture, while others such as inflation and exchange rates create short-term and immediate impacts. These forces can present both threats and opportunities. A marketer needs to understand and analyse his/her environment to be proactive in his/her actions. This action is reflected in the marketing strategy and marketing mix.

In this chapter, you will learn about the following.

• Components of environment
• Influence of environment on tourism marketing activities
• Methods of analysis of environment
• Concept of marketing mix
• Elements of tourism marketing mix
• Tourism marketing mix as total offer

INTRODUCTION

Tourism is highly sensitive to external forces and any mishaps, such as terrorist acts, wars, and natural calamities such as tsunami, which create an immediate and visible impact on tourist flow. Predicting these might be difficult but there are other forces, such as technology, new destinations, changing preferences, and so on, that are predictable. Planning marketing activities to adapt and respond to these forces can give a definite competitive advantage but it requires continuous analysis and forecasting of the external environment. The environment of tourism marketing can be understood with the help of the system's approach that takes into account all the relevant forces and factors.

TOURISM MARKETING SYSTEM

The system approach helps in logical and orderly analysis of marketing activity by stressing on marketing linkages inside and outside the firm, emphasizing the relationship of inputs to outputs, highlighting changes in environment, providing an approach for control, offering opportunities for innovation, and providing a means for measuring results (Rosenberg 1977).

Tourism marketing is an open system that has a number of interrelated and interdependent entities. This system can be arranged in a frame of internal, external micro, and external macro environment. The marketing organization forms the internal environment, the organizations or groups frequently interacting with the marketer form the micro environment, and the macro environment is made up of larger forces that affect both the micro and the internal environment (Fig 3.1).

Internal Environment

The internal environment is the core of the system and is controllable by the firm. The firm can alter it to adapt to the requirements of the external environment. It consists of marketing organization, its philosophy and approach towards marketing, and its strengths and weaknesses. This decides the preparedness and ability of the firm to meet challenges of

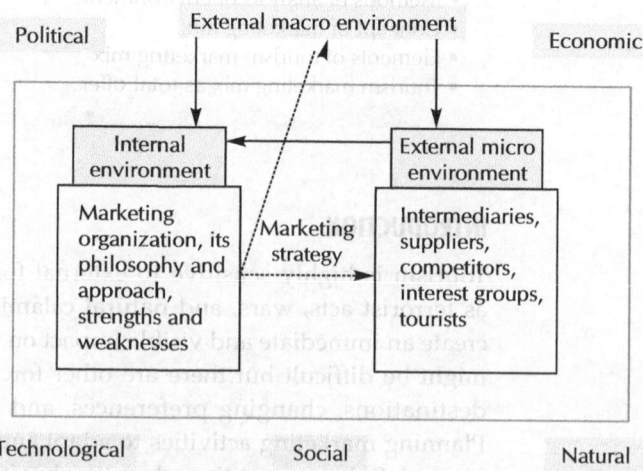

Fig. 3.1 Tourism Marketing System

marketing. For example, Indian airlines was the only player in the Indian skies for domestic routes but with the opening of the skies, the entry of private airlines, and low-cost carriers, it started discounted and apex fares. The change was made in response to the changing environment.

External Micro Environment

This is the nearest environment of the marketer that has direct and immediate effect on tourism marketing activities. All the forces and players of this environment directly participate in the marketing process. This includes the following.

Intermediaries between firm and tourists

Intermediaries or middlemen are used by the marketers to reach wider market places. Wholesalers and retailers, often called tour operators and travel agents, are used for the distribution and sale of tours. These work on commission basis for principals such as hotels, airlines, and destinations. The relation with principals depends upon industry practices and position of the middlemen. If the agents acquire a dominant position by controlling the markets, the principals will have to change their approach accordingly. For example, online travel companies are emerging as the new middlemen. As a result, even airlines are selling their seats through them than from their own portals. Indian railways is selling its tour packages through 'makemytrip.com', though it is also using its own website, 'indianrailtourism.com'.

The development of technology has led to discussion on the utility of travel agents. Many of their functions, such as ticketing, have been automated and so now they are reinventing themselves as consultants.

Suppliers

Tourism product is a composite mix of accommodation, transport, attraction, and other associated facilities. All these supplies are procured from many suppliers before assembling a product. Any change in the price, quality, and availability of these inputs will change the product and, subsequently, its marketing. These inputs depend heavily on the suppliers. Principals, such as hotels, airlines, and destinations, supply their outputs to travel agents and tour operators. If they decide to reduce the commission rates or modify the prices, the tour prices will also change. Similarly, airlines have hotels or caterers as suppliers of food. Hotels have vegetable, linen, furniture, and flower vendors for their supplies. Every firm needs to understand its suppliers and their behaviour as the quality, promptness, and assurances of the supplies influence further marketing agreements and contracts.

For example, the government of Uttarakhand has given a new set of guidelines for *Char Dham Yatra* for protecting the environment. It includes high fees for entering different areas, restricted numbers for travel to Gaumukh, and slow pace of journey to reduce the burden of vehicular traffic. These changes by the destination managers have forced all the agents to rebuild their itineraries. Another example can be of increased prices of food supplies during the inflation in 2008 that forced hotels to revise the rates or to cut down margins. The high tariffs of hotels in the country forced the agents to make changes in the package pricing.

A marketer needs to analyse the complete supply chain to understand the impacts resulting from any changes in the supply chain. For example, increased prices of food and rental space by the suppliers of hotels have forced hotels to revise prices that are reflected in the prices of tour packages of the tour operators. The heavy hike in fuel prices in 2008 has had an impact on airlines tariffs that in turn are visible in the enhanced prices of the tour packages.

Competitors

The competitors of a firm decide its relative strengths and weaknesses and force it to change its marketing approach. Competition can come from similar firms, related firms, or sometimes unrelated ones. The entry of Kuoni Travels in the Indian market has given competition to many of the existing players. Cruises are the new destinations in the Indian market that encompass travel, accommodation, food, and entertainment under one roof, taking some business away from the existing players. Luxury tourist trains take away the business of hotels, and low-cost air services promote same day to and fro travel plans, thereby saving a day's stay in a hotel. *Dhabas* along the highways in India became popular, as the food served in these modest eateries appealed to all types of travellers. Initially, the competition was among the *dhabas* only but recently big food chains, such as, McDonalds, Haldiram, Nirulas, Sagar Ratna, and so on, have started their outlets on the highways. These swanky modern spaces are competing with the old style *dhabas*. Any type of competition impacts a firm's business and thus it needs to devise suitable strategies to counter it.

Interest groups

Tourism activity may create problems for ecology, culture, and society. The society, in general, will expect the marketers to minimize the damage and to contribute something positive or create good impacts.

Some important interest groups are as follows.

Environment groups These groups are often termed as green groups and aim at protecting the environment. These watch every industry for environmental concerns and tourism is no exception. These groups ask for promotion of ecotourism, environmental certification, and so on, and may

The conduct and business of the marketer influences the interests of many groups in the society who expect marketing to be more sensitive to their needs.

influence the marketing by convincing the tourists and the government to adopt eco-friendly tours. They may demand ban on entry of tourists to national parks if the wildlife is threatened. Their efforts have led to many studies on the carrying capacity and the adoption of eco-sensitive practices by tour companies. As a result, hotels are going for ecotel labels and energy and environment (E^2) certifications, and destinations are adopting Green Palm and Green Globe labels.

Citizens groups   These groups are formed to watch sociocultural impacts of tourism on the host communities. The popularity of certain destinations creates problems of high prices, pollution, and crowded roads for the locals who then start opposing tourism. A large number of tourists make them feel uncomfortable at their own places. This strains the host–guest relationship. Tourism marketers need to keep a watch on the harmful effects of tourism to sustain tourism and their own business. Hence, practices such as community-based tourism and local participation are adopted for tourism development. Rural tourism schemes are following community-based development in India.

Tourists

Tourists or consumers of tourism decide the marketing strategy as it begins with their needs. Any change in profile, attitudes, and behaviour of consumers will have far-reaching changes for marketing. A few examples of this are as follows.

- Demand for business tourism in the country is growing with the growth of economy.
- Student tourism is increasing with the increasing popularity of international education.
- Increased incomes are boosting air travel.
- Changing food preferences are forcing hotels and restaurants to provide global cuisine and health foods.

Apart from this, tourists can also form groups to share their opinions and experiences. This can be organized if the tourists are geographically closer and can put pressure on the marketers for their rights. For example, if a flight is delayed the travellers immediately protest in a group. The complaint in the court can be a more organized form of protest. For example, budget airlines in the country were refusing refunds on discounted fares if a flight was cancelled. Recent guidelines of the government have made it clear that the fare shall be refunded or the passenger will be adjusted on the next flight, depending on the choice of the consumer.

Macro Environment

This is the larger environment in which tourism activity occurs. Any changes here influence tourism either directly or through the micro environment. It is often referred to as PEST (political, economic, social and technological). But it includes the natural environment too, more so in tourism that uses nature as a product or to create the ambience for the use of the product.

Political environment

Political environment influences tourism marketing through pressure groups, policies, rules and regulations, and legislation. All these determine the framework for marketing.

Pressure groups   These groups in society use political influence for the furtherance of certain issues. Green groups work for ecotourism, consumer groups for tourist protection, culture groups for protection of heritage, industry groups for reduction of taxes, and so on. These try to influence law-making bodies, such as the Parliament and the legislative assemblies, to create a suitable mechanism to address their concerns. For example, the opening of casinos to promote tourism has been debated in the country for the past few years. There are pressure groups for and against them. These may be opened once the pro-casino lobby gets stronger. The move has been dropped for now because of opposition from the hoteliers.

Another example can be the declaration of hotels as industry.

Policies   The government creates policies as guidelines to provide direction for the development of tourism. The Tourism Policy, 2002 guides tourism growth in India. It had identified certain focus areas that have been followed for subsequent developments. This policy talks about promotion of domestic tourism, creating a good host culture, the image of the country, and the development of infrastructure. As a result, tourism in the country was developed along these lines. Prior to 2002, the direction for tourism development was provided through National Action Plan, 1992 and the five-year plans. But the impetus to it was given by enhanced budgetary support in the tenth five-year plan. The plan provided for the promotion of rural tourism and identified places for it.

Rules and regulations   Rules regarding land allocation for hotels and tourism development, tax concessions, permits, registration of tour operators and travel agents, open sky, budget airlines, and tourism police give a direction for tourism growth.

To boost tourism, the government has made obtaining a tourist visa easier and is planning to begin offering visa on arrival. Easy access to medical visa has given a boost to medical tourism.

Laws The government regulates tourism with the help of laws that govern its different sectors. General laws for other businesses apply here as well. Legislations, such as environmental protection, consumer protection, foreign exchange management, companies act, labour laws, contract act, food adulteration act, and so on, play an important part in tourism. For example, the government has liberalized foreign direct investment (FDI) in tourism, and allowed privatization of airports, thus facilitating the inflow of essential capital.

Travel advisories Travel advisories are general guidelines issued by governments to the citizens to observe certain precautions while travelling to other countries. These precautionary guidelines can create a fear among the tourists, thus affecting the tourist inflow to particular destinations. The Mumbai bomb blasts in 1993 and 2006, the *Gujjar* agitation in Rajasthan in 2008, terrorism in Jammu and Kashmir, or insurgency in the north-eastern states are some of the instances which have adversely affected Indian tourism.

(A sample advice for US citizens is given in the case study at the end of this chapter.)

Economic environment

The general economic environment of a country influences any economic activity. The growing income levels in India in the past few years have given a boost to the service sector and tourism is one such important beneficiary. The important developments in the country's economy are as follows.

Growth of new sectors Growth of new sectors, such as information technology (IT), travel and tourism, retail, and banking has given jobs to young people. This income is finding its outlet in recreation, including travel and hospitality.

Growth of economy India has seen growth in almost all sectors of the economy, thus creating prosperity. This has the multiplier effect on consumption and is visible in increasing consumers in malls, hotels, airlines, destinations, etc.

Easy availability of foreign exchange Over time the government has eased access to foreign exchange for travelling abroad. This has spurred outbound tourism. The basic travel quota was USD 500 in 1996 but later it was increased to USD 10,000 per annum for holiday travellers, USD

25,000 per person for business travellers, and USD 1, 00,000 per academic year for education abroad.

Tax structure Tax structures bear on the price of tourism services and this is a sensitive issue. The tourism industry feels that the tax structure in the country is high compared to other countries. It is because of these reasons that the country is understood to be an expensive destination.

Inflation Rising prices put pressure on tourists' pockets, thus reducing the disposable income. The inflation in 2008 has made essential components of tourism, such as food and travel, dearer. This has made road travel, air travel, and restaurants costlier.

Social environment

The social environment decides the buying patterns of the tourists and the response of the society to tourism. The sociocultural environment of a place decides the holiday choices regarding the type of destination, activities, duration of the holiday, expenditure pattern, travel party size, and so on.
   The major elements of social environment are as follows.

Group behaviour Indians are group oriented like other Asians. For them bonding with primary groups (family) and secondary groups (friends) is very important. This makes group travel acceptable and likeable. The reference of groups in framing opinions is also very important.

Increasing role of women Traditionally, women were not given important decision-making roles in the patriarchal families. But now education and economic freedom has bestowed decision-making power on them. This has, thus, increased their mobility and their number among the travellers.

Changing mindsets of Indians The attitudes of Indians towards travel are changing. Mobility has increased as a result of globalization. As Indians are starting to travel more, the idea of tourism is being accepted. The comfort factor with new places and new activities has led to an increased domestic and outbound travel to newer places and for new activities.

Demography India is a young country with 59 per cent of its population in the working age group of 15–64 years. This segment is more mobile and forms a good tourism market.

Lifestyle changes Globalization has changed the lifestyle of people. A good number of people live in big cities and earn well but do not get enough time. Recreational activities, such as tours and eating out, have become a part of the lifestyle of these people. People take tours frequently for a change and rejuvenation.

Technological environment

Technology has completely altered the way the tourism business is conducted. Transportation technology has given faster and better vehicles to facilitate the movement of the tourists to far off places. Nowadays, it is even possible for tourists to travel to the deep seas and the outer space. Major changes have been introduced by information and communications technologies (ICT) in tourism. Internet and online distribution systems, such as centralized reservation system (CRS) and global distribution system (GDS), have changed the distribution and payment mechanism. These are used to distribute reservation and information services to sales outlets.

> The recent popularity of companies such as yatra.com, makemytrip.com, and cleartrip.com indicates the influence of ICT on tourism business.

Tourists can book their tour and other facilities from their homes and pay through credit cards. It is possible to look for the best buys from the comfort of homes. Information and communications technologies is used by marketers for promotion. All types of internet advertising and mobile advertising are examples of ICT.

Travel is the largest e-commerce category in India and online travel will increase to 23 per cent of total travel from 15 per cent in 2008. It is expected to be worth USD 6 billion by the end of 2010 (PhoCus 2008).

Natural environment

Climate and natural resources, such as mountains and hills, beaches, and forests are key resources for tourism. Therefore, it is important that these resources be managed effectively. The Davos Declaration, 2007 suggested the actions to be taken by the industry and the consumers to mitigate climate change. Studies have pointed that tourism in ecological fragile areas has led to threats to biodiversity, unsustainable and inequitable resource use, deforestation, and urban problems. This often necessitates that tourism marketing should promote nature-friendly practices. Globally, it has been realized that tourism is not as smokeless as was initially thought. The fragile destinations in India, such as hill stations and cultural monuments, have already started enforcing and encouraging the sustainable practices through guidelines for the marketers and the tourists. Environmental impact assessment (EIA) and carrying capacity analysis have become an integral part of sustainable tourism planning.

Environment impact analysis Tourism has profound impact on its environment and there is a need to assess the quantum of the impact before a product is designed. Acceptance of ecotourism and sustainable tourism as viable options forces a marketer to adapt these practices and project an image of a good corporate. Many practices are used for environment impact assessment and its conservation. The first is mandatory clearance of projects according to environmental laws of a country, the second is adopting voluntary certifications such as green globe, and the third is environmental benchmarking to constantly minimize the impacts. The latest in the list is carbon credits that take emissions of carbon as a measure.

Carrying capacity analysis   Tourism carrying capacity is the ability of a tourist attraction to bear the burden of tourism without any negative impact. It can be natural, social, economic, and cultural. The assessment of carrying capacity is made in physical as well as intangible terms. It forms a very important part of tourism planning in order to preserve the physical environment of a tourist attraction. If the carrying capacity of a tourist attraction is exceeded, it might have adverse affects. For example, the heavy rush of visitors and subsequent increase in the temperature in Amarnath, Jammu and Kashmir resulted in the melting of the *ice lingam* before the completion of the *yatra* period in 2008.

ENVIRONMENT ANALYSIS

Once you have learned the environmental forces and their impact on marketing, the next step is to analyse the environment and its impacts on the present and the future markets. This will enable a firm to take suitable action. A number of approaches are used for analysing the environment such as SWOT analysis, BCG matrix, GE matrix, ETOP profiling, etc. These identify forces in the external environment and the position of the firm in relation to these. The same force can be an opportunity for one firm and a threat for another.

SWOT Analysis

SWOT analysis is strengths, weaknesses, opportunities, and threats analysis. It is a tool that helps a firm to assess its environment to find the opportunities and threats and identify its internal strengths and weaknesses in a systematic manner. Strengths are the characteristics of a firm that increase its competitiveness. Weaknesses are those characteristics that decrease the competitiveness. Opportunities are positive environmental forces and threats are negative forces for a company. Figure 3.2 shows the SWOT matrix.

> The purpose of the SWOT analysis is to formulate strategies to take advantages of the strengths, defend against the weaknesses, find the best opportunities, and minimize the external threats.

SWOT analysis helps to match strengths and weaknesses with opportunities and threats in the environment. The perception of threats and opportunities in the external environment depends on the internal environment of a firm. Consider the case of the increasing strength of the rupee. It makes the exports expensive but at the same time makes the imports cheaper. Law and order problem in one state is a threat to its

	Positive	Negative
Internal environment	*Strengths* Advantages of a firm in • Physical assets • Human assets • Intangible assets • Financial assets	*Weaknesses* Disadvantages of a firm in • Physical assets • Human assets • Intangible assets • Financial assets
External environment	*Opportunities* • New markets • New products • New technology • Alliances • Vertical and horizontal integration	*Threats* • New competitors • Substitutes • Changing customers' tastes

Fig. 3.2 SWOT Matrix

tourism but if it diverts tourists to another state then it is an opportunity for the second state.

The following strategies can be formed after SWOT analysis.

SO   to use strengths to take advantage of the opportunities

WO   to overcome weaknesses to take advantage of the opportunities

ST   to use strengths to avoid threats

WT   to minimize weaknesses and threats

MARKETING STRATEGY PLANNING

Marketing strategy planning is advance decision-making for future marketing actions. Environment analysis is an essential prerequisite for it as it defines the conditions of the plan. The following steps are used to develop the marketing strategy.

Define the Mission

It is an answer to what the firm wants to become in the market. It can go for premium image, largest market share, or quality leadership. The mission decides the different subsequent directions of marketing.

Research the Market

The market is researched and analysed to know the customers and the competitors. It identifies the space of action for the marketers. For example, a hotel chain may learn that the top-end segment is cluttered with many players but the budget segment is under-represented and has space for profitable operations.

Set Strategic Aims

These are broad, long-term, action-oriented areas of the marketer. These can be specified in terms of the markets or products such as market penetration, market development, product development, and entering new markets.

Segment the Customers

The market is divided into homogenous groups of buyers so that each group or segment can be reached through suitable marketing activities. With the same strategic aim, activities for each segment will differ. Take the case of product development as strategic aim. One market may accept a standard product, while the other may demand a lot of adaptation according to the local requirements. In case of tours, the demand for ready-made packages and customized tours often comes from different markets and the marketer shall be prepared to deliver both.

Define Marketing Objectives

Strategic aims are developed as specific objectives to design focused plans. For example, the aim of the largest market share is converted into a number of tourists to be approached, sales per tourist, geographical coverage of the market, and so on.

Design a Marketing Strategy

Marketing strategy is designed to achieve specific marketing objectives. It is based on the marketing mix. To achieve the largest market share, the strategy is designed in terms of the product to be supported, the type of promotional campaign, the distribution channels used, the price adjustments, etc.

Set Tactical Plans, Budgets, and Programmers

The strategy is broken into workable tasks and schedules. Responsibilities are assigned to achieve the objectives. Sales volume may be broken channel wise, area wise, or according to product variants with budget and responsibilities fixed.

Monitor Progress

The performance is measured against standards to control and identify the need for any changes in the strategy.

The planning of marketing strategy has environmental analysis and marketing mix as its important components. Marketing strategy balances the marketers' goals and resources with the given environment through the marketing mix elements. The approach towards tourism marketing strategy planning is elaborated in Fig. 3.3.

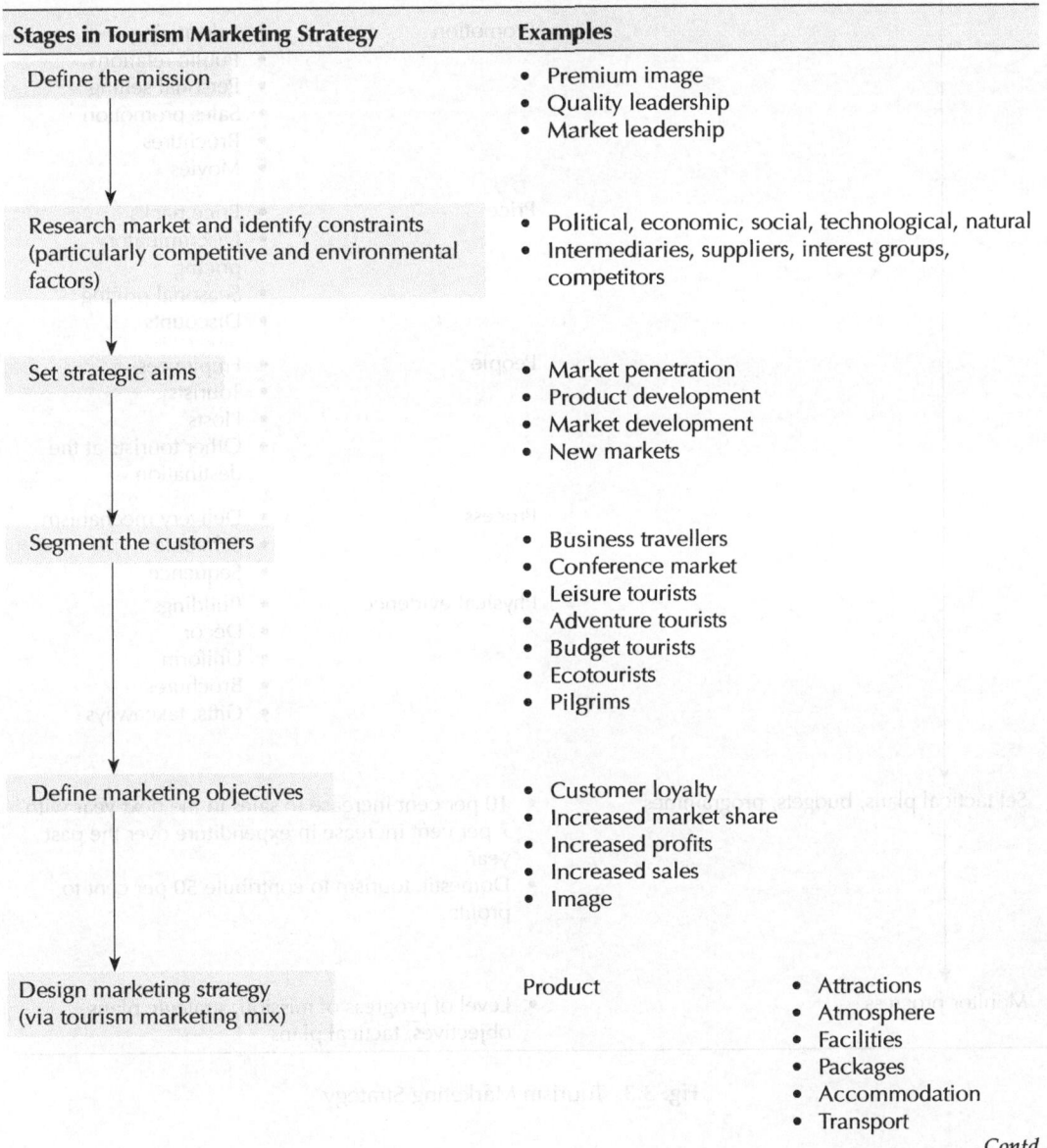

Stages in Tourism Marketing Strategy	Examples	
Define the mission	• Premium image • Quality leadership • Market leadership	
Research market and identify constraints (particularly competitive and environmental factors)	• Political, economic, social, technological, natural • Intermediaries, suppliers, interest groups, competitors	
Set strategic aims	• Market penetration • Product development • Market development • New markets	
Segment the customers	• Business travellers • Conference market • Leisure tourists • Adventure tourists • Budget tourists • Ecotourists • Pilgrims	
Define marketing objectives	• Customer loyalty • Increased market share • Increased profits • Increased sales • Image	
Design marketing strategy (via tourism marketing mix)	Product	• Attractions • Atmosphere • Facilities • Packages • Accommodation • Transport

Contd

Stages in Tourism Marketing Strategy	Examples
Place	• Location • Accessibility • Channels of distribution • Infrastructure
Promotion	• Advertising • Public relations • Personal selling • Sales promotion • Brochures • Movies
Price	• Price packs • Discriminatory pricing • Seasonal pricing • Discounts
People	• Employees • Tourists • Hosts • Other tourists at the destination
Process	• Delivery mechanism • Schedule • Sequence
Physical evidence	• Buildings • Décor • Uniform • Brochures • Gifts, takeaways
Set tactical plans, budgets, programmes	• 10 per cent increase in sales in the next year with 7 per cent increase in expenditure over the past year • Domestic tourism to contribute 50 per cent to profits
Monitor progress	• Level of progress of mission, strategic plans, objectives, tactical plans

Fig. 3.3 Tourism Marketing Strategy

CONCEPT OF MARKETING MIX

Businesses need to market right offers to the right buyers at the right time with the right prices under the right ambience and using the right systems. Marketing mix helps in it. It is a mix or a combination of tactics used to market effectively to a target market. It can also be defined as the combination of elements, tools, or efforts used to achieve marketing objectives. It is a combination of the controllable elements in marketing that are used to respond to the external uncontrollable environment.

The concept of marketing mix was given by Theodore Levitt who proposed the four Ps framework of product, place, price, and promotion.

Product

It is the offer of the marketer to satisfy a need and want. It includes the product variety and assortment, quality, features, style, brand name, packaging, warranties and guarantees, product logos, trademarks, and associated benefits.

It can be a good or a service or a combination of both. Traditionally, the term product was used for goods, as services were a less important part of the economy and not marketed in the same way. But with time, services and their marketing became important. Therefore, products can be goods such as food, car, house, books, etc., or services such as food service, car service, house maintenance, teaching, etc. The importance of the product lies in understanding the need or want that it will satisfy.

Place

Place refers to the distribution of the products to the consumers. It involves the movement of the product from the sellers to the buyers, as well as storage at different points to make these available at convenient time and locations to the buyers. The product can be made accessible in cyber space, in big shops in big cities, in rural areas or other places. In tourism, it involves the movement of tourists to places of attractions and creating facilities near the tourists for the purchase of tours. Various types of channel members are involved in this process, notably wholesalers or tour operators, retailers or travel agents, specialty operators or event organizers, and so on.

Price

It is the monetary value of the product. This is what the buyer pays to the seller, including discounts, allowances, credit terms, payment period, etc. Prices should be such that they create profit. It may be difficult for a new product to earn profit. At the time of a product's introduction, the cost is high and the demand is low. The marketer needs to plan the prices for a long period till the demand picks up and profits can be generated. Price decisions take account of a number of factors throughout the existence of a product in the market. A high-priced product may see prices coming down with growing technology and changing customer preferences. Air travel in India was once considered to belong to only the rich class but the concept of budget airlines has changed it altogether. The seasonal variations in prices and differential pricing are important aspects that affect the demand of tourism in the market.

Promotion

It refers to all the methods and tools used to give product information to the buyers and persuade them to purchase. It includes advertising, personal selling, public relations, and sales promotion. A suitable combination of these methods of promotion yields good results. Promotion includes decisions on its total plan, placing each method into the plan, deciding details of each method and the tools to be used therein.

EXPANDED MARKETING MIX

The expanded marketing mix finds application in tourism for its services orientation.

For a long time, the four Ps framework was used to target markets. But it was felt to be limiting for services that offered different sets of benefits to the consumers. Later, an expanded mix was proposed by Bitner that added three more Ps of people, process, and physical evidence.

People

People imply the human elements involved in the service experience. The most visible elements are those engaged in exchange, i.e., sellers and buyers. The people employed in the organization decide the quality of services that the customers get. The marketer should understand the contribution of people to the marketing mix and make efforts to enhance the quality of people through proper human resource management (HRM) practices. The customers are another category of people who decide the service experience through their involvement. The marketers need to know the methods of improving this experience through people.

Process

Process of service delivery decides the satisfaction of the customers. It includes the procedures, task schedules, mechanisms, activities, and routines by which a product or service is delivered to the customer. No element of marketing mix can overcome the deficiencies of poor process. An easy, on time, error-free check-in at the airport cannot be compensated by anything else.

Physical Evidence

Physical evidence creates tangibility for the intangible services. It portrays an image through physical presence such as buildings, decor, uniform, etc. Intangible services are heavily dependent on physical evidence. In creating this evidence the marketers must ensure its compatibility with the image of the product.

Each component of marketing mix has further sub-components. The framework given in Fig. 3.4 explains the marketing mix for services.

Product	Place	Price	Promotion
• Physical good features	• Channel type	• Flexibility	• Promotion blend
• Quality level	• Exposure	• Price level	• Salespeople
• Accessories	• Intermediaries	• Terms	◆ Number
• Packaging	• Outlet locations	• Differentiation	◆ Selection
• Warranties	• Transportation	• Discounts	◆ Training
• Product lines	• Storage	• Allowances	◆ Incentives
• Branding	• Managing channels		• Advertising
			◆ Targets
			◆ Media types
			◆ Types of ads
			◆ Copy thrust
			• Sales promotion
			• Publicity

People	Physical Evidence	Process
• Employees	• Facility design	• Flow of activities
◆ Recruiting	• Equipment	◆ Standardized
◆ Training	• Signage	◆ Customized
◆ Motivation	• Employee dress	• Number of steps
◆ Rewards	• Other tangibles	◆ Simple
◆ Teamwork	◆ Reports	◆ Complex
• Customers	◆ Business cards	◆ Customer
◆ Education	◆ Statements	◆ Involvement
◆ Training	◆ Guarantees	

Fig. 3.4 Expanded Marketing Mix for Services

(*Source:* Zeithaml and Bitner 1996)

MARKETING MIX OF TOURISM

Tourism as a product has its own marketing mix. Using the seven Ps framework, it can be expressed as shown in Fig. 3.5.

Marketing Mix Analysis

Marketing mix analysis provides an insight into the relative advantages of its elements and their components to get the most appropriate

Product	Place	Price	Promotion

• Attraction
   ◆ Beaches
   ◆ Theme parks
   ◆ Hill stations
   ◆ Events
• Transportation
   ◆ Trains
   ◆ Aircrafts
   ◆ Cruises
• Accommodation
   ◆ Hotels
   ◆ Guest houses
   ◆ Resorts
• Tour packages
• Terms and conditions
  of tour
• Product lines
• Branding
	• Channel type
	   ◆ Direct
	   ◆ Indirect
	• Intermediaries
	   ◆ Travel agents
	   ◆ Tour operators
	• Movement of tourists
	   ◆ Type of transport
	     used
	   ◆ Stoppages given
	   ◆ Time taken
	   ◆ Facilities en route
	• Managing channels
	   ◆ Selection
	   ◆ Integration
	   ◆ Agreements
		• Price level
		• Terms
		• Differentiation
		• Discounts
		• Allowances
		• Package prices
			• Promotion mix
			• Salespeople
			   ◆ Number
			   ◆ Selection
			   ◆ Training
			   ◆ Incentives
			• Advertising
			   ◆ Targets
			   ◆ Media types
			   ◆ Types of ads
			   ◆ Copy
			• Sales promotion
			• Public relations
			• Movies

People	Physical Evidence	Process

• Employees
   ◆ Recruiting
   ◆ Training
   ◆ Motivation
   ◆ Rewards
   ◆ Teamwork
• Customers
   ◆ Education
   ◆ Training
• Host population
   ◆ Education and
     training
   ◆ Participation
• Other tourists at the
  destination
	• Facility design
	• Equipment
	• Signage
	• Employee dress
	• Others
	   ◆ Reports
	   ◆ Business cards
	   ◆ Gifts and takeaways
		• Flow of activities
		   ◆ Standardized
		   ◆ Customized
		• Number and
		  sequence of steps
		   ◆ Simple
		   ◆ Complex
		• Customer
		  participation
		• Level of automation

Fig. 3.5 Marketing Mix of Tourism

combination. This is a continuous process as the importance of various elements keeps changing with time. If we consider the life cycle of a destination, promotion is very important in the beginning for wider awareness, the price becomes more important at maturity and growth stages to meet competition, and distribution gets prominence to reach more markets at the saturation stage.

A checklist can be used to judge relative merits of different elements of mix and their components as shown in Fig. 3.6.

Developing Marketing Mix

Developing a new marketing mix for an old product or for products similar to existing products is easy. The existing mix is used as a base for

Marketing Mix Element	No Change Required	Modifications Required	Major Change Required
Product			
Features			
Quality			
Accessories			
Packaging			
Services			
Warranties			
Guarantees			
Branding			
Place			
Channel type			
Channel length			
Channel members			
Location			
Storage			
Transportation			
Price			
Price level			
Payment mechanism			
Payment terms			
Discounts			
Differentiation			
Promotion			
Advertising			
Sales promotion			
Personal selling			
Public relations			

Contd

Marketing Mix Element	No Change Required	Modifications Required	Major Change Required
People Recruitment Training Motivation Rewards Education and counselling			
Process Flow of activities Mechanism Schedule Simple or complex Customer involvement			
Physical Evidence Facility design Employee dress Others: stationery, gifts			

Fig. 3.6 Checklist for Marketing Mix Analysis

further modifications. But if a mix is to be developed for a completely new product, no prior mix would be available for reference or analysis and modification. It is developed from scratch. The following considerations help in developing its frame.

1. Understand the importance of different elements of mix and their components for the target market in the given marketing environment. A checklist as shown in Fig. 3.7 can be used for it.

   For example, if we want to know the mix for a new destination, the analysis of potential markets brings out the fact that a new destination interests explorers, while an established one is for mass tourists. Explorers may not want luxury facilities or very low prices and often search the destination by themselves. Contrary to this, mass tourists want all the facilities that they can access in their homes, rely upon mass media for information, and are price conscious too. A marketer needs to research and find many more facts to develop the right mix for its target market and products.

2. Combine elements and their components in a tentative mix after understanding the relative importance of each.

3. Analyse the mix of competitors/substitutes and adjust the mix accordingly. A marketer may adopt a different strategy then that of the competitors or may follow the same depending upon its goals.

Marketing Mix Elements

Environment	Product	Place	Price	Promotion	People	Process	Physical evidence
Political							
Economic							
Social							
Technological							
Natural							
Competitors							
Suppliers							
Consumers							
Interest groups							
Political							

Fig. 3.7 Checklist for Marketing Mix Elements

4. Identify the requirements of different segments and adjust the mix for each.
5. Fix the budget and responsibility for each element.
6. Integrate the above for total effect.
7. Constantly monitor the mix.

To conclude, the analysis of the environment is used to develop the marketing strategy through a mix.

SUMMARY

Marketing activities are planned, developed, and executed in the external environment and are profoundly affected by it. The tourism marketing environment can be understood with the help of the tourism marketing system that is an open system with a number of interrelated and interdependent entities. This system can be arranged in a frame of internal, external micro, and external macro environment. The marketing organization forms the internal environment, the organizations or groups interacting with the marketer frequently form the micro environment, and the macro environment is made up of larger forces that affect both the micro and the internal environment. The internal environment is controllable by the firm and it can be altered to suit the requirements of the external environment. The micro environment closely surrounds the marketer and has direct and immediate effect. The macro environment is the larger environment in which the tourism activity occurs and is often referred to as PEST (political, social, economic, and cultural environment). In tourism, the natural environment is also included and it forms the main tour attraction. Any changes here influence the tourism activity either directly or through the micro environment. An analysis of this environment helps in planning the marketing strategy. A number of approaches, such as SWOT, ETOP profiling, EIA, and carrying capacity analysis are used for it. Marketing strategy planning is a systematic process that creates a road map for the firm. This follows the sequence—define mission, research markets, set strategic aims, segment consumers, design a marketing strategy, set tactical plans,

decide budgets, make programmes, and monitor progress. Marketing strategy is defined with the help of the marketing mix. The marketing mix is a combination of the controllable elements of a firm. These are designed to respond to the environment. Traditionally, the four elements of product, place, price, and promotion were discussed as a mix but the growing service industry changed that and an expanded marketing mix adding people, process, and physical evidence was accepted. The product is the offer of a firm; the place, also called physical distribution, is making the product available to the buyers; the price is deciding the monetary value of the offer; the promotion is communicating to the buyers about the offer; the people are engaging concerned parties in the exchange; the process is deciding the transfer mechanism of the product and its benefits to the buyers; and the physical evidence is creating tangible evidences for the intangibles. All these elements are integrated in a mix for the total effect.

KEY TERMS

Carrying capacity Tourism carrying capacity is the ability of a tourist attraction to bear the burden of tourism without any negative impact. It can be natural, social, economic, and cultural.

Environment impact analysis (EIA) It is the assessment of the physical impact of operating a tourism business at a place.

External macro environment This is the larger environment in which the tourism activity occurs. Any changes here influence tourism either directly or through the micro environment. It includes political, economic, social, cultural, and the natural environment.

External micro environment This is the nearest environment of the marketer that has direct and immediate effect on the tourism marketing activities. It has intermediaries, suppliers,

tourists, competitors, and interest groups in it.

Internal environment It consists of the marketing organization, its philosophy, and approach towards marketing.

Marketing environment Marketing environment is the sum total of the forces external to a firm that affect its marketing activities.

Marketing mix A set of controllable variables used by a firm to develop strategies for its target markets that is commonly explained with the four Ps framework of product, place, price, and promotion.

Marketing strategy planning Marketing strategy planning is advance decision-making for future marketing actions that acts as a road map.

Services marketing mix Marketing mix for services requires different set of strategies and is explained with the seven Ps framework of product, place, price, promotion, people, process, and physical evidence.

Sustainable tourism Tourism development that maintains and protects the tour attractions for the future. It engages in environment-friendly practices for the same.

SWOT analysis SWOT or strengths, weaknesses, opportunities and threats analysis is an environmental analysis technique.It aims at finding the best match between the environmental opportunities and threats against a firm's strengths and weaknesses.

Tourism marketing system Tourism marketing is an open system with a number of interrelated and interdependent entities such as marketers, tourists, distributors, suppliers, interest groups, and major external, political, social, economic, natural, and cultural elements.

Travel advisories Travel advisories are general guidelines issued by the government to its citizens to observe certain precautions while travelling to other countries.

EXERCISES

REVIEW QUESTIONS

1. Define marketing environment. What are its components? Discuss the impact of sociocultural environment on tourism marketing.
2. Explain marketing environment as a system.
3. What is expanded marketing mix? Why does the traditional mix not work for services like tourism?

PRACTICE EXERCISES

1. Find the different interest groups at your nearby tourist destinations and learn about their activities.
2. Identify the target market for a museum and prepare its marketing mix.

3. Analyse the marketing mix of India as a destination. What changes would you suggest and why?

PROJECTS

1. Survey a destination which has the visible physical and social impacts of tourism. Administer a little questionnaire to the tourism marketers to find how the degrading environment is influencing their marketing strategy.
2. Prepare a SWOT analysis of Taj Mahal as a tourist destination.

REFERENCES

Kotler, Philip 1995, *Marketing Management:Analysis ,Planning, Implementation and Control,* Prentice Hall of India, New Delhi.

Kotler, Philip, Bowen John, and Makens James 2004, *Marketing for Hospitality and Tourism,* Pearson Education, Delhi.

Mathieson, A. and G. Wall 1982, *Tourism: Economic, Physical and Social Impacts,* Longman, Harlow, UK.

Middleton, V.T.C. 1988, *Marketing in Travel and Tourism,* Heinemann, Oxford.

Meidan, Arthur 1984, 'The marketing of tourism,' *The Service Industries Journal,* vol.4, no.3, pp.166-186.

PhoCus Wright 2008, October, Indian Online Travel Review.

Porter, Michael E. 1999, 'Towards a dynamic theory of strategy,' *Strategic Management Journal,* vol.12, pp.95-117.

Rosenberg, Larry R. 1977, *Marketing,* Prentice Hall Inc, Englewood Cliffs, New Jersey.

Sharpley, Richard, Julia Sharpley, and Adams John 1996, 'Travel advice or trade embargo: The impacts and implications of official travel advice,' *Tourism Management*, vol. 17, no.1, pp. 1-7.

Witt, Stephen F. and Moutinho Luiz 1989, *Tourism Marketing and Management Handbook*, Prentice Hall International, Hemel Hempstead, UK.

Zeithaml A. Valarie, A. Parsuraman, and L. Leonard L. Bery 1985 'Problems and strategies in services marketing,' *Journal of Marketing*, vol.49, pp.33-46.

Zeithaml, Valarie A. and Mary Jo Bitner 1996, *Services Marketing*, The McGraw Hill Companies Inc., Singapore

Website References

Tourism and Hospitality 2007, 19 July, www.ibef.org.

UNWTO 2007, 3 October, 'Davos Declaration—Climate change and tourism—Responding to global challenges,' www.unwto.org.

CASE STUDY

TRAVEL ADVICE OR TRAVEL THREAT

Travel advisories or general travel guidelines are issued by a government to its citizens travelling to other countries to ensure their security. The following guidelines are from the US government to its citizens travelling to India.

Safety and Security

Terrorist incidents causing fewer casualties occur on a frequent basis, including a few in which American citizens were injured.

Beyond the threat from terrorism, demonstrations often cause disruption. Local demonstrations can begin spontaneously and escalate with little warning, disrupting transportation systems and city services and posing risks to travelers' personal safety. In response to such events, Indian authorities occasionally impose curfews and/or restrict travel. U.S. citizens are urged to avoid demonstrations and rallies as they have the potential for violence, especially immediately preceding and following elections and religious festivals (particularly when Hindu and Muslim festivals coincide). In addition, religious and inter-caste violence is unpredictable and occurs occasionally. In some cases, demonstrators specifically block roads near popular tourist sites in order to gain the attention of Indian authorities; occasionally vehicles transporting tourists are attacked in these incidents. Mobs have, however, attacked Indian and American missionaries and social workers as such activity provokes strong reactions in some areas. Anti-Christian violence has seen a slight increase in recent years in certain areas of India, such as in Gujarat. U.S. citizens should monitor local television and print media and contact the U.S. Embassy or the nearest U.S. Consulate for further information about the current situation in areas where they wish to travel. Finally, visitors should exercise caution when swimming in open waters along the Indian coastline, particularly during the monsoon season. Every year, several people in Goa, Mumbai, Puri (Orissa), and other areas drown due to the strong undertow. It is important for visitors to heed warnings posted or advised at beaches and avoid swimming in the ocean during the monsoon season.

Crime Petty crime, especially theft of personal property, is common, particularly on trains or buses. Pickpockets can be very adept, and women have reported having their bags snatched, purse-straps cut, or the bottom of their purses slit without their knowledge. Theft of U.S. passports is quite common, particularly in major tourist areas, on overnight trains, and at airports. Train travelers are urged to lock their sleeping compartments and take valuables with them when leaving their berths. Air travelers are advised to carefully watch their bags in the arrival and departure areas outside of airports. Violent crime, especially directed against foreigners, has traditionally been uncommon, although in recent years there has been a modest increase. As U.S. citizens' purchasing power is comparatively large, travelers also should exercise modesty and caution in their financial dealings in India to reduce the chance of being a target for robbery or other crime. Gangs and criminal elements operate in major cities and have sometimes targeted unsuspecting businessmen and their family members for kidnapping.

U.S. citizens, particularly women, are cautioned not to travel alone in India. Western women continue to report incidents of physical harassment by groups of men. Known as 'Eve-teasing', these incidents can be quite frightening. While India is generally safe for foreign visitors, according to the latest figures by Indian authorities, rape is the fastest growing crime in India. Among large cities, Delhi experienced the highest number of crimes against women. Although most victims have been local residents, recent sexual attacks against female visitors in tourist areas underline the fact that foreign women are also at risk and should exercise vigilance.

Women should observe stringent security precautions, including avoiding using public transport after dark without the company of known and trustworthy companions; restricting evening entertainment to well-known venues; and avoiding walking in isolated areas alone at any time of day. Women should also ensure their hotel room numbers remain confidential and insist the doors of their hotel rooms have chains, deadlocks, and spy-holes. In addition, it is advisable for women to hire reliable cars and drivers and avoid traveling alone in hired taxis, especially during the hours of darkness. It is preferable to obtain taxis from hotels rather than hailing them on the street. If women encounter threatening situations, they can call 100 for police assistance.

Scams   Major airports, train stations and tourist sites are often used by scam artists looking to prey on visitors, often by creating a distraction. Taxi drivers and others, including train porters, may solicit travelers with 'come-on' offers of cheap transportation and/or hotels. Travelers accepting such offers have frequently found themselves the victims of scams, including offers to assist with 'necessary' transfers to the domestic airport, disproportionately expensive hotel rooms, unwanted 'tours,' unwelcome 'purchases,' and even threats to the traveler when the tourists try to decline to pay. There have been several disturbing reports of tourists being held hostage on houseboats in Srinagar, Jammu & Kashmir, and forced to pay thousands of dollars in the face of threats of violence against the traveler and his/her family members.

Travelers should exercise care when hiring transportation and/or guides and use only well-known travel agents to book trips. Some scam artists have lured travelers by displaying their name on a sign when they leave the airport. Another popular scam is to drop money or to squirt something on the clothing of an unsuspecting traveler and during the distraction to rob them of their valuables. Individual tourists have also been given drugged drinks or tainted food to make them more vulnerable to theft, particularly at train stations. Even food or drink purchased in front of the traveler from a canteen or vendor could be tainted. To protect against robbery of personal belongings, it is best not to accept food or drink from strangers.

Some vendors sell rugs or other expensive items that may not be of the quality promised. Travelers should deal only with reputable businesses and should not hand over credit cards or money unless they are certain that goods being shipped to them are the goods they purchased. If a deal sounds too good to be true, it is best avoided. Most Indian states have official tourism bureaus set up to handle travelers' complaints.

Traffic Safety and Road Conditions   While in a foreign country, U.S. citizens may encounter road conditions that differ significantly from those in the

United States. The information below concerning India is provided for general reference only, and may not be totally accurate in a particular location or circumstance.

Travel by road in India is dangerous. A number of U.S. citizens have suffered fatal traffic accidents in recent years. Travel at night is particularly hazardous. Buses, patronized by hundreds of millions of Indians, are convenient in that they serve almost every city of any size. However, they are usually driven fast, recklessly, and without consideration for the rules of the road. Accidents are quite common. Trains are safer than buses, but train accidents still occur more frequently than in developed countries. On Indian roads, might makes right, and buses and trucks epitomize this fact. For instance, buses and trucks often run red lights and merge directly into traffic at yield points and traffic circles. Cars, auto-rickshaws, bicycles and pedestrians behave only slightly more cautiously. Frequent use of one's horn or flashing of headlights to announce one's presence is both customary and wise.

Outside major cities, main roads and other roads are poorly maintained and congested. Even main roads often have only two lanes, with poor visibility and inadequate warning markers. On the few divided highways, one can expect to meet local transportation traveling in the wrong direction, often without lights. Heavy traffic is the norm and includes (but is not limited to) overloaded trucks and buses, scooters, pedestrians, bullock and camel carts, horse or elephant riders en route to weddings, bicycles, and free-roaming livestock. Traffic in India moves on the left. It is important to be alert while crossing streets and intersections, especially after dark as traffic is coming in the 'wrong' direction (i.e., from the left). Travelers should remember to use seatbelts in both rear and front seats where available, and to ask their drivers to maintain a safe speed. If a driver hits a pedestrian or a cow, the vehicle and its occupants are at risk of being attacked by passersby. Such attacks pose significant risk of injury or death to the vehicle's occupants or at least of incineration of the vehicle. It can thus be unsafe to remain at the scene of an accident of this nature, and drivers may instead wish to seek out the nearest police station.

Protestors often use road blockage as a means of publicizing their grievances, causing severe inconvenience to travelers. Visitors should monitor local news reports for any reports of road disturbances.

(*Source:* www.travel.state.gov/travel, accessed on 23 June 2008)

DISCUSSION QUESTIONS

1. What travel advices do you find to be overreactions?
2. What can be the impact of these advices on tourists?
3. As a tourism marketer, how can you counter such advices?
4. What measures can be taken by the tour organizers to reduce risks to the American tourists?

CHAPTER 4

Marketing Management Information System and Demand Forecasting

LEARNING OBJECTIVES

In the previous chapter, you studied about the marketing environment and the marketing mix and learned how the marketing mix helps in developing an intelligent response system for environmental forces in a way that satisfies interests of all concerned. The fundamental of a good marketing mix is accurate information of the environment. For this, a marketing information system is essential. It collects the required information for decision-making of the marketing managers.

In this chapter, you will learn about the following.

• Concept of marketing management information system (MMIS)
• Structure of MMIS
• Marketing research as part of MMIS
• Transaction processing system (TPS), management information system (MIS), decision suppport system (DSS),and executive support system (ESS) in MMIS
• Demand forecasting for MMIS

INTRODUCTION

The marketing managers continuously make decisions in the form of strategy, plans, tactics, setting objectives, and so on. These decisions are based on the information available to them and the good quality of the information enhances the quality of the decisions too. Therefore, a system is required in the organizations to supply information to the marketing managers. This is called **marketing management information system (MMIS)** and is part of the larger management information system (MIS). An MIS integrates many other functional information systems such as finance information System (FIS), human resources information system

(HRIS), etc. All these are closely related. For example, the marketing profitability is concerned with finance for revenue generation and human resources for its own funding. An MMIS contributes to the bigger MIS but primarily focuses on information requirements of the marketing decisions. Marketing management information system is defined as a collection of interrelated and interdependent entities working together for common goals of collection, analysis, and dissemination of information for marketing decision-making. It has many components or entities that collect, analyse, and supply information.

MARKETING DECISIONS

Marketing decisions encompass all aspects of marketing, ranging from analysis of the market to development of the strategies and the marketing mix. Some of the major areas of decision-making are as follows.

- What will be the environment in future?
- What will my competitors do?
- How do I plan my products?
- Can I know the best price?
- What shall be the distribution system?
- How much shall I spend on promotion?
- How to find the optimum promotion mix?

The above decisions are made under an environment of complete certainty, uncertainty, and risk. Decision-making is easy in a certain environment but almost impossible in an uncertain one where nothing is known. Risk environment is a mix of certainty and uncertainty and is most common for the managers. The decisions of the managers can be broadly categorized as programmed and non-programmed. The programmed decisions are made in the same manner and apply to routine and recurring situations. Guidelines and benchmarks are used for these decisions and the information system shall be able to provide information as per the set benchmarks.

The other category of decisions is the non-programmed one. These are non-routine and non-recurring and a fresh decision is made after analysing the problem every time. These require information according to the situation. A good information system (IS) shall be able to cater to the flexible information needs of such decisions.

QUALITY OF INFORMATION FOR GOOD DECISION-MAKING

The marketing managers expect the following qualities to be present in the information.

Relevant

The information shall be relevant to the needs of the managers to assist in the decisions.

Timely

Late information is as good as no information. So the timely supply of information is necessary.

Sufficient

Information provided shall be optimum in quantity. Too much information wastes the time of the managers, and too little makes them ask for more information till it is complete.

Easy to Follow

The presentation of information shall be in such a format that the managers can understand it easily without any external help.

All these features can be built in the information only with a good information system.

STRUCTURE OF MARKETING MANAGEMENT INFORMATION SYSTEM

Marketing management information system can be explained with the help of four fields that interrelate with each other for collection, analysis, and supply of information for marketing decisions. A comprehensive framework of MMIS is presented in Fig. 4.1.

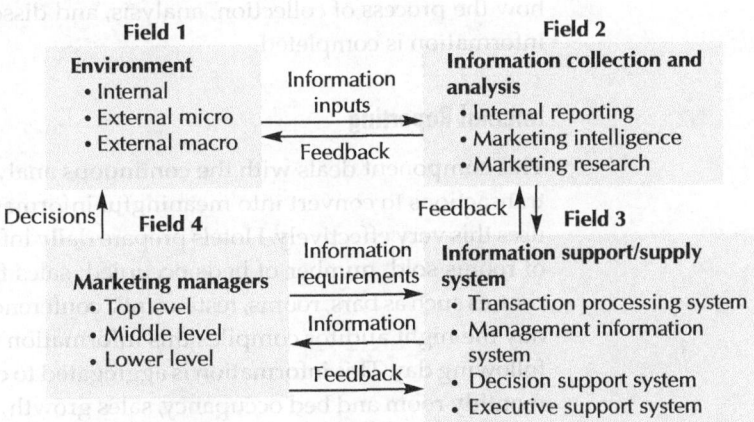

Fig. 4.1 Framework of Marketing Management Information System

In Fig. 4.1 Field 1 contains the environment of a firm. This environment keeps changing and the organizations need to adapt to these changes to survive. A relatively stable environment makes decision-making easier but it becomes difficult under conditions of uncertainty and only a good MMIS provides some certainty. The information of environment is collected by Field 2.

Field 2 consists of the systems of data collection and analysis pertaining to the environment. It includes three systems: internal reporting, marketing intelligence, and marketing research. Internal reporting processes transactions that are the result of daily exchanges of the marketer with the consumers, suppliers, middlemen, etc. Marketing intelligence supplies constant external information and marketing research caters to the ad hoc information needs which cannot be met by the other two.

Field 3 is the information support system that ensures that right information is made available to the users. The information obtained by field 2 is stored here. It has four sub-systems: transaction processing system (TPS), management information system (MIS), decision support system (DSS) and executive support system (ESS). Each of these caters to the diverse marketing information requirements of different levels.

Field 4 has the marketing managers who take decisions in an environment and demand information from Field 3 for the same. They also give feedback about the quality of the information so that the system undergoes continuous improvement.

We will discuss in detail the components of Field 2 and 3 to understand how the process of collection, analysis, and dissemination of marketing information is completed.

Internal Reporting

This component deals with the continuous analysis of the daily internal transactions to convert into meaningful information. The hotel industry uses this very effectively. Hotels prepare daily information of the number of rooms sold, number of beds occupied, sales from the different profit centres such as bars, rooms, restaurants, conferences, etc. At the end of the day the night auditor compiles this information for billing the guest the following day. This information is aggregated to calculate the weekly and monthly room and bed occupancy, sales growth, and profits per room to help the management to take the necessary decisions. A similar analysis of the daily transactions is done by travel agencies, airlines, and destinations to understand the pattern of their performance. For example, after such analysis, a destination may find that it is attracting high volumes of tourists who are spending less. It may then devise a strategy to attract the high-value tourists and to encourage the low-spending tourists to spend more.

Internal reporting feeds data into the TPS and can give very useful information if the collection and analysis is systematically done. The aggregated information from the TPS supports the management information system of marketing.

Marketing Intelligence

Marketing intelligence supplies continuous information about the external environment. The information from the external environment is collected from different sources such as competitive firms' employees, newsletters, dealers, suppliers, government reports, independent researches, reports, forecasts, etc. The information from different sources is put into a proper perspective to derive useful conclusions. It is checked for accuracy before use. For example, the high growth rates of economy indicate growth for all the sectors but if it is accompanied by inflation, some businesses may see the demand eroding.

The intelligence supplies both recurring and non-recurring information. Techniques such as data mining help in seeing the patterns in such information.

Marketing Research

American Marketing Association (AMA) defines marketing research as the systematic gathering, recording, and analysing of data about problems relating to the marketing of goods and services.

All information requirements of the managers are not predetermined. Some are ad hoc in nature. The managers put the demand and it is supplied on 'as and when' needed basis. This information may be derived from the database of the firm that is continuously built on internal reporting and the marketing intelligence, or if not found there, it can be collected separately. The collection of information on project by project basis is the domain of the marketing research. It is defined as the process of collection, analysis, and supply of marketing information.

Marketing research follows a systematic process, as shown in Fig. 4.2.

Project definition

The problem or the information needs of the managers are converted into the project definition for the researcher in terms of the purpose of the project. The researchers and managers sit together to decide it and to avoid any gaps between their understandings of the problem. A few checks are made at this stage.

- Is it justified on cost benefit basis?

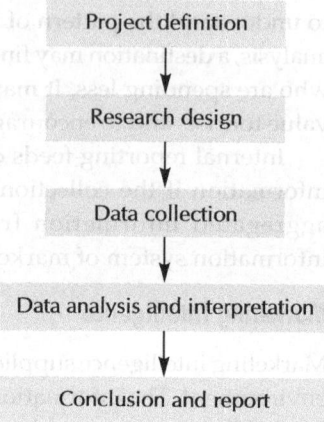

Fig. 4.2 Process of Marketing Research

- Is the research really required or can the information be obtained from the other parts of MMIS?
- Is the problem clearly stated?

If the answers to the above are positive, the process is carried forward.

For example, if the sales of a company are going down, it can look beyond the sales of the existing products and can formulate a project to identify the potential of new products and markets. The definition of the project and information needs also sets the agenda for the type of study to be conducted. In this case, it will be descriptive, if the sales data is presented in detail. It will be co-relational, if an association is ascertained between the declining sales and the promotional pricing of the competitors, and explanatory, if it is explained why the buyers are no longer buying the product.

Research design

Research design is the blueprint for conducting research. It includes the plan and structure that is undertaken to find the answers to project questions. It specifies the following.

Study design   What will be the framework of research? Some designs used in marketing are cross sectional, before–after, experimental, and historical. Cross-sectional researches are a study of a particular phenomenon in a population like studying changing preferences of the tourists. The information can be collected by contacting a sample of respondents. In before–after studies, a phenomenon is measured before and after the intervention and the gap is attributed to the intervention. These studies can be experimental or non-experimental. The preferences of the tourists can be measured before and after their exposure to the advertising campaign. Any change in their preferences is taken to be the effect of the advertising. You can measure the opinion of the tourists towards India before and after the Incredible India campaign. Experimental study is controlled where the intervention supposedly has the cause–effect relation with the outcome. This intervention is introduced to learn its impact. A tour package can be made available for different prices through different channels to judge the effect on sales. It can be done in controlled situations such as a room or an uncontrolled one such as the market. Historical designs study the trend over a time period. It can involve the past, the present, and the future. All forecasts use this design. Tourism trends are identified with this design only.

Sampling   Researches are conducted on a part of a population or a sample that is a good representative of the whole. Sampling explains the sources of information collection including the selection of the study area, the elements, and the units of data collection. A number of sampling designs are available, ranging from random to convenient. The decisions on the size of the sample, its elements, and the data collection units depend upon the accuracy desired. For example, a study of the foreign tourists in India can be based on randomly choosing the respondents or purposely selecting those who match the general profile of the international visitors to India. Either the individuals or the families can be contacted. Further, the data can be obtained on the number of places visited or the duration of holiday. The choice depends upon the information needs specified at the time of the project definition.

Measurement   What and how much information should be collected? Collecting information, even through sampling, involves cost and too much information is not always good. Specifically detailing the information measurement will help in going for the cost-effective solutions.

For example, the data of the volume of outbound tourism of India is collected from the ports and the airports. But the countries where these tourists are going collect details of their demography, psyche, and behaviour. Thus, different measurements are made on the same population as per the different needs.

Data collection

The data for research can be primary or secondary. The data that is generated for research is called primary. The already collected data for other purposes that can be used for research is called secondary.

The secondary data can be found in the following sources.

World Travel and Tourism Council (WTTC), Pacific Asia Travel Association (PATA), Federation of Hotels and Restaurants Associations of India (FHRAI), and Federation of Indian Chambers of Commerce and Industry (FICCI) are some of the major bodies keeping data on Indian tourism.

Government records: These include census, surveys, studies, statistical records, etc. For example, the data on Indian tourism is available from the Ministry of Tourism. The annual reports, tourism statistics, surveys, policies, rules, etc. give useful information. The Planning Commission and the Reserve Bank of India (RBI) can also be a source of important information.

Independent organizations: Some independent organizations conduct researches and their reports are a good source of secondary data. United Nations World Tourism Organization (UNWTO) and the other UN wings are a good source of data.

Private organizations: Some private organizations and their federations collect data. Some companies, such as American Express and Thomas Cook, also collect data for their business interests. For example, American Express has conducted studies on corporate travel across the globe.

Universities and research institutes: These conduct researches as part of projects, doctoral work, and students' dissertations and can be a source of invaluable data. A number of universities in the country are engaged in tourism research.

Media: The media brings out well-researched reports for areas of general interest. Television channels such as National Geographic and Discovery report on tourism. Magazines and newpapers cover current issues on tourism. For example, the *Amarnath Yatra, the Kailash Mansarovar Yatra,* and the *Char Dham Yatra* are extensively covered every year.

Research journals: These academic publications follow scientific rigour for the research and supply good data.

Websites: Web space is becoming a mine of information these days and many websites can give good information.

The managers use the secondary data because this is cheaper and saves time. In case this is unavailable, the primary data is collected. The primary data is collected through the following methods.

Observation: This is to look at a phenomenon closely for understanding. It can be done in a hotel to see what types of customers are coming, the party size, behaviour in the hotel, items, and quantity ordered, and so on. The same is possible for a tourist destination and an airport. Observations over a few sittings yield the necessary data. But this method is time consuming, requires trained observers, and may disturb the subjects.

Questionnaire: It is a participative method of data collection where the respondents answer the written questions. The questionnaires are sent to the participants who can fill these at their convenience and return them later. It is a simple and cheaper method but the response rate may be low. The questions may remain unanswered, making the rejection rate high. The questions may be answered without proper understanding or may be manipulated closer to ideals and norms.

A good questionnaire can overcome some of the limitations. A short, simple questionnaire may be answered well.

Schedule: A questionnaire is called a schedule if the researcher fills the answers given by the respondents. This increases the response rate and the accuracy but takes more time.

Interview: An interview is a conversation between two parties in a question and answer form. The researcher asks and notes answers. It is time consuming but the interviewees can be probed to get a good answer. Focus groups are common in marketing where a homogenous group is asked to discuss the issue for which the data is required. The moderator notes the opinions and ensures that the group does not drift from the core theme. The free discussion provides very good information on issues such as problems of tourism, how to improve tourism, security of foreign tourists, and so on.

Laboratory experiments: Tourism experience as such cannot be tested in a laboratory but certain aspects can be tested. Computer simulation can be used to give virtual experience of all the components of the tour and assess the response of the potential market.

Field Experiments: Test marketing is an acceptable practice in marketing, where a real market is used as a laboratory to test the product. Hotels with fixed locations and the airlines cannot be tested but the tour packages can be tested.

The data collected is checked for accuracy and relevance before the next stage. Then it is passed on for data analysis.

Data analysis and interpretation

The data collected is analysed with the help of suitable techniques. Statistical tools prove valuable in this. These days statistical packages like Statistical Package for Social Sciences (SPSS) are used. Thus, data is read to observe meaningful results for the project.

Research report

Finally a report is prepared that follows a systematic and an objective approach as the ideas are expressed with validity and verifiability in mind. The plan of the report depends upon the nature of the project but the following general format is followed in an elaborate report.

Introductory part It includes preface, executive summary, chapter plan, list of tables and figures, acknowledgements, authorization letter, and so on.

Report proper It has three main parts: introduction to the research area, the main part consisting of literature survey, research design, presentation, and analysis of data and conclusion. This part gives references and bibliography in internationally established styles, American Psychological Association (APA) Style or Chicago Manual of Style.

Appended parts All the information that is felt essential for the reader but otherwise does not fit in the main part is placed here such as the questionnaire and additional data.

Marketing Research in Tourism

Marketing Research in tourism is difficult because of the intangibility of the product and is not undertaken by small operators who form a big part of the industry. Hodgson (1991) identifies four broad areas of research in tourism marketing.

Measuring past and present It includes tourist flow, brand share, sales data, advertising tracking, customer profiling, quality control, and image studies.

Predicting future It covers the forecasting travel intentions and plans.

Creating future It entails product improvement, modification, and new product development.

Understanding market It relates to market segmentation, gaining qualitative insights for understanding consumer rationale, etc.

INFORMATION SUPPORT SYSTEMS

The MMIS supplies information for all levels of marketing functions. In a typical organization with a pyramid structure, three levels of decision making—operational, managerial, and strategic—are identified (Fig. 4.3). Corresponding to each level, the information support system is divided into TPS for operational decisions, MIS for managerial decisions, and DSS and ESS for executive decisions.

Transaction Processing System (TPS)

In an organization, routine and recurring operational decisions are made at the lower level. These require accurate and timely information in a

Management Levels

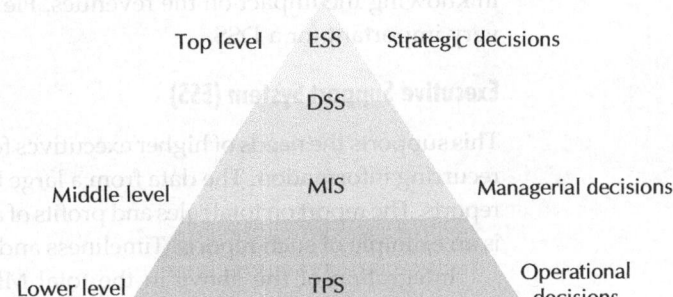

Top level   ESS   Strategic decisions

DSS

Middle level   MIS   Managerial decisions

Lower level   TPS   Operational decisions

Fig. 4.3 Decision-making and Information Processing at Different Management Levels

fixed format. A TPS provides this from the internal detailed and standard records. Technology makes this system more effective and reliable. Ticket reservation, order and bill processing, accounts, and payroll are some examples of this system. A TPS can help a ticketing agent know the daily number of tickets booked, the tickets booked destination and airlines wise, total revenues generated, revenues on different routes, and so on.

Management Information System (MIS)

We discussed earlier that MMIS is a component of MIS but within MMIS a smaller MIS is present to help the managers. We also used the term MMIS instead of MIS to avoid any confusion.

It supports management of the operations that are regular and recurring. It supplies reports in a summarized and standard format. Here too, the timelines and reliability of the information is important and technology plays an important role. The same examples of TPS can be used here to understand this. While TPS helps in the booking of tickets, MIS judges the performances of the different outlets from where the tickets are booked. In order processing, it finds profitable orders, and in billing it evaluates the effectiveness of the process, and so on.

Decision Support System (DSS)

It supports the unstructured information needs of the managers for dealing with one time situations. The information is generated from the TPS on 'as and when' needed basis. For example, a hotel maintains the complete data of bookings and their potential revenues but if at one time all the bookings are cancelled, the management will be interested in knowing the impact on the revenues. Flexibility and adaptability are very important for a DSS.

Executive Support System (ESS)

This supports the needs of higher executives for aggregated, standard, and recurring information. The data from a large base is used to prepare these reports. The report on total sales and profits of a hotel chain across the globe, is an example of such reports. Timeliness and reliability is critical for ESS.

Integration of the above in the total MMIS supplies the necessary information to the marketing managers and assists in making good decisions.

Futuristic information of the market demand is an important aspect of information needs of the managers and demand forecasting is used for it.

DEMAND FORECASTING

Demand estimation is very important in tourism as it is very sensitive to external developments. Perishability of tourism products necessitates accurate forecasting.

Managers would be very fortunate if they can accurately know the demand of their products in the market. But such a situation is not possible and the next best option is to get a good estimate of the future demand so that resource allocation can be made in an optimum way.

A variety of forecasting methods and models have been developed to forecast highly aggregated demand such as international tourist arrivals to disaggregated ones such as arrivals to a city, hotel, agency, or monument.

What is Demand?

Demand is defined as the level of estimated sales under defined conditions. For a marketer these conditions are as follows.

- Market or a defined geographical area
- Product
- Competitors' efforts
- Own marketing efforts

The estimation of demand involves projection of all these conditions. If any of these prove inaccurate, the forecasted demand also goes awry.

Demand Forecasting Methods

Many methods have been developed for demand forecasting, ranging from simple opinions to sophisticated models. All of them may yield a fair estimate depending upon the case to which these are applied. Broadly, these are divided into the following five categories.

1. Surveys
2. Judgemental methods
3. Experiments
4. Time series methods
5. Causal methods

Surveys

Surveys are a common source of information for future demand. The consumers and sales force are surveyed for demand forecasting. For consumer surveys, potential individuals and households in the target market are asked about their travel plans.

The logic is that these plans will convert into actual travel. The quality of information from these surveys depends upon the framing of the questions, the skills of the surveyors, the response rate from the buyers, and the honesty of the answers. But the consumers cannot have an understanding of the external and the larger forces in the environment that may bear on their demand in future. Consumer surveys are very useful for a new product where no other source of information exists. Sales force surveys are also used on similar lines and the people who sell tourism are surveyed such as travel agents, tour operators, and direct sales force of the company. These are asked to predict their demand for the forecast period and this forms the base of the firm's estimate. The logic here is that being closer to the customers, they understand their behaviour and being in business, also understand the impact of other external factors on the demand, thus, yielding a better figure. But they may manipulate information because the sales force targets, such as sales quotas and territories, are tied with forecasts.

Judgemental methods

These methods use the opinion and judgement of knowledgeable persons in the field to predict demand. These experts have an insight into the different market forces and their impact on future sales. This insight is converted into future sales figures. The two main methods used for this are as follows.

Expert consensus   A group of 8 to 10 experts are invited to a place and are asked to make the predictions. They are supplied all the required information to rest their predictions on solid foundation. They sit together and discuss and after many rounds of discussion may agree on a figure. The problem with this method is the availability of experts, cost of conducting the meeting, and the situations where the experts may not agree on a common figure. Another risk is that if a few group members move in a wrong direction in the beginning, the others may follow and all may end up agreeing on the wrong figure. The domineering and the vocal members may influence the others.

Delphi technique Delphi technique tries to avoid the open discussion of expert opinion and allows experts to revise their opinions in secret. A group of 8 to 10 experts gather at one place and are supplied all the input information. Each makes its estimate and writes on paper. The moderator of the group aggregates these estimates and circulates the aggregated data to the members for a review of their original forecast. The members may review and revise, and again submit the estimates. The same process of estimation, aggregation, and revision continues till all reach a common figure. This method too suffers from the problems of expert consensus, except that the dominance of vocal or aggressive members is avoided.

Experiments

Surveys and judgemental methods predict the intention to purchase and not the actual behaviour. Experiments are used to calculate the actual purchase. Test marketing is used for this. It involves the selection of a sample market where the product is launched with its marketing mix. The response of the buyers in terms of sales is observed and is used to predict the sales in the total market. The sample market can be a geographical area or a shop in a mall. Test marketing too has the following limitations.

1. The behaviour of a sample market may not be replicated in the actual market as test market conditions are more controllable.
2. The competitors may disturb the conditions in the test market to destroy the test market results.

To calculate the sales results in the total market, one more variable is needed, such as the sales of related product or the sales of whole product category in both the test and the whole market, as shown in the formula given below. The sales forecast will depend on the effective relation of sales to this variable.

$$\text{Sales forecast of product } A \text{ in the market} = \frac{\text{Sales forecast of product } A \text{ in the test market}}{\text{Sales of product category/related product in the test market}} \times \text{Sales of product category/related product in the total market}$$

Time series methods

Time series for sales is past sales data on time scale. Time series methods are based on the assumption that past trends can be used to forecast future sales. A time series is considered to be composed of four types of variations: trend, cycle, season, and random. A trend is a basic long-term pattern underlying series. Cyclic variations are sustained periods of high sales followed by low sales such as business cycles. Seasonal variations are regular, recurring fluctuations of less than a year. Random variations are the result of unexpected events, such as political events, and cannot be predicted. All the variations that cannot be explained by trend, season, and cycle are taken to be random. In forecasting that uses time series data, the effect of seasonal variations is adjusted before projecting data for the future.

The models used for time series forecasting are as follows.

Naive model   This is the simplest model that takes the next period forecast from the last period sales. This model provides accurate value if the trend is flat. The forecasted value can be adjusted for seasonal effects, if any. This assumes that there will be the same percentage increase in sales in the next period as in this period and if we take this period to be a year, the forecast is made as given below.

Next year's sales = this year's sales + per cent increase in this year's
sale over the last year's sales

Moving average method   Moving average is the average of the past periods that moves forward as the data for the next period becomes available. This method is used for forecasting sales for short periods. If the forecast is to be made for the month of May and the time cycle is 4 months, the average from January to April is taken and for the forecast of June, the average from February to May is considered, and so on.

$$\text{Sales forecast for May} = \frac{\text{Total sales from January to April}}{4}$$

$$\text{Sales forecast for June} = \frac{\text{Total sales from February to May}}{4}$$

$$\text{Sales forecast for July} = \frac{\text{Total sales from March to June}}{4}$$

Exponential smoothing   In time series, some time periods may be more important for future sales such as recent periods. In exponential smoothing, greater weightage is given to important periods. A simple form of exponential smoothing combines weighted average of this year's sales with the forecast of this year's sales. The forecasting equation used is

Next year's sales = k (this year's sales) + (1– k) (this year's forecast).

where k is the smoothing constant and its value is kept between 0 and 1. Its value is kept small if the earlier trend continues but if it changes, its value is kept closer to 1 to adapt to these changes. Its value is calculated by analysing the past data and the value, giving minimum error in forecast is chosen.

Statistical trend analysis This involves determining the underlying trend in data with the help of simple regression analysis that takes time as one variable, and forecast as another. The forecast is made assuming that a constant rate of change in sales will take place from one period to the next. For a simple linear relation, the equation is

$Y = a + bT$

Where Y = forecast variable
T = time period
a and b are coefficients calculated using regression analysis

The least squares regression technique is used to estimate the coefficients by fitting a line through the past demand data on time scale.

Causal Methods

Time series cannot be used for demand forecasting if it does not show any pattern. Then other methods are used that forecast sales based on variables other than time. Causal methods forecast sales as a result of other variables. For example, tourist arrivals may depend upon a number of factors such as events, international trends, infrastructure, etc. A model incorporating these as independent variables can be used to forecast sales. The models used for causal methods are as follows.

- Regression models
- Barometric models
- Econometric models

Regression models An equation relating sales to predictor variables is derived using multiple regression analysis. Regression analysis involves fitting an equation to explain sales fluctuations in terms of related variables. For forecast, the estimates of influencing or related variables are used with the estimated relationship. Multiple regression involves building a model to determine the predictor variables to be included in the analysis and the magnitude of their relationship with the demand. The following steps are used in building such a model.

1. Select the major predictor variables
2. Collect past data about these variables
3. Decide the relationship between these variables and the demand
4. Run the regression equation for goodness of fit and to determine the values of the coefficients
5. Repeat the past steps unless the model gives satisfactory forecasts on historical data

Barometric forecasting   A time series may correlate with another time series showing lead–lag relation. If the lead can be predicted, the lag can be predicted too. Take the case of the tourist movement that can be related to the growth of transport. There may be a lead time for the indicator after which the tourist movement follows. For example, the number of air travellers will depend upon the frequency of flights and price. Any change in the price and frequency can be taken for predicting the change in the number of travellers.

Econometric models or input output analysis   It uses a number of equations that define variable to be forecasted and other economic predictor variables. Tourism demand depends upon a large number of factors and the consideration of all becomes important in the model. For example, international factors such as global economic scene, events, and national factors such as, inflation, currency exchange, social factors, natural factors, customers, and competitors, all need to be built as the predictor variables in the model.

A summary of the different forecasting methods is presented in Table 4.1.

CHOOSING DEMAND FORECASTING METHODS

A manager would like to use a model that gives the best results in a given situation. Different methods of forecasting prove effective for different time periods. Sophisticated methods give good results for long time periods, while the simple ones are effective for short-duration forecast. A manager shall be able to choose the appropriate combination of methods by considering the following factors.

Time Period of Forecasting

Forecasting needs a range from a short duration to a long one. A hotel makes weekly estimates for weekly demands such as rooms, food, etc. The same hotel can plan its business strategy for next 10 years.

Table 4.1 Forecasting Methods

Method		Nature	Benefits	Drawbacks
Surveys	Consumer surveys	Opinion of consumers about buying intentions	Direct from buyers	Gaps between intention and action
	Sales force surveys	Aggregate of sales force opinion	Expertise of front line staff	Estimates linked with targets, quotas, and compensation
Judgemental methods	Expert consensus	Independent opinions	Biases internal to organization avoided	Diverse background of experts makes agreement difficult
	Delphi technique	Written estimates with feedback from other participants through successive rounds	Biases of group shift and thinking avoided	Group dynamics not used
Experiments	Test marketing	Sales in selected areas	Actual sales	High costs and interference of competitors
Time series methods	Naive method	Past simple average used to forecast	Easy	Past trend may not be repeated
	Moving average	Recent periods of data used	Easy	Recent periods may be different from future
	Exponential smoothing	Weightage is given to periods assessing their impact on sales	Useful for short periods	Long-term forecasts not possible
	Statistical trend	Projecting past trend in future	Easy	Not accurate if environment changes
Causal methods	Regression model	Relation built with the help of regression equation	Easy as the cause–effect relation is established based on past data	New variables are not considered
	Barometric model	Relation built with demand as lag and other variables as lead	Easy	Lead–lag relation may not follow the past pattern again
	Econometric model	Model built based on many variables	Good forecasts	Time consuming and complexity of model

Methods that can predict turning points in demand and are based on concrete data yield better results for long duration. Advanced mathematical models are useful for this. For short-term estimates, opinion-based methods give quick results.

Time Period Available for Forecasting

Sometimes immediate forecasts may be needed and only those methods can be used that give quick results. All the opinion-based methods are time consuming and cannot be used here. The computerized quantitative methods can run the past data and give forecast in a day or two.

Cost of Forecasting

The choice of method depends upon cost-benefit analysis. If the cost of using a method exceeds its benefits, it is not used.

Accuracy Required

The management decides the level of accuracy needed in the forecasts. If more accuracy is not required then less sophisticated options can be used.

Data Available

All methods use some form of data as input. A method can be used if the relevant data is available. Take the case of completely new products. In the absence of similar products, the past data is not available and only the judgmental methods can be used.

After considering all the above factors, a decision-maker can choose to use one or a combination of methods for demand forecasting.

SUMMARY

The managers need information about their environment to make good decisions. The marketing management information system meets this need. It is a collection of interdependent and interrelated entities that work for the purpose of providing information. An MMIS collects, analyses, and supplies information to the managers. Collection of information is done through internal reporting, marketing intelligence, and marketing research. Internal reporting is the recording of the daily transactions and generating meaningful

information out of it. Marketing intelligence provides information about the external environment and the information is collected from diverse sources. Marketing research provides information on project basis and after analysing the needs of the managers, the information is collected and presented as a report. It involves accurately identifying needs, collecting and analysing data, and writing the research report. The information collected becomes part of the information support system that supplies it to the users. An information support system meets the needs of all levels in an organization and has transaction processing system, management information system, decision support system, and executive support system as its parts. A transaction processing system supplies information of the internal records and the management information system of the aggregated records. A decision support system gives information about the external environment to higher levels on the basis of marketing intelligence and research and an executive support system deals with the highly-aggregated records to be supplied to top decision-makers.

The MMIS can supply information of the past, the present, and the future. The future information is estimated to help in decisions and demand forecasting is its important part. Demand forecasting is estimating future sales for a defined product, in a defined geographical area, with defined market conditions and marketing strategies. Surveys, expert opinions, experiments, time series, and causal methods are used for it. Surveys judge the intentions of the tourists and the dealers to know the demand. Expert opinion is used to collect data from experts in the field who have broader perspective. Expert consensus and Delphi techniques are used for it. Experiments use real sample markets to test the response to a product. Time series methods relate future sales to past data and the naive model, moving average method, and exponential smoothing are used for this. Causal methods establish a relation between sales and causal or predictor variables. Regression, barometric, and econometric models are used to establish the cause and effect relation.

The efficacy of a method depends upon the time period of forecast, data, and time available. An appropriate method is selected after considering all the factors.

A good MMIS and demand forecasting increase the certainty of the environment for the managers to take effective decisions.

KEY TERMS

Causal method This method establishes a relation between the demand and the variables influencing it and forecast is made on the basis of this relation.

Decision support system It supports the unstructured information needs of the managers for dealing with one-time situations.

Delphi method In this method members of an expert group individually write their forecasts that are averaged and sent back to the group members for reconsideration. Such rounds continue till a consensus is reached.

Demand forecast It is the estimate of the total amount of sales for a given product for a specified future time period and under defined marketing conditions.

Executive support system This supports the information needs of higher executives for aggregated, standard, and recurring information.

Experiments The real market conditions are simulated and sales figures obtained are used to forecast for actual markets.

Expert consensus A group of experts discuss the probable forecasts and agree on one forecast.

Internal reporting It is a system of recording and analysing daily the internal transactions to convert into meaningful information for the decision-makers.

Judgemental method This method uses judgement of knowledgeable persons in the field to predict demand.

Management information system It is a system that supplies reports in a summarized and a standard format for regular and recurring management decisions.

Marketing intelligence It is a continuous collection of external information from diverse sources in the environment.

Marketing management information system

It is system of collection, analysis, and dissemination of information for marketing decision-making.

Marketing research It is systematic gathering, recording, and analysing of data about the problems relating to the marketing of goods and services.

Naive model This predicts the next period sales from the last period sales. It is used for short-term forecast and the seasonal effects in data can also be adjusted.

Statistical trend analysis This involves determining the underlying trend in data with the help of simple regression and forecast is made

assuming a constant rate of change in sales.

Surveys Demand forecasting methods that make forecast on the basis of the information collected by surveying consumers and sales force.

Time series methods These are the methods that use past sales data on time scale to forecast future sales.

Transaction processing system It is a system of providing information from the internal detailed and standard records for routine, recurring, and operational decisions.

EXERCISES

REVIEW QUESTIONS

1. What is marketing management information system? Discuss its components.
2. Explain the process of marketing research.
3. What is the role of transaction processing system and decision support system in marketing management information system?
4. How is forecasting done with the help of the Delphi method? Discuss its advantages and limitations.
5. Classify the demand forecasting methods discussed in the chapter under the following categories.
    (a) Quantitative versus qualitative
    (b) Old products versus new products
    (c) Short term versus medium term versus long term

PRACTICE EXERCISES

1. Collect the past room sales data of a local hotel. Try to forecast the demand for the next period using simple regression on time series. How

accurate are your forecasts? Explain the reasons for your results.
2. Visit a theme park. See how the transactions are recorded and aggregated. Also study the reports prepared from this data. Try to prepare more analytical reports from this data. Suggest the decision support of these reports.

PROJECTS

1. Study the marketing information system of a travel company. Compare it with the framework prescribed in the chapter. What gaps do you observe? Will the model improve the quality of information?
2. Make a survey of the hotel managers in your city. Find the information used by them for marketing decisions along with its sources, quality, and sufficiency. What other sources of information do you suggest? How can you improve the quality and quantity of information?

REFERENCES

Chandra, Satish and Menezes Dennis 2001, 'Applications of multivariate analysis in international tourism research: The marketing strategy perspective of NTOs', *Journal of Economic and Social Research*, vol.3, no.1, pp.77–98.

Hodgson, Peter 1991, 'Marketing research in tourism,' *Tourism Management*, vol.12, no. 4.

Kumar, Ranjeet 2005, *Research Methodology*, Pearson Education, Delhi.

Kroenke, David 1989, *Management Information Systems*, McGraw-Hill International Edition, Singapore.

Nargundkar, Rajendra 2002, *Marketing Research: Text and Cases*, Second Edition, TataMcGraw-Hill, New Delhi.

Peterson, H. Craig, Lewis W. Chris, and Jain K. Sudhir 2006, *Managerial Economics*, Pearson Education.

Tull, Donald S. and Hawkins I. Del 1997, *Marketing Research: Measurement and Method*, Sixth Edition Prentice Hall of India, New Delhi.

Witt, S. F. and Martin, C. A. 1992, 'Demand forecasting in tourism and recreation,' *Progress in Tourism, Recreation and Hospitality Management*, Cooper, C. P. (ed.), CBS Publishers, New Delhi.

CASE STUDIES

1. MARKET SURVEYS AND RESEARCHES—GOVERNMENT STEPS IN

The Ministry of Tourism, Government of India carries field studies at the macro level about the growth of tourism and potential areas. It supplies information on the upcoming areas, such as cruise tourism, rural tourism, and reports on tourism in various states placing these on its site for the public to view. This helps the private players to get an overview which otherwise would be difficult to develop. These surveys and status reports available by May 2009 are as follows.

1. Perspective plan of states/union territories.
2. Reports
   - The India convention industry—size, scope and economic impact
   - Master plan for Valley of Flowers–Hemkund in Chamoli District, Uttarakhand.
   - Foreign tourist expenses on handicrafts
   - Impact of civil aviation policies on tourism in India
   - Manpower requirement in hotel industry and tour/travel sector
   - Kerala's approach to tourism development—A case study
   - Cruise Tourism—Potential and strategy study
   - Best practices adopted by the state governments, vol. - I
   - Best practices adopted by the state governments, vol. - II
   - Tourism satellite account for India— 2002–03
   - Study to assess the requirement of hotel rooms/accommodation in metro cities
   - Action plan to raise the number of foreign tourists visiting India from 3 million to 25 million in 10 years time.
3. Study reports on evaluation of plan schemes
   - Evaluation study for the plan scheme of market research—Professional services
   - Evaluation study for the plan scheme 'Computerization and Information Technology'
   - Evaluation study for the plan scheme 'Assistance to IHMs/FCI/IITTM/NIWS'
   - Evaluation study for the plan scheme of assistance for large revenue generating projects (LRGP)
   - Evaluation study in selected overseas market
   - Evaluation study on rural tourism scheme, 2007
   - Evaluation study of the scheme of incentive to accommodation infrastructure
   - Evaluation of the plan scheme for assistance to states for development of circuits/destinations
   - Evaluation of the plan scheme 'Capacity Building for Service Providers (CBSP)'
   - Evaluation of the scheme 'Domestic Promotion and Publicity Including Hospitality (DPPH)'
4. Statistical Surveys
   - Domestic tourism survey—2002-03
   - International passenger survey—2003
   - Survey on tourism statistics for the state in Goa (April 2005–March 2006)

- Survey on tourism statistics in Bihar (January–December 2005)
- Survey on tourism statistics in Rajasthan (April 2005–March 2006)
- Survey on tourism statistics in U.P. (April 2005–March 2006)
- Survey on tourism statistics in Uttranchal (April 2005–March 2006)
- Survey on tourism statistics in Madhya Pradesh (January 2005–December 2005)
- Survey on tourism statistics in Chhattisgarh (January 2005–December 2005)
- Survey on tourism statistics in Assam (April 2005–March 2006)
- Survey on tourism statistics in Karnataka (May 2005–April 2006)

- Survey on tourism statistics in Orissa (April 2005–March 2006)

Apart from these, the ministry posts information about its policies on its website. Check the website, www.tourism.gov.in about the type of information available.

DISCUSSION QUESTIONS

1. What difference will a real-time online information system make?
2. How is it different from a typical MIS developed for an organization for its use?
3. What can be the contribution of this information to the marketing efforts of the private operators?

2. EMERGENCY MANAGEMENT INFORMATION SYSTEM

The United Nations World Tourism Organization (UNWTO) has developed a global information system to manage emergency situations affecting tourism and to mitigate the impacts of natural and man-made disasters in tourism. It uses the Tourism Emergency Response Network (TERN), SOS.Travel, and travel advisories for quick dissemination of information about any untoward situation as well as measures to check it.

Tourism Emergency Response Network

The TERN is a closely-knit group of the leading tourism associations of the world, launched in 2006 for closer collaboration and cooperation amongst the decision-makers and stakeholders in tourism. The evolution of the H5N1 avian flu virus to a pandemic form and the tsunami of December 2004 were the catalyst to its formation.

Its current members are the African Travel and Tourism Association (ATTA), Airports Council International (ACI), American Society of Travel Agents (ASTA), American Hotel & Lodging Association (AH&LA), Association of European Airlines (AEA), Associación de Transporte Aereo (ALTA), Association of Asia Pacific Airlines (AAPA), European Travel Commission (ETC), International

Council of Cruise Lines (ICCL), International Hotel & Restaurant Association (IHRA), International Federation of Tour Operators (IFTO), National Tour Association (NTA), Pacific Asia Travel Association (PATA), and United Federation of Travel Agents Associations (UFTAA).

This 'network of networks' TERN works for a single cause—make travel and destinations safe for tourists.

It works on the following basic guidelines.
(a) Work closely with the UN System Influenza Coordinator, the World Health Organization (WHO) and the other involved UN agencies
(b) Share real-time information and ideas
(c) Give clear, concise, and geographically specific public messages
(d) Seek close media liaison to better spread information as necessary

The UNWTO hosts and manages TERN through its risk and crisis management (RCM).

The TERN plays a prominent role in the UNWTO's portal www.SOS.travel designed to serve the travellers and the industry partners alike as the one-stop shop emergency platform.

SOS. Travel

It is an online one stop shop where the users can access the latest critical information and communication tools in anticipation of, or in response to, natural and man-made crises with potential impacts on tourism. The system aims to support crisis preparedness in the tourism sector and assists in rapid recovery from crisis situations. SOS.travel also serves as a valuable resource for the travellers by providing in one place the tools and information they need in order to make informed decisions about their own safety and security, and to obtain assistance in case of an emergency.

Through SOS.travel, the UNWTO supports its member states in deploying the very latest developments in modern media communications to facilitate their crisis management activities. Apart from being a public site, SOS.travel offers the UNWTO member countries and destinations easy-to-use tools and procedures to create stand-by web pages that are ready when a crisis occurs.

SOS.travel serves as a hub of secure communication, facilitating the timely exchange of critical information between and among the TERN members and participating international organizations. Through the deployment of identification safeguards, the system enables the executives in different organizations facing similar challenges to better coordinate their efforts and rapidly exchange information with the confidence that the information will only be read by the intended recipients.

Travel Advisories

The UNWTO provides guidelines for the preparation of travel advisories for travellers who should be encouraged to consult these, prior to departure.

The following general norms are to be observed for these guidelines.

- Accurate, relevant and appropriate, unambiguous language without any bias and political considerations

- Updated and easy to use information
- Travel threats and risks in advisories to be specific about the geographical location of the problems and include maps and indications of distance
- Travel advisories should be specific about the nature of the threat or risk and they should be developed through a robust and considered process
- The following categories of threats and risks may be addressed
  (a) Political (due to political process)
  (b) Social (crime, delinquency)
  (c) Related to terrorism
  (d) Environmental (natural disasters)
  (e) Industrial (such as chemical or nuclear) hazards
  (f) Related to health (communicable disease status and emergencies such as epidemics)
  (g) Related to transportation systems
- Threats and risks in advisories should be under constant review and in each case should specify the date of their publication.
  (*Source:* www.unwto.org)

DISCUSSION QUESTIONS

1. How does the TERN help in preparing responsiveness to emergencies?
2. What is SOS.Travel and what is its role in managing emergencies?
3. What are travel advisories? What are the problems faced by the countries for whom such alerts are issued? What is the UNWTO's role in it?
4. Can a similar information system be used at the national level? Discuss its advantages in the Indian context?
5. Is it possible for an organization to develop its own emergency response network? Discuss.

CHAPTER 5

Tourism Markets And Tourist Behaviour

LEARNING OBJECTIVES

In this chapter, we will describe and illustrate the different aspects of tourism markets and tourist behaviour. We will look into the following areas.

- Concept and significance of tourism markets
- Types of tourism markets including important ones for India
- Tourist behaviour and buying process
- Factors affecting tourist behaviour
- Models of tourist behaviour

INTRODUCTION

Understanding tourism markets and their behaviour is the key to attain high levels of tourist satisfaction. The array of tourism markets and their behaviour makes this understanding a necessity as well as a challenge. Destination marketers face the tough task of gratifying different expectations and demands of different tourists. More so in cases of places like India that have a wide variety and range of attractions. India offers a mix of modern and oriental concurrently to different sets of visitors wanting to explore its mysticism and living with modern facilities at the same time. India has traditionally been popular among western tourists for its old world charm and is mystified as the land of rope tricks, magicians, and snake charmers.

Such a situation can be strangely paradoxical as no country can afford to target limited source countries and put all the eggs in one basket. A diversified market may yield a product basket too large with customized variations. Destination marketers are challenged for finding

An entire class of tourists abhorred a visit to India earlier for want of modern amenities but now with these in place, another class feels that it has lost its distinct charm and identity.

optimum mix of markets and products. The country's planners have to decide about factors such as what type of tourists they want, from where, and for what purposes. This is possible only with the analysis of markets and their behaviour. Market behaviour differ across regions, countries, states, cities, and further down to the level of corporates and individuals. A careful analysis of these uncovers the underlying causes as well as patterns. For example, food is a very important product of a hotel that can be consumed by guests not only for satisfying hunger, but also for entertainment, or socialization. The hotel must take into account the expectations of different types of diners for the choice of items, quantity ordered, price preferred, services expected, and time spent in the restaurant. It will help in facility planning and other aspects. Even if the basic food remains the same, value addition in the form of presentation, ambience, and services shall differ.

WHAT ARE TOURISM MARKETS?

Tourism market is a collection of marketers and tourists who come together as and when the exchange of benefits takes place. This involves the supply side of the marketer and the demand side of the tourists. Understanding of the demand side is critical for the marketers to develop and manage the supply accordingly.

Tourists are geographically dispersed and travel from their residences to destinations for tourism experience. There may not be much interaction among them either at the destination or elsewhere. They come together for a while and disperse. Hence, tourists as a group do not have a long-standing uniform identity.

Tourists' behaviour and interaction patterns with the host cultures arise from their roots, i.e., places of origin, home cultures, and plethora of other factors that define them. Different host cultures too may bring out entirely different tourist behaviour as tourists learn and adopt host cultures in their appearances and expressions. For example, an Indian may behave differently at different destinations by dressing up and behaving entirely differently from his/her daily routine. These behaviours are factored by many levels at which a tourist interacts with the host culture.

A tourist visiting Australia and Dubai will appear to be like two different persons marked by differences in appearance, behaviour, purchasing patterns, and psychological states.

TYPES OF TOURISM MARKETS

Tourism markets can be classified into different categories. These are discussed as follows.

Table 5.1 Outbound Markets of the World in 2008

Source Regions	Number of Outbound Tourists in Million	Per Cent Share
Europe	508.7	55.2
Asia and Pacific	181.6	19.7
Americas	151.8	16.5
Middle East	31.5	3.4
Africa	28.6	3.1
Origin not specified	20.2	2.2
Total	922	100

(*Source:* Tourism Highlights 2009, www.unwto.org)

On the Basis of Origin and Destination

Tourist markets can be outbound, inbound, and domestic on the basis of their origin and destination.

Outbound market/international import market

The outbound market for a country consists of its citizens travelling outward to other countries/destinations. The United Nations World Tourism Organization (UNWTO) defines it as residents travelling to another country from the point of view of the country of origin. It is considered important because tourists purchase foreign products during their stay abroad. Indian outbound tourism market is an emerging market with the current size of 8 million tourists who are travelling to countries such as Singapore, Switzerland, Australia, USA, UK, and so on. The region-wise outbound tourism markets for the year 2008 are shown in Table 5.1.

Behaviour of the world outbound markets differ considerably as found by the UNWTO for their spending pattern. German outbound has the highest overall expenditure though the per capita spending is highest for the UK (Table 5.2).

Further analysis can provide information on expenditure of one origin market at different destinations and can be helpful for the suitable product development and delivery.

Inbound market/international export market

This is the opposite of outbound markets. The inbound market for a country consists of people travelling to it from other countries. The

Table 5.2   Expenditure of Important International Tourism Source Markets (2008)

Market	International Tourism Expenditure (USD in billion)	Expenditure per Capita (USD)
Germany	91.0	1108
United States	79.7	262
United Kingdom	68.5	1121
France	43.1	693
China	36.1	27
Italy	30.8	519
Canada	26.9	810
Japan	27.9	218

(*Source*: Tourism Highlights 2009, www.unwto.org)

Table 5.3   Inbound Tourism of World Regions (2008)

Market	Inbound Market (in million)	Market Share	International Tourism Receipts (USD in billion)	Receipts Per Arrival
Europe	489.4	53.1	473.7	970
Asia and the Pacific	184.1	20.0	206.0	1120
Americas	147.0	15.9	188.4	1280
Africa	46.7	5.1	30.6	650
Middle East	55.1	6.0	45.6	830
Total	922	100	944	1020

(*Source*: Tourism Highlights 2009, www.unwto.org)

UNWTO defines it as the non-residents received by a destination country from the point of view of that destination. The UK, the USA, France, Germany are all inbound markets for India as tourists come to India from these countries. This is an instance of export because tourists purchase Indian tourism services giving precious foreign exchange. In 2008, the Indian inbound market was 5.28 million and earned 11.7 billion USD (India Tourism Statistics 2008). India comparatively has a very small inbound market. Table 5.3 shows the inbound tourism or international arrivals for world regions.

Table 5.4 World Inbound Tourism by Purpose of Visit and
Mode of Travel (2008)

Purpose of Visit	Percentage	Mode of Transport	Percentage
Leisure, recreation, and holiday	51	Air	52
Visiting friends and relatives (VFR), religion, health, others	27	Road	39
Business and professional	15	Water	6
Not specified	7	Rail	3

(*Source:* Tourism Highlights 2009, www.unwto.org)

Further analysis of inbound market highlights the different patterns of behaviour (Table 5.4).

Inbound market is very important for any country as it brings the economic benefits in the form of development, employment, foreign exchange, and so on.

Domestic market

It comprises residents travelling within the country from one place to another. India had 562.9 million domestic tourists in 2008 (India Tourism Statistics 2008). It does not involve any form of export or import. But this does not undermine its value in any way as this can act as the backbone of international tourism. It is much more stable and comparatively impervious to fluctuations vis-à-vis international tourism.

On the Basis of Purpose of Visit

Tourism markets can also be classified on the basis of the purpose of visit. Different tourists travel with different purposes and for satisfaction of different needs. This forms the basis of such classification. For example, when people travel to Goa to relax on beaches, it is leisure market and when they visit a place to attend a business conference, it is a part of business market. The same location can act as different markets depending on different needs. Also, as new purposes evolve with time, so do the new markets. These purposes can be identified in relation to both source and destination. The examples of such tourism markets can be as follows.

Leisure, holiday, and recreation markets

The main purpose of tourists of these markets is to relax and have a good time. As the tourists are not interested in any particular activity, the tourism is passive in nature rather than activity oriented. An example can be the sun, sand, and sea market of cold countries. Tourists from these markets travel to the warm beaches of the Mediterranean and South-East Asia.

Business markets

Tourists from these markets travel primarily for business purposes. The MICE (Meetings, Incentives, Conferences and Exhibitions) markets fall in this category. A major part of Indian outbound is for business purposes with forecast of 2.63 million by 2010-11 as compared to 1.54 million of leisure and holiday market.

Adventure markets

When a tourist travels to a place for river rafting or other adventurous activities, such as bungee jumping, mountaineering, hang gliding, and parasailing, he/she is a part of the adventure market. Gulmarg in Jammu and Kashmir, Auli in Uttarakhand, and Manali in Himachal Pradesh are being promoted as destinations for such markets.

Wildlife markets

Tourists travel to forest areas and national parks in order to enjoy wildlife. It usually involves activities such as watching wildlife, safaris, and staying close to nature. Tourists visiting national parks, such as Corbett and Rajaji (Uttarakhand), Gir (Gujarat), Ranthambore (Rajasthan), and Manas (Assam), constitute this market.

Voluntary markets

This is a new and emerging market where tourists make their contribution to the destinations by voluntary participation in different activities. This may include teaching villagers about health and hygiene, imparting skills for use of solar energy, and other such activities that are aimed at benefiting the local population. It involves a longer stay at the destination and closer interaction with the host population. But it requires a coordinating agency in between to help tourists find suitable destinations and activities for participating in such markets.

Student markets

Some countries or places have a large number of youth travelling to other places for education. These places are termed as student markets. Tapping into these requires facilitation in the form of admissions, visa,

A few ecotourism destinations in India are

- Thenmala Eco-tourism Project, Kerela
- Nal Sarovar Wetland Bird Sanctuary, Gujarat
- Jungle Lodges and Resorts Ltd, Karnataka
- Welcome Group Bay Island Hotel, Port Blair

travel, documentation, and related help. India is a good student tourism market with students travelling to different countries for education.

Ecotourism markets

This is tourism in natural areas which takes into account the maintenance of ecological balance of the area. This is a responsible and sustainable form of tourism. Tourists from many places are eco-friendly and prefer to enjoy the natural environment without harming it in any manner. Similarly, many destinations can be promoted as ecotourism destinations. The markets for all these places can be called ecotourism markets.

Nature tourism markets

This constitutes the markets from where tourists travel to nature areas. It differs from ecotourism markets as this might not include eco-friendly practices by visitors and can be potentially degrading for the destination. Natural areas world over attract this market.

For example, visitors from all over India visit hill stations such as Shimla, Manali, etc. However, these places are losing their charm and fast becoming over commercialized and crowded. These places attract visitors from nature tourism markets and the focus lies squarely beyond conservation and eco-protection.

Rural tourism markets

The urban areas are full of people who want to get away from all the factors of their life that are responsible for stress. They want to travel to the easy and laid-back lifestyle of rural areas. These urban locales constitute rural tourism markets and with increasing urbanization they seem to have a strong future potential. The Government of India (GoI) has identified many villages to be promoted for this market.

Urban tourism markets

Tourists travel to urban areas from rural areas and towns to feel the pace of development not seen in their places. It is often combined with business, shopping, or heritage tourism at the urban destination. People travelling to metropolitan cities, such as Delhi, Bangalore, Chennai, fall under this category.

Health tourism markets

Tourists often travel to other places for change of weather, better environs, or medical facilities. This is emerging as a new market world over and tourists from the developed countries are travelling to Singapore, Dubai, India, and South Africa, and so on, to avail cheaper medical care and to avoid the long waiting lists in their native places. Kerala is coming up with the alternate yoga therapy. Karnataka and the National Capital Region (NCR) are developing modern hospitals to tap this market. The USA, West Asia, and Europe are important health tourism markets for India.

On the Basis of Types of Tourists

Types of tourists can also be used to classify tourism markets. In this, the mental make-up of tourists with respect to acceptance of a new destination or attraction is used to classify them. Some categories based on this classification are as follows.

Explorers

These are tourists who are innovative by nature and their acceptance rate of a new destination or activity is high. Such tourists will always look out for novelty and, consequently, have a greater chance of travelling to a virgin destination that may not even have proper facilities. These have been called wanderlust by Gray.

Mass tourism markets

Most of the tourists like to go to a well-developed conventional tourist spot. Risk avoidance is a natural human tendency and this comes into picture for mass tourism markets. Famous tourist spots and attractions that are familiar to most people provide a psychological buffer to risk-averse individuals. A majority of tourism markets belong to this class.

Niche markets

These are markets whose tourists frequent well-known places that are not crowded, either because of high prices or on account of special activities offered at the destination. High-risk adventure activities fall under this category.

On the Basis of Regions

The UNWTO has divided the world tourism market into five regions. The countries in a region are geographically contiguous and have similar types of tourism development. There are five tourism markets on this basis.

Europe

It has four sub-regions of North, West, Central/East and South/Mediterranean.

Asia and the Pacific

It also has four sub-regions of North-East Asia, South-East Asia, Oceania, and South Asia.

Americas

The four sub-regions, North America, the Caribbean, Central America, and South America form this market.

Africa

It has North Africa and sub-Saharan Africa as its parts.

Middle East

It includes Egypt, Saudi Arabia, the UAE, and Bahrain

While the Americas and Europe have well-developed tourism, the other regions are catching up fast and have faster rate of growth.

TOURIST BEHAVIOUR

Understanding behaviours, expectations, preferences, and choices of tourists is essential for effective marketing. The behaviours are studied as a process from pre-buying to buying, and up to post-buying. Tourist behaviour is very context specific and not subject to general inferences. We can take the case of Indian tourists. Just knowing how they behave during foreign travel is not enough. It has to be supplemented by the knowledge of how they behave in different countries. It requires an understanding and application of dynamics of behaviour and influencing forces.

A simple purchase sequence is shown in Fig. 5.1.

At the think stage, tourists use cognitive skills to consider different options of travel, consequences of each choice, and costs–benefits of various alternatives. Choices selected at this stage move to the feel stage, when the emotional aspects of a tourist's persona help eliminate non-appealing choices, acceptable otherwise. At the behave stage, one final choice is made and decisions regarding from where to buy, how much to buy, and mode of payment, and so on are taken. Understanding of

> Travel buying is a mental and physical activity that begins early in the mind just like any other purchase. A potential tourist passes from one stage of purchase readiness to the next stage influenced by factors such as own psychology, reference groups, society, and facilitating features of a purchase.

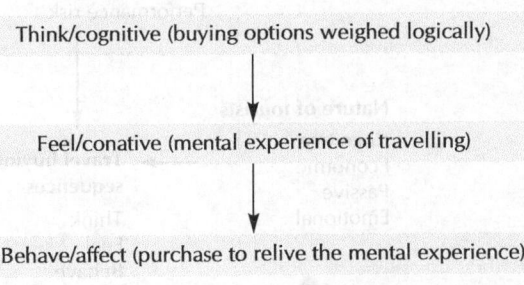

Think/cognitive (buying options weighed logically)

Feel/conative (mental experience of travelling)

Behave/affect (purchase to relive the mental experience)

Fig. 5.1 Simple Sequential Model of Purchase

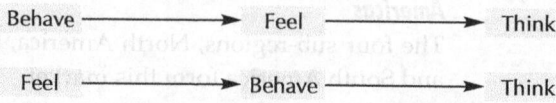

Fig. 5.2 Purchase Sequence Variations

tourists at each stage can be used to assist them in decisions by passing appropriate stimuli. They can also be persuaded to move forward through the stages and also to decide in favour of marketed offers. There can be variations in this sequence (Fig. 5.2) for urgent, emotional, and impulsive decisions. Tourists may travel to a destination under peer pressure but may not find it up to their own expectations and might later realize the futility of the tour.

Travel buying decision sequence depends upon the following factors (Fig. 5.3).

1. Nature of decision-making
2. Nature of tourists
3. Risks involved in travel purchase

Nature of Decision-making

The importance given by a buyer to different purchases differs. An important purchase may be given more inputs in terms of money, time, and effort spent. On this basis, three types of decision-making can be identified.

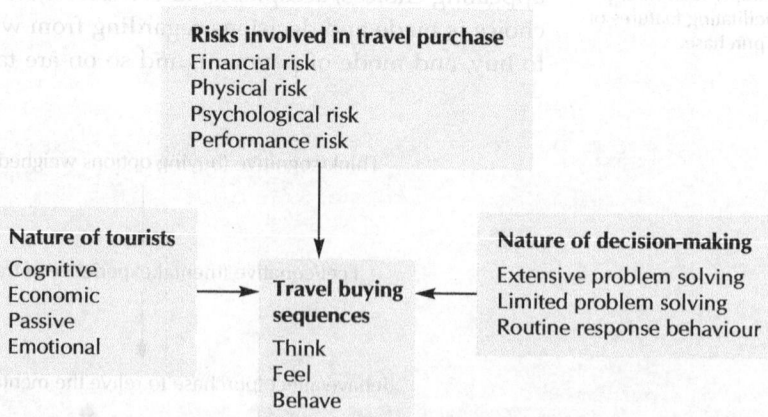

Fig. 5.3 Factors Influencing Travel Buying

Extensive problem solving (EPS)

Here, the purchase is very important for the buyer and involves large expenditure. Therefore, the buyer devotes more time and effort to search and evaluate all the options and makes the best choice. These decisions are made once in a while; hence the buyer ensures maximizing his/her returns. Purchase of high-value items, such as cars, houses, and foreign travel, come under this category.

Limited problem solving (LPS)

Here, the purchase is moderately important and involves moderate expenditure. In such cases, the buyer spends a moderate amount of time and effort for selecting an option. Such purchases are more frequent in comparison to extensive problem solving and less frequent compared to routine response behaviour. The decision-making is satisfying type to get good value than to optimize and get best value. Travel within the country falls in this category.

Routine response behaviour (RRB)

These decisions are routine, recurring, and frequent, and involve low expenditure. The buyer knows the consequences of various options and requires no effort for evaluation. The buyer repeats the past choices and spends little time and effort in coming to a decision. A business tourist's choice for frequent travel is routine response behaviour.

If a decision involves extensive problem solving, the logical sequence of buying is followed to get the best choice. But for limited and routine decisions, this sequence gets altered to give the best option in a short time.

For example, travel arrangements for tourists from West Bengal to Shimla may involve elaborate decision but it is not so for tourists from nearby places like Chandigarh.

In urgent decisions to travel, impulsive or emotional aspects may overrule the rational ones. Consequently, decision sequence may be behave–feel–think or behave–think–feel. For repeat travel decisions based on past experience, the sequence of feel–behave–think is adopted. In all types of decisions, the final experience feeds back the future decisions.

Nature of Tourists

The basic nature of tourists also affects the way decisions are taken. The same decision can be treated either as logical or emotional depending upon the individual. One person may devote more time and effort to a decision that may be taken impulsively by another. The nature of tourists impacts the purchase sequence too.

Based on nature, the four types of tourists can be identified as follows.

Economic

Such tourists give high priority to economic considerations for making decisions. Their judgement is based on best value for their money.

Passive

These tourists are passive receivers of information and their decisions are based on whatever information comes their way. The marketers continuously supply information to such buyers to keep it fresh in the memory.

Cognitive

These tourists have high information processing ability and actively search information before making decisions. They systematically evaluate the information for decision-making. The marketers can assist such buyers by supplying the information as and when needed.

Emotional

Such buyers accept information selectively and focus on the part that appeals to their emotions. This selective information is used for decision-making.

Each one of the above can find expression in the same tourist at different points of time but a group or segment can usually be characterized by one type of nature. When a buyer acts as an emotional or passive human, buying is likely to begin from feel. But in case of cognitive and economic buyers, the think stage will precede other stages. This knowledge is used by the marketers to devise strategies. For example, there is a basic difference between eastern and western cultures regarding their thinking pattern that is commonly called cyclic vs linear. People in eastern cultures think in a loop-like fashion, not giving clear direction to their thoughts towards some outcome. This makes them great debaters historically and well versed in abstract topics like philosophy. But the linear thinking of western cultures focuses on moving forward from one point to another. This behaviour gets transferred to buying and has implications for marketing communications. Similarly, other tendencies of markets should be studied in detail before planning or introducing any marketing interventions.

RISKS INVOLVED IN TRAVEL PURCHASE

Tourism purchase involves a number of actual and perceptual risks that makes buying a complex decision. These risks are discussed below.

Physical Risk

Tourists everywhere are faced with risks to their body and health from bad weather, law and order problems, diseases, accidents, etc.

Some degree of physical risk exists at all the destinations, although tourists travel to a destination after weighing all the pros and cons. Moreover, this risk can be real or perceived. In adventure sports, the risks are minimized if due security procedures are followed. Still they are believed to be hazardous. Also, some tourists travel to Jammu and Kashmir with confidence in the security measures of the government but others avoid it altogether for lack of similar confidence.

Psychological Risk

Tourists travel for a variety of psychological reasons. This may include factors such as mental peace on a religious tour, recreation in a leisure tour, and thrill in an adventure trip. There is always a risk that the requisite psychological satisfaction may not be derived from the tour. Tourists may or may not take the tour based on the acceptance of the risk.

Financial Risk

Tour purchase involves high expenditure and promises of intangible benefits. This makes tourists wary about getting the true value of their money. Correlating high expenditure with experiential benefits makes tourism a high-risk purchase.

Performance Risk

Tourists may fail to get the promised tour benefits for uncontrollable reasons. For example, tourists may experience rains and clouds instead of sunshine, cancelled flights and train services because of heavy fog, or other weather disturbances. The performance risks always exist for all nature-based tourism.

Tourists often face these risks because of the following reasons.

- Political: Terrorism, political instability, war/military conflict
- Environmental: Natural disasters, landslides
- Health: Lack of access to health care, life-threatening diseases, lack of access to clean food and water
- Poor planning: Unreliable airline, inexperienced operator, not assured flight
- Property: Theft, loss of luggage

High risk perception situations are analysed thoughtfully, while low risk perception may propel the tourists to choose a destination on the basis of emotions or feelings.

The final decision by the tourists is taken after considering and weighing all the risks. The marketers try and influence the risk perception through proper supply of information. They also assess the most likely

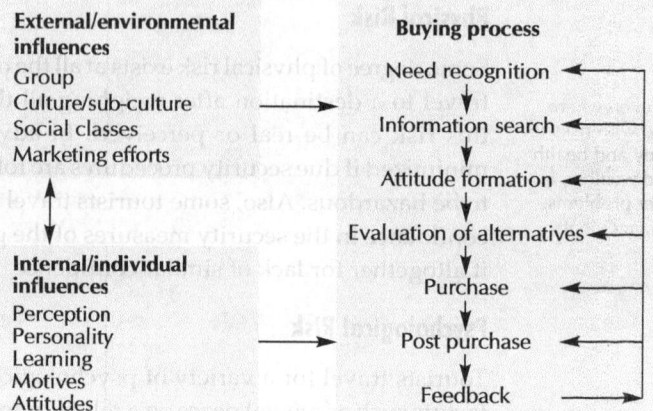

Fig. 5.4 Tourist Buying Process for Elaborate Decision-making

approach to be followed by tourists after understanding the nature of decision-making, the nature of buyers, and the risks involved. All the communication and images are built accordingly to facilitate the buying.

TOURIST BUYING PROCESS

In all types of buying the tourist moves through a process. An analysis of how and why of this process provides an understanding of tourist behaviour. A simple model of decision-making (Fig. 5.4) depicts tourist's purchase as a logical sequence influenced by individual/internal factors and external/environmental factors.

This process is directed by the following salient features of tourism purchases.

1. Holidaying is mainly an extensive problem solving (EPS) and its purchase is a well thought out activity. It can be limited problem solving (LPS) for frequent and repeat travel. It can also be routine response behaviour (RRB) for travel to nearby destinations.

2. Tourists always look for novelty and may visit a different destination each time. Destinations need to reinvent themselves continuously to provide the novelty necessary to sustain the interests of tourists.

3. Natural factors, such as geographical distance and climatic features, influence the destination selection.

4. The service characteristics of tourism affect its purchase.

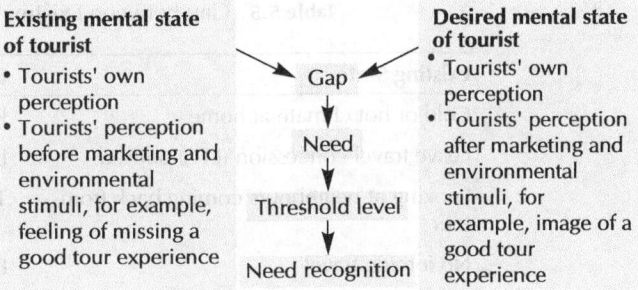

Fig. 5.5 Need Recognition

Need Recognition

Tourism is not a basic phycial need but a complex and higher order need. It is a social esteem, and self-actualization need.

Human behaviour is need based and begins with an effort to satisfy the unfulfilled needs. Need is the felt or perceived gap between the existing and the desired states of a person. This can be both physical and psychological. It holds true for tourist behaviour as well. The felt or perceived gap creates a feeling of discomfort and the tourist begins to act on it to remove the dissonance. A consumer's propensity to act increases with the increasing gap level and the act begins when it reaches the threshold level. This is the level of gap that becomes wide enough to necessitate action. It is very crucial for the marketers to identify the needs that relate to tourism and the threshold levels for different markets (Fig. 5.5). The underlying motives behind travel needs are very important to understand. For example, tourists may feel the need to travel to Haridwar for multiple reasons such as pilgrimage, leisure, business, etc. But each need will require a different facilitation for its satisfaction. Need recognition stage is where the service provider can gauge the needs and decide how to satisfy it in the best possible manner. How a tourist's need is recognized determines the behaviour of tourists at the later stages. Also, the marketer's activities at the later stages of this process are heavily influenced by the need determination stage and this is where some marketers gain an edge by having that precise incision into the psyche of a tourist.

How to recognize need?

Usually, an individual's need to travel is vague to the person himself. Although it can be recognized by surveying people to find out whether they travel for motivational purposes such as leisure, compulsions such as business, and so on. Responses may give an idea of the needs as well as

Table 5.5   Gap between Existing and Desired State

Existing State	Desired State
Cold or hot climate at home	Pleasant climate at tourist places
Leave travel concession (LTC) unused	LTC used
Looking at neighbours coming back from tour	Travelling like neighbours
No foreign travel	Foreign travel for status
Has never been to a beach	Wants to see beach

expectations of the tourists. Table 5.5 shows some features of the existing and desired state that may propel the need for the tour.

This illustration is only suggestive; a host of other features can mark both the states. Tourists themselves can identify the gap based on their perception but marketing communication plays a very important role here.

The marketers intervene at this stage to increase the perception of the gap and trigger the potential tourist to the next stages of decision-making.

> Advertisement of an affordable foreign trip can increase the felt need to travel that could not have been triggered at a higher price.

Information Search

Once tourists perceive the gap, efforts begin to fill it. Tourists start looking for information that might assist in finding the best way to do it. Information about various alternatives are gathered and weighed. The information search may be internal and immediate from the memory or external and elaborate. Memory contains information of past experiences and may be very useful if a behaviour is to be repeated. External search provides new information and is used for non-repetitive actions.

Both types of search supplement each other as given in Fig. 5.6.

The marketer may not be able to influence internal search immediately but can do so in the long run by making information accessible for external search that may add to the memory. Since tourism is a complex purchase

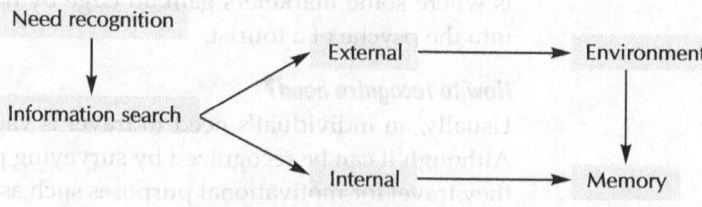

Fig. 5.6   Information Search

where the product is composite and assembled, a few components may be purchased based on internal search and others based on external search. As a result, choice of hotel brand or airlines may be repeated but not of the destination.

The marketers at this stage provide external information through sources accessed by the potential tourists. These can be websites, brochures, advertisement through news, features, outdoor, middlemen, and so on. The challenge here for the marketer is to convey the information to the right group so as to maximize the impact. This can be accomplished by getting the carrier, timings, and the message right.

Sources of external information

Tourists may collect external information from both the marketers' sources and independent sources. Each tourist market will have its own preference of sources that need to be identified for the transmission of information. Independent sources, such as word of mouth and tourist forums, may not be available to the marketers but an assessment of information flow is surely helpful to decide information content in manageable sources. Moreover, the marketers try to create a good image of their offering in independent forums by advertising there or by putting information as third party to lend credibility to it. A large number of options in the print and audio-visual media are available and the one that is most suitable can be used. For example, the Ministry of Tourism, Government of India has extensively used the Internet for its Incredible India campaign.

Types of information

Information can be simple or complex and can be presented to appeal to different faculties such as logic, morals, or emotions. Each buyer group has its own cognitive abilities and accordingly likes different types of information. Identification of comprehensive abilities of buyers with regard to type of information will aid the marketers in designing and supplying the right type of information. Different types of information can be recurring–non-recurring, historical–present–future, text heavy–picture heavy, numerical–non-numerical. Different tourists can perceive the same information as simple/complex depending on their psychological make-up and other such factors. This can be presented using three main appeals of logic, emotions, and moral (Table 5.6).

Amount of information

Giving a list of 100 hotels to a buyer and asking for a choice may not produce any decision. However, a list of 10 or 20 hotels may elicit a faster response and is easier for the decision-maker too. Judging the

> More information is not always good and may end up confusing the buyer by creating information overload.

Table 5.6 Types of Information used by Tourists

	Logical	**Emotional**	**Moral**
Simple	Online purchase of air tickets with fewer number of variables	Back to roots to trace one's ancestral places	Keep destination clean
Complex	Online purchase of air tickets with greater number of variables	Back to roots and also make contribution to improve these places	Adopt sustainable tourism

optimal amount of information suitable for target buyers helps in better management of information. The collected information is processed by the tourists and it adds to their mental make-up. The decisions at the subsequent stages are based on the mindset developed.

Attitude Formation

The information obtained contributes towards the formation or reformation of attitudes. Attitudes are mental predispositions to behave in a consistently favourable or unfavourable way towards an object/ service. Attitudes help tourists in making decisions easily by eliminating all the options viewed negatively. For example, tourists generally have positive attitudes for places such as Singapore, Switzerland, and France that receive major share of international tourism. Destinations such as India, Nepal, and Indonesia receive lesser number of tourists as these places lack the same good image. But attitudes do change overtime with additional information and the same has been judiciously used by India through its Incredible India campaign. The UNWTO, in January 2007, noted the 'emergence' of South Asia as a tourist destination, with remarkable growth of 10 per cent in tourist arrivals in 2006 that was more than double the global growth. Furthermore, it noted that the growth of tourism in South Asia was 'boosted by India, the destination responsible for half the arrivals to the sub-region.'

Awareness into why and how of attitude formation can be used to intervene and build the relevant attitudes. Attitude building is a natural process as shown in Fig. 5.7.

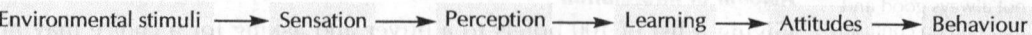

Environmental stimuli → Sensation → Perception → Learning → Attitudes → Behaviour

Fig 5.7 Attitude Formation

Information contributes to the attitude formation. Attitude provides the quick and short route to decision-making by eliminating a number of choices. Tourists form attitude for a number of reasons.

1. Utility function: Positive attitudes are developed towards a choice that gives the best value for money even if it is not the best choice on other features. Budget airlines may not give the best facilities but are preferred for the value given at a lower price.
2. Ego defensive: An option may be preferred only for status and defending the ego. A luxury holiday may be seen positively by a tourist who wants it for exhibition and sees it as a status symbol.
3. Value based: A tour option may be judged in the light of personal values of tourists. Adventure lovers may find it difficult to accept leisure holidays as an attractive proposition. Similarly, explorers usually stop going to a place that starts attracting large crowds.

The Kerela Government has created positive attitude among tourists by promoting its backwaters and nature cure. India has done the same through the Incredible India campaign.

Even the same tourist can form different attitudes for different reasons at different times. But the marketers can help the tourists see distinctive reasons in their offerings by providing right information or by highlighting specific aspects of information.

Thailand has been successful in removing the sex tourism tag attached to it. Continuous information helps in forming and reforming the attitudes.

Evaluation of alternatives

Information search gives a number of alternatives that are evaluated to determine one final choice. The process of evaluation involves decision-making based on the chosen criteria. The final choice can be arrived through a process of deletion or selection but ultimately ends with one option as shown in Fig. 5.8.

Total set is the number of options available in the market for the tourists. If a tourist wants to go for a religious tour in India, a list of all the religious places will constitute the total set.

Awareness set includes all the options known to the tourist. The tourist may know only certain important religious centres.

Inept set contains the unsuitable choices that are deleted from further consideration. The tourist may delete all the destinations requiring arduous journey.

Total set ⟶ Awareness set ⟶ Inept set ⟶ Consideration set ⟶ Choice set ⟶ Choice

Fig. 5.8 Choice Process

Consideration set incorporates alternatives to be considered for detailed evaluation. Inept set deleted from the awareness set gives this set.

Choice set has a limited number of alternatives that have good probability of selection after evaluation. For example, the tourist may consider only two or three places from west India.

Choice is the final decision for one destination. From the choice set of two or three religious destinations in western Indian, the tourist may finally choose Nashik.

The marketer's job is to ensure its presence in every set for its target market, except the inept set. This is achieved through product modifications and value-added selling by the service provider. For example, Vaishno Devi and Kedarnath often featured in the inept set of many tourists because of the arduous journey involved but the helicopter services to both the places have done away with this limitation. Information and communication about features of destinations is also used to increase the chances of their selection, as the tourists may not know all the features of destinations. For example, Sikkim is promoting its rural and community-based tourism, as most of the tourists are not aware of these features.

Evaluation is a complex process and each option can be judged either in totality or on its components. For example, a religious destination can be evaluated as a whole or in terms of components such as connectivity, infrastructure, cost, special occasion, popularity, etc.

Tourists mentally use any of the general models of decision-making for evaluation of alternatives. These are optimum decision-making, satisfying decision-making, and implicit favourite decision-making.

Optimum decision-making This decision-making supports rational choice for the best decision. It is elaborate, time consuming, and assumes that all the alternatives and their consequences are well known.

The choice criteria are also known and decided beforehand. Each alternative is evaluated on these criteria and the one with the best outcome is taken to be the final decision.

Satisfying decision-making The focus here is on satisfying or good enough decision than on the best decision. The choice criteria are known beforehand but only the important ones are used for the evaluation of a limited number of alternatives. The order of evaluation of alternatives against these criteria may change the final choice. One good alternative may not be selected when it is placed later in order and some preceding alternative is selected. The same may have been the choice if placed higher in the order. If none of the limited alternatives seems good enough in the initial evaluation, more options can be considered. This helps in taking quick decisions.

Implicit favourite decision-making   Here evaluation is made with a highly predisposed mind. A tourist likes a choice in advance and has mentally decided for it but will still carry the evaluation against other alternatives with the criteria that tend to support the initial choice. This exercise entails justification of one's initial choice and is used for self-satisfaction and rationalization.

Understanding of decision dynamics of the tourists will help the marketers in giving suitable information for evaluation. If the tourists think that security and food are important criteria in the choice of destination, then information on these should be available. Telling tourists only about the beauty of the place and the illustrious past visitors will not help in the choice. Another example can be online purchase of air tickets. If the tourist submits the connecting destinations, best buy is suggested in terms of price. This choice can be narrowed and altered by giving suitable times of flight. Specifying airlines again limits and changes the choice. It can go on if an option is further given for a refundable ticket. It explains how the criteria and availability of information on different parameters changes the final choice.

Evaluation process helps in finding an alternative and the final purchase is the next stage. Buyers may change their minds at this stage too.

Purchase

This is the stage when the transaction between the marketer and the tourist takes place. The tourist pays money and visits the destination for the experience. Both the buyers and the sellers take a number of important decisions at this stage. These relate to the quantum of purchase, time devoted to purchase, source of purchase, payment mode, and so on. (Fig. 5.9).

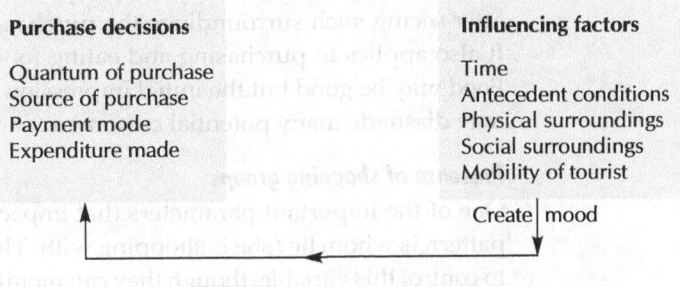

Purchase decisions	Influencing factors
Quantum of purchase	Time
Source of purchase	Antecedent conditions
Payment mode	Physical surroundings
Expenditure made	Social surroundings
	Mobility of tourist

Create mood

Fig. 5.9 Purchase Decisions

Purchase decisions depend upon the following factors that create the mood for purchase.

- Time available
- Antecedent conditions
- Physical surroundings
- Social groups at the time of shopping
- Mobility of the tourists

Time available

It will influence the hours to be devoted for shopping. A hurried shopper will rush through purchases, not visiting many shops or comparing offers, or mixing shopping with pleasure. Even in online purchases, the number of websites visited depends on the available time. Less time encourages repeat buying.

Antecedent conditions

Emotions and moods of the potential tourists just before purchase have a major impact on their perceptiveness and acceptance of offer. A tired person will try shortening the purchase process and will not spend enough efforts to look for the best buy. A good communication from the contact staff can help in uplifting the low mood.

Physical surroundings

Physical ambience includes all the aspects of the environment that are experienced through the human senses. It triggers the physical and mental reaction at the time of purchase. A good front office or reception may convince the tourists about the quality maintained in the delivery of services. For example, tourists travelling to India often complain about unkempt airports, dirty roads and parks, beggars, and so on. However, none of this forms the part of final tourism experience that may be to visit a wondrous place like the Taj Mahal. All these variables of physical surroundings do have a remarkable impact on the overall feel. As a result, after seeing such surroundings the purchases on the spot are affected. It also applies to purchasing and eating food in an unclean restaurant. Food may be good but the initial impression of non-hygienic conditions may dissuade many potential customers.

Presence of shopping groups

One of the important parameters that impact an individual's shopping pattern is whom he/she is shopping with. The marketers find it difficult to control this variable, though they can monitor the patterns and provide for suitable offerings to a group as a whole. For example, shopping for souvenirs is an important part of tourism activity and sellers can promise special gifts for escorts who accompany the tourists.

Mobility of the tourists

More mobile tourists are able to search many options for purchase from a large number of travel agents. For online purchases, access to bandwidth and the speed of connection and navigation from one website to another decides this mobility.

The marketers cannot control all these factors but can definitely influence some of these and thus affect purchase.

Post Purchase

At this stage, the tourists experience the tour and feel the gap (if any) between the promises and actual offer. This stage involves preparing for use of tour experience, experiencing, ending, and judging the tour (Fig. 5.10).

Preparation in tourism is important in terms of readying clothing, health check-ups, acquiring prior knowledge of place, and so on. It will decide the experience of the tourists when they visit a place. All usage in tourism is experiential and a prepared tourist will have better experience than an unprepared one. Different tourists can have different experiences at the same destination based on their preparedness for actual use and transfer of the preparation to use. For example, a tourist who has taken ski lessons well will enjoy a ski resort more than the one who has not done so. Ending the tour is a very important decision. Some tourists can tour a country for three days, others for thirty days. The marketers are always interested in long-haul tourists than short-haul ones.

> Tailored websites are a rage today and most operators are creating sites that come at the top in search engines such as Google. This helps attract the less mobile customers and increases access and visibility.

> In packaged tours the duration of tour is fixed but in non-packaged tours, the tourists stay at a place for as long as they like. When to close the tour also depends on them.

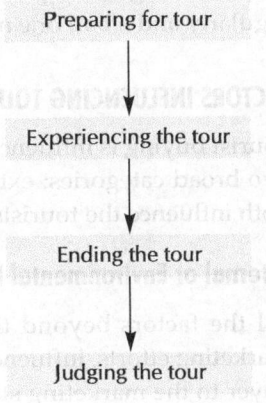

Fig. 5.10 Post-purchase Stage

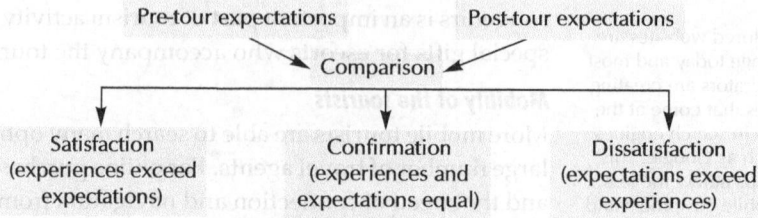

Fig. 5.11 Judging the tour

End of the tour is followed by a judgement of the tour.

Here, the tourists compare their experiences with expectations and the outcome can be satisfaction, dissatisfaction, or confirmation (Fig. 5.11). This judgment is fed back into the buying process for future purchases.

Tourists can be helped in all the post-purchase decisions by informing about the pre-tour preparation, making the best use of the in-tour period, and carrying most pleasant memories at the post-tour stage. This becomes very important as tourists usually move from one culture to another and are given information regarding cross-cultural perspectives. For example, for a visit to Hindu religious places, instructions shall be given about taking off shoes before entering the temples, covering the head, and avoiding promiscuous behaviour in public. Such tips can go a long way in enhancing the satisfaction. Apart from this, the marketers shall be cautious in building expectations. Promises that cannot be fulfilled will only create dissatisfaction.

Feedback

The post-purchase experience will influence all stages of buying process in future. A good experience may convince the tourists to take tours regularly and a bad one may discourage the future purchase of tours.

FACTORS INFLUENCING TOURIST BUYING

Tourist buying is influenced by many factors. These can be divided into two broad categories: external/environmental and internal/individual. Both influence the tourists through the buying process.

External or Environmental Factors

All the factors beyond the individual, such as groups, culture, and marketing efforts, influence the buying. These impact the reaction of the buyer to the marketing stimuli. Whether a tourist will eat local food or his/her own food, travel alone or with a group, travel to familiar places

A young college student may insist on going on a tour with friends even if the family feels otherwise, because the referral influence of a friendship group is greater than that of a family. If the family has more referral influence then the student may not go on the tour.

or new ones, are all influenced by these factors. The total effect of all these factors can be quite complex.

Groups

A tourist belongs to a large number of groups, mainly family, friends, social, and work. The number of social and friendship groups can be many. All these can inform, suggest, and persuade about travel choices. But at a particular time, the impact of the group acting as the reference group to the choice maker will be most. Any group can be the reference group if the decision-maker shares its values and is impacted strongly by it.

The influences of different groups depend on the social set-up of a place. The family may have stronger influence on Asians than on people from the western world. The involvement of a person with social and work groups too affects the reference power of these groups.

These groups are important for the marketers as information and promotion can be directly targeted at these to approach the buyer indirectly. These are very important in tourism where intangibility of services makes reference an important source of information. Table 5.7 shows the different types of reference groups important for the buyers.

All the four groups impact behaviour and a tourist may travel to a destination because his/her friends have visited the place and have spoken positively about their experiences and he/she trusts them. He/she may not travel if he/she does not trust the choice of these friends. The response can be either compliance or non-compliance to the group views. The influence of reference groups is also category specific. One group may be relied upon for leisure tours, another for adventure, and third for foreign travel. Hence, identification of the right group with the right reference power is critical for the use of group influence. Non-membership groups too play a very important role as tourists may copy their purchases in order to identify with these groups. If a particular place

Table 5.7 Reference Groups for Tourists

	Membership Groups	Non-membership Groups
Positive influences	• Family • Friends • Work groups • Social groups	• Other work groups • Other social groups
Negative influences	• Family • Friends • Work groups • Social groups	• Other work groups • Other social groups

is shown in a film, it becomes a popular tourist attraction. Celebrities from all walks of life are often used to testify the destinations so that visits of general tourists can be influenced.

Culture

Culture is the sum total of living at a place. It guides the human reactions to external stimuli through learned ways and often finds expression in the rituals, symbols, practices, language, religion, and so on. It gets reflected in use of leisure time and travel behaviour too. The marketers can customize packages if they understand the effect of culture on travel choices and practices. Culture can be defined in broad terms such as Western and Asian. It can also be classified in more specific terms such as South and Pacific Asian subcultures, Indian and Sri-Lankan cultures. Further, India has many subcultures in its different regions. Even a village has its culture. Culture helps in analysing the host–guest relation. Host culture can be xenophobic (fear of foreigners) or may like foreigners. Some cultures accept and assimilate the new and the foreign, while others reject and insist on tradition. This is a challenge for tourism that takes culture as the main product as well as the incidental product. Similarly, guest culture will have its orientations and the meeting of hosts and guests will produce varied tourism experiences. The experience of British tourists in north India can be just opposite to that in south India. The marketers cannot change the culture but can assure that hosts and guests are informed, persuaded, and trained to respect each other. Table 5.8 presents major cultural differences in the behaviour of Asian and European tourists.

> Understanding, learning, and appreciation of foreign cultures by both the hosts and the guests accentuate the good tourism experience.

Table. 5.8   Cultural Differences between Asian and European Tourists

	Asian Tourists	European Tourists
Cultural values	Group orientation, emphasis on togetherness and sociability	Individual orientation, emphasis on individualism and privacy
Rules of behaviour	Acceptable form of behaviour and indirect expression of opinions	Direct and open form of behaviour and open expression of opinions
Social interaction	Smooth relations, avoidance of disagreement, unhurried use of time, meals part of socialization	Efficiency and promptness, open disagreement, punctuality, meals not part of socializing
Body language	Formal dress, frequent smiling in social encounters, eye contact avoided, frequent body contact, use of left hand avoided, restrained gesticulation	Informal dress, smiling only to express genuine pleasure, frequent eye contact, body contact avoided, free use of both hands, unrestrained gesticulation

Table 5.9 Influence of Culture on Travel-related Activities

Travel-related Activity	Influence of Culture
Trip type	Packaged or non-packaged, long or short, similar cultures or different, distant or nearby places
Tour group	Alone or with group, small or large group, Family or friends
Activities on tour	Active or passive, shopping or no shopping, purchasing souvenirs or not, photography—less or more, interaction with hosts—less or more
Food preferences	Local food or own food, food important factor in tour choice or not
Use of travel agent	For full tour arrangement, partial, or not at all

Culture influences on specifically travel-related activities such as trip type, tour group, activities on tour, food preferences in tour, use of travel agents, and so on, as shown in Table. 5.9.

The facilitation of these activities at the destination depends on the understanding of the cultures.

Marketing initiatives

The states in India have well understood the importance of themes. For example, Kerala's theme is 'God's Own Country' and that of Madhya Pradesh is 'Heart of India'.

Marketing initiatives influence the tourists to a large extent. The range of these initiatives is broad, including development of tour services, transferring information to the buyers, promotion, facilitating purchases, and monitoring post purchase. Promotional initiatives in particular focus on assisting the tourists through the buying stages. Brand names and image is used as a tourist appeal. Destinations world over have adopted themes to market themselves such as Incredible India and Malaysia Truly Asia.

Special discounts and offers attract the tourists and propel purchase. Seasonal offers by destinations and even hotels are such instances. Frequent customer schemes reward the buyers for their repeat purchase and brand loyalty. Competitive strategies are used to snatch the competitors' buyers. The marketers need to find the right combination of these initiatives to be targeted at each stage of buying and also to help the tourists in moving from one stage to another.

All the external factors put together create a force on the tourists' buying but the internal factors determine the response to this force.

Internal/Individual Factors

A tourist is both an individual and a group member. The psychology of an individual tourist decides the reaction to external forces. Therefore, common and undifferentiated marketing initiatives may not be successful for all the tourists. For example, some tourists may take information from friends, others from newspapers, or the internet, and so on. It all depends on the personal comfort level with a source and belief in the value of information therein. Many psychological processes, such as perception, personality, learning, attitudes, and motivation, add to the behaviour of an individual.

Perception

It is the process of receiving stimuli from the environment and processing it to provide a meaning. Due to the nature of tourism services, all tourism is perception. Tourists visit a place believing it to be good based only on information. No prior experience is possible. Post visit, new perceptions may be formed that are transferred to other tourists again as information. Perception makes tourism information intensive and gives opportunity to the marketers to supply suitable information at the right time. For example, when parts of Asia were hit by severe acute respiratory syndrome (SARS) in 2002, the promotional campaign of India proved effective as many tourists opted for India. The Incredible India message of the Ministry of Tourism has coincided with the economic growth here. The two together have given a more positive message.

Personality

How a person relates to the environment forms the personality. The important personality traits for tourists are a desire to see new places and meet people. Both these traits can be of different degree. As a result, some tourists travel to familiar destinations and others to unfamiliar ones. Tourist personality is categorized as allocentric, mesocentric, and psychocentric. Allocentric tourists travel to new and unfamiliar places, while psychocentircs opt for well-known destinations. Mesocentric fall in between and prefer slightly familiar places. Just like the choice of the destination the activities during the tour too depend on the tourist's personality.

Motivation

Tourists travel to a place for different motives. The demographics of tourists may not reveal this but psychographics do bring out the reasons. For example, Delhi may have tourists for a number of purposes, such as business, heritage, shopping, pleasure, and education, while a small hill station may have only leisure tourists. Some common travel motivations can be grouped as physical, cultural/psychological, social/interpersonal and ethnic, entertainment/pleasure and religious (Table 5.10).

Table 5.10 Travel Motivations

Physical	Cultural/ Psychological	Social/ Interpersonal and ethnic	Entertainment/ Pleasure	Religious Motives
• Participation in sport and active recreation, such as, golf, walking, and so on.	• Participation in festivals, theatre, music, museums, and so on	• Enjoying the company of friends and relatives	• Watching sport-related activities, and so on	• Participating in pilgrimages
• Undertaking activities in pursuit of health, fitness, and so on.	• Participation in personal interests, that is, intellectual or craft-related activities	• Undertaking social duty occasions— weddings, funerals, and so on	• Visiting theme parks, and so on	
• Resting/relaxing —unwinding from everyday life	• Visiting destinations to enjoy their cultural and/or natural heritage qualities	• Visiting the place of one's birth	• Leisure shopping	

The behaviour of tourists at the destination is directly related to motivation. Understanding of motives of tourists can be used for customizing services. For example, all types of tourists will require hotels but business tourists will demand completely different facilities from shoppers. Putting them together in a property may not provide the right ambience to either.

Learning

Learning is deliberate and non-deliberate acquisition of new knowledge that brings relatively permanent change in the behaviour. All behaviours including travel are learned. Tourism learning is about purchase and consumption. Touring habits can be acquired from friends or from television shows. The marketers can contribute to this learning through their own inputs in the form of benefits of tours, convenience of well-arranged tours, low cost of foreign travel, and so on. Any untoward incident at the destination can make the tourists perceive the tour as risky and hence, avoid it. A counter campaign in confidence building can help in damage reversal. The promotional campaigns can be systematically targeted towards learning.

Attitudes

Insurgency in Jammu and Kashmir or law and order problem in the North-East may create the impression that the entire country is unsafe for travel. This might discourage many travellers from visiting India.

Attitudes are a settled way of thinking or feeling towards something. People have general attitudes that are transferred to the evaluation of destinations.

Attitude provides a backdrop against which additional information is seen. Changing attitude is a challenging and long-drawn process but is possible through persistent communication. Many destinations world over have changed the attitudes of potential visitors towards their attractions. India is also trying to change the attitude of its overseas visitors by enriching its product basket with medical and business tourism. Efforts are made not to allow formation of negative attitudes by taking quick action in cases of crimes against foreigners.

All these internal influences create a cumulative effect to influence the choice of tourists.

Many tourist decision-making models are used to understand cumulative impact of these internal/external forces that leads to final purchase. These models also take into account tourism specific factors like geography.

TOURIST DECISION-MAKING MODELS

General models of buyer behaviour, such as Nicosia, Engel–Kollat–Blackwell, and Howard–Sheth can explain the decision-making of tourists. But these models are not tourism specific. Many models have been derived from these models and adapted to tourist behaviour. All these models have the following commonalities.

1. Exhibit behaviour as a process
2. Focus on individual behaviour
3. Share the belief that consumer is rational and behaviour can be explained
4. View behaviour as purposive
5. Information processing is key component of decision
6. Outcome is used as feedback that influences future purchases

Three important models, namely Schmoll, Mathieson and Wall, and Moutinho are used here to explain the tourist behaviour.

Schmoll Model (1977)

It is one of the earlier models on travel behaviour and is based on general models of consumer behaviour (Fig. 5.12). But it considers travel specific features in detail and identifies the following four-stage process of travel decision.

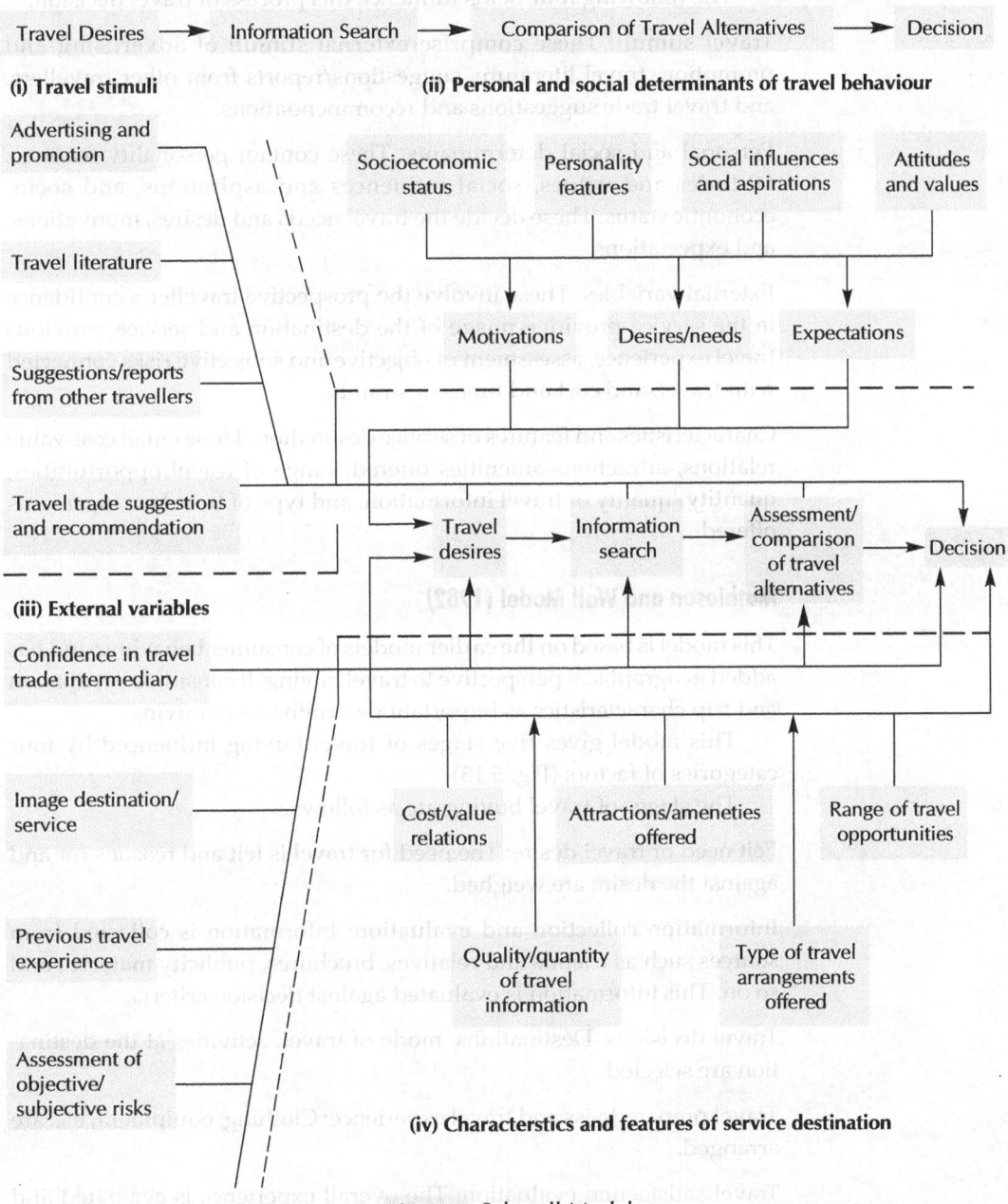

Fig 5.12 Schmoll Model
(*Source:* Cooper (ed.) 1992)

The following four fields influence this process of travel decision.

Travel stimuli: These comprise external stimuli of advertising and promotion, travel literature, suggestions/reports from other travellers, and travel trade suggestions and recommendations.

Personal and social determinants: These contain personality features, attitudes and values, social influences and aspirations, and socio-economic status. These decide the travel needs and desires, motivations, and expectations.

External variables: These involve the prospective traveller's confidence in the service provider, image of the destination and service, previous travel experience, assessment of objective and subjective risks connected with travel, and cost and time constraints.

Characteristics and features of service destination: These entail cost-value relations, attractions-amenities offered, range of travel opportunities, quantity/quality of travel information, and type of travel arrangements offered.

Mathieson and Wall Model (1982)

This model is based on the earlier models of consumer behaviour and has added geographical perspective to travel buying. It considers destination and trip characteristics as important determinants in buying.

This model gives five stages of travel buying influenced by four categories of factors (Fig. 5.13).

The stages of travel buying are as follows.

Felt need or travel desire: The need for travel is felt and reasons for and against the desire are weighed.

Information collection and evaluation: Information is collected from sources such as friends and relatives, brochures, publicity material, and so on. This information is evaluated against decision criteria.

Travel decisions: Destinations, mode of travel, activities at the destination are selected.

Travel preparedness and travel experience: Clothing, equipment, etc. are arranged.

Travel satisfaction evaluation: The overall experience is evaluated and the results influence subsequent travel.

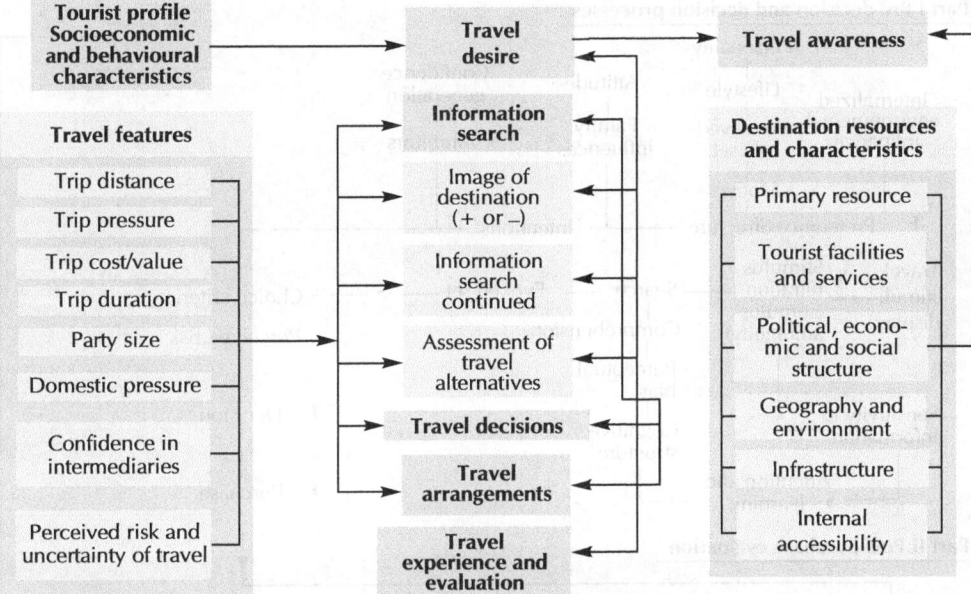

Fig. 5.13 Mathieson and Wall Model
(*Source*: Mathieson and Wall 1996)

The four categories of factors influence the buying are as follows.

Tourist profile: Age, income, education, attitudes, previous experience, motivations

Travel awareness: Image of a destination's facilities and services which are based upon the credibility of the source

Destination resources and characteristics: Attractions and features of the destinatior

Trip features: Trip type, trip distance, and perceived risk

Moutinho Model (1987)

This is a very comprehensive model of travel decision and considers three parts in buying: pre-decision and decision, post purchase and evaluation, and future decision-making. Each part is further composed of fields and sub-fields (Fig. 5.14).

Part I   Pre-decision and decision

This includes preference structure, decision, and purchase. Preference structure includes influences of family, motivation, attitudes, financial

Part I Pre-decision and decision processes

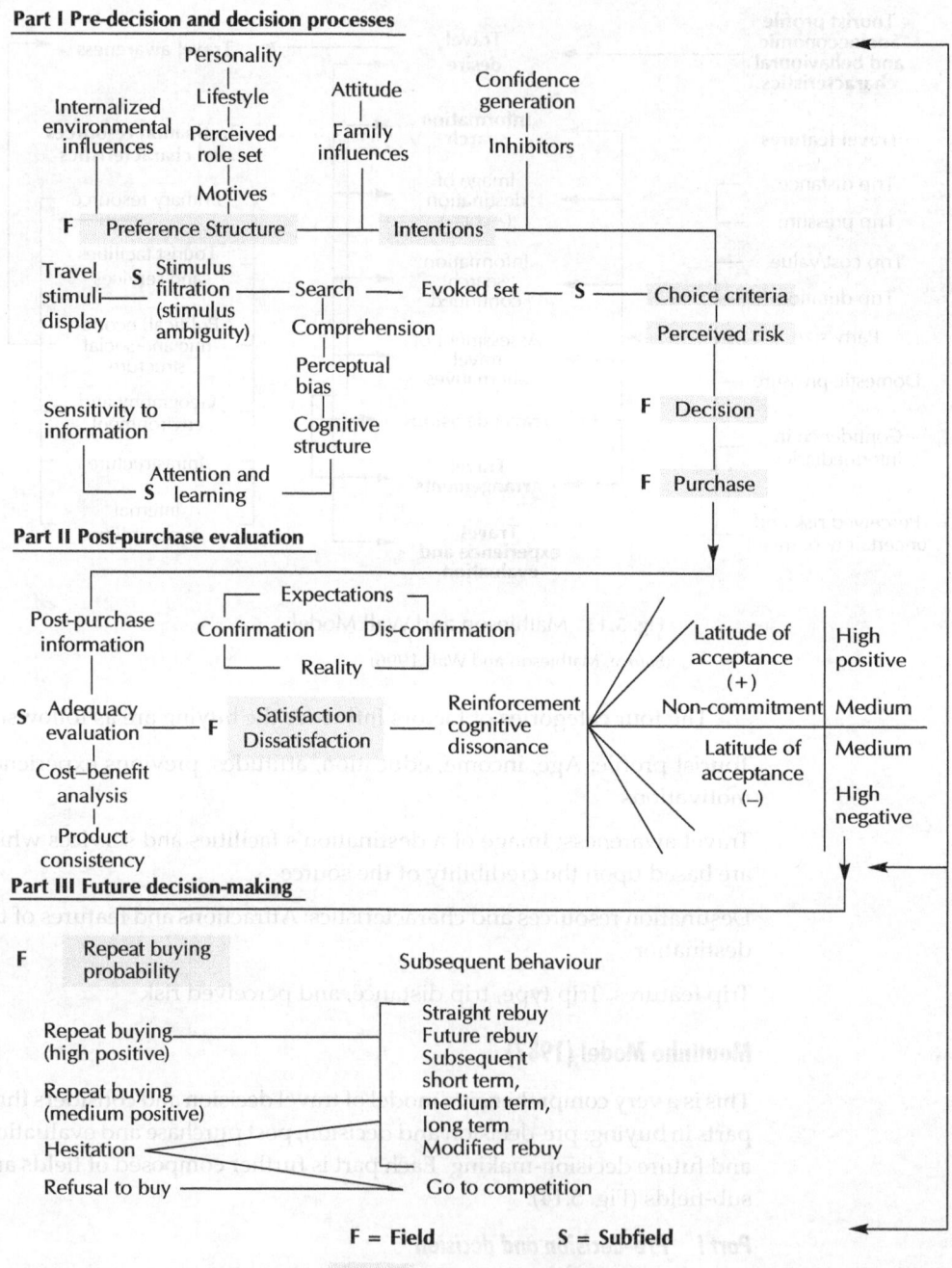

Part II Post-purchase evaluation

Part III Future decision-making

F = Field   S = Subfield

Fig 5.14 Moutinho Model

(*Source:* Witt and Moutinho 1989)

status, class and environment. All these lead to a specific intention or preference. The level of confidence, anxiety, caution, and indecisiveness towards purchase inhibits this preference. The decision and purchase fields are activated by information.

Part II   Post-purchase evaluation

At this stage, tourists develop a feeling of satisfaction/dissatisfaction that may lead to changes in future behaviour.

Part III   Future decision-making

This covers certain probabilities occurring out of the foregoing process.

This model tries to incorporate all aspects of travel purchase but the relationships between parts and fields, subfields are not clear.

But the overall travel specific models make the reader aware of the dimensions of travel purchase and tourist behaviour.

SUMMARY

The knowledge of the markets and their behaviour can be crucial for a marketer. Tourism markets have a unique nature of geographically dispersed buyers and products. As a result, the homogeneity in supply and demand is not found. Tourism markets can be of many types categorized on the basis of origin–destination, purpose of visit, and types of tourists.

Tourism markets for India are based in the USA and Europe who come for beaches, mountains, and heritage. Lately, the government is planning to diversify its market to more countries for adventure, ecotourism, medical tourism, and so on.

Insight into market behaviour is used to plan marketing interventions through suitable strategies. Market behaviour are aggregation of individual behaviour that can be of many types. Generally, these are studied as a process. Types of tourist behaviour can be well thought out,

emotional, impulsive, or a combination thereof. The nature of purchase, nature of tourists, and the perception of risks in travel buying mainly determine these.

Travel buying can be studied with the help of a simple process model containing six stages of need recognition, information search, attitude formation, evaluation of alternatives, purchase, and post-purchase. Each stage can be extensive and long drawn. The marketers have the opportunity to influence the buyers at each stage.

Travel purchase models explain tourists' behaviour and their decisions by considering the tourism-specific factors. Important models here are Schmoll, Mathiesan and Wall, and Mountinho.

All the models differ in approach and assign importance to different aspects of travel decision.

KEY TERMS

Business markets Tourists from these markets primarily travel for business purposes. The MICE markets fall in this category.

Culture Culture is the sum total of living at a place. It directs the human reactions to external stimuli through learned ways and often finds expression in the rituals, symbols, practices, language, religion, etc. It gets reflected in use of leisure time and travel behaviour.

Domestic market It comprises tourists travelling within the country from one place to another.

Ecotourism markets Tourists from these markets travel to nature areas in an eco-friendly manner and do not disturb the nature.

Groups and tourist reference groups Group is a collection of two or more persons. A tourist belongs to a large number of groups, mainly family, friends, social, and work that can inform, suggest, and persuade about the travel choices.

Health tourism markets Tourists travelling to other places for health benefits through change of weather, better environs, or medical facilities form this market.

Inbound market The inbound market for a country consists of people travelling to it from other countries.

Need recognition It is the identification of unfulfilled needs. This is the first stage in the buying process.

Outbound market The outbound market for a country consists of its citizens travelling outward to other countries/destinations.

Perception It is the process of receiving stimuli from the environment and processing these to form a meaning. It is very important in tourism due to the high intangibility component of tourism services.

Personality It is the way a person relates to the environment. For tourists, the desire to see new places and meet people is an important personality trait.

Tourism market This is a collection of marketers and tourists who come together for exchange of benefits.

Tourist buying process This constitutes the stages through which a tourist passes for taking a travel decision.

EXERCISES

Review Questions

1. What are tourism markets? Explain tourism markets on the basis of origin–destination.
2. Explain the evaluation stage of buying and the role played by attitudes of tourists at this stage.
3. What decisions are taken by the tourists at the post-purchase stage? What makes this stage important for the marketers?
4. Write a note on the role of culture in tourist behaviour.
5. How do groups influence tour purchase? Explain with the help of examples.
6. What are reference groups? How do these influence travel purchases?

Practice Exercises

1. Prepare a profile of tourism markets of Kerala's wellness tourism and identify the underlying motives of these markets.

2. India is considered a long-haul destination for international markets. Identify the possible reasons for the same.
3. Read the blogs of backpackers. What makes India a popular backpacker destination? How do backpackers differ from other groups of tourists?

Projects

1. Prepare a small questionnaire on tourists profile, motives, and behaviour. Administer it in your city and use it to understand the tourists better. You can also use it to compare tourists from different places.
2. Compare your own individual travel buying decision against the detailed travel buying process explained in the chapter. Find and explain the differences.
3. Plan a tour of three–four days with your friends.

Now compare all the decisions taken by you and the efforts taken against the buying process explained above. Do you find any variations? Try to find an explanation for the same.

4. Contact the managers of few local travel agencies and hotels. Discuss the behaviour of their tourists and customers. Now prepare a detailed report on the same.

REFERENCES

Boniface, Brian G. and Chris Cooper 1995, *The Geography of Travel and Tourism*, Butterworth-Heinemann, Oxford.

Cooper, Chris et al. 1993, *Tourism Principles and Practice*, Pitman Publishing, London.

Decrop, Alain 2006, *Vacation Decision Making, CABI* Publishing, Wallingford, Oxfordshire, UK.

Dolnicar, Sara 2005, 'Understanding barriers to leisure travel: Tourist fears as a marketing basis', *Journal of Vacation Marketing*, vol. 11, no.3, pp. 197-208.

Fodness, Dale and Brian Murray 1999, February, 'A model of tourist information search behaviour', *Journal of Travel Research*, vol.37, no.3, pp. 220-230.

Gilbert, D.C. 1992, 'An examination of consumer behaviour process related to tourism', in C. P. Cooper (ed.), *Progress in Tourism, Recreation and Hospitality Management*, vol 3, CBS Publishers, New Delhi, pp. 79-101.

Gray, P. 1970, International Travel: International Trade, Lexington Books, Massachussets.

Gursoy, Dogan and Ken W. McCleary 2004, 'Travellers' prior knowledge and its impact on their information search behaviour', *Journal of Hospitality & Tourism Research*, vol.28, no.1, pp. 66-94.

Holloway, J.C. and Plant, R.V. 1988, *Marketing for Tourism*, Pitman, London.

Kotler, Philip 1995, *Marketing Management: Analysis, Planning, Implementation and Control*, Prentice Hall of India, New Delhi.

Kotler, Philip 2003, *Marketing Insights from A to Z: 80 Concepts Every Manager Needs to Know*, John Wiley and Sons, New Jersey.

Kotler, Philip, Bowen John, and Makens James 2004, *Marketing for Hospitality and Tourism*, Pearson Education, Delhi.

Lovelock, Christopher and Jochen Wirtz 2004, *Services*

Marketing:People, Technology, Strategy, Pearson Education, Delhi.

Mathieson, A. and G. Wall 1982, *Tourism: Economic, Physical and Social Impacts*, Longman, Harlow, UK

Middleton, V. T. C. 1988, *Marketing in Travel and Tourism*, Heinemann, Oxford.

Moutinho, L. 2000, 'Consumer behaviour in tourism', *European Journal of Tourism*, vol. 21, no.10, pp. 1-44.

Pizam, A. and G. H. Jeong 1996, 'Cross-cultural tourist behaviour- Perceptions of Korean tour-guides', *Tourism Management*, vol.17, no.4, pp. 277-286.

Reisinger, Yvette and Lindsay W. Turner 1997, 'Cross-cultural differences in tourism: Indonesian tourists in Australia', *Tourism Management*, vol.18, no.3, pp.139-147.

Reisinger, Yvette and Lindsay W. Turner 2002, 'Cultural differences between Asian tourist markets and Australian hosts, Part 1', *Journal of Travel Research*, vol. 40, February, pp.295-315.

Schiffman, Leon G., and Leslie Lazer Kanuk 1992, *Consumer Behaviour*, Prentice Hall of India, New Delhi

Snepenger, David et al. 1990, 'Information search strategies by destination: Naive tourists', *Journal of Travel Research*, Summer, pp.13-16.

Venison, Peter 1988, *Managing Hotels*, Heinemann Professional, London.

Witt, Stephen F. and Luiz Moutinho 1989, *Tourism Marketing and Management Handbook*, Prentice Hall International, Hemel Hempstead.

Website References

India Tourism Statistics 2008, www.tourism.gov.in, accessed on 1 April 2009.

Tourism Highlights 2009, www.unwto.org, accessed on 28 March 2010.

Tourism Statistics at a Glance 2008, www.tourism.gov.in

CASE STUDY
SLUM TOURISM/REALITY TOURISM IN INDIA

Foreign tourists in India are interested in seeing Indian slums such as Dharavi in Mumbai and Paharganj in Delhi. It is similar to tours of favelas or shantytowns of Rio de Janeiro.

A two-hour tour is conducted for Rs 200 to 300 by local non-governmental organizations (NGOs), tour operators, and international human rights organizations. But not all are accepting such tours and some are even opposing these.

These tours are raising important issues like the following.

1. **Why are these popular?**
   - Novelty value for tourists from affluent countries
   - Exposes tourists to urban reality away from hotel rooms and tourist spots

2. **What can be the benefits of such tours?**
   - Part of the money raised from tourism can be fed back for the development of slums.
   - Negative stereotypes about the slum dwellers can be dispelled.

3. **Why are these opposed?**
   - It is a voyeuristic exercise for foreign tourists.
   - It is debasing the poor people.
   - It turns poor people into anthropological curiosities. They are captured on camera unannounced.

DISCUSSION QUESTION

1. Explain the behaviour of foreign tourists regarding the acceptance of such tours with the help of concepts such as personality, perception, learning, motivation, and so on.

CHAPTER 6

Market Segmentation, Targeting, and Positioning

LEARNING OBJECTIVES

Focused marketing becomes essential with the development of markets and increasing competition. This chapter discusses how resources can go waste if not targeted precisely and how the approaches of market segmentation, targeting, and positioning are used for it.

In this chapter, you will learn about the following.

• Concept of market segmentation
• Reasons for segmentation
• Bases of market segmentation
• Features of a good segment
• Concept and process of market targeting
• Product positioning and its strategies

INTRODUCTION

Tourists have distinct preferences. At one level, they have the generic need to travel followed by more specific needs regarding the type of travel, i.e., nature, adventure, business, and so on. This further trickles down to detailed likings for mode of transport and hotel facilities, etc. All this requires customization of the product to match the requirements of the buyers, and the marketers want to know the tourist groups with specific needs so that these can be satisfied in the best possible way. Segmentation helps in gaining a better return on their investment by using this consumer-led marketing technique, rather than randomly marketing to the general population. Market segmentation is a crucial tool that allows a population to be divided into groups of people with similar characteristics. It allows the needs and wants of each of these 'segments' or groups to be better understood. The products can then be customized and targeted to groups that display the most purchasing potential. It enables better decision-making and greater precision in serving and communicating with the target markets.

WHAT IS MARKET SEGMENTATION?

Market segmentation can be defined as the process through which tourists with similar needs, wants, and characteristics are grouped together or the total market is divided into smaller parts that share common characteristics. It helps in finding those tourists who are most interested in the firm's offers. It can be defined as the process to put existing and potential customers/travellers with similar preferences into groups referred to as market segments. Market segmentation is also used to design market mixes which satisfy the special needs, desires, and behaviour of the target market. Hsiesh, Leary, and Morrison (1992) call it a management strategy based on assumptions about the behaviour of the population sub-groups. Tourists can be divided in a number of different ways: purpose of travel (business, leisure), geography (by country), buyer needs and motivations, buyer or user characteristics, demography (age, gender, life cycle), economy (income, education, occupation), psychography (psychocentric, allocentric), geo-demography, price, and so on.

WHY SEGMENT MARKETS?

The main reason behind market segmentation is better service to the customers coupled with achievement of the firm's objectives. But the decision to segment markets depends upon the approach of the firm, market compulsions, its own resources, and profitability.

Approach of the Firm

A firm has many options to reach its markets and it can follow any of the following approaches.

Undifferentiated marketing

Here, the marketers present one generic offer to the whole market believing it to be good enough for the need satisfaction of all. This works in the initial stages of the market development when it is non-competitive. This may also work for low-paying markets where the buyers have limited resources to support multiple offers. An airline offering one type of seats and facilities to all its customers is a case of such approach.

Differentiated marketing

This can be utilized when the market is well developed with distinct preferences among buyers. The marketer can choose to satisfy multiple choices of the complete market through its numerous offers. An airline providing different facilities within the same aircraft for business and economy class, or operating different flights with different levels of facilities, is an example of such marketing.

Concentrated marketing

The market is differentiated but the firm cannot reach all because of limited resources and decides to choose the limited part of the market and build it strongly. An airline focusing only on super luxury tourists uses concentrated approach. Boutique hotels also follow this approach.

The choice of approach is strategically decided by a firm after considering the following related issues.

Market compulsions   A well-developed market will have a large variety of offers to suit all tourism needs and any operator here cannot afford to ignore differentiation, and segmentation becomes almost compulsory.

Firm's resources   Approaching markets require backup resources to support the marketing efforts. Full undifferentiated or differentiated market coverage demands large resources. A small firm limits itself to a few selected segments even if there are many good segments.

Profitability   The decision to segment markets is dominated by the returns generated post-segmentation. In the short run, the forms of returns may be to make an entry in a new area, increase market share, balance risks, but finally profits are important.

DECISIONS IN MARKET SEGMENTATION

Segmentation can be viewed as a four-step process and the marketers need to take many decisions at each stage. These steps are as follows.

1. Segment identification
2. Segment selection
3. Segment development
4. Feedback

SEGMENT IDENTIFICATION

Exploring the total market to find its segments is the first challenge for the marketers. A firm would like to know the criteria that will provide it the most accurate segments. Segments defined on multiple attributes can provide the right type of potential tourists but getting the right combination of attributes is very important.

Bases for Segmenting Tourist Markets/Types of Tourist Market Segments

This is one of the most important decisions for a marketing manager. A number of bases or criteria are used for segmenting tourism markets. Segmentation 'usually' involves combining many bases to develop a complete profile for different market segments. The total market for any product is likely to be quite wide, but by describing the differences between segments, it becomes possible to create focused and cost-effective strategies for each one.

Using any single base in isolation may not give good segment, such as simply identifying a segment as 'senior citizens' on the basis of age. Just because they are within the same age group, does not make them similar. Within this general group there are many variations. Here are a few examples.

- Age: Perceptions vary with different life spans across countries.
- Income: 'Elderly' people on pensions differ from others who are working.
- Activity levels: There is a world of difference between house-bound senior citizens and active citizens.

Using a number of criteria helps group larger number of similar people together.

Some common bases of segmentation are discussed below.

Demographic Segmentation

Demographic or population features are the most simple and meaningful bases for segmenting markets. This information is economically and easily available. Census reports of the government provide this information. This basis matches demographic profile with tourists' choices. The main demographic categories are as follows.

Age: Tourist behaviour is closely related to age, a deciding factor behind stamina, stress, and activities. Thus, adventure tours may appeal to the 18-30 age range, whereas visiting historic properties may be popular with the 25-45 age range. Age is regularly used to define the behaviour of certain markets. For instance, older people in India tend to be more inclined towards religious tours and pilgrimages, while younger people may tour for sports, entertainment shows, and so on.

Gender: It determines the consumption patterns. Hotels consider this to provide modified interiors for women travellers with tall wardrobe for long dresses and different provisions in rooms. Women give more weight to security and that decides the choice of hotels, flight timings, and so on.

Economic status: Income influences the expenditure on travel purchases. For example, budget accommodation will be purchased by people travelling on a restricted income and luxury accommodation is likely to be the choice of rich tourists.

Nationality: Some nationalities have a greater propensity to travel or indulge in certain activities than others.

Occupation: It decides the lifestyle and the choice of tourism activities. A professional, businessman, and farmer from the same income group will have different preferences. Professionals often travel for meetings and conferences.

Religion: People travel for religious purposes—Hindus to temples and other pilgrimage sites, Muslims to their centres of worship, and so on. A complete market of religious and pilgrimage tourists exists and it can be an effective basis of segmentation.

Family size and life cycle: The family remains the basic social unit. Consumption patterns are developed and taught within the family as it proceeds through a life cycle. This life cycle combined with income and occupation is used to delineate different consumer groups. 'Life cycles' change characteristics such as age, family status, and work status, prompting a change in motivation, behaviour, needs, and attitudes. 'Life cycle' analysis improves our understanding of consumer motivations and behaviours. This tool allows us to distinguish how people's travel patterns change as they enter different 'life cycles'. For example, the travel behaviour of young people with small children will be more towards places that kids like but the same couple will have different choice when the kids grow up and leave home.

> A life cycle stage indicates higher propensity to undertake an activity relative to other stage.

Geographic Segmentation

People travel for geographic reasons. This can be climate, topography, or political boundaries. The common geographic bases are as follows.

Regions: Geographic borders define a region having particular topographical features. These may promote particular type of tourism. India has the Himalayan region, the northern plains, and the southern peninsula as its regions. Each is distinct for its own tourism attractions. For international markets, the Government of India (GoI) identifies 10 regions: Africa, Australasia, East Asia, West Asia, South Asia, South-East Asia, North America, Central and South America, East Europe, and West Europe.

Zones: Travel zones are similar to regions but are more homogenous regarding tourism. The north-east and the north-west regions in India are more homogenous than the whole Himalayan region.

Countries, states, districts, and cities: These can be used if they give substantial business. India is being targeted as a separate segment by countries such as Singapore, Australia, Britain for its huge outbound market.

Climate: Tourists travel in winters to warmer places and to colder places in summers. Winter sports and summer tour packages are examples of tours propelled by climate.

Topography: The attractiveness of locales such as beaches, mountains, deserts, etc. and their tourism potential depends upon the topography. The west coast of India has beaches that are popularized for tourism; contrary to this eastern beaches have rocky coastline that is difficult to develop.

Political boundaries: Foreign travel is taken across national boundaries. Such travel may be taken for its charm than for other considerations.

Psychographics and Lifestyle Segmentation

Demographics may be too narrow to describe the wide variations in behaviour and outlook of a sophisticated market. Lifestyle and psychographic segmentation seek to remedy this situation. Psychographics classify consumers by their values and lifestyles.

Both attempt to cluster consumers into groups depending upon common interests and attitudes which will determine the way they spend their time and money. People's activities, interests, and opinions (AIOs) play a key role in decision-making and travel habits. By understanding people's AIOs and their subsequent motivations, certain sub-groups can be identified.

Lifestyle segmentation can be used to classify specific markets for particular products groups, for instance, adventure, leisure, and business.

Plog's Classification

Plog (1974) has also classified tourists based on their personality types. He has identified five categories of tourists: allocentrics, near-allocentrics, mid-centrics, near psychocentrics, and psychocentrics.

Allocentric and near-allocentric These tourists are characterized as self-confident, have an open spectrum on life, enjoy discovery and new experiences, and are more versatile. These tend to favour exotic places and the discovery of new cultures as well as the exploration of a new lifestyle. These tourists prefer to travel to new and unfamiliar places. These belong to the above average income group and are independent travellers.

Mid-centric   The 'mid-centric' segment tends to value comfort and familiarity in its travel experience. Individuals within such segment tend to view a travel experience as a means to relax and get pleasure. This category consists of majority of travellers who go to familiar places that have been populated by allocentrics.

Psychocentric and near-psychocentric   A psychocentric is considered to be an individual who tends to concentrate on life's small problems, is bound to a specific location, has generalized anxieties, and a sense of powerlessness. Psychocentric travellers tend to use travel as a means to enhance their social status and frequent famous tourist attractions. These like familiarity and travel to places similar to their home places. These are likely to be repeat visitors.

Gray's Classification

Gray (1970) has classified tourists into two categories based on motives for pleasure travel. These can be identified as distinct segments. These are sunlust and wanderlust.

Sunlust   'Sunlust' is linked to the travel to seek different or better amenities than those existing at one's local destination. These tourists travel to familiar places having well-developed infrastructure.

Wanderlust   'Wanderlust' is connected with the human desire to leave the familiar and discover different cultures and destinations. These travel to new places. A comparison of wanderlust and sunlust is given in Fig. 6.1.

Wanderlust	Sunlust
May visit several countries	Usually visit only one country at a time
More interest in foreign travel	More interest in domestic travel
Travel is an essential component throughout the visit	Travel is a minor component after one's arrival at the destination
Usually have an interest in educational programs	More interest either in rest and relaxation or being extremely active
Interested in staged/artificial physical attributes (climate is unimportant)	More interest in nature-made attributes (climate is important)
Searches for different cultures, institutions, and authentic cuisine	Seeks domestic amenities and lodging facilities

Fig. 6.1 Wanderlust and Sunlust

Behavioural Segmentation

The consumption rates and patterns for tourism purchases are used as a means of segmenting markets. For instance, tourists can be classified as follows.

On level of involvement in the activities

Every tour provides activities for engagement of visitors but the extent of their involvement depends upon their nature. A few tourists can put a good amount of time and effort in learning and participating in such activities, while others may join in passively.

Samplers and incidentals   Samplers do not usually take part in activities, but may sample one or two while on holiday, such as going on an organized canoe trip. Incidentals take part in an activity, but only as an incidental aspect of the holiday such as hiring a bike for the day.

Learners   They want to learn and experience more about an activity, with a view to future independent participation. This is a more significant market segment for activities that require a degree of technical expertise, for example, climbing, canoeing, windsurfing, etc.

Enthusiasts   These tourists are experienced and are frequent participants in activities. They will often base holidays and breaks entirely around their chosen activities. Highly independent and knowledgeable, these tourists will invariably organize their own activities.

Dabblers   These are people who occasionally take part in activities during their leisure time, and may well pursue their chosen activities while on holiday (though mostly as a secondary, not main, purpose of that holiday).

Corporate groups   These include companies and organizations using activities, in particular adventure activities, as a focus for team building, management development training, or incentive and reward days and weekends. Educational and youth groups, organized groups of school children, university students, and other youth groups also belong here.

On usage rate

This gives a very effective insight into markets as distinct marketing strategies would be suitable for different categories of users. Some common groups of tourists on the basis of usage rate are as follows.

- Frequent users
- Less frequent users
- Users
- Non-users

A company can identify the characteristics of different segments to target low use segments in order to increase the number of frequent users. Use of frequent customer programmes is very common in airlines and hotels, where frequent users are rewarded through discounted prices and additional benefits. Less frequent users are also attracted to low price per unit of increased usage.

Loyalty status

A market can also be segmented according to the degree of consumer loyalty to a product or service brand. According to Kotler (1995), the market would be classified as follows.

Hardcore loyals   These are consumers with undivided loyalty to one brand.

Softcore loyals   These are consumers with divided loyalty between two or more brands.

Shifting loyalties   These consumers switch their loyalty.

Switchers   These consumers demonstrate no brand loyalty.

Loyalty is difficult to measure as it can be spurious than real when tourists prefer a destination or other service in case of non-affordability or non-availability of other options. But loyalty can be rewarded based on user status.

Cohen's Classification

On the basis of behaviour, Cohen (1972) has identified four categories of tourists.

Organized mass tourists   They travel in groups, usually a package holiday where travel, accommodation, and food are all arranged for them by the travel agent/tour operator.

Individual mass tourists   They use the same facilities as above but are more individual about their tourist activity.

Explorers   Tourists arrange their own visit 'off the beaten track', want to meet locals, yet still use the facilities of the mass tourists.

Drifters   They shun contact with tourists, 'go native' by staying with locals, stay longer than most tourists, and do not regard themselves as tourists.

Benefit Segmentation or Segmentation by Purpose of Travel

Benefit segmentation uses causal rather than descriptive variables to group consumers. Different people buy the same or similar products for different reasons. For instance, some people will visit a restaurant because it has a reputation for good food or drink and will, therefore, seek gastronomic experience, others may visit the same restaurant to derive social benefits, or status. A business traveller will look for efficiency and prompt service, whereas a family is more likely to look for fun activities. The idea is to group tourists according to the principal benefit sought from a tour. Benefit-based segments relate to travel motivations and activities undertaken at the destinations. The important segments under this category are as follows.

Leisure market   It includes people who visit a place for pleasure. Leisure visitors can be further segmented into day trippers, overnight visitors, short break or holiday takers.

Business tourism   It is a broad sector encompassing the following.

1. Business or corporate travel by individuals, which can be very difficult to influence
2. Incentive travel—'trips of a lifetime'—offered to key personnel as an incentive or reward
3. Meetings and conferences
4. Exhibitions and trade fairs

Adventure tourism   In this type of tourism people travel for thrill and are ready to face the accompanied risk. Bungee jumping, rallies, mountaineering, river rafting, etc. are its main activities.

Farm tourism   In this type of tourism people travel to rural areas and stay at farmhouses to feel the nature and rural lifestyle.

Rural tourism   In this type of tourism people travel to villages and stay there for a complete exposure to village life.

Ecotourism   In this type of tourism people travel to natural areas and are active participants in its protection.

Voluntary tourism   Here, tourists participate actively with the locals to contribute meaningfully to the host area. It may be in the form of skill building on hygiene, English language, crafts, energy and water conservation, and so on.

Nature tourism   In this type of tourism people travel to experience the natural beauty of certain places.

Religious tourism   People travel to religious centres for peace of mind, wish fulfilment, performing ceremony, and so on.

Health and medical tourism   Health travel is undertaken for the change of place and associated therapeutic benefits or for some preventive treatments. Medical tours are curative in nature and are common in the parlance of modern medical systems as in the case of surgeries.

Business-to-Business Market Segmentation

Substantial parts of the market for tourism services is represented by other businesses, or organizations. For instance, conferences, seminars, incentive travel packages, air crew services are all aimed at other businesses rather than consumer markets. The concept of segmentation can be applied, although the bases used are likely to be different. Some of the most frequently used industrial market segments include the following.

Size of business   Market can be segmented on the basis of business generated and marketing efforts too can be proportionately directed. As a result, a firm can have large, medium, and small business with greater focus on large business.

Type of industry   Tourism services can be purchased by a number of industries. Firms selling fair and exhibition space segment their market on this basis.

Geographical region   Different geographic clusters of industries can be taken as separate segments based on assumption of similar requirements.

Type of buying organization   The type of organization will make its requirements distinct from others. A hotel will supply different type of food to airlines and corporate canteens. It will treat the two as different segments.

A marketer can use any of the above bases or their combinations to define its segment. The complex behaviour of buyers makes it very difficult to define it on limited bases. As shown in Fig. 6.2, Kuoni Academy clearly defines its adventure camp market segment for young people between the age group of 16-25 and raring to go.

SEGMENT SELECTION

A number of segments can be identified but only a few are to be selected. A marketer needs to take the following decisions at this stage.

Optimum number of segments

An organization has to decide the optimum number of segments for its markets. Too little segmentation will reduce the profits because customer satisfaction will be less where the buyers compromise on the products and too much segmentation may also be non-profitable as the costs of serving many markets tend to be very high. Unrestrained segmentation

Fig. 6.2 Adventure Camp Market Segment of Kuoni Academy

(*Source*: Advertisement in *The Times of India*, 18 April 2008, printed with permission)

may lead to an unsustainable range of product modifications and produce problems similar to market diversification.

Goodness of the segments

The designed market segments need to be good enough to assist both the sellers and the buyers in meeting their respective goals. The marketers need to build the following qualities in a segment to ensure the goodness of a segment.

Distinct and group identity   A segment shall be easily identifiable and distinct from the mass market as well as from other segments. True segments must be groupings that are homogeneous within segments and heterogeneous across groups, and thus have group identity.

Attractive   A segment should be attractive in terms of size that is profitable, preparedness to pay the market price for the offer, awareness of the product, and growth potential. The attractiveness in a segment is relative and directly related to the competitive strength and cost-effectiveness of the company. Even a small market may be profitable if the company has competitive pre-eminence.

Accessible and targetable   It means the ease and cost of reaching the segment. A segment may be easy to reach being geographically closer or through established channels of distribution and media. Such segments which are easy to reach can be persuaded not to choose competing products. Cost of reaching the market is often the deciding factor and it is essential to determine which ones will cost how much.

Self-containment—Focused   The defined segment shall not take demand from another product of company. A clear distinction between segments and products will make a segment focused. The large market is likely to have less focus.

Systematic behaviour to marketing mix responses   The market segment should meet the practical requirement of reacting similarly to a particular marketing mix. It shall also be responsive to distinct marketing and promotion effort.

Stability   Market segment should be stable with time and different market conditions.

SEGMENT DEVELOPMENT

The segments that pass the test of goodness are candidates for development at this stage. It involves detailed profiling of the chosen segments on multiple attributes to have insight into their travel behaviours. This helps in designing different product/service offerings and market mixes to get a favourable response from the segments or distinct groups of buyers. This also helps in the selection of segments at the targeting stage.

FEEDBACK—FORMING AND REFORMING SEGMENTS

Segmentation requires continuous evaluation as the preferences of tourists keep on changing with time and it involves regular identification, selection, and development to keep pace with market changes. It always happens in tourism where the character of destination shifts from new and unfamiliar to familiar mass tourist destination. A firm focusing on explorers will have to keep finding new places for its markets and if its focus is destination, it has to search new customer bases for itself.

MARKET TARGETING

Market targeting is the process of selection of segments and approaching selected markets/segments with suitable marketing mixes. Both decisions are critical for the success of a firm in the market.

Selection of Target Market

A firm has to find the most suitable markets for itself. To define the target market, it is imperative to consider a number of important issues which will help identify the segment that has the greatest potential for the organization. Some issues to consider and analyse are as follows.

- Market structure analysis
- Market opportunity analysis
- Product portfolio analysis
- Resource capabilities analysis
- Competitive analysis

Market structure analysis

Markets can be analysed for competition, changing preferences of tourists, technological advancements, and government regulations. The level and nature of competition will bear on the firm's decision to choose a market. High level of competition and reactive competitors will create a barrier for the new entrants. A company will prefer to select a market if the competition is healthy and predictable and gives space to new firms. Firms also have to adjust marketing efforts with the pace of change in preferences of tourists. Fast pace will result in constant

An ideal market will be low on competition with positive competitors, evolving technology and preferences of tourists, and less government controls. An ideal market may not be available, so a firm will go for best combination of these factors.

pressure for novelty, innovation, and advancement. Relatively more stable markets may be favoured for the longevity of such segments. Technological advancements in the markets have the same disturbing effects of not allowing a marketer to settle down. If the firm is a pioneer, the risk of non-acceptance of new technology remains, and if not, the risk of rejection of old is always there. Government regulations make a market unattractive if a firm cannot choose the best mix because of constraints in the form of rules and regulations. Additional surcharges, service tax can scuttle the pricing plans. Promotional schemes may be banned if judged as lotteries and so on.

Market opportunity analysis

Market opportunities are the cumulative outcome of many forces. Apparently, it is the opportunity in terms of current and future profits and market growth. Figure 6.3 shows the analysis of market opportunities. It considers compatibility of a firm's resources with markets as one criterion. It includes variables such as previous presence in the markets, awareness of brands, the firm's ability to satisfy buyers, and so on. The other criterion is attractiveness of market segments in terms of size, stability, paying capacity, growth potential, profitability, and so on.

Similarly, analysis can be made with the help of Boston Matrix which is based on potential market growth and probable relative market position (market share) (Fig. 6.4).

It gives the following four types of potential markets.

		Segment Attractiveness		
		Low	Medium	High
Compatibility with firm's resources	Low			
	Medium		Third best	Second best
	High		Second best	Best segment

Fig. 6.3 Market Opportunity Analysis

		Segment Attractiveness	
		Low	High
Market growth	Low	Dog	Cash cow
	High	Question mark	Star

Fig. 6.4 Boston Matrix

Stars: Here, the firm is likely to enjoy high growth with high market share.

Cash cows: The firm will have high market share but low growth.

Question marks: It will have low market share but high growth.

Dogs: It will have low market share with low growth.

This analysis suggests firms to avoid dogs and focus on other markets.

Product portfolio analysis

Firms develop product portfolio with a basket of products. Different products are targeted at different markets to distribute the risks. Sometimes, portfolio decisions force firms to search for new segments. Many hotel businesses in India have started from one segment and moved on to other segments. The Tata Group initiated with the Taj Group in the premium segment and later forayed into budget segment with the Ginger chain. The Oberoi Group also has entered into the four-star category with the Trident brand. Private airlines, such as, Jet Airways started with the domestic sector but later began operating on selected international routes.

Resource capabilities analysis

Developing marketing mix for the selected segments needs investment and abilities. All the resources, such as, financial, physical, and manpower, are assessed to see if effective targeting is possible. Limited resources may also restrain the choice of markets. Smaller companies often operate on a limited scale, while bigger ones go for larger and diverse markets.

Competitive analysis

Competition is a part of market structure but is the main plank of targeting. A firm will analyse the strengths and weaknesses of the competitors to find its unique features. It can select a market as target if

- it can offer an innovation or unique benefit; and
- it can offer the same benefit with additional advantages such as low cost, high quality, and better services.

But the competitive position of the firm in the market decides the stance taken. A market leader or the number one firm will like to be on top in both competitive edge and differential advantage in the large market. The challenger or the number two firm will always try to snatch these advantages. Both these firms often compete for the top slot. A follower or a firm that operates in the market created by the big two may be happy with little modified or copied advantages. It does not pose any immediate threat to the first two leading firms. Niche operators are small firms specializing in small markets, and their selection of segments is different from others.

A firm will choose the best markets for itself where it enjoys competitive edge and differential advantage.

DEVELOPING MARKETING MIXES FOR THE MARKET SEGMENTS

It begins with an analysis of needs of segments that are converted into product/service offerings.

Figure 6.5 shows how the needs of budget and premium tourists are converted into marketing mix.

The list is only indicative, the types of segments can be many and an equal number of mixes are possible.

The marketers and tourists differ from each other in this interface of needs and offerings. A match between the two is essential for successful targeting. Figure 6.6 indicates the differences in this interface.

PRODUCT POSITIONING

Marketing mix created for targeting different markets affects the mental make-up of tourists. It adds to their perception along with inputs of the

Marketing Mix	Budget Tourist	Premium Tourist
Product	Core product	Core with peripheral
Place	Will travel from a central place	Pick and drop facility from home
Price	Low	High
Promotion	High and impersonal	Low and personal
Process	Self service to reduce costs	Want everything to be performed by service providers
People	Less service staff	More service staff
Physical Evidence	Basic	Elaborate

Fig. 6.5 Marketing Mixes for Budget and Premium Markets

Needs	Offers
• Benefits • Status • Personalized services Point of interface • Differentiated services ⟵————⟶ • Lifestyle • Self expressions • Relate to other buyers • Assurance of delivery of promises	• Product features • Brand name • Customer relationship • Market segment • Promotion • Touch points • Online platforms • Grievance handling systems

Fig. 6.6 Interface between Needs and Offerings

marketers and other independent sources. This perception forms an image of the offer in the tourists' minds that is relative to other competitive offerings. This mental image is product position and its development by the marketer is positioning. Product positioning has the following important features.

- It is relative.
- It is focused and clear.
- It is perceptual that may or may not be similar to the projected image of the marketer.
- Position is influenced by multiple forces such as background of the buyers and the competitor's and marketer's positioning efforts.
- Communication helps in building position. It may be projected at par, below, or above the real image depending upon the nature of its target market.
- It is a continuous process. Position may change with new entrants in the market or with the efforts of old competitors or the firm may decide to reposition its products.

> A river may have the intangible components of both beauty and danger. The tangibles in the form of railings, life guards, connecting roads all add to beauty and safety and create an image of tourist attraction.

For example, two destinations/hotels/tour packages may be similar in terms of offers but not in image. As a result, one may see a rush of tourists and the other may only have a few takers.

Positioning tourism is different from products because of its service features. The core features are intangibles with the supporting tangibles, and positioning involves developing and communicating a right mix.

All resources, such as, beaches, canyons, forests, or mountains, can be converted in to tourist resources by adding appropriate tangibles.

Purpose of Positioning in Tourism

Positioning must promise the benefit the customer will receive, create the expectation, and offer a solution to the customer's problem. The solution should be different and better than the competition's solution. The position must be believable in the tourist's mind and the destination must deliver that promise on a consistent basis.

Positioning Strategies in Tourism

Tourism offers can be positioned on a number of attributes on the 6 Ps of marketing mix, and the seventh P of promotion communicates the position to the tourists. The main strategies used for positioning are given below.

Positioning on the basis of attributes

Tourism products contain a large number of attributes. Any combination of these can be chosen for creating a position. Some commonly used attributes are as follows.

Natural tourism appeal   These attributes are unique, nature-based, and cannot be copied. The Valley of Flowers, the Kashmir valley, the Himachal hills, the beaches of the west coast, the river Ganga are all positioned such. The common attributes used here are:

- Beautiful beaches: Goa, Kodaikanal
- Dense forests: National parks, tribal and hilly areas
- Sloping mountains: Kashmir
- Religiosity: Traditional seats of religion such as the *Char Dhams*, Shakti Peeths, the Kumbh Mela, Buddhist places
- Beautiful sights: Lahaul–Spiti, Kinnaur, Kausani (Uttarakhand)
- Wildlife: National Parks such as Gir, Kanha, and Corbett

This strategy works well if tourism offers possess this appeal; else other options need to be considered.

On the basis of man-made appeal   There are places that do not have natural appeal but artificial attractions are created that become the appeal. Infrastructural support and facilitation of tours through good roads, airport, and hotel facilities, etc. often become the selling point of well-developed destinations.

The common attributes used for this positioning are as follows.

- Medical facilities: They are being extensively used for medical tourism in the National Capital Region (NCR) and Karnataka
- Health and wellness facilities: Kerala is using it to promote health tourism through yoga
- Conferencing and meetings: The National Capital Region and Hyderabad are developing and positioning these facilities
- Shopping: Dilli Haat, Janpath, and Chandni Chowk in Delhi; Jaipur
- Theme parks: Amusement parks
- Forts and palaces: Rajasthan
- Highways: Well-maintained highways of Haryana and Punjab

Position on price

Generally, buyers suffer from price quality syndrome where they associate higher price with higher quality. Taking this as a basis, price is often used to create a distinct position. Budget airlines and budget hotels have a different position on price only.

Position on accessibility

The convenient reach of a tourist place can be a unique feature. Hotels located closer to airports, bus stands, railway stations, business centres, and highways often get good business. Destinations get more tourists from nearby places. Due to easy access, a large number of restaurants, hotels, and resorts are opening on highways.

Position with respect to use/application

Destinations may be marketed for specific purposes such as culture, business, or shopping. For example, Sikkim is being extensively positioned for rural tourism.

Position according to users

A particular class of tourists may be targeted for positioning. Some destinations can target only rich tourists for a variety of attractions.

Position on the basis of services

Tourism products have high intangible component and can be distinguished on the basis of service features such as the following.

Quality customer support   Tourists are given all the information and help by a supportive staff.

Timeliness, accuracy, and reliability   For example, flights that take off on time, do not create confusion in customer dealings, and are consistent in performance.

Service attributes   In a highly competitive market, product features offered by different sellers become almost similar and the distinction in positioning is created through service features such as additional and superior services. Personalized care of guests, and 24 hour services are examples of use of service attributes for positioning.

Position on the basis of image

Intangibles are best packaged in a brand that can be positioned for a unique image. Tourism offers contain large assortment of benefits that are better communicated through a brand. Incredible India has positioned India better than the earlier attempts of long details of its land. A Taj hotel or an Oberoi hotel suggest more than the features of five-star hotels.

This strategy works well if the competition has forced all features and services to be almost similar.

Positioning Process

It involves the combined use of psychological and logical approaches and begins with the analysis of the image of the product to be positioned such as a destination, a hotel, or an airline in the market. The image at this stage is psychological and is the result of existing information with the buyers. The gap between this image and the desired image is noted and now the desired image is built through a systematic information and promotional campaign. The work on the desired image is done on both the objective and subjective parts of image. The product is objectively and logically positioned on the basis of facts, functional, or verifiable features. A hotel can use facts of its star status, location, technology, etc. to position. Positioning at subjective levels uses intangibles. The objective and subjective aspects of image again crystallize as psychological positioning.

Practically, positioning is done on multiple attributes and is the result of a long-drawn process comprising the following stages.

Identify the attributes

The marketers prepare a list of attributes having a potential to create distinction. These can be in attractions, facilities, processes, or images. These help in identifying and selecting the relevant attributes.

Evaluate attributes

Identified attributes are evaluated to judge their relative position against the competitors on the following criteria.

- Unique
- Distinctive
- Superior
- Better value for money

Select attributes

A collection of attributes, out of those passing through the evaluation stage, is selected to give a complete offer to tourists. This is done with the help of position maps, where the mix of selected attributes is compared with that of the competitors. Here, the marketers have to decide if they want to follow any of the competitors' position or adopt an entirely different position.

Communicate

The selected position is communicated to the tourists through promotion. What is communicated to the tourists is the image with the underlying attributes. This stage is critical because it adds to the final position of the offer.

Ries and Trout (1981) suggest the following six-step framework for successful positioning.

1. What position do you currently own?
2. What position do you want to own?
3. Whom do you have to defeat to own the position you want?
4. Do you have the resources to do it?

5. Can you persist until you get there?
6. Are your tactics supporting the positioning objective you set?

Repositioning

The positioning of tourism products is a continuous process. It requires repositioning with changes in the environment. For repositioning too, the same process is followed.

> Repositioning is often a bigger challenge as a new image is to be built over an existing one. It cannot be done very frequently.

Goa is a popular destination for sun, sand, and sea and does not get many tourists in the rainy season. A systematic effort has been made to promote Goa in the rains for its heritage buildings. Such repositioning is adopted by many destinations to promote its off-season sales. It can also be done to change the main appeal of the destination if it has reached its decline stage. It helps in reviving the place.

Positioning Errors

While positioning tourism products, often the following errors are committed.

Under positioning

Position does not stand out for tourists who perceive it as just another brand in the market. Buyers have a vague idea of it and are not sure of its distinct or unique properties.

Over positioning

Here, the product is too specifically positioned to be termed unsuitable by majority of the tourists. Tourists have a narrow idea of the brand. A lot many adventure tours are positioned as such in the Indian domestic market.

Confused positioning

Here, tourists do not know what the product stands for. Either it makes too many claims or its position is changed frequently by the marketer. For many years, India as a tourist destination faced this problem when it was promoted as the land of all reasons and all seasons. The foreign tourists coming from source markets in Europe and the USA could not perceive so many variations in a single place. As a result, they were often not sure what India could offer.

Doubtful positioning

Tourists find it difficult to trust the marketers' claims if the benefits offered do not support claims. Till a few years back, India was perceived as a land of snake charmers and rope tricks though it had moved much ahead with modernization.

SUMMARY

The chapter discusses segmentation, targeting, and positioning (STP) as a strategy to approach markets. The tourism markets often have diverse tastes, and offering one benefit to all will not satisfy the needs. Therefore, the market is divided into uniform small sub-groups or segments. The uniformity of these segments is ensured by selecting a suitable basis of segmentation. Some of the common bases are geographic, demographic, psychographic, and behavioural. Many attributes are taken together to define a segment. Once a firm knows the different segments, it will design suitable strategies to reach the chosen segments. The decision to select target markets and develop strategies for each is market targeting. Selection of target market is the result of strengths, weaknesses, opportunities, and threats (SWOT) analysis by the firm. The firm establishes an image of its offers in the market called position. Though position is the result of many forces, yet marketing plays an important role in it. It is a deliberate process of selecting attributes on which a firm wants to establish its image and communicating it to the tourists.

Segmentation, targeting, and positioning form a continuous process with the change in market environment. It is one very effective marketing approach.

KEY TERMS

Market segmentation Market segmentation can be defined as the process through which tourists with similar needs, wants, and characteristics are grouped together or the total market is divided into smaller parts that share common characteristics.

Geographic segmentation This includes deriving segments on the basis of geographic features, such as climate, topography, etc., that influence travel behaviour.

Psychographic segmentation Segmentation on the basis of mental make-up of tourists, primarily their attitudes, interests, and opinions, is called psychographic segmentation.

Demographic segmentation Using population features, such as age, income, gender, occupation, etc., to segment market as these influence the tour behaviour.

Behavioural segmentation Segmentation on the basis of behaviour expressed during the tour such as, long or short haul, sunlust–wanderlust, allocentric, mid-centric, and psychocentric.

Benefit segmentation Benefits expected from the tour are used for segmentation, such as, adventure, pleasure, education, culture, business, rural, and so on.

Product positioning It is the mental image of the product in the minds of the target markets.

Market targeting Market targeting is the process of selection of segments and approaching selected markets/segments with suitable marketing mixes.

SWOT analysis Strengths, weaknesses, opportunities, and threats analysis is the market and resource capabilities analysis.

EXERCISES

REVIEW QUESTIONS

1. Explain the role of STP (segmentation, targeting, and positioning) in focused marketing.
2. 'Geographic segmentation is commonly used in tourism.' Why? Explain with examples.

3. What is market targeting? Explain its process.
4. What attributes can be used for positioning in tourism? How are these attributes identified and selected?

PRACTICE EXERCISES

1. Identify the STP of the nearby destination. What changes would you suggest?
2. Develop a small questionnaire to judge the position of a popular Indian destination in your home city. How close is it to the projected image? What creates the difference?
3. Identify the important target markets of India? What are the different marketing strategies used by the government for these markets?

PROJECTS

1. Study the markets of a local hotel. Segment these and prepare a profile of each segment.
2. Survey the colleges in your city and find the preferences of students for undertaking travel for higher studies. Identify the different student segments on the basis of these preferences.

REFERENCES

Chacko, Harsha E. 1996, 'Positioning a tourism destination to gain a competitive edge,' *Asia Pacific Journal of Tourism Research*, vol.1, no. 2, pp. 69-75.

Cohen, E. 1972, 'Toward a sociology of international tourism,' Social Research, vol. 39, no.1, pp. 164–182.

Gray, H.P. 1970, *International Travel—International Trade*, Lexington Books, Massachussets.

Hansruedi, M., and L. K. Eveline 2001, 'Wellness tourism: Market analysis of a special health tourism segment and implications for the hotel industry,' *Journal of Vacation Marketing*, vol.7, no. 1, pp. 5-17.

Heung, C. O., U. Muzzaffer , and A. W. Pamela 1995, 'Product bundles and market segmentation based on travel motivations,' *International Journal of Hospitality Management*, vol.14, no. 2, pp. 123-137.

Holloway, J.C. and R.V. Plant 1988, *Marketing for Tourism*, Pitman, London.

Hsiesh, S., J. Leary, and M. A. Morrison 1992, June, 'Segmenting the international travel market by activity,' *Tourism Management*, vol.13, no. 2, pp. 209-223.

Kotler, Philip, Bowen John, and Makens James 2004, *Marketing for Hospitality and Tourism*, Pearson Education, Delhi.

Kotler, Philip 1995, *Marketing Management: Analysis, Planning, Implementation and Control*, Prentice Hall of India, New Delhi.

Kotler, Philip 2003, *Marketing Insights from A to Z: 80 Concepts Every Manager Needs to Know*, John Wiley and Sons, New Jersey.

Majaro, Simon 1995, *The Essence of Marketing*, Prentice Hall of India, New Delhi.

Meidan, Arthur 1984, 'The marketing of tourism', *The Service Industries Journal*, vol. 4, no. 3, pp. 166 -186.

Middleton, V.T.C. 1988, *Marketing in Travel and Tourism*, Heinemann, Oxford.

Plog, S. C. 1974, 'Why destination areas rise and fall in popularity', *The Cornell Hotel and Restaurant Administration Quarterly*, vol.14, no. 4, pp.55-58.

Plog, S. 1987, 'Understanding psychographics in tourism research', Ritchie, J.R.B. and Goeldner, C.R. (eds), *Travel, Tourism, and Hospitality Research: A Handbook for Managers and Researchers*, pp. 203-213, John Wiley and Sons, New York.

Plog, S.C. 2001, 'Why destination areas rise and fall in popularity: An update of a Cornell quarterly classic', *The Cornell Hotel and Restaurant Administration Quarterly*, vol. 42, pp.13-24.

Ries Al and Jack Trout 1981, *Positioning: The Battle for Your Mind*, McGraw- Hill Professional, New York.

Wales Tourist Board, 'Get up and go—A practical guide to developing activity tourism', www.visitwales.com, accessed on 12 August 2007.

Witt, Stephen F. and Moutinho Luiz 1989, *Tourism Marketing and Management Handbook*, Prentice Hall International, Hemel Hempstead, UK.

World Tourism Organization 2007, *Handbook on Tourism Market Segmentation: Maximizing Marketing Effectiveness*, Madrid.

CASE STUDIES

1. POSITIONING INDIA AS A HUB FOR BUDDHIST TOURISM

A holistic development of Buddhist tourism in India assumed special significance in the light of the decision by India and China to celebrate 2007 as the 'India–China Year of Friendship through Tourism' and the designation of 2007 by India and Japan as the 'India–Japan Tourism Exchange Year'.

A study by the Federation of Indian Chambers of Commerce and Industry, Investment Information and Credit Rating Agency of India (FICCI-ICRA) proposes agenda for five-fold increase in arrivals to Buddhist sites. The study underlines the need for a multi-pronged agenda to boost tourist arrivals to Buddhist circuits in India by 400 per cent and generate upwards of USD 1 billion of revenue from these circuits by 2012.

It calls for an increase in the number of direct international flights from important source markets such as China and Japan to India and to raise the frequency of domestic flights between Buddhist sites such as Bodhgaya and Varanasi; customized rail travel packages for Buddhist sites; incentivizing private investment in creating and maintaining basic tourism infrastructure such as good roads, clean budget hotels, security, availability of guides trained to speak key foreign languages, restaurants and wayside amenities, and hygienic environment; site preservation and conservation strategies; source market, traveller-specific marketing strategies, and issuance of multi-entry visa to facilitate travel to all Buddhist circuits.

The study highlights the following.

- Thirty one million Chinese travelled abroad in 2005, only 35,000 or about 0.1 per cent of this came to India. Improving air connectivity and raising the frequency of direct flights to India from the source market is imperative. Railway connectivity between Buddhist sites is important and can play an important role in augmenting

the Buddhist traffic to these areas. There is, therefore, an urgent need to coordinate this initiative and especially design customized tour packages for the tourists with the Ministry of Railways.

- It is important to encourage public-private partnership by incentivizing investment in creating and maintaining basic tourism infrastructure such as good roads, clean budget hotels, security, availability of guides trained to speak key foreign languages, presence of restaurants and wayside amenities, and hygienic environment.

- Need for proper implementation of conservation strategies and monitoring at regular intervals to make Buddhist monuments, sites, and structures world-class destinations.

- A multi-pronged marketing strategy is required since different countries have followers of different Buddhist doctrines. This will help market the Buddhist sites in appropriate countries, target higher-spend category tourists from these existing countries, and address new markets.

- Issuance of a multi-entry visa is a key requirement for Buddhist tourists travelling on a circuit. The standard route taken by Buddhist tourists is Bodhgaya–Nalanda–Rajgir–Patna–Kushinagar–Lumbini–Sravasti–Sarnath. Hence, a multi-entry visa will enable the tourists to travel to Nepal and be back in India and save time and trouble in having to reapply for a visa in order to complete the circuit.

It calls for coordination among the multiple stakeholders, including the Ministry of Tourism, state governments, Ministry of External Affairs,

Shipping, Road Transport and Highways, Civil Aviation, Railways, and others. Such coordination is vital for the development of on-ground infrastructure and other conditions such as security, availability of trained guides, and visa facilitation.

(*Source*: Media Division, Ministry of Tourism, Government of India)

2. IMAGE OF INDIA

Image of a place plays a critical role in marketing it as a tour destination. Promoting a nation, a region, or a city requires identifying and communicating this image across different cultures. Marketing and positioning India as a tourist destination on global tourism scene was a big challenge.

The need was to create an international brand that could cut across national boundaries and cultures with ease. Prevailing images associated with India were largely negative, making it a challenge to promote it as a desirable travel destination.

Over the years, the situation has improved. With factors such as information technology (IT) supremacy, advanced medical services, and age-old healing therapies in its favour, the government made the effort to position these aspects globally, through aggressive publicity campaigns. But the big challenge still remained—How to position and brand India as one entity? India is not a single destination; it is a vast country. In size, it is bigger than 23 European countries put together. Every state of India is a unique tourism product in itself. The only way left was to establish one mother brand, with the states establishing their own identities as sub-brands. Thus, the search for a brand started. Developing a strong image for India Tourism needed brand strategy based on a well defined and unique brand personality selection of the correct positioning strategies, theme product development, consistent and appropriate advertising and promotion, and careful brand monitoring. Many Asian countries had successfully launched their branding, such as 'Amazing Thailand,' 'Ma-

DISCUSSION QUESTIONS
1. What is the importance of Buddhist tourism circuit?
2. What are the problem areas highlighted by the study?
3. Are the measures suggested appropriate and sufficient?
4. What do you suggest?

laysia Truly Asia,' 'Uniquely Singapore,' and all had reported enhanced tourist inflow.

After intensive consumer research, India Tourism, in 2002–03, made a major shift in its promotional and marketing strategy and repositioned India as a premier tourism destination in the global market. It looked into the following facts.

- What images come to mind when you think of India?
- How would one describe the experience of visiting India?
- Listing the distinctive or unique tourist attractions that one associates with India.
- Forming partnerships between government and industry and to ensure delivery of the marketing promise, infrastructure development, and partnerships with the state government to form the strategy.
- To have the India image as more focused, clear, and competitive and project the destination as a vibrant tourist destination.

The brand personality was named 'Incredible India'. Essentially, 'Incredible India' is a positioning and branding strategy that differentiates India in the global marketplace. It was developed so that all tourism offices, tour operators, and organizations promoting India as a destination could market it in a unified and consistent manner. 'Incredible India' has been built on a solid research foundation that resulted in a set of descriptors for the personality and values of India and an 'essence' that captures the underlying spirit of the country. Therefore, 'Incredible India' captured its unique spirituality, the colours of its landscapes, and the distinctive character of its people.

The positioning of India was that while others claimed breathtaking locales, the mysticism of the east, the draw of the civilization, the call of the wild, India was all that and much more.

It is a journey of mind and soul.
It is a journey of the five senses.
It is a journey of self-discovery.
It is a journey of self-fulfilment.

What has the brand campaign achieved? It has enabled India to reemerge as a destination of choice and to regain its market share. As a consequence of this brand building exercise, tourist arrivals rose dramatically. At a time when all destinations witnessed negative growth, India Tourism in 2002–04 registered a growth of 16 per cent in volume and 23 per cent in value. During 2004–05, this growth had further accelerated with India demonstrating a volume growth of 23 per cent and value growth in dollar terms of 36 per cent. International tourist arrivals crossed the four million mark in 2006, a sure shot sign of the success of this branding.

(*Source*: Travelbizmonitor.com, May 2007 and www.incredibleindia.in)

DISCUSSION QUESTIONS

1. What were the challenges for branding and positioning India?
2. How was the new theme identified?
3. What does 'Incredible India' stand for?
4. Do you feel that the growth in tourist arrivals is because of the campaign?

Tourism Product

LEARNING OBJECTIVES

Tourism experience is the result of a number of products and services that are consumed as a bundle. Both the assembler of bundle/package and the tourist have the choice of deciding inputs and their combination. It contains three basic elements: attraction, transportation, and accommodation, each with a large range of options. Understanding this product, and developing and managing it are challenging tasks. In this chapter, you will acquaint yourself with these challenges and how to overcome them. You will learn about the following.

• Concept of tourism product
• Package as a product
• New product development in tourism
• Product life cycle for tourism products
• Brand and branding in tourism

WHAT IS TOURISM PRODUCT

Tourism product is a mix of tangible and intangible elements. Kotler (1984) conceptualizes 'product' as 'anything that can be offered to a market for attention, acquisition, use, or consumption that might satisfy a want or need. It includes physical objects, services, persons, places, organization, and ideas.' This takes the concept of product beyond physical objects and can very well include tourism. Kotler's multilayered concept of product considers five levels of core benefit, generic product, expected product, augmented product, and potential product arranged in concentric circles moving from centre to periphery.

Core benefit It is the basic benefit that a consumer buys. In air travel, a tourist buys faster travel as core benefit.

Generic product   It is the basic product that delivers the core benefit. An aircraft is a generic product.

Expected product   It is a set of conditions that the buyer buys with products such as timely flights, smooth check-in, good in-flight service, etc.

Augmented product   This constitutes additional benefits that distinguish a firm's offer from competitors such as information to passengers about flight time through SMS, express check-in, extra facilities during flight, and so on.

Potential product   This includes possible value additions that may be made in a product in future. Some of these might relate to application of technology that is at testing stage, such as virtual tours, while others may concern with upgradation of product when the buyer is ready for these such as space hotels.

Medlik and Middleton (1973) conceptualize tourism product as a bundle of activities, services, and benefits that constitute the entire tourism experience. This bundle consists of five components: destination attractions, destination facilities, accessibility, images, and price. According to Smith (1994) a tourism product consists of five elements in a series of concentric circles. The core is tangible and more controllable by management but the outward progression marks more intangible elements and greater consumer participation. The tourism product is a synergistic combination of these elements. These elements are as follows.

The physical plan   This is the core of a tourism product where the main attraction is produced. It can be natural such as landscape or waterfall, or facilities such as conference hall, theme park, hotel, etc.

Service   Service refers to the performance of specific tasks required to meet the needs of tourists. A hotel needs management, front desk operation, housekeeping, maintenance, and food and beverage (F&B) provisions to function as a hotel.

Hospitality   Consumers expect 'enhanced service' or 'something extra'. Hospitality is that 'extra' provided above professional service.

Freedom of choice   Freedom of choice refers to the necessity that the traveller has some acceptable range of options for a satisfactory experience. Even a package tour gives some freedom.

Involvement   This is participation by consumers in some degree in the delivery of services. Tourism is known to be a participative activity.

Hegarty (1992) explains tourism product through the following components.

Environment   It is the raw material of tourism that gives a tourist destination its particular appeal. It has natural, cultural, and social elements.

Activities   These are based on and derived from the environment. For example, trekking, rafting, mountaineering, sightseeing, fishing, horse riding, and so on.

Accommodation   A tourist must have a place to sleep and eat.

Transport   There must be ways of getting around the destination.

Services   There are various services that support tourism such as information, health, booking, and customs.

Infrastructure   Tourism cannot work without roads, airports, telephones, and so on.

All the above-mentioned authors have defined tourism as a combination of many elements as summarized in Fig. 7.1.

The relative importance of these elements depends upon target markets. In a new or undeveloped market competition is at the core. As it develops and competition increases, differentiation is created through augmentation. After some time intangibles and services take the front seat in augmentation.

Based on the above discussions, tourism product can be understood as shown in Fig. 7.2. It has the components of attraction, access, and accommodation. Features of these components can be basic for a generic product or enhanced for a specific product. The environment in which this product is experienced adds to the total tour experience.

Kotler	Medlik and Middleton	Smith	Hegarty
Core benefit	Destination attraction	Physical plan	Environment
Generic product	Destination facilities	Service	Activities
Expected product	Accessibility	Hospitality	Accommodation
Augmented product	Images	Freedom of choice	Transport
Potential product	Price	Involvement	Services
			Infrastructure

Fig. 7.1   Elements of Tourism Product

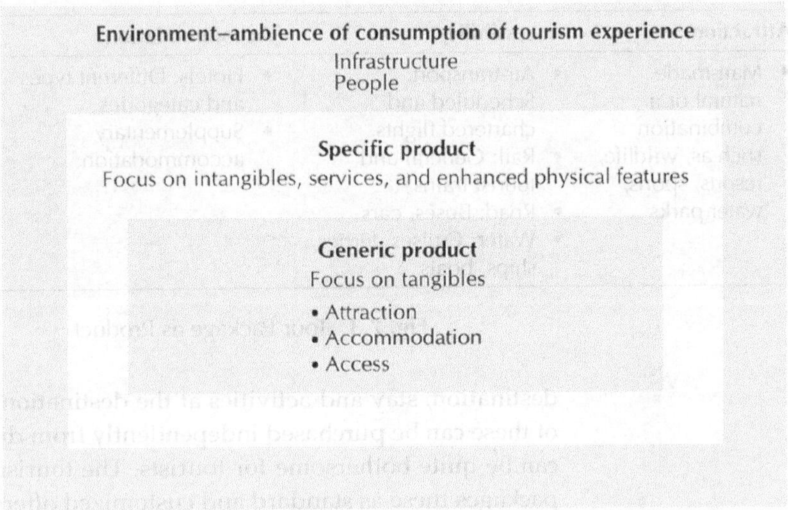

Environment–ambience of consumption of tourism experience
Infrastructure
People

Specific product
Focus on intangibles, services, and enhanced physical features

Generic product
Focus on tangibles

• Attraction
• Accommodation
• Access

Fig. 7.2 The Tourism Product

Tourism Product from the Perspective of Sellers, Buyers, and Society

A product is viewed differently by different participants in marketing. The marketers consider it an offer in terms of its features. So a tour package for a marketer means duration, itinerary, departure and arrival points, type of hotel, number and type of meals, escort facility, insurance, airport tax, and so on. Buyers on the other hand look for benefits of each feature. Tourists are interested in every benefit and service they need from departure day to arrival day. Duration of tour for tourists means number of days away from home, itinerary means what they get to see, type of hotel signifies associated comforts, and inclusive meals imply number, type, and cost of additional meals, and so on. The concepts of the marketers and tourists may not match. Society is the third party as it shares its resources for tourists. Packaged tours to them may imply mass tourism, congestion, pollution, resource shortages, and so on. A good product should be able to balance the interests of all parties as in the case of ecotours and sustainable tourism.

> A tour package is offered as a product that involves a number of elements to satisfy all tour-related needs.

TOURISM AS A PACKAGED PRODUCT

The total tourism experience is the outcome of a number of smaller experiences resulting from the use of a wide range of products and services. These are consumed at the stages of tour preparation, travel to

Attraction	Accessibility	Accommodation	Arrangements
• Man-made, natural or a combination such as, wildlife, resorts, sports, water parks	• Air-transport: Scheduled and chartered flights • Rail: General and tourist trains • Road: Buses, cars • Water: Cruises, ferries, ships, boats	• Hotels: Different types and categories • Supplementary accommodation	• Escorts • Foreign exchange • Visa • Passport • Emergency arrangements

Fig. 7.3 Tour Package as Product

destination, stay and activities at the destination and travel back. Each of these can be purchased independently from different suppliers but it can be quite bothersome for tourists. The tourism industry bundles or packages these as standard and customized offers.

The four main elements of total tourism experience are attraction, accessibility, accommodation, and arrangements and each of these can further have many options as shown in Fig. 7.3.

The four elements and their sub-elements provide a wide range of choices in the development of packages. Packages can be of the following types.

- Ready made: A standard package is prepared.
- Made to order/tailor made/customized: The package is prepared according to the customer's demand.
- Ready made but flexible: Changes are made in standard packages to meet the demand of tourists.

A package is offered with the complete itinerary. It has day-wise specifications from the first day of the tour to the last day. An example of tour package is given in the case study at the end of the chapter.

Advantages of Package

A package is a standard offer that gives value to tourists as well as marketers.

Value to Tourists

A package provides certain values to buyers such as price utility, time utility, functional utility, etc.

Cost savings Package tours are less expensive as supplies from different principles are bulk booked in advance leading to economies on large volumes.

Efficient A package covers a number of activities not possible in an un-packaged tour.

Feedback A package is experienced by a large number of tourists giving opportunity to potential tourists to get feedback before finalizing the purchase.

Benefits to marketers
Packages provide the following benefits to marketers.

Exposure to a large market Low prices make packages attractive to large markets and help in establishing brand name in the mass market.

Profitable Low costs help in getting good returns on money.

There are negative aspects of package products such as non-disclosure of all costs to tourists. Advertised costs may differ from actual costs if tourists are asked for additional payment for services essential to a tour. A package may include too many destinations/attractions to be comfortably covered, making it a touch-and-run type of experience. Similarly, if the market is competitive prices may fall, leaving little profits. On the other hand, customized tours operate on high margins.

DESTINATION AS A PRODUCT

A place or a destination as an attraction is an important part of the tourism product. It has both tangible and intangible elements and is marketed to tourists in different forms and images.

As a Physical Product

Physiography, culture, and history of a place are offered in potential markets, for example, sand dunes of Jaisalmer, Pushkar fair (Fig. 7.4), Goa carnival, and the Taj Mahal. The problem with this approach is that often features liked by tourists are highlighted and the community or the environment may be completely ignored. For example, local residents in Goa and Pushkar have opposed commercialization of their festivals and presence of foreigners therein.

As a Cultural Experience

New places and new experiences away from home and routine are offered for experience. Rajasthan is offered as a cultural experience to foreign tourists. Festivals like Holi (Fig. 7.5) at Rajasthan and Vrindavan, and Dussehra at Kullu are marketed as tourism products.

Fig. 7.4 Pushkar Lake as Physical Tourism Product
(*Photo Courtesy:* Poras Chaudhary)

Fig 7.5 Holi Festivities as a Cultural Experience Tourism Product
(*Photo Courtesy:* Poras Chaudhary)

Fig. 7.6 Sand Dunes of Jaisalmer

(*Photo Courtesy:* Poras Chaudhary)

As Images

Destination is associated with symbols and marketed as images. India is marketed as Incredible India for a journey of mind, body, and soul. Religious places are marketed for mental peace and spiritualism. Jaisalmer in Rajasthan is offered for its images of sand dunes (Fig. 7.6).

MANAGING PRODUCTS

A business takes a number of decisions relating to products offered by it, mainly the following.

Product mix decisions: How many products to offer in the market at a particular time?

Product line decisions: How many product lines to offer?

New product decisions: When shall a new product be added? When shall products be modified? When shall an old product be discontinued? What shall be the level of marketing efforts devoted to different products? How to develop a new product?

Product design decisions: What features shall be present in the product?

With all the above decisions a firm can keep a tab on its profitability, market share, and market leadership.

Product Mix Decisions

Product mix is the total basket of products offered by a firm.

Product mix is important for both sellers and buyers. Buyers need variety and expect a large range to be made available. Marketers want to maintain profitability and cannot risk a limited range as a product might loose its popularity with time. Limited range does not hedge against such risk. When the product basket is large, risk is spread across a large number of products and if a few of these fail, others provide profits to the marketer. But one possibility can be peanut buttering or spreading resources too thin over a large number of products, thus increasing expenses but reducing profitability as the products do not get appropriate support. Marketers need to balance the need for variety for consumers, high risk of a limited range and high costs of a large range. Competition in the market also forces adoption of a large range. The mix decision is a continuous process as buyers' preferences undergo change over time. It is an important managerial issue and depends upon the following factors.

- Needs of consumers for variety
- Offers of competitors
- Risks of limited range
- Resources of marketers
- Dynamism of market-changing tastes
- Life cycle of products

Product Line decisions

Product line is a collection of related products.

A firm may offer a number of lines and many products within each line. A travel agency may have lines of inbound and outbound tours along functional lines such as adventure, leisure, business, and so on. A number of lines are maintained to hedge against risks in one line and are balanced with increased costs.

Product mix and line are closely linked, as a line can be altered to change the mix.

New Products, Modified Products, and Old Products Decisions

These decisions are made to maintain profitability. When old products stop yielding profits, they are either withdrawn from the market or modified and given a new lease of life. New products are also introduced to balance the mix. The complete basket or portfolio of products is managed in view of the life cycle of each product and required level of profitability of the firm (Fig 7.7). A firm will try to have a few products at maturity stage and others at introduction and decline stage. As an old

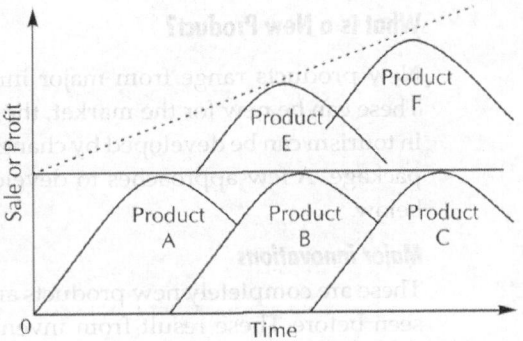

Fig 7.7 Product Portfolio

product is phased out, another will take its place. The number of products is based on profit goals of a firm, availability of resources to maintain different products, and market requirements.

Marketing Inputs Decisions

Each product does not need the same level or type of marketing effort. It can only be decided on the basis of potential and the existing status of the product. Environmental forces too play a role in it. Products showing more potential are given more inputs.

Product Design Decisions

A detailed profile of each product is prepared covering the following dimensions.

        Core benefits: Design, quality, convenience

        Services: Guarantees and warrantees, values

        Augmentation: Packaging, branding

        Features to be included in a product depend upon a firm's competitive position in the market, its objectives, and resources.

        An example of tour package in Fig. 7.3 shows how these aspects are incorporated in a product. Discrete products, such as hotels, airlines, and destinations, are also designed in the same way.

NEW PRODUCT DEVELOPMENT

Developing new products is an important decision for a firm. A successful product can change the fortunes of a business; therefore, a systematic approach is followed for new product development (NPD).

What is a New Product?

New products range from major innovations to minor style changes. These can be new for the market, the firm, or the buyers. New products in tourism can be developed by changing or modifying an element of the package. A few approaches to developing new products are discussed below.

Major innovations

These are completely new products and services that a market has never seen before These result from inventions or from market expansions, where products available in one market are taken to other markets that are yet to see these.

The innovation can be in the product such as space hotel, or in the process such as reverse auction system for a hotel where buyers are asked to quote the prices and the hotel decides if it can sell at the price asked. Process innovations can also be offered as major innovations when new ways are used to deliver existing products such as online sales of travel products.

Minor innovations

New products and services are offered for a market that is already served by existing products that meet the same generic needs.

New services for the currently served market

These represent offers to existing customers for a service not previously available from the company, although it may be available from other companies.

Products–service line extensions

These represent augmentations of the existing service line. For example, addition of budget airlines by an existing operator or vice versa.

Products–service improvements

These represent the most common type of service innovation. For example, adding new theme restaurants.

Style changes

These represent the most modest service innovations, although they are often highly visible and can have significant effects on customer perceptions. Changes in colour, uniform, and design are part of style changes.

New Product Development Process

The ending of old products and introduction of new ones are important managerial decisions. New products are systematically developed, be it a destination, a hotel, or a package. In cases of destinations, attractions, and hotels large investment is needed, hence management should ensure high success rate of its new products. For this, a systematic approach called new product development process can be followed, which would have the following stages.

- Idea generation and screening
- Conceptualization—blueprinting
- Prototype development
- Commercial viability analysis
- Product development
- Market testing
- Launch or introduction in the market

The development of a tourist circuit using the above stages is explained in Fig. 7.8.

Idea generation and screening

New products follow new ideas. Therefore, the first step is to generate good ideas. A number of sources can be tapped for this. Consumers can be asked to offer suggestions, dealers can pass on their ideas, personnel in the organization can generate ideas, competitors may provide clues, experts can advise, or conscious and deliberate processes like brainstorming can be used. What is important is to create an environment for idea generation, where ideas are not blocked for fear of being ridiculed or not taken seriously. Further, there should be a proper follow up of ideas to carry forward for development. At the screening stage, experts judge the viability of ideas for development into products. Errors of dropping good ideas or working on bad ideas should be reduced to a minimum.

Conceptualization—Blueprinting

The idea needs to be converted into a concept. This concept is a detailed statement of how and what the product will do. A blueprint is prepared for the same. Such conceptualization helps in evaluating and improving ideas. For example, in World Heritage Site listing a blueprint of unique features of a proposed site and the development plan is prepared even before applying for consideration. Screening is done again at this stage and ideas with conceptualization problems or those that are not good enough are not processed further.

Prototype development

A small model is prepared to give a real picture of the idea. Computer simulation has made this process easier. A new destination can be seen with different proposed models of development. What may not be

Idea Generation and Screening

Ideas about new circuits are obtained from different sources. These circuits are screened on bases such as length of tour, time taken to cover the route, etc. A good tour will not have too much travel and too little time for attractions. The theme of the circuit is also evaluated. Religious circuit cannot be combined with adventure spots simply because of their proximity. Availability of connecting transport, hotels at the destination, or potential of development are taken into account.

All circuits passing this stage are carried further for conceptualization.

Conceptualization—Blueprinting

The connecting destinations and their main attractions are depicted on a map along with the time of travel and the tentative time required for different attractions. These blueprints are evaluated by experts and unsuitable ones are dropped at this stage.

Prototype Development

A movie of tour taken by tour developers on the proposed circuit can be prepared. This can reveal irritants such as quality differences across different states regarding roads, hotels, safety-security, and attitude of hosts.

Commercial Viability Analysis

The above-mentioned movie can be shown to tour operators, travel agents, and potential tourists to judge their opinion. It is important to know both attitudes and intention to behave. If the market looks attractive, it is taken to the next stage for development.

Product Development

The circuit is finally developed and necessary clearances from the concerned governmental bodies are obtained. It may also involve investment on infrastructure.

Market Testing

Now the circuit is offered to a limited number of operators to plan the tours. If the response is encouraging it may be opened to all, otherwise modifications can be made based on feedback.

Launch or Introduction in the Market

Now the circuit is opened to all to plan and take the tour.

Fig 7.8 Developing Tourist Circuits

understood through concept can be made clearer by using models. The response of potential tourists can also be gauged by showing virtual tours.

Commercial viability analysis

An initial estimate of commercial viability is made at this stage in terms of future market size and profitability. The proposed product may be very good but may not be acceptable to the market to generate viable sales volumes. If a newly developed product is too expensive, it cannot be established as a regular product since it would not have a good market size. Commercial tours to outer space are one such example.

Product development

All concepts that pass the test of commercial viability are taken up for development as product. A few variations from the original concept may be experienced but good conceptualization and prototyping solves this problem.

Market testing

A product is tested in the market on a limited scale under conditions similar to actual ones. It can be offered as a free sample or as a regular product through chosen distribution channels. The selected test market should be a good sample of the total market. The response of the test market is taken to be indicative of total market behaviour. Everything including product, channels, promotion, competition can be tested. However, two basic drawbacks of market testing are the competitors' manipulated responses to damage test results and the initial euphoria of market for a new product. Otherwise, this testing gives good results.

Launch or introduction in the market

At the final stage, the product is rolled out in the market. It may be done in a phased manner moving from one market to another or in one go. It depends on the firm's strategy. While a phased launch gives time to make corrections if needed, a complete roll out deters competitors by not leaving space for them to respond.

The steps in new product development try to ensure that the final product is acceptable to the market. Despite this, products fail.

DESTINATION DEVELOPMENT

Destination is an important product in tourism and often forms the main attraction or purpose of taking the tour. Old destinations can be improved to enhance their images, new dimensions can be added to an existing image or completely new destinations can be developed with new

Tourism product development involves heavy investment and requires that the process is followed meticulously to get high success rate.

The important aspect of destination development is to build substantial pull in it and the process of development is same as for NPD.

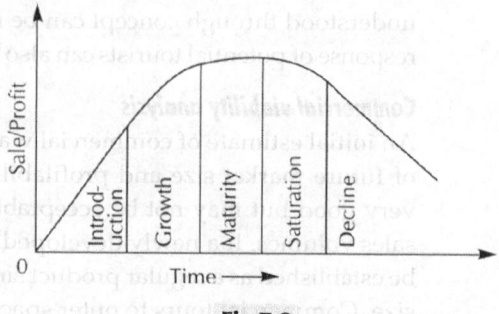

Fig 7.9

themes and structures. Delhi is given a new image with the revamping of infrastructure for the Commonwealth Games 2010. The post-event tourist traffic may be lured with the new spruced up look. Hyderabad has developed HITEX (an exhibition/meeting centre). Pragati Maidan in New Delhi is a similar example that has given a new meaning to the city for business tourism. Surajkund in Haryana has been developed from scratch into a very attractive destination. Chokhi Dhani in Jaipur is a good example of the use of innovative concept to build a new product. Theme parks, museums, and science centres fall in the same category.

A destination takes long time to break even, as the time gap when the destination is opened to visitors and when any measurable results are visible, such as number of tourists or tourism revenues, tends to be long. The lead time before results are visible in visits or profits is more for destinations and requires constant back up of suitable marketing strategies.

PRODUCT LIFE CYCLE

> Every product has a limited period of existence in the market during which it moves through different stages. Product life cycle is the commonly used term for these stages.

Product life cycle (PLC) begins where new product development ends.

Product life cycle is the status of a product on time scale from introduction to end in terms of its sales and profits. A standard life cycle is conceptualized as a bell-shaped curve as shown in Fig 7.9.

Five stages—introduction, growth, maturity, saturation, and decline—are identified in product life cycle. The time span of these stages depends on host of factors such as competition, marketing strategies, external environmental forces, etc.

Some important features of PLC are given below.

- All products may not follow standard bell-shaped pattern as in the case of fashions and fads.
- A life cycle can be as long as 100 years or very short, say one year or less.

- It is possible to prolong a life cycle through proper marketing strategies.
- A life cycle can be for a generic product, a specific product, or a brand.

PLC Stages

A standard product life cycle is explained as a bell-shaped curve having five stages from beginning to end. Each stage is marked by certain features that help a firm to identify its own stage. It helps a marketer to plan for the future.

Introduction stage

This is the stage when a product is first offered in the market. At this stage:

- A product is not known to buyers, so sales are low.
- The initial costs of developing and launching the product are high. Economies of large scale are also absent because of limited scale production. So profits are usually very low.
- Competition is absent.

Marketing strategies at this stage focus on creating awareness and increasing sales. Specific strategies are as follows.

Product related   A product should be such that it cannot be easily copied. The patent or initial heavy investment deters competition for some time.

Price related   Initial prices are very difficult to set in the absence of existing models. But depending upon the positioning requirements, premium or low prices can be set. High prices help in quick recovery of costs and low prices discourage competitors.

Place related   Distribution channels offering easy access to target markets are selected but their terms and conditions are also assessed very carefully.

Promotion related   Promotion is kept high to gain the attention of the market and the focus is on creating awareness.

Growth stage

At this stage product awareness increases and it starts gaining acceptance. The other features are as follows.

- Competitors join in after seeing acceptance.
- Awareness increases with the joint efforts of all marketers.
- Promotion remains at same high levels but the focus shifts to fighting competition.
- Sales and profits start increasing.

Marketing strategies commonly used at this stage are discussed below.

Product related   Small modifications or additions in the product may be made to gain edge over competitors.

Price related   Prices may be modified in view of competition but image and position is kept in mind. Generally prices are lowered.

Place related   A few more channels may be added to increase reach into the market.

Promotion related   Promotion remains high and also gets competitive. The purpose is to create awareness as well as to meet competition.

Now the competition moves towards giving more services to buyers and suitable strategies regarding people, process, and physical evidence become very important.

Maturity stage

The features of this stage are as follows.

- The market becomes fully aware.
- Competition gets intense.
- Sales and profits continue to increase as market is still growing.

The marketing strategies at this stage are discussed below.

Product related   Modifications or additions in the product continue.

Price related   Prices are modified and often reduced in view of competition.

Place related   More channels may be added to increase reach into the market.

Promotion related   Promotion remains high and also gets very competitive. The purpose is to meet competition.

The focus of competition shifts to good service, good ambience, and a total experience.

Saturation stage

Here, marketing strategies of the maturity stage are continued.

- The market becomes stable at this stage.
- New competitors do not enter.
- Sales stabilize at this stage.
- Profits start going down because of heavy cost of competing. As a result, some marketers start moving out.

Decline stage

- At this stage the market loses interest in the product as new and better options come in. Technology and changing tastes play an important part in it.

- Profit and sales decline.
- Marketers plan exit strategies from the market.

The strategies at this stage deal with this exit plan. These are as follows.

Shut shop and leave   Some marketers close business and leave the market.

Stay on   Some marketers stay on in the hope that others will leave and the market may generate profits once no competitors are left.

Milking   Some marketers keep operating and stop all expenditures. Whatever revenues are generated is acceptable.

Second life cycle

It is possible to give a new lease of life to a product by entering into new markets or by finding new uses. A product may be at different stages of its life cycle in different markets. This strategy is often used by multinational companies. Finding a new use for the product also gives it a new life. For example, Kerala tourism has moved from backwaters to health tourism and Uttarakhand from religious tourism to adventure tourism. In the second life cycle, the product begins its journey again from introduction and continues with the same process. Figure 7.10 shows how a new life begins at time points T_1 and T_2.

DESTINATION LIFE CYCLE AND TOURISM AREA LIFE CYCLE

The concept of product life cycle is applied to discrete tourism products such as hotels, airlines, and attractions. Attraction is considered to be the main product in tourism and others are seen as augmentation. For any tourism activity to happen, attraction is created first. All attractions have a life cycle including destinations. As Plog (2001) has put, 'We can visualize a destination moving across a spectrum, however gradually

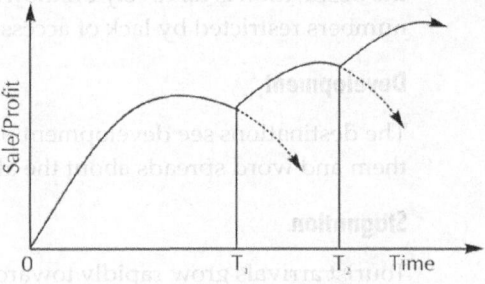

Fig. 7.10 Second Life Cycle

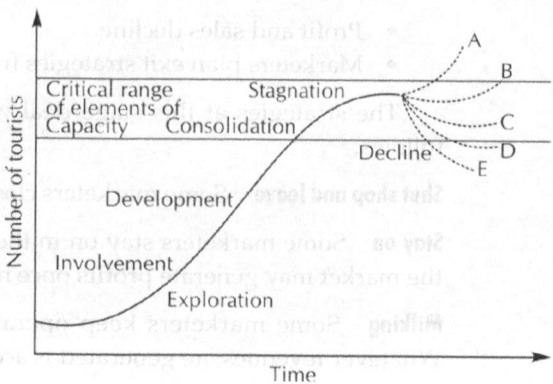

Fig 7.11 Tourism Area Life Cycle
(*Source:* Butler 1980)

> The concept of life cycle is applied to destinations as TALC or DLC. It is defined as the stages a destination goes through, from exploration to involvement development, consolidation, stagnation, rejuvenation, or decline.

and slowly, but far too often inexorably toward the potential of its own demise. Destination areas carry with them the potential seeds of their own destruction, as they allow themselves to become more commercialized and lose their qualities which originally attracted tourists.'

Destination is defined as a place that has some form of actual or perceived boundary, such as the physical boundary of an island, political boundaries, or even market-created boundaries.

Destinations are different from products as these experience tourism even before commercialization and it continues after the decline of popular tourism.

Butler proposed the tourism area life cycle (TALC) model of a tourist destination that identifies the stages of exploration, development, consolidation, stagnation, and decline (Fig 7.11).

Exploration

This is the beginning of a destination for tourism activities. At this stage the destination is relatively unknown and visitors initially come in small numbers restricted by lack of access, facilities, and local knowledge.

Development

The destinations see development of amenities as more people discover them and word spreads about the attractions.

Stagnation

Tourist arrivals grow rapidly toward some theoretical carrying capacity, which involves social and environmental limits. The rise from 'exploration' to 'stagnation' often happens very rapidly, as implied by the exponential nature of the growth curve.

Decline or Rejuvenation

A destination would decline if it follows trajectories C, D, and E as shown in Fig. 7.11. This will happen if the very attractions that created the destination are lost. However, it may continue to draw some tourists with increased consumption and unsustainable development but not for very long.

The destination can be rejuvenated through proper planning by increasing the carrying capacity and reducing negative impacts through sustainable practices. It then follows paths A and B.

According to Plog, it is possible to identify the phase of a life cycle of a destination. He correlates various tourist personality types with phases in a destination life cycle (Fig 7.12).

Plog identifies the following phases of a destination life cycle and personality types of tourists visiting the destination at these phases.

Discovery

At this phase the destination is little known and venturers visit it in search of new discoveries and unexplored areas. Through word of mouth, the area begins to attract more tourists.

Discovery—Development

At this phase venturers are followed by near-venturers. This creates the first major wave of visitors. These are more demanding in terms of services and this initiates development of the destination.

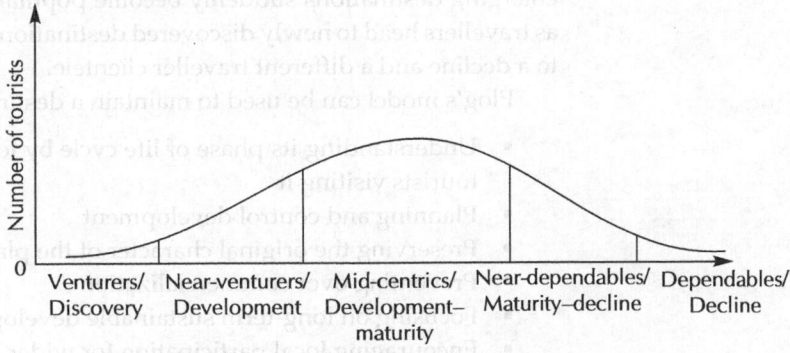

Fig 7.12 Plog's Model of Destination Life Cycle

Development

At this phase the destination gains media attention and is reported. This brings mid-centric travellers. Growth continues and becomes visible in the number and value of hotels, jobs, and revenues. The negative effects are not yet seen. But now, venturers and near-venturers leave the area and mass tourists arrive. This phase is crucial because when a destination is really booming, no one cares about planning or controls. For this reason, it is important to take action at this stage to manage development and define a long-term vision.

Maturity—Decline

At the development stage a destination is too often lax in its regulations: the number of hotels continues to grow; fast-food restaurants pop up everywhere; shops, movie theatres, and other forms of entertainment multiply; and wholesalers develop packages. The area starts to get 'touristy' and there is unchecked development. The destination is unable to resist the easy money of tourism and unsustainable development. Under such pressure, the destination loses its distinctiveness and looks like any other destination. The centrics now stop coming and the near-dependables start to frequent the area.

Decline

Decline is now inevitable. The destination now only attracts dependables, who prefer to visit and revisit well-established known places. Though often more loyal, this clientele spends less, stays a shorter time, and is less active. The destination becomes less lucrative. Deserted by the other tourist segments, the market gets smaller. It happens quite often that emerging destinations suddenly become popular and then are ignored as travellers head to newly discovered destinations. Overcrowding leads to a decline and a different traveller clientele.

Plog's model can be used to maintain a destination by:

- Understanding its phase of life cycle by looking at the profile of tourists visiting it
- Planning and control development
- Preserving the original character of the place
- Preventing over commercialization
- Focusing on long-term sustainable development
- Encouraging local participation for wider benefits

	Product Life Cycle	Tourism Area Life Cycle	Destination Life Cycle
Stages in life cycle	Introduction	Exploration	Discovery
	Growth	Development	Discovery–development
	Maturity	Consolidation	Development–maturity
	Saturation	Stagnation	Maturity–decline
	Decline/second life cycle	Decline/rejuvenation	Decline

Fig. 7.13 Stages in PLC, TALC, and DLC

PRODUCT LIFE CYCLE, TOURISM AREA LIFE CYCLE, AND DESTINATION LIFE CYCLE

The concepts of TALC and DLC are derived from PLC but the terminology used is different as applied to a destination. Figure 7.13 compares the three.

BRAND AND BRANDING

Branding is the process of creation of brands. Building brands is a long-drawn process and involves establishing an image in consumers' minds.

One of the goals of a marketer is to have a distinct identity for its products offered in the market. This is generally achieved by establishing an image of the products highlighting their features. Brands are used to communicate this image to the buyers. A brand is a unique identity and symbol of a product signifying its image and associated benefits. It can be a name, a logo, a symbol, a design, or a combination of all these. A brand name becomes a trademark after legal protection.

Features of Brands

The purpose of brands is to build an image of a product and communicate this image to the market. A good brand has certain features that help in it. These are given below.

1. Brand should be associated with the image. The name, logo, or symbol should be reflective of the brand and its benefits, or the company image. For example, Ginger and Lemon Tree for hotels; makemytrip.com, yatra.com, cleartrip.com, and ezeego.com for online travel firms.
2. It should act as a good communication tool and should be easy to pronounce, recognize, and memorize. For example, Palace on Wheels, Royal Orient, Eurail, etc.
3. It should be legally protectable and be fit to be registered under Trade Marks Act.

4. It should attract attention. For example, the Golden Arches of McDonald's, the Maharaja of Air India.
5. It should distinguish and offer competitive differentiation.
6. It should create brand equity. Brand equity is the value of a brand calculated by the gap between future expected revenue of branded product and an equivalent unbranded product. A positive equity acts as a barrier to competitors.

Types of Brands

Brands are created in many ways with the basic purpose of including all the essentials of a good brand name. Some common branding strategies are discussed below.

Individual brands

A separate brand name is given to each product of the marketer. This is not seen in tourism industry because of high investment in product development and associated risks of building brands from the scratch. Such brands are used for consumer goods to improve overall performance but costs can be high.

Corporate brands

The name of the organization is used as a brand. It is a much seen practice in the industry with organizations such as Disney, Oberoi, Tata, India Tourism Development Corporation (ITDC) using their names with many of their products. Haryana Tourism Corporation (HTC) has named its motels on highways using names of birds such as parakeet, skylark, *koyal*, red bishop and uses HTC with it. Jet Airways uses the brand Jetlite for low-cost air services acquired from Sahara. This branding helps in extending the benefits of a name to all products and saving costs.

Umbrella brand or family branding

One brand is created for related products. This strategy is often used by hotels for their premium and budget hotels. Tata uses the Taj Hotels brand for its five star properties and the Ginger Hotels brand for medium-priced properties. The purpose is to gain benefits of both common and independent brands.

Private brands or manufacturer's brands

Branding can be done by manufactures or distributors. Tour operators can brand packages specifying the category of hotel and may not name the hotel at all, but the brand ensures quality. This branding is called private branding. If done by principal, it is called manufacturer's brand.

BRANDING IN TOURISM

Branding in tourism involves creation of brands for diverse products such as hotels, agencies, airlines, tourist trains, destinations, etc. It is important because of the specific nature of tourism offers. The following salient points are worth noting in this context.

1. Tourism is a complex, high-involvement purchase decision. Branding simplifies choice making and shortening extensive problem solving.
2. Branding assists in countering intangibility. The physical attributes and symbolic meaning of a brand sets off intangibility.
3. Branding conveys consistency across multiple outlets and through time, overcoming variability of tourism services.
4. It reduces risk associated with a perishable product.
5. It facilitates precise segmentation.
6. Brands provide the focus for the integration of producers' efforts. Everyone in the organization knows what the brand stands for and works accordingly.

Destination and place branding is a challenging task in tourism. Let us discuss destination branding to understand this.

Destination Branding

Destination brand refers to the overall impression that the destination creates in the minds of potential tourists, including its functional and symbolic elements. The brand encompasses the destination's physical attributes, services, attractions, name, logo, reputation, and the benefits that these provide to the visitor. A recognizable brand facilitates a tourist's choice of destination because it encapsulates what the destination has to offer (Hankinson 2004).

It creates a superior and distinctive proposition for the destination and imparts meaning above and beyond the functional aspects of the destination.

This involves marketing activities (1) that support the creation of a name, symbol, logo, word, mark, or other graphic that both *identifies* and *differentiates* a destination; (2) that convey the *promise* of a memorable travel *experience* that is uniquely associated with the destination; and (3) that serve to *consolidate* and *reinforce* the recollection of pleasurable *memories* of the destination.

Functions of Destination Brand

According to Hankinson (2001), place branding performs the following four main functions.

1. Brands as communicators, where brands 'represent a mark of ownership, and a means of product differentiation manifested in legally protected names, logos, and trademarks'.
2. Brands as perceptual entities 'which appeal to the consumer senses, reasons, and emotions'.
3. Brands as value enhancers, which has led to the concept of *brand equity*.
4. Brands as relationships, where the brand is construed as having a personality which enables it to form a relationship with the consumer.

Berthon, Hulbert, and Pitt (1999) identify the following functions of brands for buyers and sellers.

For buyers

1. Identification of product: Brands such as McDonald's, Café Coffee Day, and Sagar Ratna give a quick identification of the type of product available.
2. Reduces search costs: A brand name means many attributes at one place. It reduces the effort of searching attribute-wise information for the product, saving both time and money.
3. Assurance of quality: Brand name assures a level of quality, be it premium or economy.
4. Reduces perceived risk: Brands give assurance and unwritten guarantee of the products. A belief is established that a good brand will not let its customers down. This builds confidence among buyers.
5. Facilitates premium pricing: Brands help in pricing beyond functional value. The difference in prices of a five-star and a four-star hotel may follow image than costs and branding is central to it.

For sellers

1. Image: A good brand carries an image that is added to the image of the seller. It builds an image of the firm and gives status and prestige.
2. Reduces risks: A good brand reduces many risks. Sellers feel confident about the performance of a good brand. It also reduces

psychological risks related to non-performance or non-acceptance of a brand.

3. Familiarity which facilitates repeat purchase: Good brands bring more buyers, including repeats.
4. Facilitates new product innovations: New products are easily accepted in the market if coming from a marketer having established brands. Here, the image of existing brands extends to new brands.
5. Coherent message facilitates market segmentation: Brand communicates an integrated picture of a product as a personality that attracts particular consumer personalities and this automatically creates segments. Brands can also be created to be targeted at different market segments.
6. Facilitates promotional efforts: A brand name helps in promotion through its image and its communicative aspects such as being recognizable, memorizable, and so on.
7. Facilitates loyalty: A brand name facilitates loyalty in purchasing and acts as a symbol around which a relationship is built.

Challenges of Destination Branding

The benefits of destination branding are many, but it is difficult and challenging for the following reasons.

Not considered essential

Place marketing and branding are not considered essential even today. India started its Incredible India campaign as late as 2002. The integration of different states and themes of tourism under this umbrella brand began much later.

Takes time

It is a long process and requires continuous messaging to the target market, coupled with management of features used in the brand. Either of the two cannot produce results separately. The final impact is created after a long time.

Defining destination as a product is difficult

A destination may have a number of features and balancing them all in one image and using product concepts for it, such as bundling and positioning, might be difficult.

Limited budgets

Destination branding is often not considered a serious issue for branding and funds are not allocated. Who should pay for it also becomes an issue.

Often the responsibility gets distributed between private and public sector. But in India, it is solely the job of the government and budget allocation competes with many other heads. In developed countries, the contribution of the private sector is larger than the state share.

Politics

Who decides the image of a destination? A number of interest groups might claim their right to be a part of destination brand building. These might not be experts. The politics in this might make this very difficult. For example, religious attractions in India are controlled by individuals who oppose all efforts of a government takeover or improvement of facilities. And brand building is not possible in the absence of these changes.

External environment

The external environment influences branding effort. It includes competitive brands and their efforts and forces like law and order situation. Incredible India least requires murders of tourists, agitations in the country, road blockades, flight cancellations, congested airports, etc.

Creating differentiation

A destination needs to be different from others. All beaches or religious destinations cannot be branded in the same way. The unique selling proposition (USP) of each must be found and communicated.

Associating brand with lifestyle and emotions

The development of such experiential relationships can be seen in tourism marketing campaigns aimed at diaspora populations.

Recent marketing campaigns aimed at the Indian diaspora have sought to engage second- and third-generation Indians who are now living outside India to rediscover their roots.

This has been done not just through the production of images in the Incredible India brand but also through the organization of specific events that bring the diaspora population together for key experiences such as festivals (Hannam 2004).

TRADEMARKS

Trademarks play a very important role in giving a different image to a firm's offers just as brands do. Brands get copied or imitated, leading to loss of market but trademarks are legally protectable symbols. This prevents the use of similar confusing marks by competitors and protects consumers from being deceived about the origin and quality of a product.

> Successful tourism marketing seeks to make an emotional attachment with the consumer's lifestyle by being credible, deliverable, and sustainable.

> A brand name gets recognition with time as a result of comprehensive marketing efforts but trademarks get legal recognition by following the procedure of registration.

The laws of trademarks are country specific and Trademarks Act, 1999 applies in India. However, to establish trademarks in the minds of consumers, marketing communication is used as in case of brand names.

A firm may register whole of its brand name as a trademark or a part or any other mark that is not included in the brand. Law does not restrict use of separate brand names and trademarks. It is the marketer who wants the similarity in two for convenience in image building.

The following are important features of trademarks in India.

1. Registration of services is allowed for service marks and of goods for trade marks. Trade marks identify goods and are displayed on goods, while service marks identify source of service and are displayed in advertisements.

2. The registration of a trademark confers upon the owner the exclusive right to the use of the registered trademark. This is indicated by using the symbol (R) with goods or services for which the mark is registered. The owner can seek relief from infringement in appropriate courts in the country. The exclusive right is however subject to conditions entered on the register such as limitation of area, of use, and so on.

3. 'Mark' includes a device, brand, heading, label, ticket, name, signature, word, letter, numeral, shape of goods, packaging, combination of colours, or any combination thereof.

4. 'Trademark' means a mark capable of being represented graphically and capable of distinguishing goods or services offered by one person from those of others. It may include shape of goods, their packaging, and combination of colours.

5. 'Service mark' means service of any kind which is made available to potential users and includes the provision of services in connection with business of industrial or commercial matters such as banking, communication, education, financing, insurance, chit funds, real estate, transport, storage, material treatment, processing, supply of electrical or other energy, boarding, lodging, entertainment, amusement, construction, repair, conveying of news or information, and advertising.

6. The registration of a trademark is for a period of 10 years and may be renewed from time to time in accordance with the provisions.

7. The registration of a trade mark, if valid, gives to the registered proprietor of the trademark the exclusive right to the use of the trademark in relation to goods or services for which the trademark is registered. It also gives the proprietor the right

to obtain relief in respect of infringement of the trademark in a manner provided by this act.

Tourism services can be also registered under this act. This has given a completely new dimension to product decisions in tourism. The old Trademarks Act, 1958 provided only for registration of products but the new Trademarks Act, 1999 follows the lines of the World Trade Organization (WTO) for trade-related aspects of intellectual property rights (TRIPS). A tourism marketer needs to take decisions for trademarking along with branding to get a competitive edge in the marketplace.

To sum up, all product decisions are very important for marketing mix and should fit into the total plan for synergistic effects.

TOURISM PRODUCTS MARKETING STRATEGIES

All strategies used for marketing of tourism products are important but a few are critical and worth discussing separately. These relate to the nature of tourism products. We have understood that tourism can be offered as a packaged product but each input of the package can also be marketed separately as a complete product. This is done through specific marketing strategies for accommodation, transport, destination, and so on. Moreover, the nature of tourism product is so complex that in most cases seasonal demand is observed making seasonal marketing a fit case. The characteristics of tourism offers make sampling almost impossible that are often substituted by familiarization tours. Familiarization tours are used not as a substitute of sample but as the best possible alternate available for services. It means that marketing tourism products requires a thorough understanding of their nature and adoption of appropriate strategies. A detailed discussion of these specific strategies will help you in understanding and appreciating marketing of tourism products.

Accommodation Marketing/Hotel Marketing

Stay arrangements form an important part of tourism and are offered on commercial and non-commercial basis. Commercial stay includes hotels and alternate accommodation such as motels, paying guests, rest houses. Non-commercial stay includes *dharamshalas*, economical Young Men's Christian Association (YMCA) hostels, and so on. The range of stay facilities is wide and so is the diversity of marketing practices used. Hotels are an important type of commercial accommodation and commonly adopt the following marketing strategies.

Positioning location as an attraction

The location of the hotel or the room decides its value. A room facing a beautiful beach is more expensive than a room without a view. Hotels exploit this feature and highlight the location advantages to clients. A suburban hotel cannot be as attractive to tourists as a city hotel will be for its proximity to attractions. All new hotels face the problem of attracting clients as these are usually located away from the city due to non-availability of land in the city. Such hotels use appeals other than location.

Low price as attraction

Hotels in the outskirts of the city keep prices low to attract guests. The low price lures price-sensitive or low-budget tourists if the cost of transportation is not much. This strategy cannot be used by premium hotels interested in high-end clientele.

Brand name as an appeal

Tourists travelling to far-off places are anxious about the quality of hotels. Their uncertainty is reduced by using known brand names. Hotels cash in on it by buying a franchise of well-known hotels and using the name to get loyal guests. The franchise also helps in adopting benchmarks of the brand, thus upgrading a local hotel to the international level. Such appeal is difficult for a stand-alone hotel.

Unique benefits as attraction

Hotels may develop a loyal clientele by building unique attractions. It may be personalized service, a unique concept like heritage or old world charm. Boutique hotels operate on this concept. Hotels offering spa as the main attraction also use this strategy.

It is for the hotel to identify its unique appeal for its market. Even a budget hotel may have this appeal. For example, most of the five-star hotels in Goa are located in the south. These have their own beaches as an appeal but the hotels in north Goa appeal to tourists as these are closer to the hustle and bustle of Goa.

Transport Marketing—Airlines, Rails, Cruise, and Road

Transport is one of the main components of a tour experience and tourists purchase it for to and fro travel to the destination as well as for ground travel. Any combination of transport facilities can be used by the tourists. Take the case of a tourist travelling to Pondicherry. The person can fly to Chennai and then take a cab or bus to Pondicherry. Once there, rickshaws, autos, or motor bikes can be used for local movement. The marketing strategies used depend on the mode of travel. Some of the common strategies are given below.

Low price

Budget airlines, public transport system, railways, all use low price as a selling point. Low travel cost saves a lot of money for the tourists that can be used elsewhere.

High-end services

A travel facility may offer premium or luxury services. Luxury aircrafts, stretch limos, and trains, such as the Royal Orient, fall in this bracket. These are preferred by tourists who do not mind paying more for additional services.

Benefits offered

The ease of availability and flexibility in services are used as special benefits. Car rentals offer anytime, anywhere service through toll free numbers. Such benefits give access to a market that values these benefits.

Competitive offers

The benefits offered and value provided may be more relative than absolute. An airline may offer increased facilities or decreased prices as a reaction to other airlines in the market.

Destination Marketing

Each destination is different and unique and the marketing strategies adopted by each also tend to be unique. The important strategies are discussed below.

Selling core value

Every destination has a main feature which attracts tourists. For example, Goa is known for beaches, Manali for hills, Rajasthan for forts, and Kerala for ayurveda. Each place should identify its core appeal and promote it to potential markets.

Selling additional values

The core appeal may be marred or enhanced by other attractions of a destination such as connectivity, cleanliness, and law and order. These values can be used in addition to core value to market a destination. But using only secondary appeal for marketing will not help in the absence of a main appeal.

Seasonal Marketing

Seasonality involves predictable and uncontrollable variations in demand over time.

All the above elements of tourism face the problem of seasonality of demand from tourists as very few destinations can be year-round attractions.

Seasonal patterns can have peak demand over hours, days, weeks, months, years, and so on. The demand tends to be seasonal for the following reasons.

Climate

Changing weather conditions at different times of the year at the destination and source affect the demand pattern. For example, a country like India has different weather conditions in a year, particularly in the north. As a result, people from north India travel to warm places in winter and cooler places in summer. South India gets visitors from the north in winter but in summer the hill stations of the north receive heavy rush of tourists.

Holiday season

Time availability is an essential precondition for a tour. A good amount of travel coincides with holidays, be it summer break of schools and colleges or holidays in the festival season. Countries like China declare official holidays to encourage tourism. In India, the tourism industry studies the holiday calendar of the government to prepare tour packages.

Festivals

Tourists travel from one place to another to attend festivals. Most religious festivals in India follow seasonal pattern. *Kanwad*, the festival of collecting water from holy rivers before *Maha Shivratri* in the *Shravan* month of the Hindu calendar, generates a large amount of movement leading to blocking of half side of the road on the Delhi–Haridwar highway. Travel organizers organize trips for such festivals.

Seasonal demand creates a gap between demand and supply when facilities fall short in the rush period and remain empty otherwise. The following marketing strategies are used to overcome seasonality.

Market diversification

A destination may be marketed in a number of countries having different weather and holiday patterns. As a result, when demand from one country goes down, others fill the gap. For example, Thailand gets its tourists from the west in its winters and in summers it receives visitors from India.

Product diversification

A destination can be developed with multiple attractions that will make people visit it at different times of the year and for different reasons. One common strategy adopted is creation of meetings, incentives, conferences, and events (MICE) facilities as business tourism is supposed to be less sensitive to weather variations.

Creation of artificial attractions, such as theme parks and museums, help in diversifying a destination.

Price differentiation

Price is a very effective tool used to regulate demand. In the peak season, facilities are made available at high prices to shift price sensitive tourists to off-season. Prices are reduced in off-season to lure these price-sensitive buyers. Goa does not get many tourists in summer and most hotels here reduce prices substantially to attract tourists.

Value packages

It also amounts to savings for the buyers when prices are not altered but more features and benefits are offered at the same price. For the standard price of bed and breakfast, complimentary lunch and dinner may be given.

Familiarization Trips

All the components of tourism have a high unit price and a high service element. As a result, buyers can only be told about the benefits and no sampling or test experience is possible. This becomes a barrier in convincing buyers about benefits offered, as telling alone does not result in selling.

Familiarization trips or fam trips use the concept of opinion leadership for adoption and diffusion of products and services to be sold. It involves a complimentary offer to people who can pass the word about their experiences to the potential market. The market trusts their word and makes purchases based on their recommendation. The groups used for fam trips are usually media personnel, travel agents, government officials, and so on. Media personnel write about the experiences that are read by millions of potential buyers. Government officials prepare for agreements between different countries to promote tourism. Travel agents recommend tours to their clients.

There are certain conditions for fam trips to be effective. These are as follows.

> Tourism industry has adopted the concept of familiarization tours, commonly known as fam trips, to substitute for samples.

1. Fam trip users should be opinion leaders, meaning that individuals who are offered fam trips must have the capability of influencing other buyers.
2. It is important that experiences of fam trip users are shared by opinion leaders in their respective circles. It helps pass the message to the potential market.

3. These opinion leaders must pass positive information. Opinion leaders are valued for their good opinion, yet effort should be made to garner a positive word.
4. The market should act positively. Fam trips are considered productive when sales are generated.
5. There is a lead time between fam trips and the resulting demand as words generated from fam trips take time to diffuse in the market.

These tours help in giving initial exposure to a product. Fam trips are used for a new product at the initial stages of product life cycle. Once it establishes as a brand, other strategies become more relevant.

SUMMARY

Tourism experience is a result of using a number of products. The assembled nature of a tourism offer gives tourists the option of choosing from many combinations. A tourism product is defined as a combination of tangible and intangible elements. Kotler and Smith have given a multilayered concept where the centre is the core tangible benefit and intangibility increases towards the periphery. Medlik and Middleton, and Hegarty have proposed a bundled concept of a tourism product. Therefore, a package of stay, travel, and attraction is a product and so are all its elements. Tourists can buy independent elements or a package. Marketers need to develop their products to maximize satisfaction of buyers as well as to achieve their business goals. This entails decisions for developing product mixes, new products, managing product life cycle, branding and trademarking.

Product mix is the total number of products offered by a firm and product line is constituted by related products in that mix. Well-planned lines and mix give a firm a basket of products that hedge against risk and also help in future growth. Development of new products helps a firm in keeping pace with changing consumer preferences. It involves constant and systematic efforts. The new product development process is followed for it. This process involves the stages of

idea generation, conceptualization–blue printing, prototype development, commercial viability analysis, product development, market testing, and launch or introduction in the market.

The development of destination is different as it cannot be tested like movable items. Once a product is launched in the market, it begins its journey. Its cycle, from introduction to its last stage when it is withdrawn from the market, is termed as product life cycle which is divided into stages of introduction, growth, maturity, saturation, and decline on a time scale in terms of sales and profits of the product. Butler has introduced the concept of tourism area life cycle and has identified the stages of exploration, development, stagnation, decline, and rejuvenation. Plog has offered the model of destination life cycle and this identifies stages according to profile of tourists visiting destinations. The destination at its stages of discovery, development, development–maturity, maturity–decline, and decline is frequented by venturers, near-venturers, mid-centrics, near-dependables, and dependables.

A product needs a distinct identity in the market that is provided through branding. It is the process of giving a recognizable identity to a product in the form of a name, a symbol, or a combination. Branding in tourism involves creation of brands for diverse products such as hotels, agencies, airlines, tourist trains, destinations, and so on. Brands are beneficial and offer value to both sellers and buyers. Destination branding is a challenge and involves deciding the image of a place that sustains for a long time. Brands are given legal protection through trademarks. Trademarks Act, 1999 of India prevents the use of similar and confusing marks by competitors and protects consumers from being deceived about the origin and quality of a product.

All product decisions help a firm in building its lead in the market.

KEY TERMS

Brand Brand is a unique identity and symbol of a product signifying its image and associated benefits.

Destination brand Destination brand refers to the overall impression that the destination creates in the minds of potential tourists, including its functional and symbolic elements.

Destination life cycle It is defined as stages through which a destination passes from introduction to decline.

Fam trips Fam trips are complimentary tours given as samples for experience to select persons.

New product It is a product that has new or improved features for its markets or sellers.

New product development The process of development of new product which involves idea generation, conceptualization or blueprinting, prototype development, commercial viability analysis, product development, market testing, and launch or introduction in the market.

Package tour It is a tour in which all the components are bundled.

Product Anything that can be offered to a market for attention, acquisition, use, or consumption and that might satisfy a want or need is called a product. It includes physical objects, services, persons, places, organization, and ideas.

Product life cycle (PLC) It is defined as stages in the life of a product in the market—from introduction to growth to maturity to stagnation and decline measured in terms of its sales/profit figures.

Product line Product line is a collection of related products.

Product mix Product mix is the total number of products offered by a firm.

Seasonal marketing It is marketing according to the seasonality of demand.

Tourism area life cycle It is defined as the stages a tourism area goes through, from exploration to involvement to development to consolidation to stagnation to rejuvenation or decline.

Tourism product A bundle of benefits that give a total tourism experience is called tourism product.

Trademark Trademark means a mark capable of being represented graphically. It is used to distinguish goods or services of one person from those offered by others. It may include shape of goods, their packaging, and combination of colours.

EXERCISES

REVIEW QUESTIONS

1. What is a tourism product? Explain the need for balancing the product portfolio.
2. How are product line decisions associated to product mix?

3. Explain Plog's destination life cycle and compare it with product life cycle and tourism area life cycle.

4. What is a destination brand? What are its benefits? Also discuss the features of a good brand.

PRACTICE EXERCISES

1. Study new and old destinations in your area. Compare their features with phases of destination life cycle and tourism area life cycle. Prepare a critical report of your observations.
2. Collect all packages of a local travel agent. Arrange according to lines. Do you find the mix balanced?

PROJECTS

1. Make a little survey of tourists coming in your city. Find the value of destination as a brand compared to other similar destinations. Try to find reasons for the differences in perceived value of the brand. Also prepare a brand plan based on your findings.
2. Collect information about development of a destination in your area. Did it follow the NPD process? What process did it follow? Assess.

REFERENCES

Berthon P.R., J.M. Hulbert, and L.F. Pitt 1999, 'Brand Equity: Brand Management Prognostications', Sloan Management Review.

Blain, Carmen, Stuart E. Levy, and J. R. Brent Ritchie 2005, 'Destination branding: Insights and practices from destination management organizations', *Journal of Travel Research*, vol. 43, pp. 328-338.

Butler, Richard 1980, 'The concept of a tourist area cycle of evolution:Implications for management of resources', *The Canadian Geographer*, vol. 24, no.1, pp. 5-12.

Clarke, Jackie 2000, 'Tourism brands: An exploratory study of the brands box model', *Journal of Vacation Marketing*, vol. 6, no..4, pp.329-345.

Hankinson, G. 2001, 'Location branding: A study of the branding practices of 12 English cities', *Brand Management*, vol. 9, no. 2, pp.127–142.

Hannam, K. 2004, 'India and the ambivalences of diaspora tourism, in Coles, T. and Timothy, D. (eds), *Tourism, Diasporas and Space:Travels to Promised Lands*, pp. 246–260, Routledge, London.

Hannam, K. 2008, 'Tourism geographies, tourist studies and the turn towards mobilities', *Geography Compass, vol.* 2 no. 1, pp.127–139.

Hegarty, E. Joseph 1992, 'Towards establishing a new paradigm for tourism and hospitality development', *International Journal of Hospitality Management*, vol

11, no. 4, pp. 309-317.

Kotler, Philip 1984, *Marketing Management: Analysis, Planning, and Control*, Prentice Hall, Englewood Cliffs, New Jersey.

Lichrou, Maria, O'Malley, Lisa and Patterson, Maurice 2008, 'Place-product or place narrative(s)? Perspectives in the marketing of tourism destinations', *Journal of Strategic Marketing*, vol. 16, no. 1, pp. 27-39.

Medlik, S. and V.T.C. Middleton 1973, 'The tourism product and its marketing implications', International Tourism Quarterly, 3, 28–35.

Ooi, Can-Seng 2004, 'Poetics and politics of destination branding:Denmark', *Scandinavian Journal of Hospitality and Tourism*, vol. 4, no. 2, pp.107-128.

Plog, Stanley 2001, 'Why destination areas rise and fall in popularity', Cornell Hotel and Restaurant Administration Quarterly, vol. 42, no. 3, pp. 13-24.

Smith, L. J. Stephen 1994, 'The tourism product', Annals of Tourism Research, vol. 21, no. 3, pp. 582-595.

Zeithaml, V.A. and Bitner, M.J.1996, *Services Marketing: Integrating Customer Focus Across the Firm*, McCraw-Hill Higher Education, New York.

CASE STUDY
TOUR PACKAGE OF KAILASH MANSAROVAR

The following package of Kailash Mansarovar includes a number of essentials of the tour and the left out facilities are separately mentioned.

16 days fixed departure overland tour to Mt Kailash Mansarovar by 4500 CC Toyota Land Cruisers (4WD Vehicles)

Day 01 Arrival Kathmandu

Arrive Kathmandu. Transfer to pre-booked hotel from Tribhuvan International Airport and overnight stay in the hotel.

Day 02 Temple visit in Kathmandu

After breakfast, half day sightseeing tour of Pashupatinath Temple and Budhaneelkantha. Evening at leisure in Kathmandu. Agency will obtain Chinese VISA in Kathmandu on this day. However, travel permit for Tibet would be applied well in advance.

Day 03 Drive Kathmandu to Nyalam (3700 m)

After breakfast, drive to the frontier town of Nepal at Kodari enjoying a scenic drive through Dhulikhel. From here, a short walk to the friendship bridge for the drive to Zhangmu, the main entrance of Tibet, China at the height of 2,300 m which is about 145 km from Kathmandu. In Zhangmu, you will be received by guide from our Tibetan counterpart. After all the immigration formalities at the check post here, journey continues for another 35 km which can take almost 3 hours through the up-winding road to Nyalam with beautiful scenery as the drive brings us for the overnight stay at Nyalam (3,700 m). The lodges and guest houses here are very simple and basic. Overnight at Hotel Nyalam or similar.

Day 04 In Nyalam for acclimatization

This whole day is dedicated for acclimatization at Nyalam. We will be going for a short trek of about three hours in Nyalam itself. Overnight at Hotel Nyalam or similar.

Day 05 Drive Nyalam to Saga (4600 m) 240 km/ 6-7 hours drive

After breakfast, drive through the windswept territory passing many villages and camps of Yak herders with the distance view of snow capped mountains. We will be passing through the first highest pass of Lalung La Pass (5000 m) where a superb view of high Himalayas can be seen from Gaurishanker, Shishapangma to Langtang Himal. Drive past Khunmen Tso, Sinling, Karru Ongchen and Peigutso Lake (4400m). We continue driving crossing the river 'Yarlung Tsangpo' known as Brahmaputra, to reach Saga (4600 m) covering 240 km In a 6-7 hours drive. Overnight stay at local guest house.

Day 06 Drive Saga to Prayang (4750 m) 255 km/ 6-7 hours drive

After breakfast, drive to Prayang (4750 m) covering 255 km in a 6-7 hours drive through the windswept territory passing many villages and camps of Yak herders with a distance view of snow capped mountains. On this day the road is quite flat, hence the drive will be comfortable compared to other days. Overnight stay at a guest house/ Hotel Prayang.

Day 07 Drive Prayang to Hor Quo (4560 m) 223 km/5-6 hours drive

After breakfast, drive to Mayum River for 112 km and have lunch. Thereafter, drive to Hor Quo (4560 m) 223 km/5–6 hrs. We continue driving crossing Mayum La pass (5200 m) and arrive at Hor Quo. Today is the day of lifetime, as we will

(*Source:* Taken verbatim from Oriental Vacations And Journeys Pvt. Ltd., New Delhi , India, printed with permission)

have the first view (darshan) of the Holy Mt Kailash and Holy Lake Manasarovar. Camp on the bank of Holy Mansarover Lake. Overnight stay at the camp.

Day 08 Mansarovar Parikarma (4520 m) 115 km/ 4-5 hrs. and drive to Darchen (4620 m)

After breakfast, it is a day for Puja and holy bath in the holy lake. We will be doing Mansarovar Parikarma by Jeep (4520 m) covering 115 kms in 4–5 hours. On the way, we will stop near Trugu Gompa for a holy bath in the Holy Lake Mansarovar. We will be setting separate bathing tents for changing clothes. During this parikarma, we will have a picnic lunch on the bank of the Holy Lake Mansarovar. Time permitting, we will visit Chui Gompa. Afternoon drive to Darchen (4620 m). Darchen is located beneath the majestic holy Mount Kailash, a small village with a couple of guesthouses. During the auspicious pilgrimage time, this place will be flooded with pilgrims with hundreds of tents all around.

Day 09 In Darchen for acclimatization

After breakfast, we will proceed for our acclimatization exercise with a short trek to Serrlung Monastery and to Nandi Parvat which offers an excellent view of Mount Kailash. We will be staying overnight in Darchen and will prepare ourselves for Kailash Parikarma. Overnight stay at Guest House in Darchen.

Day 10 Drive to Tarboche (13 km) and trek to Dirapuk (4860 m) 7 km/5–6 hours.

After breakfast, drive approx. 13 km to Tarboche, the trek starting point of Kailash Parikrama. Tarboche is also known as the outer 'Asthapath'. The first day of our Kora is a gradual walk with multitudes of other local pilgrims chanting and praying. The trail leads us to few ups and downs till we reach our camp/guest house at Dirapuk (4860 m) covering 7 km in a 5-6 hours trek. Camping on the nice grassy meadows with a view of, the north

west face of Mount Kailash. Those not feeling fit to continue parikarma will drive back to Darchen and wait for the Parikarma group to return. Overnight stay in Camp/Guest house.

Day 11 Trek to Zuthulphuk (4760 m) 18 km/ 9-10 hours.

Today our circumambulation (Kora) leads to the much higher side of the holy path just beneath the Holy Mount Kailash. The walk will bring us to one of the highest point at Drolma La, at 5,200 m before descending to the gradual field towards Zuthulphuk for overnight stay after 5–6 hours walk. Zuthulphuk (4760 m). The distance is 18 km covered in 9–10 hours.

After early breakfast, group will set off as the sun's rays break over the ridges above. After the footbridge, the trail rises up a rocky slope. Take this gently but steadily. It soon reaches a level walk. The peak of Mount Kailash rises to the right and can now be seen linked to a long spur, which joins the eastern ridge. This is the top edge of the glacial valley from which the Lhachu (Divine River) flows.

This day is the climax of the holy journey and is the most difficult day of our journey. One has to pass through Drolma La Pass at 5680m—the highest altitude on this tour. Physically, it is the most arduous day. At the pass is a large boulder depicting Tara, festooned with prayer flags. Here too, Tibetans leave a memento of themselves such as a tooth, a lock of hair, or even a personal snapshot.

After perhaps 30 minutes, we descend a steep, rock-strewn path to the valley below. Just below the pass is Lake Tu-je Chenpo Dzingbu (Gauri Kund), 'The Pool of Great Compassion'. Take great care now because it is easy to sprain your ankle or worse. You must negotiate steep staircases down to a snowfield. The only way down is to jump from boulder to boulder across a large rock fall. On the ridge above is a formation known as the Lekyi Ta-ra (Axe of Karma).

A final steep descending staircase brings

you to the valley floor. From here it is about 5 hours to the day's destination with no shelter in between. It is vitally important to remain on the right-hand side of the river, the west bank. If not, you will get trapped, unable to cross it. The walk now becomes very pleasant and relaxing (as long as the weather is clear and there is no howling gale). The path follows the gentle slope of the valley over grassy fields and clear brooks for several kilometres before it narrows and turns further south to merge with another valley before reaching Zuthulphuk, the 'Miracle Cave' of Milarepa. Overnight stay in the second camp.

Day 12 Zuthulphuk to Darchen trek 10 km/4–5 hours and drive to Prayang (4750 m)

The morning can be spent exploring the caves and visiting the temples and shrine that has been built around Milarepa's cave. A married elderly couple supervises the temple, which is usually an active residence for over half a dozen Tibetan devotees, helpers, or relatives who continuously busy themselves with the tasks of maintaining the buildings.

One imagines Milarepa's disciples meditating here. Many of the caves contain meditation platforms, self-contained by dry stone walls which separate them from their cooking partitions and entrance areas. It is well worth the short climb up to these caves before beginning the final stage of the trek. The winding gradual tracks finally ends our holy pilgrimage walk covering 10 km in 4-5 hours. Once we reach at the trek end point near Darchen, our land cruisers will be waiting to take the group back to Prayang by tracing

our footsteps returning home leaving the Holy place. (Those who could not do parikarma would be waiting to welcome other group members at this point.) Overnight stay at Hotel Prayang.

Day 13 Drive Prayang to Saga (4600 m) 255 km/ 6-7 hours drive

After breakfast, drive to Saga. Overnight stay at local guest house.

Day 14 Drive Saga to Nyalam (3700 m) 240 Km/ 6-7 hours drive

After breakfast, drive to Nyalam. Overnight stay at Hotel Nyalam or similar.

Day 15 Drive Nyalam to Kathmandu

Drive downhill to Zhangmu and Friendship Bridge where transportation awaits for our final leg of journey to Kathmandu of 150 Km in 8–9 hours. After reaching the Friendship Bridge, we will be leaving our vehicles and will walk on the other side of border for approximately 15 minutes towards Nepal Immigration Post where our coach for Nepal would be waiting for us. Our border guide will assist in shifting our belongings to Nepalese side of the bridge. Overnight stay at Hotel in Kathmandu.

Day 16 Fly back to your home with memories of Mount Kailash and Holy Lake Mansarovar

After breakfast, you are free for souvenir shopping and other independent activities. Transfer to International Airport to board your onward flight.

Departure dates and rates for 2008
Kailash Mansarovar Yatra – 16 Days using 4500 CC landcruisers

Tour No.	Arrival in Kathmandu First Visit	Depart for Kailash	Arrival in Kathmandu Second Visit	Departure from Kathmandu	Remarks
1.	30th April	02nd May	14th May	15th May	
2.	13th May	15th May	27th May	28th May	Full Moon
3.	27th May	29th May	10th June	11th June	
4.	10th June	12th June	24th June	25th June	Full Moon and Saga Dawa Festival
5.	24th June	26th June	08th July	09th July	
6.	11th July	13th July	25th July	26th July	Full Moon
7.	24th July	26th July	07th August	08th August	
8.	10th August	12th August	24th August	25th August	Full Moon
9.	24th August	26th August	07th Sept	08th Sept	
10.	07th Sept	09th Sept	21st Sep	22nd Sept	Full Moon
11.	16th Sept	18th Sept	30th Sept	01st Oct	
12.	25th Sept	27th Sept	09th Oct	10th Oct	

Indian Passport Holders:
INR 64,999/- per person on twin sharing basis
INR 69,999/- per person on single occupancy basis

Foreign Passport Holders/NRIs:
USD 1,999 per person on twin sharing basis
USD 2,199 per person on single occupancy basis

(VISA Fee supplement for US Passport Holders would be USD 60 per person)
(Twin sharing/single occupancy will only be applicable in Kathmandu and Camping whereas at all other places, dormitory/twin/triple sharing accommodation will be provided)

The above cost includes:
Airport transfers in Kathmandu, twin sharing accommodation at 4 star hotel in Kathmandu (Shanker or equivalent) with daily breakfast, lunch and dinner, transportation Kathmandu/Tibet border/Kathmandu by non-A/C coach,

Camping arrangement backed by Nepalese Sherpa crew on full board basis, hiring charge of sleeping bags, transportation inside Tibet by Deluxe 4500 CC Japanese Land Cruiser (4 pax per land cruiser), necessary Yak and Yak men to carry your luggage (one piece per person only) for Kailash Kora, applicable entrance fees to visit monasteries, normal Tibet Entry Visa fee, and half day sightseeing tour of Kathmandu valley.

Special Inclusions:
We will provide one down jacket and a duffel bag which must be returned after arrival in Kathmandu, a certificate on successful completion of Holy Yatra which retains nostalgic memories even years after undertaking this once-in-a-lifetime pilgrimage.

The above cost excludes:
Travel and medical insurance, rescue evacuation cost in case of emergency, insurgent fee approx.

INR 500 per person, airport tax, extra cost in the event of landslide to hire additional transportation or porterage on the Arniko highway (INR 500-700), beverages, photography charges, porterage at the airports, laundry, tips, telephone calls, other expanses of personal nature, airfare to Kathmandu and back, yak/pony hiring charges for riding during Kailash Parikarma and anything not specifically mentioned in the clause, 'The above cost includes'.

DISCUSSION QUESTIONS

1. Study the tour details very carefully and list elements used in designing the complete tour package. Discuss each element as a product.
2. How does this package help a tourist in comparison to a non-packaged tour?
3. What are the benefits of non-packaged tours?
4. How does the given tour information help in understanding the bundled tourism product?
5. Do you suggest any modifications in the elements or information of the package?

CHAPTER 8

Tourism Distribution

LEARNING OBJECTIVES

A travel agent is the most popular and visible face of tourism distribution. It gives information, advice, services, and assists in purchase. Tourists feel comfortable when all the tour components are managed under a single window. But it takes a long chain and value enhancements at various levels before the benefits reach the tourists.

In this chapter, we shall explore how distribution channels transfer values to tourists and what are the important issues in selection and management of these channels. The focus will be on learning the following.

- Concept of tourism distribution
- Distribution channels in tourism
- Management of channels
- Developments in tourism distribution

INTRODUCTION

The distribution element of marketing mix is very important for a firm that concerns with transfer of goods and services from the manufacturer to the buyers and all the activities therein. The whole system of managing channels and members, maintaining inventory and logistics to make benefits available at convenient locations for customers is essential backup for good distribution. A right distribution system can give an edge to the firm but at the same time a weak system can prove to be a trouble spot.

The tour experiences take place at destinations such as mountains, beaches, forts, cities, and resorts, etc. that are immovable sites. This requires movement of tourists from their places of residences to the place of consumption. The convenience and facilities of this movement decide the accessibility of tourism attractions. The place utility is created

The concept of distribution applies to tourism in a different set up of inseparability of tourism products. It necessitates simultaneous production and consumption and implies that both sellers and buyers shall be present at the time of tour experience.

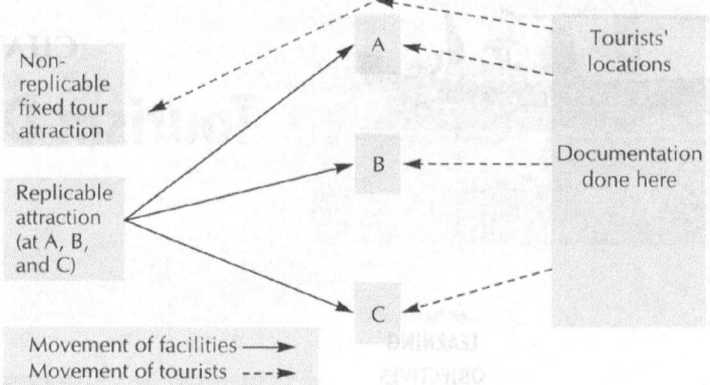

Fig. 8.1 Physical Distribution in Tourism

by moving tourists, unlike goods that are physically transported near the consumers' locations to create this utility. The documentation part of distribution and transferring movable services is performed near the tourists' locations (Fig. 8.1).

For example, ticket, visa, and passport formalities are completed at tourists' place and then tourists move to destinations for tour. The non-replicable natural attractions or historical monuments have only one fixed location but facilities, such as, a hotel or a fast food chain, can open its branches at a number of places to be in close proximity to the consumers.

The unique features of distribution in tourism make it a challenging task but at the same time can give competitive advantage.

TOURISM DISTRIBUTION

Tourism distribution is transfer of tour and associated facilities from the suppliers to the tourists through the tourism distribution system. It delivers many benefits to the tourists. These are as follows.

1. Accessibility and availability: Attractions are made available conveniently by arranging transfer of tourists.
2. Information: Tourists get information about places, flights, trains, routes, costs, and so on.
3. Counselling and advice: Tourists may not be able to decide about travel destinations and plans and may ask for advice.
4. Arrangements: Tourists want arrangements to be made for them so that they have minimum hassles on tour.

5. Buying: Tourists want the buying facility at one place where they can make payment and get proof of purchase such as tickets, vouchers, etc.
6. Documentation: Tourists want suppliers to do the necessary documentation or help them in it, particularly, for visa and passport.

Tourism distribution system is a complex, informal global network of independent businesses which form the 'travel distribution chain'. This network allows the consumers to research, book, and pay for tourism products. It is concerned with two important areas.

1. Physical movement of tourists from their residences to the destinations.
2. Selling and distributing products near tourist locations.

All the functions in the above areas can be performed either directly by a firm or with the help of intermediaries. The decision depends on the effectiveness and cost of choice. Maintaining its own network can be expensive for a firm as it may not have enough resources for the same. In such cases, middlemen are preferred. Using middlemen may give cost advantage but the firm will have less control over these agents. So the decision is taken after considering all the factors discussed below.

Physical Movement of Tourists

Tourists travel from their own places to various destinations for tour experience. Their decision to travel to a place is influenced by the following factors.

- Distance between source and destination
- Time required for travel to the destination
- Infrastructure for travel between origin and destination
- Facilitation of this movement

Tourism marketers can control and manage only the arrangement and the facility part. New infrastructure of roads, airlinks, rail lines, and faster connectivity make the way for changes in the arrangements. The pictures of the road from Katra to Vaishno Devi Shrine in Jammu and Kashmir before and after development clearly show the impact of roads in facilitating physical movement of tourists (Figs 8.2 (a) and (b)).

To facilitate movement of tourists, the following considerations are used.

Route of the tour

As a thumb rule, the shortest possible route shall be chosen for cost and time savings. But direct flights or trains may not be available or the roads

Fig 8.2 (a)   Vaishno Devi Route before Development

on direct route may be bad. In such cases, an alternate longer route is
selected. In tourism, a number of attractions are packed in a single tour
and a circuit is taken that covers a number of destinations.

Stopovers en route

A tour can be of many days and tourists will need rest and food in
between. It is planned in advance as to how many stoppages will be
allowed, where, and when.

Time available for tour

Tourists have limited time with them and this factor decides what
places are covered in a tour and how much time is spent at each
place.

Mode of the tour

Mode of the tour or transport depends on the liking of the guest, cost of
travel, and availability of a mode. A tourist may prefer the toy train to go
to Shimla for its charm, even if the journey time is more. A flight may be

Fig 8.2 (b) Vaishno Devi Route after Development

considered expensive. Road journey may be preferred for viewing locales and the flexibility of taking breaks.

Attitude and fitness for journey

It is very important to know the tourists' comfort with the length of the tour. People may or may not like to travel to far-off places. Most of the international travel is dominated by regional travel, indicating the tendency of tourists to be closer to home and familiar places. Other reasons, such as high costs of long distance travel, may also be attributed to it. As the cost of travel comes down tourists shift to distant sites.

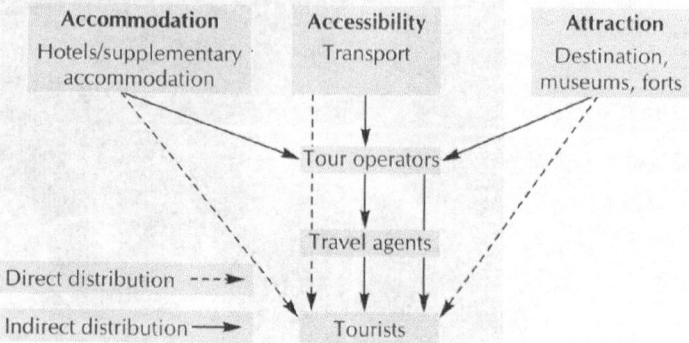

Fig. 8.3 Direct and Indirect Distribution of Tourism Services

The nature of journey also determines if a tourist can go to a place or not. Tourists going to religious places, such as Amarnath, Kailash Mansarovar, etc. undergo medical tests before being allowed to travel on the difficult routes.

Selling and Distributing Products near Tourists' Locations

Tourism as a discrete product can be sold directly to the tourists who will purchase different services from different suppliers or indirectly through middlemen. As a complete assembled tour, middlemen may sell it directly or through other middlemen. Different mechanisms are developed for selling directly and indirectly. Direct selling is done through sales force and websites. Indirect selling is made through a chain of middlemen, also called the distribution channel. The direct and indirect distribution and sales of tourism is shown in Fig. 8.3.

For indirect selling different types of middlemen can be used at different levels (Fig. 8.4). The involvement of different middlemen and the functions attributed to them depend on the industry practice.

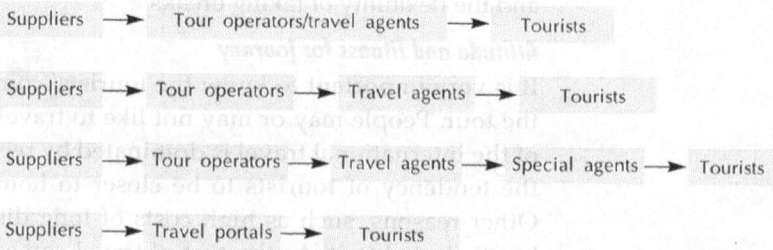

Fig. 8.4 Middlemen in Tourism Distribution

Principals	Channel members
Gives expertise and brand	Ensure service standards
Financial assistance	Financial commitment
Incentives	Local knowledge
Training	Local offices
Controls	Assemble products
Geographical exclusivity	Market coverage
Preferential purchase	Customer service
Promotional support	Promotional support
Guaranteed supplies	Inventory management

Fig. 8.5 Functions of Suppliers/Principals and Channel Members in Distribution Chain

The participants in the distribution channel perform many functions to add value to the offer. The choice between direct or indirect selling is based on these functions.

In using middlemen, a marketer will be interested in finding what functions can be performed by its channel members and if there is sharing of functions, what type of arrangements can be made. The relation will be based on mutual benefit to both parties. The functions performed by both are shown in Fig. 8.5.

Functions performed by principals

The functions performed by principals are discussed below.

Give expertise and brand name   The tourism products belong to owners or suppliers such as a hotel room to hotelier, an airlines seat to air-transport firm, etc. Destinations are excluded from the control of marketers as they are national resources. But artificial destinations, such as theme parks and resorts, are supplied by marketers. When it is given to middlemen, the brand name and related services are transferred for sale. A tour package of travelling by simple train, air-conditioned (AC) coaches, luxury trains is not the same. Palace on Wheels is a luxury tourist train and has a well-established brand name. Expertise and brand is a very important consideration for middlemen to choose one supplier over another.

Financial assistance   Financial support is provided by principals that give the inventory for sales to its regular agents without advance payments. But for others, only limited assistance may be provided.

Incentives   Benefits in the form of commission, schemes, and familiarization tours are offered to middlemen as motivators for higher sales. Sales promotion schemes are also used as incentive.

Training   Training of agents in handling the firm's products yields better results. It includes product knowledge, different schemes, insight in tourists' behaviours, and so on.

Controls   In the distribution channel, the members need to be kept together for synergistic effect. Bigger and dominant principals control the whole chain, deciding the conditions of agreement. For example, in the tourism industry, agents are less powerful than the principals, as a result the commissions offered by airlines or hotels are decided by principals leaving little scope for conflict.

Geographical exclusivity   Firms give exclusive geographical sales rights to agents. An agent in a zone may be selling all products of a firm. If this right is given to many agents, then internal competition may begin.

Preferential purchase   A supplier gives its quota to its agents on preferential basis. If any stock remains, then it can be sold to others.

Promotional support   Principals maintain memory of their brands in market through promotional efforts, thus making the job of agents easier.

Guaranteed supplies   A travel agent will provide guaranteed availability of airline seats, hotel rooms, entry tickets, etc. to its clients. Any turn down will erode the credibility of the suppliers. Suppliers need to ensure guaranteed supplies to its agents.

Functions performed by middlemen

Middlemen at different levels share functions among them. These are discussed below.

Service standards   Principals expect their products to be packaged in sync with their image. This requires following certain service standards. Agents guarantee these standards. For example, hotels use franchising to gain a wider reach and fix the standards of servicing for all franchisees. Franchisees have to ensure that the standards are maintained.

Financial commitment   Agents give financial commitment for office location and minimum guaranteed business. This eases the funds position of the principals.

> Agents have better knowledge of local markets. They understand the buyers, know their languages, have contacts, and can connect to the customer easily.

Local knowledge   The local knowledge of agents cannot be acquired easily by the principals if they open their offices. This is one of the most important functions of agents and the reason behind the use of intermediaries.

Local offices and support   Agents establish offices in different parts of the market, covering villages and small towns. This is backed by manpower support at these places. This organizational support is very useful for the suppliers.

Market coverage   A network of agents provides a better market coverage. The agents have the presence in markets and proper selection will give exposure to principals in the concerned markets.

Customer service   Responsibility of customer service at the local level is borne by the agents. It includes information, counselling and advice, documentation, buying support, and so on.

Promotional support   All agents support the promotional efforts of principals by having their own promotional plans and budgets.

Buying inventory   Agents purchase stocks from principals to sell further. In Indian tourism industry, many practices prevail. Big agents can get stocks without any advance payments and make all payments after sales. Small agents pay part advance for stocks. In some cases, agents are asked for a bank guarantee that is kept with principals. This acts as security and the amount of guarantee depends upon the stocks required.

By managing demand and supply   Agents are able to balance demand and supply at the local level through suitable strategies as and when needed. They know the price at which packages will sell on a particular day and use the flexible pricing accordingly.

Jointly performed functions

Some functions are jointly performed by both the suppliers and the agents.

Market information and research   Suppliers carry market research at the broader industry level and micro-level efforts are made by the agents.

Risk distribution   Suppliers bear the risk while selling to long-established dealers as no advance payment is taken. But other agents buy the stocks from principals and then sell it further. They may also undertake the responsibility of unsold stock. This risk is more for small agents who rely on small market and sales may not happen for any unforeseen reasons.

The above discussion on functions of principals and agents is general in nature and these vary depending upon the power of channel members. If channel members are bigger and stronger then they can control the channel. A big hotel or an established airline may not depend on middlemen but a small stand-alone hotel or a new airline may not be able to sell without the agents. The distribution of functions also depends upon the agreement between the two.

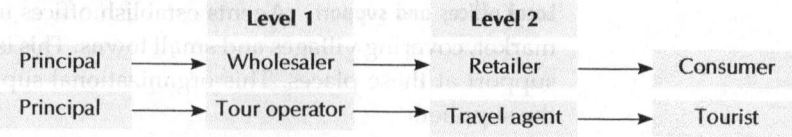

Fig. 8.6 Distribution Channel

DISTRIBUTION CHAIN/CHANNEL

World Tourism Organization (WTO, 1975) suggests that 'a distribution channel can be described as a given combination of intermediaries who cooperate in the sale of a product. It follows that a distribution system can be, and in most instances, is composed of more than one distribution channel, each of which operates parallel to and in the competition with other channels.'

Distribution channel is used for indirect selling. It can be understood to be a collection of independent organizations that enter into an agreement for distribution and function as a chain. The participating organizations are called channel members. Figure 8.6 shows a distribution channel.

This is a simple channel as there can be more members at different levels.

Channel Design Decisions

If the suppliers have decided to sell through middlemen then decisions are taken as to: How many middlemen to use? How to distribute functions among the channel members? How to manage the channel members?

Deciding channel members

A firm can decide not to use any middlemen at all if its market is small and it can reach there directly. It gives a complete command over distribution. But if the market grows or is dispersed then reaching tourists directly can be difficult and expensive. Here the firm prefers middlemen.

The following channel members participate in the distribution of tourism.

1. National or regional tourism organizations
2. Tour operators
3. Travel agents: outgoing and incoming
4. Online travel distribution firms
5. Specialized agents

National or Regional Tourism Organizations

These are government bodies that enter into tourism as suppliers and regulate the national resources of the place or tourist attractions. A country or city is not given to private operators but the government organizations plan and manage these in the larger interest. The Ministry of Tourism acts as the national tourism organization in India. The various state tourism corporations act as regional bodies that develop and promote tourism in the framework of the national body.

These play a very important role in the initial stages of a destination when it is not profitable and gets very less tourists. At this time, the private operators do not invest but the government tourism bodies perform the following foundational functions.

- Formulate national tourism policies and strategies
- Deal with international tourism issues
- Advise other agencies on tourism interests
- Make investment attractive in tourism
- Manage crisis
- Fill the gaps left by private sector
- License and regulate private operators
- Hotel/restaurant classification
- Training and education in the sector
- Tourism product development
- Market research and statistics

Tour Operators

These are wholesalers who bulk buy from principals, prepare tour packages, and give to travel agents for further selling. These are manufacturers or designers of packages. They add value through design. Costing, designing, and packaging are their important functions. A package can be developed as standard or customized. A standard package is fixed that is prepared first and sold later. Tourists do not have any option to alter it in any way. A customized package is adapted to the varied needs of the buyers. A comparison of standard and customized packages is given in Fig. 8.7.

Adaptation to the needs of the markets and customization of packages and allowing for customer participation is one of their important roles that make other channel members dependent on the tour operators. In today's competitive times, mass customization is becoming a popular approach in tourism which produces individually customized products and services at the price of standardized mass produced alternatives. Different levels of customization are possible in package design and delivery such as the following.

Adaptive customization

A standard but customizable package is given to the tourists who can alter it themselves. Different modules of package can be offered to tourists who can mix and match to prepare their own package. For example,

Standard Package	Customized Package
Appeals to mass markets that are price sensitive	Appeals to tourists who look beyond economic value and want the package to offer extra facilities
Costs are less as benefits of bulk purchase of inputs are obtained	Costs increase
Profits increase through high volume sales	Profits increase through value as higher prices can be charged
Better quality can be offered as focus confines to limited packages	Quality improves because of useful inputs received from buyers
It can be effective if market is undifferentiated	It is used when market is differentiated

Fig. 8.7 Standard versus Customized Packages

pre-defined package tour may be adapted according to the preferences of tourists by adding extras.

Cosmetic customization

A standard package is offered but its representation is changed for different groups of tourists as per their needs such as changing the name, making it available from different delivery points, changing the advertising or promotion, and so on.

Transparent customization

Packages are continuously improved or customized with the changing likes of tourists but the name given or representation is not changed as the buyers remain connected to it. The buyers in this case feel the increased satisfaction from the customization without knowing about it.

Collaborative customization

A package is the result of discussion between the seller and the buyer where both try to understand and adjust to each other's opinions.

Customerization

A completely buyer-centric package is built to order. The design is initiated by the buyers. This approach has been adopted by online travel firms that can prepare a product after getting the requirements from the buyers. These are transferred to the sellers to prepare the package.

Approaches to customization

The approaches to customization are shown in Fig. 8.8.

The operator can offer its package anywhere on a scale between completely standard and completely adapted. Apart from the preferences

Generic Customization	Customization in Tourism
Standardization	Pre-defined packaged tour
Adaptive customization	Adaptation of pre-defined packaged tour as using add-on offered
Cosmetic customization	Selection of different distribution-delivery systems, e-tickets, printed ticket
Transparent customization	Personalized services, for example, SMS alerts for flights cancellations, delays, new benefits
Collaborative customization	Collaborative design of travel products between supplier and customer
Customerization	Flexible itineraries determined by the traveller

Fig. 8.8 Customization in Tourism

of the buyers, many other factors in the environment influence customization. These include competition in the market that force firms to offer variety, cultural factors that force tourists to demand additional facilities of own food or other home-like facilities than those available at the destinations. Economic prosperity also makes tourists shell out additional money for more services.

Considering all the factors, packaging or tour designing is done by the operators.

The availability of good tour operators in the market makes distribution effective. The Ministry of Tourism, Government of India provides for recognition of tour operators, adventure tour operators, and domestic operators. By December 2008, their number was 479, 25, and 30, respectively.

Travel Agents

These are retailers in tourism who buy from the wholesalers and sell to the tourists for commission. A market may be dotted by large and small agents but certifications and recognition keeps a check on quality. The Indian government has a system of recognizing agents on the basis of their infrastructure, manpower, and processes. In December 2008, India had 348 recognized agents. Travel agents link wholesalers and tourists. They add value through the reach in the market and personal consultation. They are closer to market and build personal rapport with the consumers. Their credibility in the market makes it easier to sell through them. In tours spanning a number of countries, more than one agent is used for handling the tour. These are called outbound and inbound agents. Even tour operators doing retail can link similarly as outbound and inbound

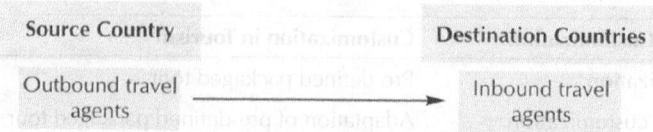

Fig. 8.9 Outbound and Inbound Travel Agents

operators. A travel agent marketing packages of Australia, New Zealand, and the UK makes all the arrangements within India and is the outbound agent. For the arrangements at respective destinations, the inbound agents in different countries are used (Fig. 8.9).

The inbound operators/agents are also called destination managers. These are very important in international travel and perform the following functions.

- Act as single local contact point and eliminate the need to contact many suppliers
- Make all arrangements at the destination
- Advise on itinerary preparation and packaging
- Give local expertise
- Simplify payment

Online Travel Companies

These are new intermediaries and are also called cybermediaries. These emerging new-age companies stock both discrete and assembled products and also suggest the best buy to the tourists. They are present on the World Wide Web and may not physically own any supplies but purchase from outside and assemble packages or just display them. These are offered for sale through the Internet and give enough choice to the tourists with a vast assortment and consultation. They also give good options for air and hotel bookings. They follow a completely different strategy than offline travel agents. Travel agents try to sell the high-priced packages with all the inclusive benefits but they suggest the best buy for the lowest priced offer among similar products.

Existing agents also adopt the online presence as an additional channel and use it for information and transactions. A practice followed is to use the web presence for information only and transactions are encouraged offline.

Online firms can be general such as indiatimes.com that sell everything including travel, or specific ones selling only travel tours such as makemytrip.com and yatra.com.

The online firms follow different commission policies resulting in differential pricing of the same product on different sites. This erodes the credibility of the product as the buyer will navigate through a dozen sites before choosing the one giving lowest price.

Online companies offer high level of customization through dynamic packaging because of the modular nature of their products. The buyer can select flights after specifying destinations, time, price range, airlines, etc. Dynamic pricing is also possible as supplies and demand are instantly known.

A principal looks for the following features for hosting its products on a site.

- Commission required and level of promotion offered
- Rate parity on different sites and with traditional offline agents
- Business expected to be generated
- Affiliate sites that operate in main site
- The information maintained onsite
- How the site is marketed

Specialty Agents

These deal with specialized products, such as conferences, meetings, casinos, etc., and connect sellers and buyers. These can act as brokers or agents. A number of agents specialize in leave travel concession (LTC) packages of government employees and are well versed in completing the documents as per official requirements. Conference handlers know their clients and their requirements.

General Sales Agents (GSAs)

These agents represent other companies/principals/wholesalers and market their products. A firm appoints GSAs on cost–benefit analysis and wants high level of business through them. A GSA performs the following functions.

- Imparts expertise of dealing with similar products
- Provides booking facilities
- Represents products in trade and consumer shows
- Gives feedback on market trends

In India, the travel industry is in the developing phase and the distinction in the roles of different middlemen is blurred. A tour operator may sell directly to the tourists, can sell through the travel agents, can have online presence, and can also deal with special products. But as the market will grow, consolidation may begin. That will make the functions more distinct.

Decisions on Length of Channel

For wider reach and penetration, a number of middlemen at different levels may be selected simultaneously (Fig. 8.10). It shows four levels

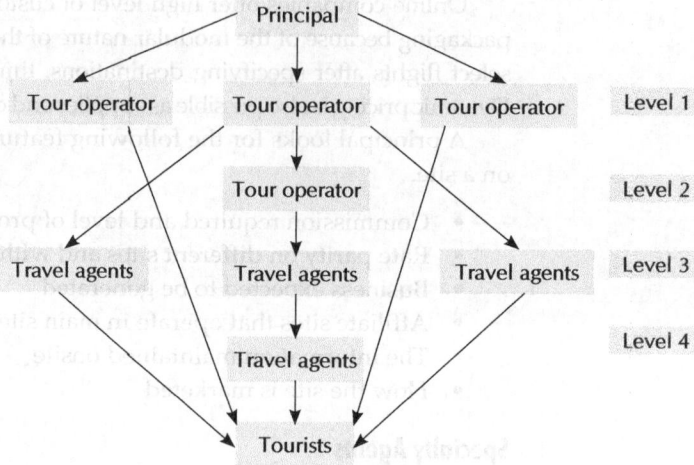

Fig. 8.10 Channel Length

in the channel and different members used at each. There can be less or more levels and members. But it shall be ensured that

- they do not compete with each other,
- the costs do not increase in a long chain,
- efficiency does not decline,
- control of the chain is easy, and
- there is coordination among all members.

Tourism market in India is full of small travel agents and it is very common for them to keep changing principals for a better deal. Principals also keep looking for agents for better service. This affects the quality of services, as well as long-term relations with the customers become difficult.

Channels in India

The distribution mechanism of Indian tourism industry is not fully mature. Its main features are as follows.

1. It is multilayered and has multiple intermediaries.
2. It has a large number of small agents who have low financial standing.
3. Volume of business is low and competition is intense. Small agents want to offer all services and undercut other channel members as well as prices.

4. Functional specialization for services is very little.
5. There is lack of destination specialization.
6. Local agents do not have travel experience and do not purchase directly from the suppliers but depend upon the bigger operators and purchase bundled or package services.

Managing Channels

The relation between channel members depends upon the agreement between them. A part of this agreement is written as a contract and the other part is implicit as per customs of the trade. The issues of administration and motivation are other important aspects of channel management.

Motivation of channel members

Channel members need motivation to push products in markets. Incentives, training, and support are used for this. Intermediaries will be motivated to sell and serve if they know how a hotel or a destination best meets the needs of its clients. This is further strengthened by more commissions and incentives for higher sales.

Administration of channel

Channel is a collection of independent entities that come together for mutual benefit. There might be problems of control of this loose chain. The following approaches are commonly used for it.

Corporate control   A firm may have its presence at all levels by operating all supplies and distribution. It means owning airlines, hotels, and agencies under one umbrella. This makes control easy being under the same management. But this is possible only for very large firms. And all firms may not like to go for such integration.

Contractual control   A detailed contract may be prepared specifying all terms and conditions, leaving no scope for aberrant actions. Violation may be made difficult through penalty clauses. The problem with this approach is that all issues cannot be foreseen to be put into contract clauses.

Administered control   The control is exercised by the bigger and dominant member that regulates the behaviour of every member by using informal power.

Managing conflicts among channel members

Tourism distribution has certain peculiar characteristics that create conflicts in the channel. Some of the main reasons for differences are as follows.

Profit margin Agents earn through commission offered by the principals. Each wants a larger share of this profit and when prices come down because of competition, squeezing profits often lead to conflicts.

Financial commitments Principals want greater financial commitment from agents and agents expect more support from the principles. Both fail to come up to each others expectations.

Service commitments Parties may fail to meet the requirements of agreement and if this violation happens too frequently, relations are strained.

Dominant behaviour of big channel members The small and fragmented agents cannot competitively negotiate with the big principals and may get a lower deal. They always look out for better deals than sustaining long-term relations. The same applies to small and medium hotels that are dependent on agents for exposure and sales in the market. Agents focus on their profits and market shares and sell at lower prices, thus harming a hotel's bottom line and image in the long run. Such hotels remain in a strained relation with the agents.

A good agreement, meeting obligations, motivational techniques, and control systems are used to handle all conflicts and get the best output from the channels.

Developments in Distribution

In earlier times, agents or direct presence in the market were the only choices available to approach the market. Agents were independent and this made control difficult and direct presence in market had higher costs. Technology has changed it. Internet has brought together buyers and sellers at a very low cost. This has made direct presence in virtual world very easy and cost-effective. Buyers too like to shop for the best purchases than relying on one or two agents. This has even raised the issue of the demise of the travel agency business. Some of the functions of travel agency, such as information, buying, advice on best buy are performed very well through the Internet. The agents are reinventing their role to perform high-level functions such as advising, consulting, and service support. They have also adopted technology for better interfaces with customers and for efficient management of their internal operations.

SUMMARY

Tourists want tour experiences and the marketer's job is to make these available. This requires moving tour benefits to tourists such as giving tickets, assisting in documentation, opening hotels or resorts in their towns. A large part of tourism experience takes place at immovable sites such as hills, beaches, etc. and it requires moving tourists from their places of residence to destinations. The access of tourists to both movable and immovable benefits is made possible through a distribution system. This is a network of distribution channels. Five types of intermediaries, i.e., tour operators, outbound and inbound travel agents, online travel distribution firms, specialized agents, and national or regional tourism organizations form a channel. Tour operators are wholesalers who assemble packages and sell to travel agents who further retail them. Online travel firms use the Internet to reach consumers as well as middlemen. Specialized agents handle special tour products such as casinos and exhibitions. National and regional tourism organizations act as suppliers that are responsible for maintaining tourism resources.

Suppliers need to decide about the length of channels, types of channels, and types of members to be used. This is decided based on sharing of functions among the concerned parties. Channel being a set of independent organizations faces the problem of maintaining unity. Members conflict for reasons such as profits and controls, and reduce performance below the optimum level. This is managed by adopting strategies to control and motivate the members. Corporate, administered, and contractual are the control methods used for this.

The growth of the Internet and online companies is changing the rules of distribution and consumers are bypassing the established channels for purchasing services such as airline and train bookings. This is increasing profitability for tourists and suppliers but is forcing middlemen to adopt newer roles as consultants and advisors.

A good distribution system can make a firm competitive when all other elements of marketing mix are equal.

KEY TERMS

Administered control Here, the channel members are controlled by the informal power of the bigger and dominant member.

Channel members The participating organizations in the distribution channel are called channel members. Tour operators and travel agents are channel members in tourism.

Contractual control Here, a detailed contract specifying all terms and conditions is used to control channel members.

Corporate control When all channel members operate under one management and control is exercised centrally, it is called corporate control.

Distribution Distribution is the transfer of goods and services from suppliers to buyers. It includes all the activities to be performed in the process and creates place utility for consumers.

Distribution channel It is a collection of independent organizations that enter into an agreement for distribution and function as a chain.

Principals/suppliers These are the members of a distribution chain who prepare the goods and services. These are manufacturers such as hotels, airlines, destination developers, etc.

Specialty agents These deal with specialized products such as conferences, meetings, casinos, and connect sellers and buyers. These can act as brokers or agents.

Tour operators These are wholesalers who bulk buy from principals, prepare tour packages, and give to travel agents for further selling.

Tourism distribution Tourism distribution is the transfer of tour and associated facilities/services

from suppliers to the tourists through tourism distribution system.

Tourism distribution system It is the network of tourism distribution channels used by suppliers to reach their markets.

Travel agents These are retailers in tourism who buy from wholesalers and sell to tourists for commission. They link wholesalers and tourists.

EXERCISES

REVIEW QUESTIONS

1. What are the decisions taken in arranging travel of tourists to the destination?
2. What is the distribution channel? What functions are performed by the channel members?
3. Explain the distribution chain in tourism and the role of different channel members in it.

PRACTICE EXERCISES

1. Visit the local travel agencies. Find out how they benefit from channel agreements. Also ask them the problems of agreement. What makes them change principals?
2. Visit a hotel with a franchise agreement. Ask

about the conditions of franchise and the benefits involved. Also ask why it is difficult to sell independent properties.

PROJECTS

1. Make a survey of hotels, agents, and operators. Collect information to find their functions. Do these match the functions discussed above? Explain any variation.
2. Study the different itineraries to a destination and find the travel plan in each. What factors have been considered in planning transport arrangements of tourists? Prepare a report.

REFERENCES

Anckar, Bill 2003, 'Consumer intentions in terms of electronic travel distribution: Implications for future market structures', e-Service Journal, vol.2, no.2, pp. 68-86.

Bennett, Marion M. 1993, August, 'Information technology and travel agency—A customer service perspective', Tourism Management, pp. 259-256.

Bitner, Mary J. and Booms H. Bernard 1982, 'Travel and tourism marketing: The changing structure of distribution channels', Journal of Travel Research, vol.20, pp.39-44.

Buhalis, Dimitrios 2000, 'Relationships in the distribution channel of tourism: Conflicts between hoteliers and tour operators in the mediterranean region', International Journal of Hospitality and Tourism Administration, vol.1, no.1, pp. 113-139.

Chaudhary, Manjula 2006, 'Tourism marketing in India—Role of public and private sector', Tourism in India: Policy Issues and Implications, Department of Tourism, Kurukshetra University, Kurukshetra, India, pp. 132-156.

Cooper, Chris, et al. 1993, Tourism Principles and Practice, Pitman Publishing, London.

Gilmore, James H. and B. Joseph Pine 1997, January–February, 'The four faces of mass customization', Harvard Business Review, pp. 91-101.

Kotler, Philip, Bowen John, and Makens James 2004, Marketing for Hospitality and Tourism, Pearson Education, Delhi.

Lovelock, Christopher and Jochen Wirtz 2004, Services Marketing: People, Technology, Strategy, Pearson Education, Delhi.

Middleton, V.T.C. 1988, *Marketing in Travel and Tourism*, Heinemann, Oxford.

Ministry of Tourism, Government of India 2008, India Tourism Statistics.

Sharda, Shalini and Douglas G. Pearce 2006, 'Distribution in emerging tourism markets: The case of Indian travel to New Zealand', Asia Pacific Journal of Tourism Research, vol.11, no.4, pp.339-353.

Sigala, M. 2006, 'A framework for developing and evaluating mass customization strategies for online travel companies', *Information and Communication*

Technologies in Tourism, Hitz, M., Sigala, M., and J. Murphy (eds), Springer Computer Science, SpringerWien, New York.

Wind, Jury and Arvind Rangaswamy 1999, June, 'Customerization: The second revolution in mass customization', eBusiness center.

Witt, Stephen F. andMoutinho Luiz 1989, T*ourism Marketing and Management Handbook*, Prentice Hall International, Hemel Hempstead, UK.

WTO 1975,Distribution Channels, World Tourism Organization, Madrid.

CASE STUDY

TRAVEL AGENTS IN INDIA—REDEFINED BUSINESS

Travel agents occupy an important place in the travel distribution chain. The main source of their revenues is commission from airlines for selling air tickets and rest of the revenues come directly from tour buyers for the services rendered. Travel agents have acted as arms of airlines for reaching markets and sell around 85 per cent of air tickets.

But the global recession and ease of reaching buyers online made airlines rethink about the commission and they decided to withdraw it. This strategy was initially adopted in the USA and was soon followed in other countries. It came to India in November 2008, when airlines declared that they would stop paying commission to agents from 1 November 2008 and the three Indian full service airlines Jet, Air India, and Kingfisher with several other international carriers stopped paying 5 per cent commission on the ticket prices. Airlines cited international practices and high costs as the reasons behind it. It created a stalemate in the market and agents opposed it vehemently and even declared that they will stop selling tickets without commission. The four Indian operators agreed to pay a 3 per cent commission to travel agents on the total fare including fuel surcharge and basic fare, instead of the 5 per cent on the basic fare earlier.

But the other airlines did not relent and instead asked the agents to levy a transaction fee of Rs 350–10,000 per ticket in lieu of the commission. Agents started levying this fee but with an apprehension that at present airlines also levy the transaction fee and the prices of tickets obtained through agents and airlines offices are the same, but in future, airlines may stop charging this fee, leaving agents in a disadvantageous position. Moreover, airlines may give incentive deals on their websites.

The reduced commission reflected on the incomes of agents and small agencies from this highly unorganized sector resorted to their own cost-cutting measures. They have voluntarily started giving up International Air Transport Association (IATA) accreditation or are defaulting on payments required for its continuation. An IATA accreditation enables an agent to get a commission from all IATA airlines, hotels, and transporters. In 2008, 123 agents did not have their accreditation renewed. This fee is USD 550 for a new applicant and USD 90 for the existing one, and also involves a bank guarantee varying from Rs10 lakh to Rs1 crore for every IATA agent. The IATA agency accreditation is voluntary but offers an agent many benefits such as access to a global network of accredited airlines and travel agencies, standardized procedures to ensure fair dealings with airlines, and visibility and credibility on premises and websites among others.

In such a tough situation agents are adopting newer service-fee driven model of revenue generation that has features like the following.

- Personalized service
- Focus on selling holidays than tickets
- Higher value additions
- New product and service ideas
- Expanding into the leisure business where commissions on non-air products remain high (cruise, hotel, etc.)
- Specialize as niche players for specific leisure products (for example, destination weddings, student travel, group travel, cruises, etc.)
- Tailored service fee by segmenting consumers according to services required and willingness to pay for services.

Service fees are a valuable source of revenue but require strict management for maximizing yield. Apart from this, travel agents also need to control other operational and staff costs without affecting the service to consumers.

In view of recent developments travel agents found it difficult to adapt to this new model and lobbied for its reversal. As a result,

Director General of Civil Aviation (DGCA) issued a directive to international carriers on 5 March 2010 to resume the commission to agents that can be mutually fixed between them and agents after considering market factors. The reasons cited were that high transaction fee was imposed on customers and airlines were giving discount to big agents as productivity bonus, thus scuttling healthy competition in market. But the basic issue is how long can the agents restrain global trends.

(*Source:* Livemint.com, accessed on 4 June 2009, 4 hoteliers.com, accessed on 29 January 2008, and traveldailynews.com, accessed on 17 July 2007, eyefortravel.com accessed on 1 April 2010.

Discussion Questions

1. Will travel agency business end in future with online business to consumer (B2C) business model evolving when principals might bypass agents or completely withdraw commission?
2. What can be the other sources of income for agents in the absence of commission?
3. How can travel agents balance cost reductions and added services to tourists?

Tourism Pricing

LEARNING OBJECTIVES

This chapter will get you acquainted with the basics of pricing and tourism pricing. After reading this chapter, you will be able to understand the following.

- Concept of price and pricing
- Factors affecting tourism pricing
- Methods of pricing
- Pricing strategies
- Price fixation in tourism

INTRODUCTION

Tourism products consist of a combination of goods and services. Goods form the core product and services provide the differential advantage. For example, a tour package consists of tangibles such as food, travel, and accommodation. This is the basic constituent that will be provided by most service providers. However, the intangible part that includes quality of service and add-ons provide that extra edge to the tour seller. This requires extra effort on the part of the seller. However, the results more than make up for it. The intangible component or the service part increases as we move on the spectrum towards high-end tourism offerings. Pricing in tourism involves deciding monetary value of both tangibles and intangibles. Ordinary pricing methods, such as cost plus, can be used to fix prices of tangible components. However, the real challenge lies in the pricing of intangibles.

One of the current practices is closely monitoring the competition and pricing your product depending on their prices. But this technique is useful only when there is parity in offerings of different providers. Also, prices in tourism fluctuate with season, days, time, demand–supply, markets, and occasion. This makes tourism pricing a difficult task where

Take something as unique as space tourism. How do you put a price on experience? And then the provider has to include factors like safety. Add to this the environmental concerns that may possibly put a ceiling on the number of visitors. Taking all the relevant variables into account and then making the pricing decision is a cumbersome and difficult process.

costs, profit margins, salability, fixed capacity, fluctuating demand, and a host of other factors are to be balanced.

CONCEPT OF PRICE, IMPORTANCE OF PRICING, AND PROCESS OF PRICING

Price is the monetary value decided for exchange of goods and services between buyers and sellers. Both parties want maximum benefits from this exchange. While a seller primarily aims at covering costs, earning a decent profit coupled with a number of other long-term and short-term objectives, buyers simply want best value for the money paid. An interplay of a large number of forces decides the final price that will be acceptable to all. Finding the suitable price figure is a continuous process.

Importance of Pricing

Pricing or the process of fixing the prices is a very important decision for any firm due to the following reasons.

Most flexible component of marketing mix

Price is the most flexible marketing mix component that can be altered very quickly to adapt to competition, increasing costs, government regulations, and so on. Changing the rest of the components, such as product, process, people, promotion, and others, is a long process. Therefore, pricing is frequently used to modify the marketing mix.

Important to set price right in the beginning

Finding the right price is a very critical decision. A wrong price set initially is very difficult to correct. If high prices are set in the beginning, customers may shift to low-priced offers of competitors and reducing the prices may not bring them back. Initial low price may cost sellers lost profits and attempts to increase prices later may not succeed as buyers may not accept the new value. This is especially true in a price-sensitive market like India. Just because price is easily alterable does not mean sellers should play around with it to find the right fit. If customers start perceiving a firm as price untrustworthy then it can cause irreparable damage to the firm.

Builds value and image

Customers use price figures for perception building. A premium product backed by high prices enhances its brand value and appeal in the mind of the consumer. Price is used as a tool for positioning, particularly in services where it is one of the visible elements. Marketers try to assimilate price perfectly with rest of the marketing mix to create the right value and image.

Part of sales promotion

Price is used to encourage sales over a short period in the form of discounts, price packs, loyalty schemes, and so on. The strategy is to increase sales in lean periods by building new consumers who might be encouraged to try a service once the new price matches their spending level. It is not intended to shift existing buyers from peak to low season. It should also not encourage the sales force to push all sales in the off season and achieve sales targets. The organization must have proper checks in place whenever they go for sales promotion based on price. Price has to be fixed in a manner that the objective of sales promotion is achieved.

Important factor in final tour decision

Price is a major determinant in tour decisions. Research studies have shown that an increase in relative cost can be shown to be linked to a fall in market share in travel from every origin country. The cost of tourism to the visitor includes the cost of transport services to and from the destination and the cost of ground content (accommodation, tour services, food and beverage, entertainment, etc.). Both types of costs are relevant to the travel decision. Changing costs in particular destinations relative to others and price adjustments for exchange rate variations are regarded as the most important economic influence on destination shares of total travel abroad.

Process of Pricing

Using a rigid, well-defined process for fixing the price is not possible. The process requires many variables to be considered and reconsidered simultaneously. However, the following sequence does help in taking pricing decisions although some of the steps can overlap.

Take stock of marketing strategy

Marketing strategy formulates a long-term road map for a firm and all decisions are made in accordance. Pricing decisions should take the firm closer to the intended position specified in the firm's marketing plan. Market analysis, market segmentation, targeting, and positioning decisions are noted to ensure that pricing be done accordingly.

Study marketing mix decisions

Price is only one of the elements of marketing mix and should be strategically linked with other elements. It should not work at cross-purposes with other components. A study of other elements conveys what is to be achieved through pricing.

Estimate demand curve with price

Price elasticity analysis of demand of a tourism offer will give an estimate of demand at different levels of prices. This is important because a firm may have other objectives such as quantity to be sold.

Understand environmental factors

The prices of competitors, changes in costs because of increasing input costs, taxes, and government laws/regulations should be studied for their impact on prices.

Set pricing objectives

A firm must decide its objectives of pricing. Multiple objectives can be set but these should supplement each other. A firm cannot possibly fulfil dual objectives of market share and high prices at the same time.

Develop price with price methods

Now the final price can be decided with the help of a suitable price method. This price takes into account all the major considerations.

The sequence of steps in the pricing process is iterative as most of the factors accounted at each stage change with time, leading to price revisions. But prices should be kept stable for a good enough duration to enable tourists to take decisions. Most pricing in tourism specifies the validity period of quoted prices.

FACTORS INFLUENCING TOURISM PRICING

Tourism pricing is influenced by a large number of factors relating to supply, demand, and the environment. The cumulative effect decides the final price.

Supply-side Factors

Supply of tourism services is characterized by perishability, geographical restrictions, and domination by intangibles, and with consumption that takes place instantly with production. All this affects pricing. The specific supply-related factors affecting prices are discussed below.

Perishable

Tourism services tend to perish if not consumed. These cannot be produced in advance and stored for later use. For example, if a place has a carrying capacity for 5,000 tourists per day, it will host 35,000 in a week. It cannot host all tourists in one day. Tourism services are to be consumed as and when produced. Unsold rooms, aircraft and train seats, theme park entry tickets, and so on cannot be sold for any other day. As a result, if average occupancy is 50 per cent in a year, price accounts for 100 per cent of the cost as tourists have to bear the cost of maintaining supplies throughout the year. This makes prices high, which can be lowered with higher occupancy.

Intangible

Tourism services are dominated by intangibles and putting a monetary value for these is very difficult. Pricing night view of Taj Mahal differently from day view is dependent upon its perceived value in the minds of buyers apart from a host of other factors. It is very difficult to convince a tourist that one scenic view of Taj can be priced differently from another. Intangibility is used by the hotels to price rooms differently depending upon the view from the windows of the rooms. A room facing sea will be perceived differently from the one facing a road but the question is of converting these differences in monetary figures.

Geographically restricted operations

All tourism services come defined with geographical constraints. A diner's clientele can get services at a particular place only where the diner is placed. Tourists can enjoy a national park only after getting there. This limits the potential of the restaurant and the park only to people who get there. This result in supply being confined to a market and the economies of scale does not come into picture as a very potent factor. It leads to higher prices.

Fixed capacity

Tourism supplies have a fixed capacity. A double hotel room cannot accommodate more than two guests. An aircraft can carry only a limited number of passengers. Fewer customers will imply empty seats and more will mean turndowns. Since supplies are limited, prices tend to rise in relation to demand. The suppliers use overbooking to ensure full capacity utilization and to hedge against no shows, but it can be highly inconvenient to customers to travel to airport with a non-confirmed or waiting ticket only to return in case all customers with confirmed tickets turn up.

Substitutes

Availability of substitutes increases total supplies and tourists shift to different options for reasons such as higher prices, non-availability, and so on. Low-cost airlines have substituted high-end train travel in India. Paying guest accommodation is being promoted in New Delhi to substitute for shortage of hotel rooms. However, all components of tourism cannot have relevant substitutes.

Information technology (IT) is trying to dispense off with the geographical restrictions by providing real-time imagery from tourist places. However, this simulated experience is limited to the senses of sight and sound only and has been largely unsuccessful in replicating real experience.

A national park, a mountain, or a beach is entirely unique and non-substitutable.

Wherever substitutes are not available, prices tend to increase with demand. This is visible in case of tourist destinations that become much more expensive in peak seasons.

Costs

Costs decide the minimum level of revenue to be charged from buyers. But if costs are high because of inefficiencies of production, prices too are unreasonably high. Costs of tour packages are often not in the hands of marketers, when most of the components are bought from other suppliers. Both fixed and variable costs are accounted for pricing, and allocation of fixed costs across multiple offers makes calculation of unit costs difficult. Activity-based costing (ABC) is used to calculate costs in tourism and at the national level, satellite accounting practices are being adopted.

New developments in the environment also enhance costs. Impact of tourism on climate and use of carbon footprints is likely to increase the tourism costs in future.

Objectives of the marketer

Prices make an important contribution towards achievement of a firm's objective. If the goal is volume, prices are set low to penetrate the market, but if it is to create a premium image, prices are set high, as tourists tend to relate high prices to high quality. For profit maximization objective, high prices can be set and for a middle-range image, medium prices are set. Other objectives, such as revenue maximization, survival in market, etc., are also considered. Tourism marketers set prices in accordance with desired objectives.

Competition

Competition in the market increases supplies, reduces inefficiencies, and brings down prices. Heavy competition in the international market has made travel to some international destinations affordable to the Indian middle class. Tourists from India are travelling in large numbers to Singapore, Malaysia, Thailand, and Dubai because of competitive prices.

Demand-side Factors

Tourists' opinion about services affects demand as well as perception of price. The specific demand-related factors affecting prices are discussed below.

Value perception

Value perception of price is subjective and varies among and within market segments. It also varies with time and location. This develops because of readiness to pay for non-monetary considerations. There are multiple non-monetary costs that a tourist bears such as time costs (unnecessary waiting time or queues to get services), physical costs (bad weather, bad seats, unwanted efforts), and psychological costs (perception of risks, efforts required). A tourist may be willing to pay more to avoid all these costs and any offer that takes care of these is likely to have high value perception.

Level of demand

The level of demand impacts prices. High demand leads to high prices as tourists compete among themselves for the experience. This phenomenon is often observed at unique destinations with demand throughout the year. Suppliers increase prices to increase revenues. However, prices cannot be increased beyond a limit because steep increase in prices may dampen demand.

> Tourists pay more for luxury hotels, all inclusive packages, and business seats in aircraft based for the high value perception of additional services even though the costs may not justify the prices.

Demand pattern

Tourism demand is often marked by seasonal fluctuations with majority of tourists travelling during the tour season for the best experience. As a result, demand exceeds capacity in peak period and facilities remain underused in the off season. Prices are adjusted to match the demand pattern and also to influence demand to balance it with supply. High prices are charged in the peak period to make up for any loss of revenues from low prices of lean times. India has seasonal demand because of its climate. It gets international tourists between September and March, while the rest of the year is off season because of hot weather. It becomes expensive during high demand period. But prices are slashed in off season to get price-sensitive tourists.

Exhibition effect

All purchase decisions are not dominated by economic reasons. Non-price factors, such as prestige and status, play a very important role in the final buy. Tourists may select a tour for the associated status and show value while giving secondary consideration to price. In such cases, prices are fixed at higher levels to make use of the price quality syndrome where buyers believe that higher the prices, higher the quality. In such cases, higher prices do not decrease demand; rather they increase it by raising the prestige attached to the tour. For example, foreign travel in India is considered a status symbol and tourists prefer to opt for it at higher prices than low-cost domestic tours.

Environmental Factors

External environment constitutes many forces that directly or indirectly shape demand and supply factors and price.

Tax structure

The tax structure in the form of surcharges, airport tax, luxury tax, and service tax adds to the cost and final prices. India has a high tax structure for tourism and that makes it a high-priced destination. Further, provisions of service tax stipulate that it is to be charged from tourists and the government decides the service tax in per cent on final price. Consequently, when service tax rate is changed, final prices change immediately. Over time, service tax in the country has grown from 5 per cent to the current 10 per cent.

Market structure

Type and level of competition in the market has a direct bearing on price. Competition can be easy or intense, negative or positive, with similar or dissimilar products, government regulated or free. Less competition results in creation of artificial scarcity by service providers that enables them to charge higher prices. Positive or healthy competition usually leads to reduction in prices but negative competition can lead to a cut-throat situation such as when some players enter cartels or collusions to weed out competition from the market. Competition in similar product market implies higher price sensitivity among tourists. Tourists choose one adventure destination over another for its low prices. But dissimilar product competition will not result in as much price sensitivity, as tourists will not easily shift from an adventure tour to leisure tour only because the latter is cheaper. The government also regulates prices and competition. It discourages formation of cartels or groups of a few big suppliers to control prices and restrain new competitors from entering the market.

Government policies

Marketers have to abide by government policies on prices. India has a dual price policy wherein foreigners pay in dollars and Indians in rupees for the hotel accommodation. Foreigners always end up paying more as the dollar remains relatively stronger. The entry fees of monuments are also fixed at different rates for Indian and foreign tourists. When a tour package is prepared, such price differentials are reflected in the tour cost.

Exchange rate fluctuations

All international travel is affected by the exchange rate of the currency of the destination as well as origin country. It directly influences price competitiveness of destinations relative to each other. Each country would like to have stable currency exchange rates to enable tourists to take decisions.

All the above variables form critical inputs for pricing decisions in tourism.

METHODS OF PRICE FIXATION

Price fixation involves deciding monetary value of a tourism offer. Initially, only costs can be calculated that are to be recovered through suitable pricing. Nothing is known about price levels that will yield maximum demand or profits. The right price is deduced after many adjustments and readjustments. However, a good starting estimate can be found through cost-based, buyer-based, and competition/market-based methods of pricing.

Cost-based Method

This method is seller oriented. Cost is calculated and the required mark up is added to it to get the price figure.

$$Price = Costs + Profits$$

This is a simple method but the following issues need special consideration.

Calculating the cost

This involves deciding the cost of producing the tour product and service. The total cost has a variable and a fixed component. Fixed cost remains constant irrespective of output. The cost of a hotel building and related infrastructure is a fixed cost irrespective of occupancy there. The variable cost changes with the quantum of output. The costs of maintenance and guest service are variables and relate to occupancy numbers.

All fixed and variable costs are added to get the total cost. But sometimes fixed costs and variable costs are common to different products. For example, in the case of construction and annual maintenance of roads the costs are shared by tourists with general public and transporters of cargo.

For calculation of costs a firm can opt for either full distribution of costs or use only the incremental costs as explained below.

Fully distributed pricing Common costs are allocated among different products and prices for each are set to recover the assigned part of cost. The methods for cost distribution tend to be arbitrary and affect the prices set. Consider the example of use of roads for tourists, general public, and cargo. Fixed cost can be divided equally among the three and variables in proportion to the level of use by each category. But if there are different types of maintenance costs accruing to different users, then the costs as well as prices calculated will change.

Sometimes such full allocation of costs makes the price non-competitive or unjustifiable. The same price for general public and tourists for travel between Pune and Mumbai is not acceptable. It will require a different system such as considering incremental costs.

Incremental costs   These are additional costs that would not be incurred if a product is not produced. Let us take an example of a road. The costs for construction and maintenance of a road exist even without tourism. However, if the road is used by tourists, there would be additional costs of maintaining extra buses, and bus terminals to facilitate tourism. These are incremental costs. So in order to promote tourism on a circuit, only incremental costs can be used to lower prices.

All products cannot be priced on incremental cost basis and overall prices set shall recover total costs.

Return on investment   Once a firm has decided cost allocation, the next step is to decide the method of return on investment (ROI) and the time period to recover the fixed costs. This will change the total cost to be recovered per year. A fixed cost of Rs 1,00,000 spread over five years will require Rs 20,000 per year for recovery, while it will be Rs 10,000 per annum if distributed over 10 years.

Deciding mark up or profits

The mark up can be an absolute figure or a percentage of cost. It can be calculated by considering either the firm's expected profits or industry standards. If a firm's expected profits are high, prices too will be high. However, industry standards may be followed to keep parity with other suppliers, although prices can still vary if costs are different.

This method completely ignores customers' perspective but gives a definite idea of the floor level or base level of prices. This can be a useful method if a new product, having no similar products to use as benchmark, is to be priced.

Buyer-based Method

This method of pricing takes into account the customer's perspective as the starting point. Buyers are assessed for their willingness to pay for a particular service. The initial assessment is fine-tuned yielding final price figures. This technique entails more of a psychological approach than a mathematical one, although it does not make sense if the perceived price is less than the cost. Also, if the perceived price is too high and is fixed as such, tourists may feel cheated later, hurting the image of the firm. The gap between perception and costs can be bridged through modifications in the offer. If the perceived price is lower than the cost, suitable value additions may be made to the product. This will push the perceived price to a higher level. If the perceived price is very high, additional features can be given to justify the high prices. This method indicates the maximum acceptable level of price. It is very effective in tourism pricing, as costs of all intangibles cannot be worked out. Particularly, the costs associated with damage to natural areas are almost impossible to calculate. Thus, eco tours are premium priced on the basis of perception of tourists. The intangible benefit of environmental protection is considered by buyers as a good enough feature justifying higher costs.

Competition-based Method

This is also called the going rate method. This is a very useful method if the market contains similar product offerings. The marketer fixes the price at the level of competitors. It is an easy method that does not require any cost calculations or market surveys to find out buyers' opinions and results in higher acceptability by the buyers who are already buying at the same price. But the problem of different costs and different perceptions remain and following the collective wisdom may not yield results. The imitated price may also not help in recovering costs or in creating a good image. One restriction here is that it can be a suitable method for challengers or followers but not for leaders. A market leader will always maintain its unique and distinctive position and that includes the price.

PRICING STRATEGIES

Pricing strategies are used by firms to tune prices to objectives, changing environment, and rest of the marketing mix. These can be formulated taking into view both long-term and short-term goals. A number of strategies can be used simultaneously to focus on multiple goals. Important pricing strategies are given below.

Market Coverage Pricing

A firm may follow a strategy that targets the whole market or one particular segment therein. Depending on this, it adopts pricing strategies that yield the requisite results. These strategies are as follows.

Market skimming

It is a high value–low volume strategy. The offering is priced high to maximize profits and recover costs quickly. This is an effective strategy in case of products with short life cycles. A short life cycle curtails competition, as competitors cannot easily copy products in a timely manner. Another case where this strategy can be followed is when the offer has no relevant substitutes and buyers are ready to pay high prices. The drawback of this approach is the compulsion to lower prices with the entry of competitors which creates the feeling of being cheated among all the earlier buyers.

With such pricing in place, the number of tourists who visit a destination will be low but the profit margin per tourist is sufficient to make it lucrative. This strategy can be very valuable as fewer tourists imply less ecological and allied damages that emanate from it. Kerala tourism has adopted this strategy very successfully for its wellness and holistic health tourism.

Market penetration

This is a low value–high volume strategy. A very low price is fixed for the offer to reach a large number of buyers and earn profits. Profits here lie in numbers as opposed to margins in skimming. The focus here is maximizing market coverage with lower profit margin from each buyer. This strategy can be used if the size of the price sensitive market is large, a product is easily copied, or a product is not unique to justify a high price. Early sellers get the advantages associated with economies of scale and the low prices act as a barrier to the entry of further competition. This pricing has the limitations for a seller as he/she may be perceived as a low-end specialist making his/her entry into high-end offerings difficult.

This may not be a very good strategy from the ecological perspective as mass tourism harbingers problems such as pollution. This strategy is being used by budget airlines such as Go Air and Indigo. Domestic tour operators in India depend heavily on this pricing strategy.

Pricing Mix Strategies

A number of strategies can be fashioned by combining price and quality (Table 9.1). Some are as follows.

Premium

A high quality tourism experience is provided at high price. All luxury tours come under this strategy. For example, tourist trains such as Palace on Wheels and Deccan Odyssey. Luxury hotels also follow this pricing. This approach succeeds when an excellent image of the tour is created and buyers perceive quality to be high enough to justify prices.

Budget

Price is kept low and quality offered is also the same. Quality is compromised by cutting down on extras and keeping services to the

Table 9.1 Pricing Mix Strategies

		Quality	
		Low	**High**
	High	Rip-off	Premium
Price	**Low**	Budget	High value

basics. Budget airlines, budget hotels, no-frills tours use this pricing strategy. Price-sensitive tourists prefer such pricing and forgo some services for the low price.

Rip-off

A high price is charged for poor quality. Price is not justified but tourists buy based on false perception of good quality. It can be used when tourists are not aware of the quality and pay the price out of ignorance. This is commonly used by shops in Asian countries where bargaining is the norm. Foreign tourists may purchase at the initial quoted price that could be very high. This pricing can also be used by unethical sellers or fly-by-night operators who do not have long-term interests in the market.

High value

A high quality tour experience is offered at low price. This gives very good value to the tourists. This pricing is possible only in a highly competitive market, where sellers try to outdo each other to gain maximum share of market. An example of high-value pricing is medical tourism in developing countries. Internationally certified medical care is offered at a fraction of the price in developed countries with benefits such as no waiting time, the best doctors, and highly personalized nursing and care.

Discount Pricing

Discount pricing strategy is used to give impetus to sales. It is a short-term strategy to motivate tourists to take advantage of reduced prices. This pricing cannot be used over a long period as it may lead to tourists perceiving discounted prices to be real prices and the attraction of lowered prices may be lost. Discounts can be offered in various forms such as the following.

Seasonal discounts

Price discounts are offered during off season to increase the sales and maximizing capacity utilization.

These discounts attract price-sensitive tourists who want the experience at lower rates. Hill stations offer such discounts during winter and beaches float this pricing in the rainy season. This type of pricing is very commonly used throughout the industry.

Exhibit 9.1   Quantity Discounts of yatra.com

Travel Miles with Yatra Miles Program!
Yatra.com offers its customers a chance to earn Yatra Miles on their online domestic flight bookings. These Yatra Miles can be used to avail discounts on further air bookings (domestic) done through yatra.com. It recognizes and rewards new and regular customers with loyalty points or Yatra Miles.

(*Source:* www.yatra.com, accessed in February 2008)

Quantity discounts

Discounts are offered on bulk buying to encourage large volumes of sales. Hotels give special prices to airlines, travel agents, embassies, and companies who use a large number of rooms continuously. Group bookings are also given special rates. An excellent example is the frequent flyer scheme offered by airlines. Frequent travellers are given points on each flight that can be redeemed for future travel and special gifts. They also enjoy associated facilities such as special lounge and food offers. This prompts the customer to use the same airline again and again to continue enjoying the benefits. Exhibit 9.1 shows such a scheme at yatra.com.

Price discounts

Discounts are given on a specified amount of purchase to encourage tourists to spend more. Tour packages may be sold on discounts with more discounts on high-end packages than low-end ones. This may lure tourists into purchasing high-value packages for the sake of discounts. An example of price discounts in tourism is exhibited in Exhibit 9.2

Time discounts

Demand of tourism services also fluctuates with time of the day. Discounting the price for the lean time helps in increasing sales during these hours, while reducing rush during peak time. An example of time discount is the happy hours scheme in most restaurants and pubs.

A typical pub gives a 20 per cent discount from 6 p.m. to 8 p.m., which is not a favoured drinking time among users. However, the discount attracts quite a healthy number to enable pubs to utilize their capacity better.

Cash back

A part of the total sales value is given back as refund to the tourists after completing the tour. This ensures that the purchase is made first and refund is offered later (Exhibit 9.3).

Exhibit 9.2 Price Discounts from makemytrip.com

Hotels			
City	Star rating	Regular	Special
Goa	2	Rs 1904	Rs 1456
Chennai	2	Rs 1660	Rs 1500
Mumbai	2	Rs 2350	Rs 2128
New Delhi and NCR	2	Rs 1869	Rs 836
International Airfare Deals			
From	To	Regular	Special
Delhi	Singapore	Rs 16,920	Rs 14,100
Mumbai	Dubai	Rs 12,999	Rs 11,599
Chennai	Bangkok	Rs 13,499	Rs 12,399
Delhi	New York	Rs 32,909	Rs 29,799

(*Source:* makemytrip.com, accessed in February 2008)

Exhibit 9.3 Cash back from yatra.com

Holiday in Thailand with 51 per cent cash back for companion's travel on 45 days advance booking.

(*Source: The Times of India*, accessed on 15 April 2008)

Package Pricing

Also known as bundle pricing, this is the most common form of pricing in tourism where a product is assembled and sold as a package. Basic components, such as stay, food, transport, and destination, are combined to make a complete tour and the overall price is quoted. A package costs less to the tourist than the combined cost of individually purchased components. An example of package pricing is shown in Exhibit 9.4.

Differential Pricing

A very flexible approach to pricing is adopted in tourism to balance capacity and demand, and to maximize revenues. This is done by selling the same service at different prices to different tourists.

A hotel may price same type of rooms differently, based on their locations. A room with a scenic view may be priced higher than a room with an average view.

Exhibit 9.4   Dazzling Dubai from makemytrip.com

Price Rs 27,999 (indicates—per person rates—applicable on 2 persons staying together sharing the same room) for 3 nights, validity up to 24.3.2008

Inclusions:
   Return airfare
   Normal visa fee
   3 nights accommodation
   Daily breakfast
   Half day city tour on private basis
   Return airport transfers on private basis

(*Source:* makemytrip.com, accessed in February 2008)

A seller may also charge less for a room if a customer comes in at a late hour as the room might remain unsold if the tourist goes back. Budget airlines sell the same seats at different prices. Apex fares or tickets for advance bookings are cheaper. Early bird offers of conferences give cheaper prices to initial bookings. Museum entry tickets are priced differently for different market segments. Dual pricing in India fixes different prices for Indians and foreigners for the hotels and monument entry tickets.

Psychological Pricing

Pricing is done to psychologically appeal to tourists. Use of certain digits in the prices may have better effect on buying. It may include the use of digits 999 to give the false impression of low price and to convince tourists to consider the option. For example, the Ginger chain advertises its hotel rooms beginning from Rs 999 only to give the impression of a three-digit price. But overall stay there may cost much more. The same is done for pricing of tour packages as well. Similarly, numbers ending with 0 and 5 are used (Exhibit 9.5). It is believed that use of certain digits has a positive influence on customers.

Promotional Pricing

Special price offers are made to boost sales. These are of limited duration and may have conditions attached as shown in Exhibit 9.6. But these do lure tourists to plan purchases on low prices.

Geographical Pricing

Transportation is a very important component of tourism accounting for a substantial part of tour cost and is given due consideration in pricing.

Exhibit 9.5 Psychological Pricing

SOTC world famous tours

9-day Egyptian Wonders	Rs 62,999
11-day Jewels of China	Rs 1,05,999
9-day Scenic South Africa	Rs 1,18,999

Cleartrip.com

Roundtrip flights anywhere in India	Rs 599

Indiatimes Travel

Lowest Travel Fares Challenge Domestic Travel

Jaipur to

Bangalore	Rs 1995
Hyderabad	Rs 2200
Guwahati	Rs 2500
Kolkata	Rs 2200
Delhi	Rs 500
Mumbai	Rs 1025

Cox and Kings Tours

South African adventure	Rs 1,11,999
Land of Pharaohs	Rs 45,999
Sri Lankan soujourn	Rs 37,999

(*Source:* Advertisement in *The Times of India*, accessed on 31 March 2008)

Exhibit 9.6 Promotional Pricing

Roundtrip flights anywhere in India at just Rs 599 from cleartrip.com

Conditions:

On GoAir network
On bookings 5 days or more prior to departure date
For first 6,000 bookings between 20 February 2008 to 5 March 2008
For travel up to 15 April 2008

(*Source:* cleartrip.com, accessed in February 2008)

Marketers may absorb a part of the cost of travel and can come with different geographical pricing strategies. A tour package may consist of travel from Delhi airport to destinations and back. At the same price, it may also offer free pick and drop facility to tourists from any central location or from their homes. In the first case, tourists will bear the cost of travel to and from airport, in the second, from central location, and none in the third case. Geographical pricing gives consideration to the cost of physical movement of tourists and decides who will foot the bill.

PRICE FIXATION IN TOURISM

Pricing in tourism involves fixing the price(s) of destinations, hotels, tour packages, attractions, and so on. An expensive destination with a premium image has all facilities suiting the image and pricing. Tour pricing offers greater flexibility to buyers and they can choose according to their paying capacity. A three-day tour experience may be purchased rather than a seven-day tour to cut costs. Such flexibility of pricing is not possible for other services. Important pricing decisions in tourism are revenue management, price structure, and payment mechanisms.

Revenue Management

Tourism demand varies across different market segments and with time and place. Revenue management considers these variations and maximizes revenues by setting prices according to the predicted demand levels among different market segments. The least price sensitive segment is allotted capacity first at higher prices. Then the second segment is allotted capacity at lower prices and so on. A higher price segment books closer to time of consumption. For example, tickets for a flight may be offered at Rs 2,000 for those who book one month in advance, Rs 3,500 for booking between 15 to 30 days before the flight, and Rs 6,000 for bookings between 14 days and three hours before the flight. The number of tickets for each category is also planned beforehand. This pricing strategy is successful based on the following two conditions.

1. Prediction of demand in a given slot is made with reasonable accuracy.
2. People of a target slot do not jump to other slots. If high-paying customers shift to advance bookings at low fares, capacity in high fares will remain unsold.

Price Structure

A firm may have a large product mix with a number of product lines and offers. Its prices must have internal consistency, i.e., the difference between various lines and items shall be justifiable based on certain criteria. For example, in an aircraft, the difference between business and budget seats is justified on the basis of legroom, food, and other such facilities. If the same airline flies both luxury and budget aircrafts, the price differential should be justified. The same is applicable to tour packages of different durations in the same circuit. An effective price structure will lead to higher sales and better customer satisfaction in the long run.

Payment Mechanism

Payment mechanism in tourism deals with collection of payment and mode of collection. Tourism services are often sold through middlemen both online and offline. Collection centres have to be provided where tourists can pay money. If railway tickets are booked through automated teller machines (ATMs), it acts as a collection centre for tourists and other passengers. Tourists are widely dispersed geographically. Thus, proximity and ease of use of a collection centre is critical as it supports achievement of the pricing objectives. Mode of payment is equally important as different modes of payments result in different receipts at seller points owing to differential middle-layer service provider charges. For example, payment through cash and cheque is different. Cash will give more money to the seller, while a bank will charge processing charges for the cheque leading to lower receipt for the service provider. Marketers have to decide how to get the payment. It can be through cash, credit cards, cheques—banker's and personal—travel agent vouchers, online account transfer, and so on. Each has its liquidity, risk and value, and a balance between all should be established.

Thus, we can see that tourism as an industry has some special characteristics that impact pricing decisions and differentiate it from pricing of goods and services of other domains.

SUMMARY

Price is the monetary value of goods and services and fixing this value right is critical for the success of a firm in the market. Price depends on a multitude of factors such as costs, demand, supply, and environment. Their effects on prices are analysed with the help of appropriate pricing methods. The cost-based, buyer-based, and competition-based methods are commonly used in tourism industry. Once a price level is determined, pricing strategies are used to respond to the continuously changing environment. The strategies often used are market skimming, market penetration, price–quality combination, discount pricing, geographical pricing, and differential pricing. The seasonality of tourism services makes discount prices a common practice.

Revenue management is a very important technique for the pricing of fixed capacity tourism services such as airlines and hotels. Prices are fixed at different levels based on the sales estimation at each level. It leads to maximum capacity utilization and yield. Deciding the price structure of the total mix and the payment mechanism are other important and related considerations.

KEY TERMS

Budget pricing It is a pricing strategy in which low prices are fixed and is associated with low quality of products.

Buyer-based pricing It is a method of pricing where the perception of buyers is used to decide the price.

Competition-based pricing It is a method of pricing where the prices of competitors are taken as reference.

Cost-based pricing It is a method of pricing where cost is taken as the basis for fixing price. A profit margin is added to the cost to get the final price.

Differential pricing When different prices are fixed for different markets for the same products and services it is called differential pricing.

Discount pricing In this pricing, temporary price reductions are made to encourage sales.

Geographical pricing It is pricing based on the location where the service is delivered.

Market penetration It is a low value–high volume strategy to enter the market. Price is kept low to be able to reach a large market. Margins are kept low but large sales make this strategy profitable.

Market skimming It is a high value–low volume strategy to enter the market. Price is kept high

to target a small market and high margins from each customer make it a profitable strategy.

Package pricing It is the pricing of a bundle of products and services.

Premium pricing It is a pricing strategy where a high price is fixed to build a high-end image of a product. The product quality is also kept high to support the price.

Price Price is the monetary value of a product or a service.

Promotional pricing Pricing to encourage sales is called promotional pricing.

Revenue management Revenue management maximizes revenues by setting prices according to predicted demand levels among different market segments.

EXERCISES

REVIEW QUESTIONS

1. What is pricing? Discuss the factors affecting tourism pricing.
2. What is the importance of cost-based pricing? What aspects are to be considered in this pricing method?
3. Explain different types of discount pricing offered in tourism. What is the role of such pricing?
4. What are the major issues of price fixation in tourism?

PRACTICE EXERCISES

1. Conduct a tourist survey to gather tourists' perception of discount pricing.
2. Can differential pricing be considered unethical? Ask tourists to get their opinion.
3. Calculate prices of hotels in your area on the basis of costs, buyer perceptions, and competition. What is the difference between

the three? How would you balance the three in fixing the final price?

4. Interview tourists to find the importance of non-price considerations in their choices. How do these factors influence pricing decisions?

PROJECTS

1. Prepare an itinerary for a nearby tourist destination. Do a small survey of the market to find a suitable price for it. Fix three price levels— optimistic, pessimistic, and most likely. Survey the market again to get the right price. What have you learned about pricing? Note your experiences.
2. Collect rates of hotels, taxis, and entry tickets in your city. Prepare tour packages of different durations and calculate costs. Now fix the prices of each. Compare these prices with the popular packages of the city. Try to find the reasons for the difference.

REFERENCES

Lovelock, Christopher and Jochen Wirtz, 2004, *Services Marketing: People, Technology, Strategy*, Pearson Education, Delhi.

Chaudhary, Manjula and S.S. Boora 2008, 'Medical tourism in India: Trends and competitive advantages', *Journal of Tourism*, vol. 9, no.1, pp.109-127.

Gilbert, D.C. 1996, 'Revenue management and airline loyalty schemes', *Tourism Management*, vol. 17, no.8, pp. 575-582.

Holloway, J.C. and R.V. Plant 1988, *Marketing for Tourism*, Pitman, London.

Kotler, Philip, John Bowen, and James Makens 2004, *Marketing for Hospitality and Tourism*, Pearson Education, Delhi.

Kotler, Philip 1995, *Marketing Management: Analysis, Planning, Implementation and Control*, Prentice Hall of India, New Delhi.

Kotler, Philip 2003, *Marketing Insights from A to Z: 80 Concepts Every Manager Needs to Know*, John Wiley and Sons, New Jersey.

Dwyer, Larry, Peter Forsyth, and Prasada Rao 2001, 'PPPs and the price competitiveness of international tourism destinations', Paper presented at the joint World Bank–OECD seminar on *Purchasing Power Parities—Recent Advances in Methods and Applications*, Washington D.C., 30 January–2 February.

Middleton, V.T.C. 1988, *Marketing in Travel and Tourism*, Heinemann, Oxford.

Witt, Stephen F. and Luiz Moutinho 1989, *Tourism Marketing and Management Handbook*, Prentice Hall International, Hemel Hempstead, UK.

Website References
www.makemytrip.com
www.cleartrip.com
www.yatra.com

CASE STUDY

BUDGET PRICING—MEDICAL TOURISM IN INDIA

India's medical tourism is estimated to bring revenue of $ 2.2 billion per year by 2012. It specializes in selective treatments for chosen markets as shown in Table 9.2.

Table 9.2 Markets and Products of Medical Tourism

Country	Number of Foreigners Treated in 2002	Number of Foreigners Treated in 2003	Major Source Areas/ Countries	Specialized Treatments Offered
Thailand	600,000	973,532	USA, UK	Cosmetic surgery, organ transplant, dental treatment, joint replacements
Jordan	126,000	130,000	Middle East	Organ transplants, fertility treatment, cardiac care
India	100,000	150,000	Middle East, Bangladesh, other developing countries	Cardiac care, joint replacements, lasik
Malaysia	85,000	129,318*	USA, Japan, developing countries	Cosmetic surgery
South Africa	50,000	NA	USA, UK	Cosmetic surgery, lasik, dental treatment
Cuba	NA	NA	Latin America, USA	Vitiligo, night blindness, cosmetic surgery

(*Source: Businessworld* 2003 and 2005)

Competition for medical tourism is highly specialized. For North American patients, Costa Rica is the chosen destination for inexpensive, high-quality medical care without a transpacific flight. South Africa gets cosmetic surgery patients from Europe, and many South African clinics offer packages that include personal assistants, visits with trained therapists, trips to top beauty salons, post-operative care in luxury hotels, and safaris or other vacation incentives. Argentina ranks high for plastic surgery, and Hungary draws a large number of patients from Western Europe, and the USA for high-quality cosmetic and dental procedures that cost half of what they would in Germany and America. Dubai is scheduled to open the Dubai Healthcare City by 2010 that will have the largest international medical centre between Europe and South-East Asia. India has its own advantages in cardiac surgery and joint replacements. Lately,

the profile of tourists coming to India is changing from (SAARC) nations and the Middle East to the USA, the UK, and Canada.

India is positioning itself as a low cost alternative in medical tourism, as shown in Table 9.3

This low-cost alternative is becoming an attractive option for tourists who are choosing modern medical centres in India.

This low pricing option is accused of not addressing the following important issues.

- Lack of follow-up care. The patient is in hospital for only a few days, and then goes on the vacation portion of the trip or returns home. Complications, side effects, and post-operative care are then the responsibility of the medical care system in the patient's home country.
- Most of the countries that offer medical tourism have weak malpractice laws,

Table 9.3 Comparative Costs of Medical Treatment in India, USA, UK, and Thailand

Nature of Treatment	India	USA	UK	Thailand
Partial hip replacement	$4,500	$18,000	*	*
Full hip replacement	$3,000	$39,000	*	*
Orthopedic surgery	$4,500	$18,000	*	$4,500
Cardiac surgery	$4,000–$9,000 or £6,000	$30,000–$50,000	(Private care) £30,000	$7500–$14,250
Knee surgery	$4500	$16,000	(Private care) £20,000	$7000
Bone marrow transplant	$30,000	$400,000	$1,50,000	$62,500
Liver transplant	$40,000–$45,000	$500,000	$2,00,000	$75,000
Neurosurgery	$8,000	$29,000	*	*

Contd

Nature of Treatment	India	USA	UK	Thailand
Gall bladder surgery	$7,500	$60,000	*	*
Dental care				
Tooth extraction	*	*	*	$30
Two dental bridges	*	$5,200	*	*
Filling	$20 to $40	$300 to $400	*	*
Root canal	$200 to $400	$3,500	*	*

*Figures not given were either not available or were quoted with a wide range in prices in different sources.

Note: Figures are estimated in US dollars or UK pounds; figures vary due to prices charged by different medical centres and patient profile and do not include travel and accommodation costs.

(*Source:* IBEF Research, Ministry of Tourism Govt. of India, www.health-india tourism.com accessed in February 2008)

so a patient has little recourse to local courts or medical boards if something goes wrong.

- There are growing accusations that profitable, private-sector medical tourism is drawing medical resources and personnel away from the local population, although some medical organizations stress that medical tourists help in generating revenues that are used to improve services for locals.

Discussion Questions

1. Do you feel that a country's medical facilities should be extended to outsiders when the country has very poor public health system?

2. Discuss the issues of organ trade in the name of medical tourism.

3. Do you feel low cost is a good enough reason to motivate people to seek medical facility? Identify other motives of such tourists.

CHAPTER 10

Tourism Promotion

LEARNING OBJECTIVES

Tourism promotion is informative and persuasive communication aimed at target markets. It helps in achieving marketing objectives such as selling, image development, market share, etc.

In this chapter, we will discuss the following.
• Concept of promotion and promotion mix
• Developing promotion for tourism
• Advertising
• Personal selling
• Sales promotion
• Public relations
• Important promotion tools in tourism

INTRODUCTION

Promotion can be defined as persuasive communication of a marketer with its target market to achieve marketing objectives. Promotion is a part of marketing communication which is a much broader term. Communication can have many goals other than promotion. Integrated marketing communication is the commonly used term in marketing. It includes all communication by a marketer with its market and promotion is its most visible part. The other elements of marketing mix are also used for communication. Consider an example of a tourist planning to take a tour. Promotion will persuade him/her with necessary information, discounts, and schemes. But the salesperson, other people purchasing the same services, ambience of transport vehicle, destination, price, distribution channel, all will transfer messages. The tourist combines these messages with the promotional messages to develop an understanding of the tour. The more unified these are, the easier it is for both the tourists and the marketers to effect sales.

PROMOTION AND COMMUNICATION

Promotion follows the process of communication. It includes sender, encoding, message, channel, receiver, decoding, feedback and has all the limitations associated with this process (Fig. 10.1).

This process as used for promotion is presented in Fig. 10.2.

Marketing communication uses the process of human communication, but the buyers cannot be expected to understand and behave the way the marketer wants. At best, they can be convinced.

> Promotion creates mental images in the target market to get sales.

In tourism promotion, developing messages and communicating these to potential tourists is a challenge. The dominance of intangibility in tour products makes it very difficult to frame concrete messages and non-ownership of tour products further complicates it. How do you convince and motivate a buyer for a purchase that is not concrete, cannot be possessed, and usually is an extensive problem-solving type of buying decision. Tourists are communicated the future experiences through images and abstract words such as exotic, heavenly, serene, out of this world, and so on.

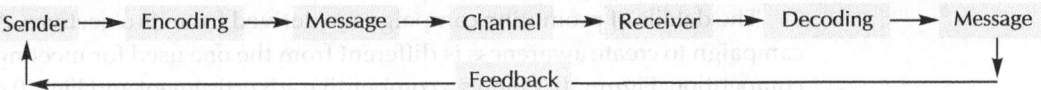

Sender → Encoding → Message → Channel → Receiver → Decoding → Message

Feedback

Fig. 10.1 Process of Communication

Step in Communication Process	Role in Communication	Role in Promotion/Marketing Communication
Sender	Originator of message	Creates promotional message
Encoding	Converts idea or thought into message	Coverts product feature and benefits into promotion theme and message
Channel or medium	Transfers message from sender to buyer	Transfers message from sellers to buyers such as TV, newspapers
Receiver	Destination of message	Buyers who receive the message
Decoding	Message is changed back to thoughts, ideas for understanding	Buyers find meaning into promotional message
Feedback	Receiver response to message is judged to know if it is understood	Buyers' response in terms of attitude or sales indicates the understanding of message

Fig. 10.2 Process of Marketing Communication

OBJECTIVES OF PROMOTION

Promotion contributes to the achievement of broader marketing goals and some of its specific objectives are as follows.

- Create awareness
- Generate interest
- Stimulate sales
- Meet competition
- Create image

The objectives of promotion depend on a number of factors such as goals of a firm, nature of market, and buyers. The buyers' position on buying process stage is used in building suitable promotion to assist them in moving from one stage to another. If we take the simple AIDA model of buying process, the stages attention, interest, desire, and action are used to decide the objectives.

For example, for a new entrant in the market, the immediate objective of promotion is to get attention. After this, the focus changes to generating interest and so on.

The details of promotion campaign are derived from its objectives. A campaign to create awareness is different from the one used for meeting competition. Figure 10.3 shows a competitive advertisement and Fig. 10.4 shows an advertisement to create awareness. An analysis shows that the presentation of the two is entirely different.

PROMOTION MIX

Promotion mix is the combination of different methods of promotion. Each method is suitable under different conditions and a right combination can be very powerful. Advertising, personal selling, sales promotion, and public relations (PR) are commonly identified methods of promotion as part of this mix.

- Advertising is defined as paid, non-personal communication for mass market by an identified sponsor.
- Personal selling is person to person selling. This is personal communication used for small markets.
- Public relations entail all the activities for building good relations with various publics of the firm. The goodwill generated through it promotes the product.
- Sales promotion is the use of short-term measures such as discounts, gifts, etc. to increase sales.

Lowest Hotel Prices.
No guarantee needed.

A Hotel Booking is about more than just price, Only Travelguru offers you India's largest collection of 30,000+hotel user reviews, advanced maps to locate, full list of amenities, high-quality photos & the lowest prices tool insist on more hotels, more information and more inclusions for the same price. **Guarantee your stay with Traveguru.**

Hotel Name	City	Travelguru special rates*	Make my trip rate*	Yatra rate*
Monarch Luxur (4*)	Bangalore	6555	7083	8865
Royal Orchid Central (4*)	Bangalore	5509	5608	5708
JP Churchil Hotel and Suites (4*)	Bangalore	3980	5429	Not Available
Victor Exotica Beach Resort (3*)	Goa	2352	2795	2834
Estrela Do Mar Beach Resort (3*)	Goa	1500	1514	1540
The Orchid (5*)	Mumbai	11553	12114	14014
Empire Royale Hotels (Un-rated)	Mumbai	3712	3750	4171
Le Royal Maridien (5*)	Mumbai	11273	Not Available	Not Available
Sarthak Resorts (3*)	Manali	1177	1251	1440
Hotel Snow Park (3*)	Manali	1829	2255	Not Available
Ginger Hotels	Across India	Upto 20% off	Not Available	Not Available

GET UP TO **50%** OFF
WITH YOUR VISA CARD.*

CALL **1800-102-4878**
from all major mobile operators
022 40304878 : www.travelguru.com

travel**g**uru™
India's Largest Hotel Network

*Conditions Apply. Rates are per room per night or double occupancy inclusive of taxes
†Rates given are extracted from the published data available on the respective websites at on 6th June 2008.
Check-in Date *05/06/08 & Check-out Date 14/06/08 Business Destination and Check-in Date 12/06/08 & Check-out Date 16/06/08 (Leisure Destination)

Fig. 10.3 Competitive Advertisement from travelguru.com
(*Source:* TravelGuru, printed with permission)

A firm needs the right promotion mix for best results. This is a difficult decision for the manager who considers all the relevant factors and then decides the mix. Sometimes it requires many alterations before a good mix is obtained. This mix changes with any new development in the concerned influencing factors.

Fig. 10.4 Advertising Campaign to Create Awareness by
ezeego.com

(*Source*: Cox and Kings, printed with permission)

FACTORS AFFECTING PROMOTION MIX

Promotion mix depends on a large number of factors and their cumulative effect is considered to develop it. Some of the important factors that affect mix decisions are discussed below.

Goals of Promotion

Different promotional methods produce different results. For creating awareness and for reminding, advertising is very effective. Sales promotion works best when sales need push in a short run. Personal selling delivers if the market is small and the product is complex, requiring one-to-one relationship. Public relations is needed to supplement other efforts.

Nature of Buyers

The market and its segments may show different behaviours in evaluating products. If it is rational and cognitive, personal selling provides the essential support. But for passive and emotional buyers, advertising and sales promotion help. Public relations can support in both the cases but the type of PR activities valued by each segment may differ.

Nature of Product

Complex products need one-to-one relations to transfer the information, while simple products are easy to mass market. So, increasing complexity leads towards more personal selling. Advertising and sales promotion suit simple offers. For example, high adventure tours or specialized tours are not promoted through advertising. Ready-made tour packages to popular tourist places are promoted through advertising and sales promotion schemes.

Life Cycle Stage of Product

At each stage of the product life cycle, the knowledge and attitude of the market changes and promotional efforts too are made accordingly. At the introduction stage, advertising works well for building awareness in mass market. At the growth stage, the need is to meet competition and the focus of advertising shifts at highlighting the competitive aspects. Sales promotion is used at maturity, saturation, and decline stage. Personal selling can be useful throughout, depending on the size of the market. It can be used if the market is small. Public relations is useful at each stage.

Level and Type of Competition

The leader in the market can meet competition better by sales promotion and advertising. A similar strategy can be adopted by the challenger. Niche or small specialized players can bank on personal selling to maintain their position. Public relations is good for all but give effective results for big firms who use it to publicize their socially responsible activities. For example, an advertisement about wildlife tours will have more effect if at the same time articles are published to show how tourism contributes to the preservation of wildlife. Higher level of competition forces the market to fight for space in the consumers' memory. This purpose is well served by advertising and sales promotion.

The impact of the above considerations on promotion mix is shown in Fig. 10.5. These are only indicative; the actual decision depends upon a number of other factors as well.

Influencing Factors		Promotion Mix			
		Advertising	Personal Selling	Sales Promotion	Public Relations
Goals of promotion	To create awareness	*			*
	To generate interest	*		*	
	To build desire	*	*		
	To lead to action or purchase	*	*	*	
Nature of market	Rational	*			*
	Emotional	*		*	*
Nature of product	Simple	*		*	*
	Complex		*		*
Life cycle stage of product	Introduction	*			
	Maturity	*	*		*
	Growth			*	*
	Decline			*	
Level and type of competition	Leader	*			*
	Challenger	*			*
	Followers			*	
	Nichers				*

* Indicates the use of a promotional method

Fig. 10.5 Factors Influencing Promotion Mix

DEVELOPING PROMOTION PLAN

It involves preparing an integrated plan that answers the following questions for the marketers.

- Whom to say?
- What to say?
- How to say?
- Where to say?
- How often to say?
- At what cost?
- Has everything been said well?

The above are answered in a well-designed promotion plan. It is systematically developed through a process of promotion planning (Fig. 10.6).

Deciding the Target Audience—Whom to Say?

Decision on the target audience of the promotion directs the rest of the promotion. Profiling of the market in terms of their demographic, psychographic, and behavioural features will give knowledge about its level of awareness and action. The promotion of the firm can either strengthen the existing level or try to create new levels. For example, if ecotourists are chosen as audience, they would like to hear only about ecotourism or sustainable tourism offers.

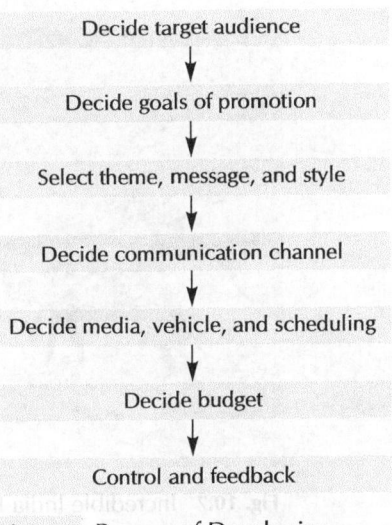

Decide target audience
↓
Decide goals of promotion
↓
Select theme, message, and style
↓
Decide communication channel
↓
Decide media, vehicle, and scheduling
↓
Decide budget
↓
Control and feedback

Fig.10.6 Process of Developing Promotion Plan

Selection of Goals of Promotion—What to Say?

Goals of promotion depend on the status of the target market and the marketing goals of the organization. These aim at mobilizing the market towards marketing goals. Some common goals are as follows.

- Create awareness
- Build attitudes
- Build sales
- Reinforce purchases
- Reduce cognitive dissonance

The goals of promotion shall consider the SMART criteria, i.e., goals shall be simple, measurable, achievable, realistic, and timely. The subsequent decisions of promotion build on these goals.

Decide the Theme, Message, and Style—How to Say?

For every communication, a theme or a core idea is chosen. A theme is the underlying concept for everything in a particular attraction.

Tourists need to be told of the main attraction of a destination. Ministry of Tourism, Government of India has used incredible charm of its different attractions such as beaches, hills, villages, cities for establishing its tourism image and the theme-based slogan selected is 'Incredible India' (Fig. 10.7). Similar approach has been earlier followed by Malaysia and Thailand with their slogans 'Truly Asia' and 'Amazing Land'.

Fig. 10.7 Incredible India Print Advertisement of Ministry of Tourism, Government of India

(*Source*: Annual Report 2007, Ministry of Tourism, Government of India)

The other features, such as good roads, hotels, Information counters, local transport, emergency services, tourist police, etc., add to the theme. The core idea is conveyed to the tourists through messages. A message can be presented in different styles using different appeals. The following three main appeals are used in messages.

1. Emotional: Messages try to stir the emotions of tourists who may develop positive feelings for a destination and purchase it subsequently. The commonly used emotions are love (honeymoon packages), thrill (adventure), pure (nature), and peace (pilgrimage).
2. Rational: Messages use logic to sell products. Features such as cost, extra services, proximity of destination from source, connectivity, etc. can be highlighted. This is commonly used in business tours.
3. Moral: The theme of ethics and responsible behaviour is built in the message. Ecotourism and sustainable tourism use this.

More than one appeal may be used simultaneously and depending upon the target market, an appropriate appeal is selected. For example, tourists may be asked to follow environment-friendly practices on a religious tour by conveying the following messages.

'Leave the resources for future generations.' (Emotional)

'If you do not respect environment, the place might end in your life-time.' (Rational)

'The nature is worshipped as God in Hindu religion. (Moral)

Decide Communication Channel—How to Transfer Message to Tourists?

Marketers come across the following three main problems in promoting and communicating tourism destinations.

- The target market is spatially remote.
- The culture of the source market is different from the destinations.
- Promotion is to be focused on those most likely to visit the destination.

These markets can be effectively reached through intermediaries who are physically, culturally, and psychologically close to tourists. These include tour operators, travel agencies, travel media, and opinion leaders.

Decide Media, Vehicle, and Schedule—Where and When to Say?

Many media are available for communication. Each has its pros and cons and is suitable under different conditions. A right mix of media can be selected after finding a match between needs of the marketer, the tourists, and the suitability of media.

The important media options are as follows.

- Print media: Newspapers—daily or weekly; magazines—weekly, fortnightly, biannual, annual; journals—monthly, quarterly, biannual, annual; directories—yellow pages, brochures
- Audio media: Radio
- Visual: Outdoor—billboards, displays
- Audio-visual: TV, films
- Internet
- Events

A comparison of the main features of important mass media used in tourism is presented in Table 10.1.

Earlier, tourism in India was not promoted much but recently almost all the media are used for it.

When the media has been chosen, the decisions for vehicle and timing become important. Vehicle is a specific programme or space in a medium. If a hotel has decided to use hoardings then it shall also finalize about the location and numbers of these. Similarly, for TV, decisions about channels, programmes, and time of shows are taken. These are critical and must match the media habits of the target market. Advertisement through TV will be useless in villages with heavy power cuts. Showing business news on sports channel will not deliver results.

Table 10.1 Media Available for Promotion and their Features

Features	Print Media	Audio Media	Audio-visual Media	Internet
Frequency	From daily to annual	Daily	Repeated in a day	Whenever user wants or surfs
Reach	Large, depending upon circulation	Was very popular and is again reviving with FM channels	Spreading fast	High penetration
Credibility	High, supposed to be trustworthy	High	Low	Medium
Target market	All from villages to cities	Rural and urban	Urban	Urban
Cost	Low	Low	High	Low

Decide Budget of Promotion—At What Cost?

Many of the above decisions may need a review when the firm allocates resources. The above decisions provide what should be done but a marketer may not have the funds for the same. The following methods are used for budgeting.

Objective and task based

A firm decides what ought to be done and what will be the cost of each activity. This becomes the budget for promotion. This is a good approach as funds are allotted objectively.

Per cent of sales method

A per cent of the previous year sales is taken to be the budget for the following year. Usually, industry standard is followed for fixing the quantum of per cent. It is a very easy method but lacks sound judgement. Because if sales go down in a year, more promotion shall be required to boost sales but this method lowers the promotion. And the industry wisdom of following some per cent like 10 or 20 may not be good for every firm. A market leader will need a different budget than small operators.

Competitive parity

The budget is taken to be the same as that of competitors. It is an easy method because the firm is only copying the figures but the problem is that competitors' information may not be correctly available and their goals may be different from those of the marketer.

Affordable method

The marketer decides to spend the affordable amount on promotion. It is an easy but not a good method. The marketer may spend less when more promotion is required.

Develop Control and Feedback System—Has Everything been Done Well?

A firm decides in advance the checks to measure performance of promotion. Yardsticks based on goals as well as mechanism of performance evaluation are developed. These can be subjective such as changes in attitudes, perception; or objective such as sales and profit figures. Feedback is used to improve the promotion plan for the next period. However, for any control system it is very difficult to segregate the impact of different components of promotion mix on the results of promotion.

COMPONENTS OF PROMOTION MIX

Similar to the development of overall communication plan, each component of the mix is planned. The general process of development of these plans follows the same pattern but the details of each component with regard to objectives, applications, tools, and media used are different.

Advertising

Advertising has emerged as an important form of promotion that is used to communicate to a very large audience. It has acquired a very prominent place in tourism with the growth of economies and acceptance of tourism as an activity. In common parlance, it is often equated with promotion.

Developing advertising plan

Advertising plans are developed by carefully integrating them with promotion mix and entail the following decisions.

Decide target market   The target market for advertising is usually large as it allows reach at low cost per buyer. A common message for all makes it highly impersonal. But there are many routine purchases where repetition reinforces the message and stimulates purchases. This can be used for building initial awareness in extensive problem solving situations. The markets for tourism advertising are identified in source countries or locations on the basis of purposes and activities of tour such as pilgrimage, adventure, education, and heritage. Figure 10.8 shows the market identified by Cox and Kings on the basis of monsoon period in India.

Decide goals of advertising   Advertising is commonly used to create awareness, reinforce messages, build and position brands. Goals can also be specified in sales and profit figures. A clear specification directs the efforts towards these goals.

Decide theme, message, and style   Advertising offers large options in this regard. Out of many product and service features, an appropriate combination is chosen for the target market. A destination may use the theme of beauty as well as business to attract both leisure and business segments. Message is prepared on this theme and either emotional, logical, or moral appeal or a combination is used.

Advertising in tourism promotes intangibility and presentation strategies for services can be used for this, as shown in Table 10.2

Fig. 10.8 Target Market of Monsoon Package of Cox and Kings

(*Source*: Cox and Kings, printed with permission)

Table 10.2 Advertising Strategies for (Tourism) Services

Strategy		Description
Physical representation		Show physical elements representing core benefit, for example, hotel located on beach, comfortable seat in aircraft, luxurious rooms
Documentation	System documentation	Document components of service delivery, for example, available conference facilities, number of aircrafts, number of destinations. Fly to Chicago everyday ad by Air India documents system.
	Performance documentation	Document performance benefits, for example, energy saved, guests satisfied, awards received. Singapore Airlines calls itself the most awarded airlines.
	Consumption documentation	Obtain and present customer testimonials, for example, comments in guest books. The use of Simon Jones, a golf pro in Emirates ads is such a case.
Episodes	Service consumption episode	Show customers benefiting from the service consumption, for example, photographs of tourists on tour
	Service performance episode	Note an actual event/service delivery incident, for example, incident reports, guest comment cards
	Service process episode	Write steps of a service process, for example, how to organize a conference
	Case history episode	Present an actual case history of specific events, for example, cases of customer care

Decide media, vehicle, and schedule Any media such as print, audio, audio-visual, or outdoors can be used for advertising but the factors of reach, frequency, impact, and cost are considered before selecting one. Reach is the number of individuals approached by a medium, for example, the number of persons reading a particular newspaper or watching a TV programme. Circulation figures for newspapers and rating points for television are taken to be indicators of reach. Frequency is how often a medium approaches its audience. Newspapers do it daily, TV programmes three or more times in 24 hours, and magazines in a month or less. Impact is deciding if advertisement in one medium has effectively led towards its goals. Inserting advertisements in one newspaper or page may have greater impact than others. Cost is judged in relation to reach, frequency, and impact and the medium giving maximum cost advantage for the same reach, frequency, and impact is chosen.

Scheduling is deciding the pattern of advertisements on time scale. It can influence the impact of advertisement positively if it is timed with the perceptiveness of buyers. In tourism, this is clubbed with holiday seasons and events.

Take the case of the Cricket World Cup. It has a great pull in the Indian market and tour planners advertise heavily just before it.

Decide budget Budget may lead to revision of plans if the costs exceed it. Any of the methods used for promotion budgeting can be used hereto.

Develop control and feedback system It is very essential to know if advertising is achieving its goals. This is done constantly to know if any corrections are needed at any point of time. The effectiveness of advertisement is judged in comparison to its goals. Generally, these include attitudes and sales. Surveys are used to judge the effectiveness for attitudinal impacts. Recognition and recall tests find if the advertisements are noted, recognized, and remembered. Sales analysis is done to find the difference between sales before and after advertising. In all the control methods, it is important to remove the effect of extraneous factors, such as inflation, recessions, counter efforts of competitors, new product in market, etc., to know the real effectiveness.

Public Relations

Public relations is used to promote a firm and its offerings by creating a general goodwill in the market that is transferred to products and services. All the interest groups and general public are target markets for PR activities with which good relations are carefully cultivated. Public relations plan is developed with this market in mind and its goals complement the broad goals of marketing and specific goals of promotion.

Develop PR plan

The following needs to be done to develop a PR plan.

Identify target market of PR The target markets for PR are international and national tourism bodies, general and travel media, governments, tourist forums and groups, environment groups, pressure groups, community, etc. It includes almost everyone whose word matters in shaping the opinion of tourism products.

Identify goals of PR The goals of PR are derived from the goals of promotion and the purpose is to complement that. For example, the Government of India is not only promoting its brand 'Incredible India' through extensive advertisement campaigns but is also building on PR by ensuring that no adverse travel advisories are issued in its major source markets. Similarly, it tries to get positive coverage in media. Some common goals of PR are to fight negative coverage, to build image, to get positive word of mouth, and so on.

Select theme, message, and tools Public relations involve the use of logical and moral approach and messages are prepared based on tools used for it. Tools used for PR can be many and the major ones used in tourism are as follows.

Sponsorships: Sponsoring events shows the involvement of business in social causes and gives exposure to the sponsor along with publicity of the event. Events can range from very large such as Olympics to very small such as sports or cultural events in a school or college. Each gives exposure at different level. A host of events, such as quiz shows, talent shows, games, exhibitions, can be sponsored.

Scholarships: Many organizations give scholarships to students at different levels. This builds the reputation of good corporate citizen for a firm.

Promoting social causes: Social causes, such as safe driving, healthy eating, good public behaviour, women's education, employment generation, maintenance of parks, roads, shelters, and so on, can be supported. Organizations even create infrastructure, such as cyclone shelters, road dividers, for this. Free of cost education or capacity building in tourism can be another initiative in this category.

Media relations: Media is supplied news and features about the firm as people trust media more than advertisements. Even events are organized to create news and get noted. The Indian Premier League (IPL) is an example of how an event is kept vibrant by involving the media actively.

Relations with interest groups: Interest groups, such as suppliers, shareholders, dealers, know an organization better and any negative word from them affects its interests. Liaison is maintained with the concerned interest groups to avoid any negative word.

Familiarization trips: This is an acceptable practice in tourism industry where media personnel are taken for a free tour and all the information is provided to them. Their writings of the tour experiences act as testimonials. Travel writers and food critics are involved in it. This tour can also be given to a group leader who has the potential of bringing group business.

Select media, vehicle, and scheduling Even PR gets reported through media though it is not paid. Selection of the right media gets better value for every penny spent. Tourism programmes on television, articles in travel magazines, travel supplements, etc. are used for PR and maximum coverage is obtained in the holiday season.

Decide budget   The methods for deciding the budget are the same as for promotion in general.

Decide feedback and control system   Feedback can be obtained in terms of positive opinion about the firm and its offers. Sales targets are not used here as these are indirectly achieved.

Sales Promotion

Sales promotion is the use of short-term measures to increase sales. The objective is to introduce short-term interventions that boost sales in the lean period and carry over the effect on future sales, even if these interventions are removed. Sales promotion can be direct and targeted at tourists or indirect that is targeted at intermediaries who push the sales to tourists. The process of developing a plan for sales promotion follows the lines of general plan but the tools used for this need separate discussion.

Sales Promotion Tools

Sales promotion tools can be either for trade promotion or consumer promotion. These are as follows.

Trade promotion tools
These are targeted at middlemen to motivate them to push sales in the market for additional benefits and incentives. The benefits offered are as follows.

Margins   High profit margins are given as motivators. Higher sales will mean higher profits to dealers.

Gifts and incentives   Gifts and incentives in cash, kind, and travel can be given to increase sales. Offers of free tickets, packages, etc. are quite common in the tourism industry.

Consumer promotion tools
Incentives are given to tourists to attract them for sales.

Price discounts and concessions   Prices are reduced in the off season to motivate tourists to take tours. It reduces the effect of seasonality. Sometimes certain costs, such as airport taxes, may be absorbed by the marketers.

Gifts and lotteries   Tourists may be offered assured gifts or limited gifts through lotteries on purchases during a particular period.

Price packs   More benefits can be offered on pre-packaged holidays, thus pushing the sales of the complete bundle.

Product enhancements   More features may be offered at the same price such as welcome drink, additional meal, free pick and drop facility, etc.

One or any combination of the above may be used to get the desired level of sales. However, sales promotion schemes shall not negatively affect the sales in other periods. It is quite possible that tourists wait for discounts before finalizing purchases. It will reduce the revenues of the firm. The decisions for duration of these schemes and quantity of benefits to be passed to the markets are other important aspects of sales promotion. Too long duration or little incentives will not motivate the buyers and too short duration and large incentives may make the buyers suspicious of the marketers' intentions. Market forces develop the acceptable levels of standards after some time.

Development of Sales Promotion Plan

For the development of an effective sales promotion plan, the following process is followed.

Decide target market

Sales promotion uses extra incentives to push sales and its market is usually price sensitive. It involves those tourists who find touring during season expensive or those tourists whose travel is independent of season. Corporate travellers belong to the latter category. These travellers frequently travel for work and travel companies use this market for bulk sales by offering extra incentives.

Decide goals of sales promotion

The main objective of sales promotion is to give spurt to sales in the short run. But the specific goals can be:

- Increase sales in the off season
- Increase sales against competitors' pressures
- Increase sales in the periods of recession
- Increase sales while tourists' preferences are changing
- Increase sales at the decline stage

Decide theme, message, and style

Theme can be according to the type of promotion such as price-offs, packages, free gifts, etc. Message is prepared around the theme and the style can have many options.

Decide media, vehicle, and scheduling

Sales promotion schemes use advertisement to pass the message. So the media used can be radio, TV, Internet, newspapers, and magazines. The scheduling is done just before and during the period of schemes.

Decide budget

The general budgeting approaches of promotion apply here too.

Control and feedback

Control mechanisms are developed around the goals of sales promotion and it is checked if these are achieved or not. Variations are analysed and fed back to decide the goals in future.

Personal Selling

It is person-to-person selling where persuasive efforts are made to convince buyers to make purchases. Compared to other methods it is personal, where message can be presented as per the needs of buyers. It too complements the goals of promotion and is very important in tourism for all institutional sales. The sales between principals or agents and with corporate buyers are made through it. Its costs are high because of more time and efforts included but can be justified by the business and profits generated thereafter.

The process of development of sales plan and personal selling follows the same general steps but understanding its process is important for its effective implementation.

Sales Process

It is the process carried from soliciting customers to making presentations, executing sales, and maintaining customer relations. It follows a systematic approach and involves the following steps.

1. Pre-approach
2. Approach
3. Presentation
4. Meeting objections
5. Closing the talk
6. Follow-up

Pre-approach

At this stage, the salesperson identifies the potential buyers to whom calls shall be made. This has lead generation and selection as its parts.

Lead generation   Leads are the prospective customers. These can be obtained by referrals from the existing clients or by analysing available databases of consumers and identifying those that have profiles similar to the existing customers. The assumption is that there is similarity among buyers.

Lead selection   Identified leads may have suspects in between who need to be eliminated. Leads are classified as hot, warm, and cold. Hot leads have high potential to purchase, warm leads do not show initial enthusiasm but have latent potential, and cold leads do not exhibit any promise. Hot leads are identified for approach and warm leads are watched till the right time or are persuaded persistently.

Collecting information and knowledge about leads   Information about potential buyers is collected regarding their needs, likes, and dislikes. This will help in altering presentations accordingly. This will also help the salesperson in selecting the right time, place, and mood for the buyer. The information about hot leads is obtained from sources such as past purchase history and telephonic interactions.

Approach

This is the greeting and meeting stage. The buyer is to be approached in an acceptable manner. Made up appearance by the salesperson may spoil the ambience. If this goes well, rest of the presentation becomes easy. Selection of right greetings, opening lines, topics of conversation are important here. These are used to create ambience and in no case will become the focus and create diversion from the main topic.

Presentation

This is the time of narration of the product. It includes opening the talk and making presentation.

Opening the talk takes off from approach. It sets the mood for narration. The salesperson begins telling about the product as soon as he/she notices that the buyer is ready to listen. Presentation involves detailing the product features and benefits to customers. The style of presentation is chosen in view of the types of customers and products. It can be canned or fixed where a memorized talk is made. It is used if the product is low priced and does not require much explanation. This saves money as highly qualified manpower is not needed. Travel agencies use this approach through their sales teams who visit potential tourists and make such presentations. Those showing more interest or potential are approached through experienced sales teams for interactive talk. The other styles of presentation are adaptive and consultative selling. In adaptive selling, the initial part of the presentation is structured, and then the salesperson stops for reaction or query from the buyer and again starts with the next part that is participative in nature. This gives opportunity to the buyers to talk between presentations and the talk is adapted to meet the buyers' needs. The talk is prepared in a manner that it includes most of the probable queries and objections. The third style is consultative selling that is highly interactive and customer focussed. Here the buyer is allowed to talk about his/her needs and expectations from the product. This judgement of needs is built into presentation to explain to the buyer how the given product best meets the needs. The buyer can intervene in between with any query that the salesperson answers. Technology is very effective in tourism presentations where films, brochures, and virtual tours make more impact.

All the different styles can give good results under different situations but tourism, being a high-value product, is suited for consultative selling.

Meeting objections

The buyers may have many objections to the information given during a presentation. These may be logical or psychological. The salesperson needs to understand these for a sympathetic and convincing response. For example, if tourists find the package expensive, a solution of financing through banks may be offered along with paperwork to be done by the salesperson. This is a very important stage as good responses from the salesperson persuade buyers to place orders.

Closing the talk

This is the time when the salesperson ends the talk. It is judged by the response of the buyers who either ask for the product or another presentation, or just express disinterest. If sales do not take place in the first presentation but potential is seen, another presentation may be made in future.

Follow-up

Follow-up of sales is very important to maintain long-term relations with buyers and to ensure that the product performs as promised. Sometimes performance can be below par for a lack of knowledge or training on the part of users. It is the case with long distance travel where acquainting tourists with preparation for the tour and culture of the destination will enhance the tour experience.

Developing Personal Selling

Personal selling also needs planning and development and uses the following process.

Decide target market

Personal selling is expensive and time consuming and using it for mass market with low value per sales will not be viable. Therefore, the market for personal selling in tourism contains big customers who purchase in bulk and negotiate terms and conditions. These are corporate buyers such as travel agents, business houses, institutions, group travellers, etc. Door-to-door selling is not yet used in tourism as in consumer goods.

Decide objectives

Personal selling supports the goals of promotion but sets the objectives for the salesperson. Objectives are made specific to help in evaluation and control.

These can be

- sales quota for products (separate for old and new),
- coverage of sales territory,
- profits generated,
- cost effectiveness, and
- participation in sales contests, etc.

Decide theme, message, and style

Talk is developed around themes, in order to improve performance, reduce costs, or better post-sales support. The message is completely structured for canned presentation and loosely for adaptive selling, and none for consultative selling.

Decide aids and scheduling

Aids are very effective in sales presentation. These add to the value of the seller's talk and range from simple pamphlets to compact discs (CDs) and virtual tours.

Sales presentations are scheduled when other factors encourage demand such as holiday season, festivals, fairs, and business meets. On day-to-day basis, the talks are made after taking appointments from buyers.

Budget

Any one of the budgeting methods discussed earlier for the development of promotion plan can be used for personal selling too.

Control and feedback

Control is based on objectives set for sales force. A feedback helps in revising goals for future.

IMPORTANT PROMOTIONAL TOOLS IN TOURISM

A few promotional tools, such as brochures, events, and movies, are more apt for tourism because of their distinct nature.

Brochures

Brochures are popular form of promotion used for direct sales. These are defined as booklets or pamphlets used for sales and promotion. The marketers mail these to the potential buyers or use for personal selling. These create initial interest that can later culminate in purchase under the right circumstances. Mailing is used to keep market aware of the firm's latest offers. A lot of effort goes into designing simple, effective, informative, and attractive brochures. The elements of design and aesthetics are used for this. It can provide detailed information with photographs and testimonials. This has the following advantages.

- It can be targeted more specifically.
- If retained, it will have greater reminder value.
- It can also have secondary or pass-along audience. When a brochure is passed from one person to another, those also read who were not originally or primarily targeted.

Events

Events are organized occasions of significance. These are used to promote and highlight the tourism potential of a destination. Without events, the destination may not garner the necessary exposure.

Attracted by events, tourists visit a place and get to see its attractions that may become popular later.

The following and many more types of events are used for promoting tourism.

International trade fairs

International trade fairs, such as auto, technology, and electronics, bring large number of buyers and sellers to a place, and who are likely to spread the word about the products showcased there.

Cultural fairs

Destination-specific festivals, such as Pushkar fair, Kullu Dussehera, Surajkund craft fair, Goa carnival, bring a large number of tourists to these places.

Cultural events

Cultural events, such as film festivals, dance shows, musical events, laser shows, etc., bring the destination in news.

Historical commemorations

Historical commemorations, such as the 350th anniversary of completion of the Taj Mahal in 2004, attract tourists.

Commercial fairs

Commercial fairs, such as craft fairs, trade fairs, silk *mela*, carpet *mela*, bring a number of people to a place.

Sports events

Sports events, such as the Indian Premier League (IPL), show that tourism can be promoted in smaller cities by organizing such sports events.

> Olympics are used to promote countries and cities on a large scale. India is organizing the Commonwealth Games in 2010 in New Delhi and hopes to promote it for tourism.

Movies

Movies are good tools for tourism promotion where destinations are used as a backdrop for a story. The destination gets noticed as much as the characters for the following reasons.

- Use of high-tech medium and high-profile spokesperson.
- The colours of the movie, sound system, ambience of the theatre, and high profile actors at a tourist place substantially increase recognition.
- Vicarious interaction
- Films allow complete perceptual integration and closing in the minds of viewers.
- It soft sells and does not carry the hard-sell impression of advertising.
- It makes image construction easy. An exposure to short advertising slots or print advertising cannot get attention needed for construction of comprehensive destination image. Movies give the advantage of long exposure.

Many destinations selected and shown in movies became popular among tourists. New Zealand and Australia are places where Indian outbound increased after watching movies such as *Dil Chahta Hai*. All hill stations in India were used as locales in movies before becoming popular among tourists. Even religious tourism gets a boost after a movie or serial on it.

SUMMARY

Tourism promotion is persuasive communication for the target market. It follows the general rules of human communication and applies it to marketing. The goal of promotion is to contribute to marketing goals but it has its specific objectives in terms of attitudes and sales behaviour of the market. Promotion is carried out with the help of different methods and together these are called promotion mix. Advertising, sales promotion, personal selling, and public relations are elements of promotion mix. Advertising is a paid form of non-personal promotion by an identified sponsor. Sales promotion is the use of short-term measures to increase sales. Personal selling is person-to-person selling through presentation and public relation creates goodwill in the market by maintaining relations with different groups. This goodwill gets converted to sales. The marketers

need to decide the composition of promotion mix that depends upon a number of factors such as objectives of promotion, product life cycle, nature of product, nature of market, and competition. The entire promotion plan and each element of promotion are developed by following a systematic approach. It includes the steps of deciding target audience, goals, theme-message style, media-vehicle scheduling, budget, and developing control and feedback system. Sales promotion and public relations need decisions on tools to be used, advertising on types of advertisements, and personal selling on sales approaches. Brochures, events, and movies play a very important role in tourism promotion.

KEY TERMS

Advertising It is a paid form of non-personal communication by an identified sponsor.

Consumer promotion It is a sales promotion for buyers and end-users.

Integrated marketing communication It is the total communication of a firm with its markets.

Leads Potential customers are called leads.

Media Media are the channels used for communicating such as radio, television, newspapers, and magazines.

Message It includes the details of product benefits communicated to buyers.

Personal selling It is one-to-one communication of a marketer with its buyers to promote and sell its products.

Promotion Promotion can be defined as persuasive communication of a marketer with its target market to achieve its marketing objectives.

Promotion mix It is combination of different promotion methods available to a firm and consists of advertising, public relations, personal selling,

and sales promotion.

Prospecting Prospecting is the process of identifying potential customers.

Public relations It is communication of a firm with its different publics to build good relations.

Publicity It is a part of public relations which is a non-paid form of non-personal communication.

Sales promotion Sales promotion includes short-term measures used to increase sales.

Schedule The pattern of promotion on time scale in a medium is called schedule.

Theme Main benefit of the product communicated to markets in a promotion campaign.

Trade promotion Sales promotion for middlemen is called trade promotion.

Vehicle Vehicle is a specific programme or space in a medium such as a film or serial at prime time, sports page, business story, and so on.

EXERCISES

REVIEW QUESTIONS

1. Explain promotion with the help of process of communication.
2. What are the different sources of information for buyers? What is the role of integrated marketing communication in it?
3. What is promotion mix? What are the major factors that influence promotion mix decisions and how?
4. What is promotion plan? How is it developed? Elaborate in the context of personal selling.
5. Explain selling process.

PRACTICE EXERCISES

1. Visit a hotel in your city and find the methods used for maintaining public relations. Are they similar to those discussed in the chapter?
2. Keep a watch on sales promotion schemes of hotels. Note the types of schemes offered. Which schemes are used more often and which less often? Why? Identify the causes.
3. Visit travel agencies to find the extent to which off-season discounts help. Can it be substituted by diversifying markets to balance the fluctuating demand?

PROJECTS

1. Accompany a salesperson going on calls for tour products. Observe carefully and note every aspect. Compare it with the selling process discussed in the chapter. What else have you learned? Prepare a report.
2. Collect different types of tour advertisements. Identify goals, themes, messages, and style in each. Prepare a comparative chart.

REFERENCES

Baker, Julie 2006, May 1, 'Advertising strategies for hospitality service, *Cornell Hotel and Restaurant Administration Quarterly*.

Hummon, David M. 1988, 'Tourist advertising, ritual, and American culture', *The Sociological Quarterly*, vol.29, no.2, pp.179-202.

Holloway, J.C. and R.V. Plant 1988, *Marketing for Tourism,* Pitman, London.

Kotler, Philip, John Bowen, and James Makens 2004, *Marketing for Hospitality and Tourism*, Pearson Education, Delhi.

Kotler Philip 1995, *Marketing Management: Analysis , Planning, Implementation and Control,* Prentice Hall of India, New Delhi.

Majaro, Simon 1995, *The Essence of Marketing*, Prentice Hall of India, New Delhi.

Meidan, Arthur 1984, 'The marketing of tourism', *The Service Industries Journal*, vol.4, no.3, pp.166 -186.

Middleton, V.T.C. 1988, *Marketing in Travel and Tourism*, Heinemann, Oxford.

Mittal, Banwari 1999, 'The advertising of services: Meeting the challenge of intangibility', *Journal of Service Research, ,* vol. 2, no. 1, 1999, pp. 98-116.

Mossberg, Lena 2007, 'Marketing approach to the tourist experience', *Scandinavian Journal of Hospitality and Tourism*, vol.7, no.1, pp.59-74.

Laws, Eric 1995, *Tourist Destination Management*, Routledge, London.

Riley, Roger W. and Carlton S. Van Doren 1992, 'Movies as tourism promotion', *Tourism Management*, vol.13, no.3,pp. 267-274.

Witt, F. Stephen and Luiz Moutinho 1989, *Tourism Marketing and Management Handbook*, Prentice Hall International, Hemel Hempstead, UK.

CASE STUDIES
1. ATITHI DEVO BHAVA

The Ministry of Tourism, Government of India initiated the domestic promotion and publicity including hospitality (DPPH) scheme in 2004, to create general awareness amongst the domestic population about the potential tourist destinations in the country and develop the domestic tourism market in India.

The scheme had four region specific campaigns, namely, (1) North-East campaign, (2) Central India campaign, (3) South India campaign, and (4) Eastern India campaign along with one special Buddhist site campaign.

In addition to the region-specific campaigns, two general campaigns, namely *Atithi Devo Bhava* and 'Indian for India' were also introduced to create a general awareness about tourism amongst the people of the country.

The campaign employed a mix of all the major mass media such as TV, radio, newspaper, and magazine.

Over Rs 25 crore was spent under the DPPH schemes across the two categories of media, namely print and electronics. The details of money spent are as under:

- Over 70 per cent of the total expenditure was on the television media, followed by 20 per cent on the newspaper media. Radio and magazines accounted for 7 per cent.
- Within the television media, the entertainment channels accounted for more than 54 per cent of the total spend, with news channels accounting for 35 per cent. Movie and sports channels did not account for any significant component.
- From a distribution perspective, all India campaigns accounted for 74 per cent of the expenditure.
- About 24 per cent of the total campaign expenditure was spent on *Atithi Devo Bhava* social awareness campaign.

The effectiveness of this campaign was evaluated by MARCH (Marketing Consultancy & Research) that gave the following findings.

Reach of Campaign
- The overall reach amongst the three target segments, namely general public, current tourists, and service providers, was impressive at more than 60 per cent. It was highest (85 per cent) for the service providers segment and lowest (42 per cent) in the general public segment. In the tourist segment, half of the respondents were aware of the campaigns.
- From a specific campaign perspective, the *Atithi Devo Bhava* had the highest reach of 47 per cent followed by the North-East region specific campaign with a reach of 39 per cent.

Efficiency (Ratio of reach to spend)
- Radio and magazines are the most efficient. However, owing to the lesser audience for both these media they can be only used as a supporting media to the TV and newspaper.
- Amongst specific promotion campaigns, the *Atithi Devo Bhava* , the 'Buddhist Site Campaign', and the 'North-East Campaign' were more efficient when compared to the other campaigns. The all India nature of these campaigns leads one to conclude that the regional campaigns are relatively less efficient when compared to all India campaigns.

Impact of Campaign
- Awareness
  The awareness of 62 per cent (overall campaign reach taking all respondent categories into consideration) is significant and reflects positively on the media selection and content. Amongst this group, 37 per cent expressed that they were 'interested'

to take a trip, which is another significant factor in support of the campaign. Further, only 12 per cent confirmed the use of the advertisement information to help 'plan' their trip. It is a very positive sign given the fact that the DPPH campaign was meant to create awareness and did not include information related to planning a trip.

- Social
  Amongst the service provider target, 60 per cent expressed the view that their respect, attitude, and behaviour towards the tourists increased after seeing the promotional campaign *Atithi Devo Bhava*.

- Economic
  Overall at least 50 per cent of the service providers felt that there was some amount of increase in tourist arrivals as a consequence of the DPPH campaign. This in turn had a positive impact on their earnings.
  (*Source*: Study on Evaluation of the scheme 'Domestic Promotion and Publicity including Hospitality (DPPH),' Ministry of Tourism, Government of India.)

DISCUSSION QUESTIONS

1. Was it correct to bundle a number of themes under DPPH?
2. What are the other important criteria on which the campaign could be evaluated?
3. What other important media could have been used?
4. Should the campaign have been prepared with other goals along with awareness?

2. PROMOTING INDIA

India is a large country with varied attractions spread over its vast expanse of thousands of kilometres. Tourists can experience a variety of culture, people, and languages not seen elsewhere. The product India presents challenge when it comes to building brand around a theme. It was as late as 2002 when the Government of India adopted the Incredible India theme. It was taken to be an umbrella brand and within it were included a variety of products, such as, rural tourism, adventure tourism, cultural tourism, business tourism, and so on.

The theme was heavily advertised to create an awareness of brand India. Along with this, efforts have been made on all fronts. India is promoted through overseas offices of Ministry of Tourism. Festivals of India are organized in major markets to showcase its features. Participation is ensured in travel marts. Agreements were made with other countries, the recent ones being with France and Greece to promote India in those countries. India and Greece stressed the importance of interaction between the private stakeholders of the two countries to develop better understanding of the tourism products in India and Greece through participation in tourism fairs and exhibitions.

The Memorandum of Understanding (MOU) with France endeavours to promote tourism co-operation in the area of tourism administrations and management by exchanging expertise, human resource development (HRD), and product development. Both the countries promise to help each other in marketing tourism and will share market research for this purpose. They will also cooperate in the area of trade and tourism investment; travel-related services as well as training programme between the respective private sectors of both the countries.

The government had been so concerned about the shortfall in tourism growth that it proposed the Tourism Promotion Bill, 2002 to have a policy and plan for the promotion of India.

The bill was never passed but indicates the seriousness for promoting India.

DISCUSSION QUESTIONS

1. Explain the promotion methods used for India.
2. Is selling a package similar to marketing a nation?
3. What other strategies do you suggest to promote Indian tourism?

People in Tourism

The human element is an important part of the services marketing mix. In services, such as retailing, banking, or insurance, the service experiences of consumers are made within the built environs with controlled surroundings and managed behaviours. It is not so in tourism, where major experiences are in spaces outside and in the presence of many people. A big part of the behaviour of people is natural and untrained. These spaces and people create settings for the experiences tourists have.

In this chapter, we will discuss people who build tourism experiences and their roles in creating these settings, also called servicescapes, vacationscapes, and tourismscapes. The focus will be on learning the following.

- Encounters in tourism
- Managing tourism experience through people
- Managing people
- Important practices to manage people

INTRODUCTION

People are an important component of the tourism marketing mix. The simultaneity of production and consumption requires active involvement of both sellers and tourists in a tourism experience.

All human elements have been researched and discussed in tourism. Hosts–guests relations, and the informal sector and its manpower are often considered to enhance tour experience. The major problem with the people aspect of tourism is that tourists and sellers understand the importance of their role, but society and indirectly involved sectors do not because tourism is not the only priority for them. As a result, we come across instances where minor irritants, such as behaviour by airport staff or taxi drivers, spoil the whole tour experience.

Tour experiences resulting from these interactions can be understood through encounters and service encounters.

> Tourism experience is gained in external non-controllable environment and all other people present at the destination, such as service providers, residents, group members, and tourists, affect this experience.

ENCOUNTERS

Encounters view marketing in a much broader context rather than a simple economic exchange. Encounters can be explained as human interactions in the economic sphere as peculiar productive processes. Two 'affecting factors' influence the outcomes of these processes. The first is the motivations and intentions of interactants, which direct the use of their resources. Indeed, these can be either addressed to increasing one's personal advantage, even to the detriment of the other, or to benefiting both parties—possibly the other more than oneself. The second factor is the external environment, an expression that includes laws that regulate a branch of economic activity, the prices that prevail in a place and a particular time, and the social characteristics of the meeting place (Gui 2004). An encounter between tourists and a marketer can be productive only if both enter into the relation with a win-win approach and the environment supports their presence. A destination with a hostile local population will not let this to be productive or satisfying.

SERVICE ENCOUNTERS

These are interactions between employees and customers. Employees are products of firms and are used to create more products as experiences. Every encounter should be meaningful and a series of these create relationships with the tourists. A firm can have the following three types of interactions with its buyers.

Encounters

These are one-time relations and it does not matter to the customer who the service provider is. The customer is interested only in good service. There is no attachment either to the brand or the company or the person delivering the service.

Relationship

Relationship is a long-term bond where the buyer identifies with the service providers. A customer may go to a restaurant and ask for the same waiter. After some time they understand each other and develop familiarity. This enhances the service experience.

Relationship with a Brand

The buyer believes in the guarantee of a brand and gets attached to it. Such a person may go to a favoured restaurant without bothering about the service person.

The type of interaction depends upon tactics in service encounters and the service climate. Tactics involve use of emotions with customers. Front line staff is trained in basics of good behaviour. The level of emotions engaged in encounters is decided by how heartfelt or superficial their greetings to the guests are. Service climate is the organizational culture of service-oriented behaviours and passion for service among employees.

Encounters where both employee and customer are emotionally engaged have shown to be more financially effective. To enhance service, encounter approaches, such as human sigma, are being developed on the pattern of six sigma that measures the effect of these service encounters on the financial profitability of a firm.

> Employee and customer engagement is very important in service encounters. Such customers are emotionally attached to the firm and employees are more committed and energized.

SERVICE ENCOUNTER QUALITY

It is often referred to in literature as service quality and includes the following dimensions (Berry and Zeithaml 1988).

1. Tangibles: Physical facilities, equipment, and appearance of personnel
2. Reliability: Ability to perform the promised service dependably and accurately
3. Responsiveness: Willingness to help customers and provide prompt service
4. Assurance: Knowledge and courtesy of employees and their ability to inspire trust and confidence
5. Empathy: Caring, individualized attention the firm provides to its customers

All dimensions involve people. It means that a quality service experience without people is not possible.

MANAGING PEOPLE AND ENCOUNTERS IN TOURISM EXPERIENCE

At the time of the encounter, a tourist's experience is formed by the presence of seven categories of people. These are tourists themselves, service providers, informal sector service providers outside the control of the marketer, residents of the area, other tourists, group members, and facilitators (Fig. 11.1).

Tourists

The level of involvement of tourists in a tour and activities depend upon intangibility, complexity, and flexibility of the tourism product. If a tour activity demands high level of involvement and tourists are not

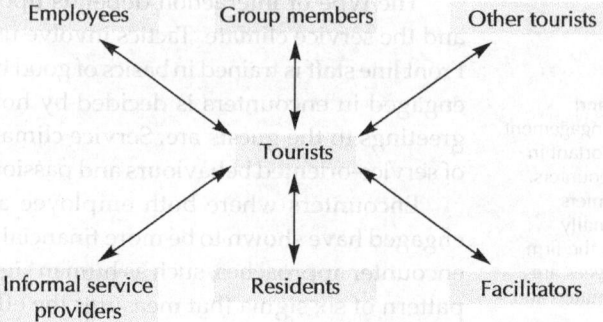

Fig. 11.1 People in Tourism Service Encounters

prepared for it, then it will create dissatisfaction. A tour inclusive of visits to museums and art galleries will dissatisfy tourists who fail to appreciate these. For a firm, it is very important to understand its market segments and their readiness for involvement before marketing tours to them. A low-involved tourist is more suitable for leisure and standard tours than for activity-based customized tours. Table 11.1 shows the relation between different involvement levels and characteristics of a tour.

This clearly indicates that some tours are suited for more involved tourists. Therefore, a marketer should try to find a match between the two. This can be done by managing involvement through preparation as is done in the case of skiing lessons for novices.

Another important factor that affects tour experience is tourist expectations. High expectations often lead to problems in case of non-fulfillment during encounters. Tourists must understand what they want and what is possible. Asking for something which is not possible builds frustration. Gaming (hunting of animals) is not allowed as a tourist activity in natural areas in India and if a tourist insists for it then it will only cause dissatisfaction.

> Tourists need to know the difference between service provision and servility. Marketers need to manage these expectations by telling tourists how much is possible.

Table 11.2 Involvement Level of Tourists versus Tour Features

		Tour Features		
		Intangibility	Complexity	Flexibility
Involvement level	Low	Low	Low	Standard
	Medium	Medium	Medium	Semi-customized
	High	High	High	Customized

Tourists cannot be pampered at the cost of environment or local sensibilities. More realistic expectations can be built through proper promotion to avoid such issues. Strategies used to manage tourists are:

- Building realistic expectations
- Building awareness about their role in the experience
- Training
- Assisting and counselling

Employees of the Firm

Employees form the visible face of the company for tourists. Usually, front line staff that comes in direct contact with tourists for the delivery of services is considered to represent the firm. But for a firm, back-office people who support all front functions are equally important.

Employees are the most controllable element in a service encounter and are also called service agents. Service agents are, in a real sense, the face and voice of the organization. They are routinely required to embody and enact what the organization espouses and to mute any misgivings they may have about the organization and their role. Moreover, when they enter the service role each day, they are typically expected to enact the role professionally and not allow extraneous factors, such as personal problems, to impair their performance. Symbols like uniformed employees are routinely used by firms to convey a certain image to customers as depicted in Fig. 11.2.

Uniformed employees as service agents

Walt Disney Company has built service ethic in its culture and all new recruits are trained in it. They are even made to learn a new language to imbibe the service culture as depicted in Table 11.2.

> Bad food cannot be compensated by good service of a waiter. All employees of a firm need to adopt the firm's service culture in their work, attitude, and actions.

Fig. 11.2 Uniformed employees

Table 11.2 Service Culture at Walt Disney

Common Language	Disney Language
Employees	Cast members
Customers	Guests
Crowd	Audience
Work shift	Performance
Job	Part
Job description	Script
Uniform	Costume
On-duty	Onstage
Off-duty	Backstage

This cultural learning helps in building a service ideology among employees.

Though the overall approach of the management decides the organizational culture but human resource management (HRM) practices purposely focus on building and managing service orientations among employees. Some commonly used HRM practices for managing employees for effective customer interactions are the following.

Managing employees

Managing employees for effective customer interactions involves use of both short-term transactional interventions like counselling and long-term transformational interventions of human-resource practices. Human resource management interventions begin from recruitment and span over complete employee life cycle till exit from the organization. The following practices are specifically used to this effect.

Transactional Interventions

These create awareness among employees about good relations with tourists and assist in building capability for the same.

Building awareness

Employees may not know the effect of service encounters on tourists' experience, firm's bottom line, and on their own selves. As a result, employees provide service by following specified procedures without being involved in them. The service may be good but will lack that extra input. This will create monotony for the employees who repeat the same procedure for every customer. Awareness programmes for the employees can convert their indifference into active involvement.

Training in relationship building

Creating awareness cannot teach the art of relationship building. The next step is to train employees in cultivating relationships with tourists. They should be exposed to dynamics of interpersonal relations and practices to be used for maintaining them. It has to be understood that good relations lead to repeat purchases and higher level of satisfaction.

Training in behavioural flexibility and professionalism

Training in specific and discrete behaviours for service providers, such as smiling, greeting, thanking, and making small talk with customers, can have a profound impact on how customers feel and evaluate the service encounter.

> Firms should employ practices that increase the frequency with which their employees display these desirable behaviours.

Managers should also provide adequate training to foster greater friendliness in service employees. All these behaviours should be used with a high level of professionalism in giving services. A smiling waiter who does not know how to serve cannot satisfy guests and a well-trained waiter without a smile will be as ineffective. A right combination of both will do the needful.

Training for empathy

Employees need to know what it feels to travel for 15 hours before reaching a hotel. Empathy is most demanded by a travel-weary person. A little training can help build an empathetic attitude.

Training in interpersonal skills

The total tourism experience is the result of many little experiences put together. These are assembled at one place through a complex network of human interactions. Interpersonal skills assist in managing these interactions better. An employee in a hotel should be able to find alternate accommodation for overbooked customers and also be able to convince guests to accept the change by putting these skills to use.

Training in non-verbal communication

In a service encounter, a lot is conveyed through silent language. Employees should be exposed to impressions of grooming, greeting, etiquette, and body language. Learning about cross-cultural differences is essential. Tourists can read much in the body language of employees and vice-versa.

Improving physical surroundings to improve performance

Physical surroundings affect the performance of employees. Good working conditions are essential to get the best out of them. Their behaviour should be backed by the systems of the organization.

Transformational Interventions

Human resource management (HRM) practices are used to select people with service aptitude and to develop appropriate behaviours in them through training supported by motivational and other systems. All these efforts are geared towards encouraging effective encounters. Internal marketing is the popular term used for it.

Recruitment and selection

It is the responsibility of the firm to find and hire only those who have the potential to be in the tourism industry. Selection procedures should be able to check personality and technical skills. Tourism is a people-centred industry and people skills are as important as job skills. This is more important in a country with high unemployment, where people apply for the jobs without any liking or temperament.

Training and development

Training can be used as a short-term measure for correcting behaviours, and at the same time can be part of a long-term intervention. It can be integrated in employee development and career planning programmes. Training can cover job as well as people skills. Nowadays soft skills training is accepted as an integral part in the service industry, including tourism.

Motivational plans

> A culture of goodness should be cultivated where employees accept good service as the only way of doing a job. Anything contrary should be abhorred all together.

It is a challenge for the employees to be always at their best behaviour overcoming personal problems, or even issues such as unreasonable demands of customers. Motivation schemes of a firm can encourage employees to always be at their best behaviour. Employee empowerment, decentralized quality control, counselling, and family benefits are instances of such schemes.

Compensation

Compensation should have built-in schemes of rewarding good and professional behaviours. This will reinforce the desired behaviours among all employees.

Cultural control

Cultural control focuses on internalization of values by employees. Here employees regulate their own behaviour rather than being controlled by any external system of checks and balances.

Other Tourists in the Group

> A tourist by himself/herself may be happy with the tour but becomes critical if other group members do not like the tour.

Tourists usually travel in groups that may be small or large. Group members affect a tour experience. The dynamics of groups, like group-think, guides its members.

This is very important in countries where people travel in groups with friends and relatives. The tour managers should study who are in the group and who are its dominant members that shape opinion. The group and its members can be satisfied by encounters liked by dominant members. Tour managers should study the size and composition of its tour groups, and roles of different members therein for effective services.

A group can be managed better by identifying the leaders and maintaining constant communication with them.

Other Tourists at the Service Encounter Scene

Tourism is experienced in an external environment where other tourists are also present. Tourists at a destination interact to share opinions and knowledge, and offer reassurance about their purchase. This information is considered to be objective and experience-based. This interaction changes the frame in which tourists evaluate experience. Now it is not bound by an advertisement or a sales brochure but includes people and their stories. As a result, a satisfied tourist with fulfilled promises starts feeling dissatisfied if told about a better deal by others. This is a challenge for the service providers because other tourists cannot be controlled by them.

Residents

Residents are an important part of a tour experience. They can create an ambience spanning from warm welcome to complete hostility. Friendliness creates environs where locals allow tourists to participate in their activities for closer interaction. This gives a higher level of satisfaction to the tourists. Residents can also turn hostile and hostility ranges between indifference towards tourism to open opposition to the presence of tourists in their areas. Marketers need to play an active role here as they cannot risk taking tourists to unfriendly surroundings.

Local residents oppose tourists if they feel any of the following.

- Tourists are spoiling their environment (it can be cultural or ecological).
- Tourists are responsible for their problems such as high prices, shortage of water, and power.
- They have become outsiders in their homes.
- They do not derive any benefits from tourism.
- Tourists are symbols and opposition to tourists is likely to be noticed fast even to get other issues heard.

Most of these indicate alienation of locals from tourism. To overcome these, approaches like community-based tourism are gaining popularity.

Informal Service Providers

Even in a completely packaged tour, some experiences lie beyond the domain of controlled delivery. A tea shop, a phone booth, laundry, parking, etc. create these experiences. People engaged in these services derive livelihood from the host population and tourists, but may not understand the importance of tourism or effect of their interactions on tourists. These interactions should be included in designing pleasant encounters. Awareness and training programmes can be very effective here. The Ministry of Tourism, Government of India is training taxi drivers, airport staff, and service staff in small eateries to ensure good encounters for tourists at every point.

Facilitators

Many people provide services to tourists as facilitators. These are not controlled by marketers and can have a different set of norms and practices for dealing with customers, as handling tourists is only a small part of their job. But for tourists, interaction with them is an essential component of a tour. Airport staff, police, and the government are such facilitators. Appreciating the value of all these in tour experiences, some states in India, such as Himachal Pradesh, have created tourism police. Airports are being rebuilt for a world-class experience. Officials posted there are asked to be more sensitive to tourists.

> Long clearance time at an airport, indifferent staff, police lacking exposure to tourism culture, difficulties in getting visa and passport, etc. spoil a perfectly packaged tour.

IMPORTANT PRACTICES OF MANAGING PEOPLE AND SERVICE ENCOUNTERS IN TOURISM

The practices of customer relationship management (CRM) to build customer satisfaction and loyalty are gaining acceptance in the tourism industry. Customer relationship management focuses on creating satisfying encounters by managing people. Internal marketing targets employees to get the best out of them. Capacity building programmes are used to fill manpower needs at lower levels and also to create the right aptitude in informal service providers and facilitators.

Customer Relationship Management

Customer relationship management deals with the important dimension of relations between sellers and buyers. It is the result of continuous satisfying encounters. It implies entering into, building, maintaining, and sustaining relations with customers. A firm establishes long-term relations with customers as it is benefiting. Customers too find it advantageous. The benefits of long-term relations are as follows.

Benefits for customers

Customers gain the following benefits from their relations with marketers.

Performance benefits   Receive satisfactory service, gain confidence in purchase, and experience low risk in purchase.

Economic benefits   Special pricing to regular buyers translates into savings for buyers and sellers too are assured of a stable market. Airlines, hotels, and other agencies use frequent customer schemes in different forms to give economic benefits to customers.

Social benefits   Relations build familiarity, recognition, friendship. After some time, both the seller and the buyer understand each other well and it makes choice-making easy.

Benefits for marketers

Marketers get assurance of loyal customer base through the following.

Stable market   Satisfied customers repeat purchase, thus ensuring a regular market.

Profitable customers   Satisfied customers pay more for services increasing profits.

Customer satisfaction   Good relations help marketers perform better, which enhances satisfaction.

The benefits prompt both to stay together. But the marketer needs to sustain this relation using CRM strategies because of competition in the market. Other competitors may also use similar strategies.

CRM as a Process

Customer relationship management is a process where the focus is on customers and use of tools and techniques is secondary. It involves the following steps.

1. Collecting customer information
2. Building customer database
3. Eliciting customer requirements
4. Analysing customer requirements
5. Building requirements into products and services
6. Creating personalized communication
7. Delivering requirements through personalized communication

Collecting customer information

Knowing the customers is the first step to understanding their needs and delivering desired benefits. This begins with collecting information about them. This is obtained from past purchases, databases available in the market, primary surveys, interviews, feedbacks, complaints, and suggestions.

Building customer database

The collected information is organized in a database. A good database will be relational with many interfaces to make retrieval of information easy on different dimensions. Marketers need foresightedness to predict the type of information required in future and provide for the same in the database.

Eliciting customer requirements

From the database, requirements of customers are identified regarding their preferences, buying capacity, tendency to repeat past purchases, desire for novelty, quantity bought, frequency of purchase, and so on. This helps in balancing supplies with demands.

Analysing customer requirements

Customer requirements are analysed to find the reasons behind behaviours. Otherwise the changes in behaviour will be difficult to foresee. For example, brand loyalty may be real where customers like the product, or spurious where customers do not like the product but patronize in the absence of worthwhile substitutes. Similarly, high frequency of purchase may be accompanied with low quantity. It may be because of low disposable income of buyers or past habits. Similar analysis on almost all dimensions of requirements is essential to gain insight in buyers' behaviours.

Building requirements into products and services

Products and services are developed according to requirements of customers. The requirements are translated into benefits that in turn are specified as product features and accompanying services.

Creating personalized communication

A personal communication is developed to convey the products–services offered and associated benefits to deliver satisfaction of requirements. A good offer may not find takers in the market if not communicated well. In such cases, buyers fail to comprehend the suitability of products for their needs.

Delivering requirements through personalized communication

Products and services are offered to the customers through personal communication. At the delivery stage it conveys the suitability of products and at post-purchase stage, reassures buyers about their choices. Small problems, if any, are also sorted by helping in understanding product features and usage.

The above is a continuous process where every exchange adds to the database that is used for furthering knowledge about customers and delivering enhanced satisfaction to enter into a stable relation with customers.

Techniques of CRM

It involves using techniques that help in collaborating with customers and sustain relations.

Focused marketing

Detailed information about buying habits of customers is collected and products are marketed according to buying habits. In tourism industry this is done by maintaining a guest history sheet. Complete details of past purchases of guests and their likes, and dislikes are recorded. On every future purchase, customization is done to best match requirements of the guests. This has given a set of loyal clientele to world famous brands such as Four Seasons hotels, Singapore Airlines, and Disneyland.

Call centres

These are automated response centres where customer queries and complaints are taken. Easy navigation through it will satisfy a customer who will use the same company again and again. A number of queries and complaints are repetitive in nature that can be easily mechanized. In such cases, a route is provided where machines forward the customers' requests to the right desk or person. An example of call centre can be taken from Indian Railways that uses the unique number 139. It can be dialed from anywhere in the country without any standard trunk dialing (STD) code. It gives information about trains, fares, bookings, etc.

Call centres use SMS, fax, and e-mail as value-added services for customers.

Customer services

Customer calls and complaints should be backed by personalized service. It is the backbone of good CRM. All calls or queries are not repetitive in nature. A few always require an open mind and a fresh approach. It is essential to connect customers to a link in the organization that can give individual attention and solution of the problem.

CRM software

This is required to effectively collect and analyse data, maintain call centres and customer service. It makes the job of database management very effective. Organizations have the option of using either ready-made software or getting a customized one developed. Many types of software are available in the market and the choice depends upon usability and cost.

Interactive websites

Travel portals are emerging as new-age usability between tourists and suppliers. These can be opened by pure online firms or by those having offline presence. Websites can be static pages or dynamic where real-time transactions can be executed. An easy to use and trustworthy site enhances customer experience and satisfaction. The importance of such sites is being recognized in the Indian market and firms ranging from railways in public sector to small, standalone private hotels are using these to generate business and build customer satisfaction.

Internal Marketing

It is targeted at internal customers (employees) and markets the concepts and schemes to them to deliver satisfying customer experiences that help in achievement of firm's objectives. Employees are prepared and empowered to deliver quality service. It uses all the concepts of external marketing such as identifying employees segments based on their attitudes towards service, designing training and motivational programmes appropriate for each segment, and controls. The focus of internal marketing is the link between employee behaviour, customer experience, and organizational goals (Fig. 11.3).

Key concepts of internal marketing include the following.

1. The employees must understand that their behaviours and organizational goals are closely related. Goals give the standards of performance and behaviours implement the performance.

2. The link between employee behaviour and customer experience should be clear. This is a major contributor to experience along with other factors.

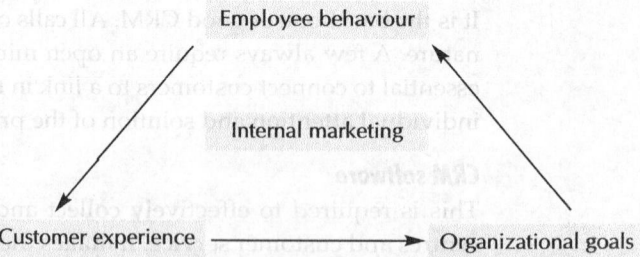

Fig. 11.3 Internal Marketing

3. Customer experience directly links to organizational goals.
4. Continuous efforts should be made for getting right employee behaviour.

Implementing internal marketing

Internal marketing is implemented through the following approach.

1. Segment the employees on the basis of their attitudes and behaviours regarding customer service.
2. Identify the approach suitable for each segment. The common approaches are:

Telling — Employees are explained the importance of expected behviours.

Selling — Importance of behaviours is convincingly told to the employees. Both soft and hard selling can be used for this.

Persuading — Persuasion is used to get desired behaviours from employees. It may involve use of incentives too.

Participating — Employees are made to initiate efforts in regulating their behaviours. Counselling, discussions, and meetings are used for this.

3. Support the employees in right behaviours. This requires interventions for behavioural improvements and using complete human resource management to get expected behaviours. We have already discussed it in detail as part of managing employees.

Capacity Building

Capacity building programmes aim to build skills and aptitude in different categories of people. Their main target is to fill the manpower requirements at lower levels through short-term courses. The unskilled staff already engaged in jobs is also imparted skills for higher productivity. It also includes awareness-building efforts for the host population, the facilitators, and the informal sector.

SUMMARY

People are an important component of a tourism marketing mix. The tourism experience depends upon sellers, tourists, other service providers, residents, and tour group members. Some people understand the importance of tourism but others may not and their behaviours or encounters with tourists might spoil the whole tour experience. Customers can look for one time encounters or relational long-term encounters. In long-term encounters, customers get attached to the service provider or brand. Long-term relations give marketers a brand-loyal market and consumers get good service. The difficulty is created in encounters with other service providers, tour group members, and other tourists at the destination who are not directly concerned with marketing. These too have to be marketed the idea of creating a good service environment.

The main focus of the firm remains its internal environment and it manages its employees and customers for the same. Internal marketing and customer relationship marketing are used to improve it. Internal marketing is marketing the philosophy of the firm to its employees and training them to deliver necessary values. Transactional and transformational interventions are used for this. Transactional

interventions include building awareness, training in relationship building, behavioural flexibility and professionalism, empathy, interpersonal skills, non-verbal communication, and improved physical surroundings. Transformational interventions use recruitment, selections, orientations, etc. to control employee behaviours.

Customer relationship management implies entering into, building, maintaining, and sustaining relations with customers. These improve encounters because both the marketer and the customer gets to know each other better with every transaction.

The improved encounters will create an environment where tourism can be experienced better.

KEY TERMS

Customer relationship management (CRM) It implies entering into, building, maintaining, and sustaining relations with customers.

Employee and customer engagement Engaged employees are more committed and energized, and engaged customers are emotionally attached to a firm.

Internal marketing It is targeted at internal customers (employees) and markets the concepts and schemes to them to deliver satisfying customer experiences that help in achievement of the firm's objectives.

People People constitute the human element in tourist encounters. The main encounters are between tourists and employees of firms but encounters outside the firm are also important.

Service encounter quality It is also called service quality and is judged on features of tangibles, reliability, responsiveness, assurance, and empathy.

Service encounters Encounters at the time of experiencing a tourism service are called service encounters.

Transactional interventions These are short-term interventions in the form of training to employees to improve quality of interactions.

Transformational interventions These focus on improving behaviours of employees in the long run and include human resource management practices of recruitment, training, and cultural control.

EXERCISES

REVIEW QUESTIONS

1. What is the people element of a marketing mix? What is its role in developing marketing strategy in tourism?

2. What is employee and customer engagement? Discuss its role in service experience.

3. What are service encounters? Explain the factors deciding quality of these encounters.

4. What are different categories of people influencing service experience in tourism? Discuss.

5. How are employees managed for effective service encounters?

PRACTICE EXERCISES

1. Survey tourists at your place and find their experiences. Explore their involvement levels. Do you find a link? Present in a brief report.

2. Visit all hotels in your city. Note how you are welcomed at the reception. Are there any noticeable differences in their customer handling? Write your experience in the light of your perception of good service.

PROJECTS

1. Prepare a small questionnaire for management and survey local hotels to find CRM practices used in them. How are these similar to or different from the ones used in the text?

2. Ask tourists in your city the reasons for their preference for specific suppliers. How much is because of CRM? Also find the reasons behind changing suppliers? Is it still CRM? What do you learn about CRM from this exercise? Present in a report.

REFERENCES

Ashforth, E. Blake et al. 2008, 'How service agents manage the person role interface', Group Organization Management, vol. 33, no.1, pp. 5-45.

Gutek, Barbara A., Bennet Cherry et al. 2000, 'Features of service relationships and encounters', Work and Occupations, vol. 27, no.3, pp. 319-351.

Berry, L. L., A. Parasuraman, and V. A. Zeithaml 1988. 'The service-quality puzzle', Business Horizon, 31(5), 35-43.

Bitner, Mary Jo 1992, April, 'The impact of physical surroundings on customers and employees', Journal of Marketing, vol. 56, no. 2, pp. 57-71.

Bitner, Mary Jo et al. 1990, January 'The service encounter: Diagnosing favourable and unfavourable incidents', Journal of Marketing, vol. 54, pp. 71-84.

Collins, Jim and Jerry I. Porras 2002, Built to Last, Harper Business Essentials, New York.

Green, Kenneth W. and Subrata Chakrabarty 2007, 'Organisational Culture of Customer Care: Market Orientation and Service Quality', Int. J. Services and Standards, vol. 3, no.2, pp. 137-153.

Gui, Benedetto 2004 'Exchanges? Encounters! A note on Economics and interpersonal relations', Group Analysis, vol. 37, no.1, pp. 5-15.

Gwinner, Kevin P. et al., 1998, 'Relational benefits in services industries: The customer's perspective', Journal of Academy of Marketing Science, vol. 26, no. 2, pp. 101-114.

Fleming , John H. et al. 2005, July–August, 'Human sigma', Harvard Business Review, pp. 107-114.

Harris, Kim, and Steve Baron 2004, 'Consumer-to-consumer conversations in service settings', Journal of Service Research, vol. 6, no.3, pp. 287-303.

Leo Y. M. Sin et al. 2006, 'The effects of relationship marketing orientation on business performance in the hotel industry', Journal of Hospitality and Tourism Research, vol. 4, pp. 407-426.

Luong, Alexandra 2005, 'Affective service display and customer mood', Journal of Service Research, vol. 8, no. 2, pp. 117-130.

Parasuraman, A. et al. 1985, 'A conceptual model of service quality and its implications for future research', Journal of Marketing, vol. 49, pp. 41-50.

Parasuraman, A. et al. 1988, 'SERVQUAL: A multiple-item scale for measuring consumer perceptions of quality', Journal of Retailing, vol. 64, pp. 12–40.

Parish, J. T. et al. 2008, 'The effect of servicescape on service workers', Journal of Service Research, vol. 10, no. 3, pp. 220-238.

Raajpoot, Nusser 2004, 'Reconceptualizing service encounter quality in a non-western context', Journal of Service Research, vol. 7, no. 2, pp. 181-201.

Yagil, Dana 2001, 'Ingratiation and assertiveness in the service provider—Customer dyad', Journal of Service Research, vol. 3, no. 4, pp. 345-353.

CASE STUDY
HOSTS AND GUESTS

Host and guest relation is a key component in building overall tourism experience. Their attitudes and behaviours towards each other create this experience. It has been observed that some countries have the right type of tourism culture with a welcoming host population, while others can be just the opposite to the extent of being xenophobic. The case of Goa can be taken here, which gets a good number of tourists and has been internationally popular for its friendly culture, but with time, locals are getting alienated and it is reflected in their behaviour. Researches indicate a feeling among local people (despite their involvement) that the gains from tourism are not substantial. There is a growing feeling that large hotels and external groups are cornering the economic benefits, while the local population has to bear the social and environmental burden. There have been instances of locals fighting to prevent major hotel projects, such as the proposed Japanese village at Morjim, and also extension programmes of hotels.

Similarly, tourists from some countries are very sensitive to their hosts and can be very demanding. According to an international survey by Expedia. fr, Chinese, Indians and French are rated as the most obnoxious tourists. Out of 21nationalities, they occupy the twenty first, twentieth, and

nineteenth positions. The criteria used for rating are communication with locals, loud, insensitive to local cultures, etc.

To an extent such perceptions and behaviours are the outcome of cross-cultural differences. Tourism involves meeting of cultures and otherwise acceptable behaviours come as shock in host–guest interactions. For example, the British and the Americans are known to be punctual, whereas Asians have a laidback attitude with respect to time. Similar contrasts can be observed at almost every moment of interaction. The Indian habit of staring is offensive to westerners who want their privacy to be respected.

Overall, a comprehensive awareness programme for both hosts and guests can go a long way in enhancing the tour experience.

(*Source*: time.com, 4 July 2008, Third World Network Features)

DISCUSSION QUESTIONS
1. What makes some countries better hosts than others for tourists?
2. Why are Indian tourists rated low on behaviour?
3. What factors decide the nature of host–guest relations?

CHAPTER 12

Process in Tourism Marketing

LEARNING OBJECTIVES

This chapter deals with the very important aspect of transfer of tourism services to buyers. It begins with the concept of process or service delivery followed by its objectives and benefits. It covers the following elements of services delivery.

- Procedures
- Mechanisms
- Time and cost management
- Balancing capacity and demand

INTRODUCTION

Process is an important element of tourism marketing mix because of the service-intensive nature of tourism. Service as an activity can be defined as a process aimed at creating value for the customer and service marketing, therefore, is to invite customers to understand and use the processes to get maximum value.

A bad experience at airport checkout with unnecessary delays or non-cooperative staff can negate all the good experiences of the tour, making the total experience dissatisfactory. The total tour experience involves a number of services, different methods of services delivery, and a large number of people involved in transfer of these services to the tourists. A right combination of all these is a prerequisite for smooth transfer. A good delivery mechanism will ensure services at the right time, in the right form, at the right place, and in the right manner. Timely flights, quick airport clearance, smooth hotel transfer, and easy hotel procedures are all examples of effective delivery. Individually, each service provider has a different process; however, the tour operator faces a challenge in assembling the heterogeneous processes and giving a unique character to the grouping.

In tourism, delivery of services or the process of transfer of services to tourists plays a significant role in the total tour experience.

The special nature of tourism—particularly the dominance of services, heavy dependence on people, and variety of procedures—makes it imperative that service delivery processes be studied and improved constantly.

PROCESS OF SERVICES TRANSFER AND ITS OBJECTIVES

The process of transfer of services can be viewed as a series of steps from the seller to the buyer, where each step creates value in terms of quality, time, convenience, cost, and experience to the buyer.

When the four Ps of the original marketing mix was extended to seven in case of services, process was listed as an additional element. It involves procedures, task schedules, mechanisms, activities, and routines by which a product or service is delivered to a customer. It is an operating system of workflow activities and their integration. The main objectives of service process are discussed below.

Improved Service Availability

Tourists want the best possible experience and they often blame travel arrangements, even for factors such as bad weather or lack of preparation at their own end. This puts even greater focus on service delivery mechanisms. A great service experience needs to be ensured through proper delivery. For example, tourists may be given a package after discussing weather and other uncontrollable factors, so that they know what may be expected. A little change in process from simply selling to consultative selling changes the mindset and expectations of tourists and also their post-tour satisfaction.

Simplified Delivery

Tourists prefer simple procedures. Filling out a large number of forms and giving too much information can be confusing and cumbersome. This may negatively impact the tour experience. Continuous process improvement through technological advancements and process reengineering is the only way towards simplification. A tour operator has the option of offering his/her services through retail agents, call centres, or websites. Tourists use the option that they believe is the simplest. Multiple options are maintained because different market segments may have different perceptions of simplicity. More choices can be added with time, to cater to demands of every segment and continually move towards ease of use and simplicity on the spectrum.

Flexible and On-demand Delivery

Tourism supplies are real time and may not match demand. For instance, if a 56-seat tourist coach is to begin a city tour at 10 a.m. then 56 tourists must be available. If the number of tourists is less the capacity of the coach will be left underutilized and if more tourists turn up, then some will have to be turned down. Therefore, suitable process should be used to make the supply flexible and balance with demand. In this case, advance booking may solve the problem. A hotel may rent facility part- time if needed and a travel agent can customize packages. Effective process can adjust product elements, prices, benefits, and features according to demand.

Cost-effective

Tourists want savings and prefer avoiding unnecessary expenses.

Optimal product designing and changes in process of delivery lead to substantial amount of savings. For example, direct bookings of hotels and airlines without middlemen have led to significant gains to tourists. Revenue management practices and use of advance bookings at low fares are also proving beneficial.

Guarantee

Faulty processes often ruin the final service or product. A minimum level of service must be guaranteed to the customers and service providers should strive to always exceed it. Lack of response from contact numbers, wrong information, no channels for registering or handling complaints are some instances of a service guarantee going awry.

ELEMENTS OF PROCESS

The building blocks of tourism process or the important elements of service delivery in tourism are:

- Activities and flows
- Procedures
- Mechanisms of transfer
- Time taken in transfer
- Cost of transfer
- Involvement of tourists in transfer

Activities and Flows

A process can be understood with the help its activities and their interrelationships. This process flow can help in identifying bottlenecks or failure areas. Improving these will improve the whole process. Processes can be improved either by setting a standard for each activity and finding the right flows to reach these standards or by continuously upgrading the process against its own benchmarks.

> Quality of service assurance is one of the key contributors to a successful service delivery process.

> An ecotourism destination can improve its processes by adopting a certified system, such as green globe, and following all the steps to maintain its standards. It can also improve by continuously evolving its own processes without using an external certification system.

All activities in a process are important and can be divided into back-end and front-end activities. While front-end activities are visible to tourists, back-end ones are not visible but affect the former. Each activity can be broken down further for in-depth analysis. This may unveil the real problem areas that affect the process. For example, the conversion rate of overbooking can give information about satisfaction among tourists. Waiting lines and crowd at the airport can suggest measures for improvement. Poor sanitation in toilets may emerge as the main factor that spoils the whole tour experience.

Figures 12.1 and 12.2 show activities and flows for handling a travel request and online booking of tickets.

Procedures of Transfer of Services

The procedures for transfer have been adopted from shop floor manufacturing processes and the following three or a combination is used.

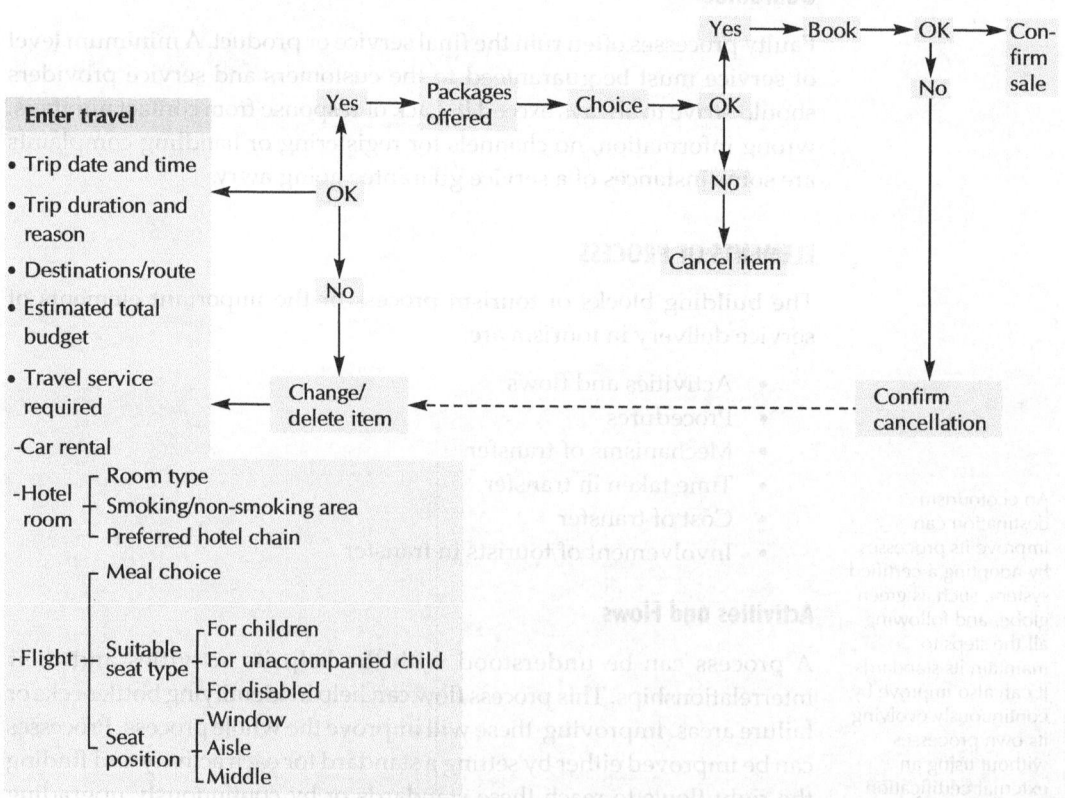

Fig.12.1 Activities and Flows of Handling a Travel Request

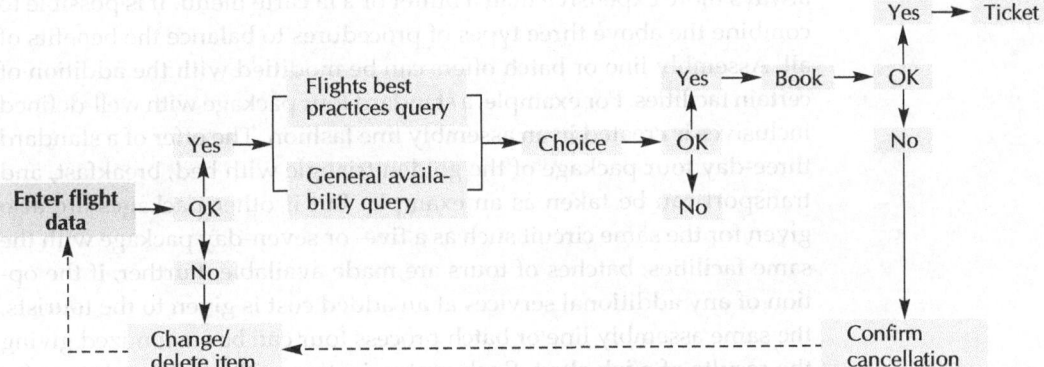

Fig. 12.2 Activities and Flows of Online Booking of Tickets

Assembly line

This includes preparing the tourism offer in a standard form on a continuous basis and selling the same to a line of customers. Fast food restaurants use this process to prepare their popular meals and serve to a queue of customers. 'Mac meal' of McDonald's is one such example. Giving rides to visitors in an amusement park is another instance of an assembly line service transfer procedure.

Batch processing or intermittent operations

This involves preparing a product or service in batches and then selling. Tourism offers are often prepared and sold in batches. These batches often differ on the basis of their constituents. Assembling tour packages for the same circuit but with different facilities/features is a batch process. Here, facilities are what account for variance in batches. This process creates a gap between production and consumption as tour packages are assembled and sold to be used only at a later date.

Job shop

Each offer is prepared as per the requirements of tourists. This procedure makes each offer different from another and is commonly used to serve a niche market. Customized tour packages fall in this category.

Assembly line offers are cost-effective, highly standardized, and uniform, and are suitable for mass marketing. Batch process offers have more variety to meet diverse tastes of tourists. Each batch by itself is uniform but because of variations between batches, overall costs are more than assembly line offers. Job shop develops a tailored product in accordance with needs of customers and consequently proves expensive in absence of economies of scale. A sit-down meal with ordered menu is always more expensive than a buffet or à la carte menu. It is possible to combine the above three types of procedures to balance the benefits of all. Assembly line or batch offers can be modified with the addition of certain facilities. For example, a standard tour package with well-defined inclusives is created in an assembly line fashion. The offer of a standard three-day tour package of the golden triangle with bed, breakfast, and transport can be taken as an example. But if other packages are also given for the same circuit such as a five- or seven-day package with the same facilities, batches of tours are made available. Further, if the option of any additional services at an added cost is given to the tourists, the same assembly line or batch process tour can be customized giving the results of a job shop. Such customization, either for batches or for individual tourists, is more economical as it is created on the already available standard model.

Mechanisms of Transfer

Each firm can decide its own set of mechanisms to transfer services on the basic foundation of action orientation, services to the tourists, effectiveness, and efficiency. The common elements of communication, information, cost, and time are included in mechanisms of delivery. Some crucial elements of tourism service transfer mechanism are as follows.

Communication

Constant communication with tourists helps in incisively piercing their psyche, enabling a service provider to see their fears, wants, and understanding of how it all operates. Fundamental beliefs can be understood and altered only through constant communication.

> Constant communication with tourists and all the parties involved in the delivery process helps in identifying trouble spots and in correcting these before any damage is done.

For example, a tourist may give details of his/her tour needs but the marketer needs to go beyond the basics to fathom the mind and know the subjective goals and fears of the client. This understanding is used to educate tourists before preparing the final blueprint of a tour.

Information and knowledge management

A complete data based management system to give necessary information and advice is required by tourists. They may want to know about travel preparations to be made, shopping tips, special arrangements for enjoying the tour, and so on. Such seemingly trivial information goes a long way in ensuring effective delivery. To meet this need, tour organizations provide standard answers in the form of guidelines and frequently asked questions. This is backed by a query-based system to supply required information. Information and communication technology (ICT) has strongly altered this aspect of service transfer and knowledge dissemination has become very convenient. The challenge is to provide the right knowledge to the right consumers in a timely and economical manner.

Safety

Safety is the prime concern of tourists and any threat or risk can tarnish a good process. It can pertain to hygiene, sanitation, or law and order. Tourists have to be ensured of their safety during a tour. Recently, the Government of India gave guidelines to foreigners to ensure a smooth tourism experience in India. Many tourists avoid going to Kashmir due to safety considerations, despite it having some of the most amazing scenic locales.

This factor becomes even more important when you are targeting masses because safety is one of their foremost and most basic criteria.

Environment management

Services are transferred in an external environment that often affects the perception of process. A satisfying experience in a hotel may not guarantee a repeat visit if the tourist experienced other hiccups such as bad taxi services, poor guides, etc. The whole cluster of services forming the whole tourist experience must fall in place for a good environment.

Services 24 × 7 × 365

Handling tours is a constant process. Tourists may want services anytime. The concept of giving it for 24 hours, 7 days a week, and for 365 days has become an accepted practice. Most tourism sellers have come up with call centres or interactive websites that never stop working.

Complaint handling

Even the best offers and processes may generate complaints on account of subjective evaluation by clients. Marketers here have the responsibility to listen and solve issues in a mature manner. The old dictum 'customer is king' should be followed. An effective complaint handling system helps in settling any grievances. Moreover, complaint analysis also brings out the problem areas that need action. If the same complaint is being received time and again, it implies re-looking into the service and its delivery, rather than simply settling the complaint. This also yields better word of mouth publicity compared to any other mechanism.

Time Taken in Transfer

Time taken in transfer of services is an important issue of delivery and can decide the satisfaction levels of customers. This is a big issue in tourism services because of limited capacity and simultaneous production and consumption. Tourists often come across the following situations concerning time.

Long booking time

Due to limited carrying capacity and huge demand, booking for the use of services is made for a tourist at a time only when supply is available. Although this gives a certainty to the tourists about accessing services at a future date, it dampens the initial enthusiasm and charm.

Queuing and waiting time

Forming queues and waiting at the time and place of consumption can be an uncomfortable experience for customers. But it is used in restaurants, airports, railway stations, and museums.

Overbooking

Supplies are overbooked to ensure full capacity use. Any cancellations are adjusted against overbooking. This exercise is based on estimates of cancellations and overbooked tourists may have to alter travel plans when waiting tickets are not confirmed.

Apart from the above, if procedures are inefficient and slow, the time taken in transferring services will prevent a customer from enjoying a satisfying experience.

Cost of Transfer

Every tourism service transfer costs the firms and the environment. The costs pertaining to service providers are visible as those of infrastructure at the destination, manpower used, facilities, and resources. Indirect and invisible costs are also incurred such as impact on natural resources, environment, society, and culture. Factoring all the costs can provide a true picture of profitability. For example, ecotourism costs more because damage is charged through high pricing to cover future regeneration. If such pricing is not done, hotels or travel agents might earn profits, but the destination as a whole may not.

Involvement of Tourists in Transfer

Tourists may be asked to actively participate in the transfer process to save cost, time, or for a better experience. If a tourist helps with luggage and moves to the room without a bell boy, the cost of transfer is reduced. Giving orders on counters, making payments, and collecting food in fast food outlets help tourists save both time and money. All budget facilities let tourists or customers contribute to the work. Tourists are involved in certain services for enhanced experience as in adventure tourism, voluntary tourism, and ecotourism. A tourist who is well trained in adventure activities will enjoy them better. A tourist who understands ecotourism will contribute more to it than simply paying more for it. Voluntary tourists must be genuinely enthusiastic about the voluntary activities to make meaningful contributions. The involvement of tourists depends upon the nature of services which can be high contact or low contact. Low-contact services are received by tourists without any participation in the design, as in the case of standardized tours. Everything, from places to duration, is fixed and the tourist only experiences it. But in high-contact services, suggestions from tourists are invited to decide every component of the tour. So what the tourist experiences is decided by him/her.

MANAGING PROCESSES IN TOURISM INDUSTRY

Processes in tourism are managed through guidelines and standard operating procedures (SOPs). All recurring, routine, and programmable processes can be managed through SOPs, but for flexible ones guidelines are used for controlling delivery of services. Guidelines are given to tourists, hosts, and service providers for effective delivery. There can be guidelines for protecting heritage, respecting tourists, or caring for the environment (Exhibits 12.1, 12.2, 12.3, and 12.4). Most of these guidelines involve active participation of tourists for effective delivery of services. Tourism service providers use external certification to improve their processes as well as for their market value. All certification systems, such as ECOTEL, Green Globe, and ISO are process guidelines. Further, for efficient delivery of services, process-based software, such as CRS and SAP, are used.

Exhibit 12.1   Guidelines for Foreigners in Himachal Pradesh

1. All foreign tourists visiting the state should seek help of authorized travel agencies only.
2. Foreigners wishing to stay overnight must stay only at authorized guest houses/hotels. They are required by law to fill Form-C and it is the duty of the host to foreigners to supply this information within 24 hours to the concerned police station.
3. In case you are interested in trekking, please move in groups of at least 5 persons and inform the nearest police station of your proposed trekking route. Engage only registered porters/guides while undertaking treks. It is advisable to go for trekking on routes identified for this purpose by the HP Tourism Department and halt at designated camping places only.
4. Please exchange foreign currency only at authorized places.
5. It is safer to carry travellers cheques and a limited amount of cash while touring.
6. All tourists are advised to stay away from drugs and drug dealers and refrain from indulging in any illegal activity.
7. Foreigners who wish to overstay, should contact the nearest Foreigners' Regional Registration Office or the *sadar* police station in the towns.
8. Some areas in Himachal Pradesh have been designated as protected areas and are not open to foreigners without permits.

(*Source:* www.hppolice.nic.in)

Exhibit 12.2 General Guidelines for all Adventure Sports in India

1. Every group taking part in adventure sports must be accompanied by a person designated as a 'leader'.
2. Leaders must possess appropriate qualification and skills as indicated in relevant chapters of this document.
3. Every person joining a group engaged in adventure sports must receive an introductory training and leaders should be satisfied that they have acquired the skills necessary to participate.
4. Leaders should have first aid certification and must be competent to impart first aid training and be able to use stretchers.
5. Leaders should be familiar with search procedures and should brief all group members in these procedures.
6. All group members must be familiar with the use of radios, where these are being used.
7. Leaders should be familiar with helicopter operations, know how to approach a helicopter, and procedures for being winched up and down.
8. Leaders should be proficient in the use of maps and compasses in any weather by day or night.
9. Leaders should be satisfied that all members are medically fit to take part in adventure sports.
10. Leaders should satisfy themselves that equipment to be used meets all safety norms for each adventure sport, all inspections have been carried out as recommended by the manufacturer, and are fit for use.
11. Under no circumstances should the capacity rated by the manufacturer of adventure sports equipment be exceeded, any unauthorized modifications except as additional safety measures be carried out, or sub-standard material used.
12. Information regarding nature of activity, area of operation, period of activity, possible hazards, persons to be contacted in an emergency, and a list of members should be given to the concerned safety and rescue committees.
13. Suitable hand-held devices with graded distress signal capabilities should be made available to adventure tourist groups at suitable prices when available in India.
14. A qualified doctor should be available on call.
15. Communication facilities, such as mobile telephones, walkie talkies, etc., should be available.

(*Source:* www.tourism.gov.in)

Exhibit 12.3 Guidelines for Safety and Security of Foreign Tourists

1. Be wary of strangers.
2. Hire taxis and auto-rickshaws from pre-paid booths. Otherwise, insist on going by the meter. Note the number of taxi/auto-rickshaw.
3. It is safe to travel in India. However, take some precautions such as avoiding isolated places and going out alone late in the night.
4. Avoid developing familiarity with strangers.
5. Use public transportation or transportation hired from approved operators. Do not accept lifts from strangers.
6. Purchase food and drinks from authorized stores only and avoid accepting food/drinks from strangers or co-passengers.
7. Do not open your hotel room without the safety latch.

8. Some parts of India are still traditional and conservative. It is, therefore, advisable to dress appropriately.
9. Dress codes for religious places can include covering your head, being barefoot, and so on.
10. Being from a different country, chances are that you might attract some attention, especially in the smaller towns.
11. It is advisable to use clean toilets available in places such as hotels and restaurants.
12. Drink only bottled water. In restaurants insist that you get a sealed bottle.
13. Eat non-vegetarian food only in good restaurants.

(*Source: The Indian Express*, 18 March 2008)

Exhibit 12.4 Code of Conduct for Ecotourism in Sikkim

1. Conserve Sikkim's natural and cultural heritage.
2. Do not trample high altitude vegetation, do not pick any flowers or medical plants.
3. Do not disturb wildlife or its habitats.
4. Do not allow clients to purchase endangered animal parts or antique cultural artifacts.
5. Support local conservation efforts and income generation activities.
6. Avoid use of fuel wood. Use alternative fuels.
7. Use kerosene, LPG (or other non-wood fuel) for all cooking, heating, lighting including that by staff and porters.
8. Discourage campfire, encourage camp fun.
9. Follow safely rules when carrying, storing, and using kerosene and gas.
10. Leave all camps and trails clean.
11. Separate and properly dispose of litter, burn burnable, bury biodegradable, and carry out all other non-biodegradable materials for deposit at designated trash site or for recycling.
12. Use toilet tents on all treks, set up and use toilets tents in an environmentally sound manner to avoid pollution of water sources (at least 100m away).
13. Use established campsites and kitchen sites, avoid trenching around tents.
14. Practice conservation.
15. Avoid fuel-consumptive menu items such as baked foods and large menu selections.
16. Repackage food into reusable plastic containers to reduce waste.
17. Reduce waste by replacing also.
18. Practice proper hygiene and sanitation.
19. Teach all staff about personal hygiene, sanitary, kitchen, and camp routines.
20. Properly treat drinking water and uncooked vegetables for clients.
21. Dispose of washing and bathing water well away from streams, use biodegradable soaps.
22. Take responsibility for staff and porter welfare.
23. Provide adequate warm clothing, sleeping cover, shoes, snow gear, food for cooking, stoves and fuel, and take care of hired staff.
24. Periodically train staff in first aid, guide responsibilities, sanitation, etc.
25. Properly brief clients before leaving on a trek.
26. Address cultural do's and don'ts, environmentally friendly behaviour, safety precautions, proper dress and respect for local beliefs, people, and religious sites.
27. Plan days for proper altitude acclimatization when ascending, know how to identify and treat high altitude illness, and how to provide emergency rescue.

(*Source:* www.sikkim.nic.in)

Exhibit 12.5 Standard Operating Procedures in Hotels

Buffet Service
- When regular banquet tables are used for buffets, they will be skirted. Buffet tables will be illuminated at night from above or below with dedicated lighting.
- Each buffet set-up will have at least one showpiece or decoration without compromising fire safety.
- Cold dishes will be served and kept cold, and will be placed on the buffet 15 minutes before guest arrival.
- Hot dishes will be kept hot, without drying out.

Dishonoured Reservation
In the event of an overbooking, due to unforeseen stay-over or any other circumstance, and if a room is not available to a customer holding a confirmed reservation (prior to 18:00 hours), or a Guaranteed All Night Reservation, and where it is not possible to upgrade the customer, the Guest Services Manager/FO Manger or Manager On Duty must meet with the customer and
- Explain the circumstances and reason for the situation (i.e., customer staying over)
- Apologize to the guest
- For 6:00 pm (18:00) reservations—The Hotel or Resort must reimburse the customer for the difference, if any, in the first night's lodging rate, if the customer arrives by 6:00 pm.
- For Guaranteed All Night Reservations—Arrange and make offer for the hotel to pay the first night's accommodation, including equivalent accessible accommodation for travellers with disabilities, at another comparable and convenient accommodation facility.
- Reimburse the customer for any reasonable expenses incurred by the change, including transportation and the cost of telephone calls to notify family.
- Refund any advance deposit, in addition to the payments described above.
- Take any additional measures necessary to satisfy the customer if the customer is still not satisfied.
     The General Manager/Manager on Duty is required to personally contact the customer on that night or the following morning by telephone. They must apologize for the situation, and enquire into the customer's satisfaction with the alternate accommodation.
     All turned away customers with guaranteed reservation will receive pick-up arrangements the following day, VIP treatment, a note or call from management and a room upgrade.
     Guests with confirmed but non-guaranteed reservations arriving after deadline will be assisted by Front Office agent or Duty Manager to arrange alternative accommodation. This accommodation will be at the customer's expense.

For routine and repetitive activities SOPs are used. Most hotels have standard processes for carrying out work of different departments, be it front office or food service. Some examples of hotel processes are shown in Exhibit 12.5. Online booking of air tickets is also an example of SOP (Exhibit 12.6).

Exhibit 12.6 Standard Operating Process of Booking a Flight

For online bookings of air tickets, a well-defined process is followed. Similar processes can be followed for trains, hotels, and car rentals if they use well-designed distribution systems.
     The process of booking of flights can be used for finding information about flights before actual booking. It gives information on available flight connections, flight prices, best prices, etc.

Contd

Determining Available Flight Connections
Procedure
1. Choose 'flight'.
   The Flight Request dialog box appears.
2. Enter the place of departure and destination. You can enter the name of a town or an IATA location abbreviation. The system only recognizes towns defined with an IATA location.
3. Enter the departure date. If you also want to choose the return flight now, enter the return flight date.
4. You can also enter a time for the outbound and return flight (optional). Depending on availability, the system lists 15 to 20 flight connections, first direct flights, then indirect flights with stopovers.
5. You can choose outbound and return flights.
6. In the Flight Availability dialog box, the currently available flight connections and flight classes for the required route are displayed. Here, you can choose a flight that is then pre-reserved for a certain period of time and is available for online booking. It also displays information about flight class, flight number, departure location, arrival location, flight duration, priority (F = First, B = Business, E = Economy, S = Special Rate, and waiting list.

Determining the Flight Price
The reservation system cannot deliver prices while you are querying the availability of flights because the flight price depends on the combination of all the flights required for a trip (for example, outbound and return flights).

You, therefore, determine the total flight price after you have completed your flight selection. The flight price is required so that later the ticket can be issued by the travel agency to complete the booking process.

Choosing 'Price' function first calculates the total price of the flights and then displays all the travel services with their prices.

The existence of a price is a prerequisite for issuing a flight ticket. If the system cannot determine a current price you can carry out the price determination at a later date, or use a different booking class and restart the price determination.

Querying Best-price Flight Connections
You can also display the best-price flight connections for the whole trip with the help of best-price function. You can use the best-price query for single flights or when requesting several flights for a trip (this is where you see the advantage of the best-price query). The advantages of this query come from the fact that flight prices are influenced by a number of factors—there is no single fixed price per leg of flight. Influencing parameters are, for example:
- Outward and return flight
- Stopovers or round trips
- Days chosen for the trip
- Duration of stay

The best-price query determines the optimum price for all the flights in a travel plan taking any special booking conditions for individual flights into consideration.

When you use the best-price query, you do not have to start an availability query for each individual flight. You are also guaranteed to find flights for which there is a price in the system. The determination of a price is a prerequisite for issuing the ticket to complete the booking process.

Choose Flight
1. The Flight Request dialog box appears.
2. Enter the place of departure and destination. You can enter the name of a town or an IATA location abbreviation. The system only recognizes towns defined with an IATA location.

Contd

3. Enter the departure date. If you also want to choose the return flight now, enter the return flight date.
4. You can also enter a time for the outbound and return flight.
5. If you do not enter a time, the system determines the cheapest flight of the day.
   If you enter a time, the system determines the cheapest flight for the time given, +/- 2 hours.
6. Choose flight.
   If you require more flights for your trip, repeat steps 1 to 5.
7. Choose best-price flight.
   The Flight Recommendation dialog box appears.
8. Select the required combination and choose 'Continue'.

DEVELOPMENTS IN SERVICE PROCESSES IN TOURISM

Processes are constantly engineered and reengineered for the improvement and the resulting current developments in tourism are as follows.

Elimination of Non-value Adding Steps

In budget airlines, many in-flight services have been dropped that were considered unnecessary for the core flying experience. Most of the fliers do not require food for a three-hour journey and they would rather have savings than food that they do not desire.

Complete service process is critically evaluated to see the contribution of each step to the final experience. Each step is reworked to see how it can be improved or substituted by more effective ones. It leads to elimination of steps that make negligible contribution. For example, passengers are required to report at Indian airports three hours before international flights because of infrastructural limitations. But once this is put in place, this step may be substituted by shorter reporting time.

Self Service

Participation of tourists in the services is becoming acceptable across all sectors. No longer would an agent suggest a suitable flight, rather tourists themselves will search through different websites to check availability of flights and prices and choose one. Same is the case with train bookings and hotel bookings.

Direct Service

Information and communication technology (ICT) has made it easier for the marketers to do away with middlemen and sell directly to buyers. This can be done through call centres and interactive websites. A large number of tourism marketers are venturing into it for its benefits.

Bundling of Services

Tourism services were always sold as packages or bundles but now this is gaining new grounds. Different service providers are joining hands to reward their regular customers by allowing incentives at different points of future purchases. A hotel customer may get the rewards on tour package from the agent or vice-versa. Airline miles are an example of very common premium incentive. Many airline miles can be substituted for discounts in hotels.

Redesign Physical Aspects

Services are always consumed with the help of tangibles. If these tangibles are redesigned, processes too will change. Information and communication technology has dramatically changed the transfer of tourism services whether it is use of computers, websites, or online transactions.

The above developments in the tourism delivery processes have altered the complete look of travel business in a very short time.

CAPACITY-DEMAND MANAGEMENT OF TOURISM SERVICES— USING PROCESSES

Tourism services are marked by on-demand real-time delivery requiring a flexible production system. Managing a perfect match between demand and supply is not possible because of fixed capacity and capacity constraints, fluctuating demand, and simultaneity of production and consumption. This affects the effective delivery of services. In order to tide over this, strategies aimed at processes are used to manage both the capacity and demand.

Managing Capacity/Supplies

Capacities in tourism services are fixed, yet efforts are made to introduce flexibility.

Tie-up with other suppliers or using cluster approach

A hotelier can tie-up with other hotels in the vicinity to accommodate its extra customers. Other hotels can also send their extra guests on reciprocal basis. This arrangement creates a bigger pool of rooms and guests that faces less demand–supply imbalance. Such grouping or cluster approach is used by destinations in a slightly different version where a circuit is promoted to physically distribute tourists to many places. As a result, supplies are not burdened.

Adjustable fixtures

A large hall in a hotel can be used for banqueting, conferences, and meeting rooms by installing movable partitions. Heavy traffic during season can be handled through temporary road diversions and dividers.

Open public spaces can be converted into temporary parking. All these are instances of using adjustable features to increase capacity.

Upgrading Tourists to high-end services

High-end services have low demand than medium or lower-rung services. Any unsold services in this class can be offered to tourists as low price services and 'the resulting emptied capacity of lower class can be allotted to waiting non-confirmed tourists. This will augment the overall capacity. Tourists may be transferred from low-end services to high end- either for free or nominal charges if excess capacity in higher services is available. Indian Airlines has started the scheme of transferring budget class travellers to business class only with the payment of Rs 100 and Indian Railways offer the vacant seats in the higher class to overbooked passengers of lower class without any extra charges.

Fast procedures

Evolving fast procedures can increase the ability of the receptionist or booking clerk to serve more customers. It can be done by simplifying procedures or by training employees in working more efficiently.

Cross-training of employees

Employees can be trained in multiple tasks so that when needed they can be shifted from low-rush areas to high-rush areas. This may not work for technical and specialized jobs but can be used for general jobs where the adhoc team can assist the core team.

Automation

Mechanization of operations increases efficiency and capacity. Tele check-in for flights reduces rush at the airports. Transacting through websites has reduced the jobs of sales agents. Online ticketing systems book tickets as programmed.

Involvement of customers

By involving customers in service transfer, some tasks can be shifted to the customers. For instance, self service in a buffet system does away with the need of a large serving staff. Providing photocopiers and fax machines during meetings and conferences for self operation also does the same.

Using more employees during rush time

Sometimes it is not possible to relocate employees from one area to another either because of heavy rush in all areas or for lack of cross-training. In such a situation, more employees are deputed on part-time basis during rush hours. People who prefer to work part-time are kept on rolls and are called when required. This helps in managing supply at a low cost.

Increasing service areas

If the rush is very heavy, more service areas are created to increase supply. Check-in facility inside the room for reserved bookings is an example. More service stations in banquets also serve the same purpose. For destination management, the case of Ajanta caves shows the way, where tourists are led to caves through three routes of left, right, and centre. This spreads the crowd and creates more capacity. The same strategy is planned for flight check-in at Delhi airport. Once metro gets connected to the airport, passengers boarding from a few metro stations can check-in at the station instead of the airport.

Increasing service hours

If facilities are kept open for a longer period, the tourist rush will spread across the period of time and more tourists can be catered to. This is done in case of support services, such as call centres and websites, that function round the clock. The same has been done for Taj Mahal by opening it for night view. Hotels and restaurants can also use this strategy but within government regulations.

Schedule down time during low-demand period

Organizations need to conduct certain activities that restrain supplies such as repairs, renovation, employee holidays, training programmes, internal meetings, and so on. These should be scheduled during off-season, without disturbing supplies in the high-demand season.

Managing Demand

Some ways to manage demand are discussed below.

Overbooking

Overbooking is a common practice in service industry, where more supplies are sold than capacity because some customers always cancel their plans at the last moment.

More units are sold than available, as some tourists may not turn up. The non-used capacity is allotted to overbooked customers. This method helps in full capacity use. This practice has drawbacks too, as all overbooked customers do not get the supply and may have to return disappointed. The number of overbooking is dependent on the past trend of cancellations or no-shows.

This practice is extensively used in railways, airlines, and hotels.

Queues or waiting line

Services are produced as and when the demand is generated. Customers understand and accept the fact that some time lag will be there. This time lag is used to make customers wait for their turn on the basis of first come, first served. This helps in regulating demand according to the pace of service production. Restaurants use it for allotting tables and serving food. Airlines use it for issuing boarding pass and railways for booking tickets on counters. The caution to be taken with a waiting line is that it should be within the acceptable limits, otherwise tourists will be dissatisfied.

Price discounts and high prices

Temporary reduction of prices by time and quantity can increase demand. Similarly, raising prices during peak season can also diminish demand. Price changes are easily and immediately possible, except for the fear of retaliatory competitive actions. However, this method is regularly and commonly used in the tourism industry.

Change product elements

New demand can be created by introducing new elements in the product. Events can be planned in the lean time to attract tourists. These can be meetings, exhibitions, film festivals, sports, food festivals, shopping fairs, cultural events, and so on. For example, tourists may not visit beaches and hill stations during the rainy season, but events like business meetings can generate additional demand.

Bookings

Bookings put customers in a queue and confirm the availability of the service at a later time. It defers the demand to the period when supply will be available. It is convenient to both the sellers and buyers and is often used as a reservation system in all sectors of the tourism industry.

Non-price incentives for lean period

All buyers may not be price sensitive and changing their demand pattern requires non-price incentives such as unique features and special events during off season. It may be in the form of prizes, surprise gifts, meeting celebrities, and so on.

Extras

Tourists may like a little extra benefit thrown in at the same price. Bundling extras in the same package may appeal in the low-demand season. For example, accommodating a child free of cost with parents can be a big lure. A tour package where taxes are absorbed by the seller is also a big attraction.

　　The above discussion makes it clear that a large number of options are available to marketers to work on both supply and demand sides. A judicious combination or mix of methods can go a long way in balancing capacity and demand.

SUMMARY

Tourism service process or delivery of tourism services involves procedures, task schedules, mechanisms, activities, and routines by which a product or service is delivered to a customer. It is an operating system of workflow activities and their integration.

The main objectives of service delivery are to build improved, simplified, real-time, on demand, guaranteed, cost-effective services.

The process of service delivery includes activities and flows, procedures, mechanisms of transfer, time and cost of transfer, and involvement of tourists in transfer.

The service delivery is managed through guidelines and standard operating procedures (SOPs). Guidelines are for non-recurring processes and SOPs for recurring ones. Both help in effective delivery.

Tourism service delivery has seen many innovations such as on line transfers, mechanization, self-service, direct service, etc.

The biggest problems in tourism processes are the imbalance between capacity and demand. Many methods are adopted to balance the two. To manage supplies or capacity cluster approach, adjustable features, fast procedures, cross-training of employees, automation, using more employees during rush hour, increasing service areas, and increasing service hours are used. On demand side, overbooking, waiting line, price discounts, product mix, bookings, non-price incentives, and extras are used.

Managing delivery effectively can provide a competitive edge to a firm.

KEY TERMS

Booking/reservation Booking/reservation means confirming delivery of services at a future date and time.

Cluster approach A cluster approach involves selling a number of destinations in a geographical area to spread the tourist traffic to a wider area.

Cross-training It is the training of employees in multiple tasks.

Overbooking Booking more than the capacity to hedge against no-shows is called overbooking.

Process of services transfer/delivery of tourism services Tourism service process or delivery of tourism services involves procedures, task schedules, mechanisms, activities, and routines by which a product or service is delivered to customer. It is an operating system of workflow activities and their integration.

Queues Tourists have to wait in queues for their turn to get services.

Standard operating procedure It is a sequence of activities used to carry out a job.

Upselling Selling premium services with low demand to tourists to lessen the burden on more popular services is called up-selling.

EXERCISES

1. Define the concept of process in tourism.
2. What developments are currently taking place in the tourism services delivery?
3. Explain different types of procedures for delivery of services with the help of suitable examples.
4. What are the objectives for reengineering of services?
5. How can capacity be managed to balance with demand?
6. Is it possible to manage demand? How? Explain.

PRACTICE EXERCISES

1. Study the food service process of a restaurant and fast food joint in your city. Prepare a flow diagram of each. Now identify the differences.
2. Try to book an airline ticket through a website. Write the process. What problems did you encounter? Are these because of customer involvement required?
3. Study the travel packages of a local agent and find out how different service mechanisms are built into these.

PROJECTS

1. Make a small survey of tourists and ask for problems in service delivery at different points. Identify the problems arising out of bad processes. Suggest improvements.
2. Prepare the general guidelines for foreign tourists wanting to visit temples in India. Also mention the logic behind each guideline. Now conduct a survey of foreign tourists and ask their opinions about these guidelines. Identify the problems of process now. Rework till you reach a satisfactory stage.

REFERENCES

Curran, James M. et al. 2003, February, 'Intentions to use self-service technologies: A confluence of multiple attitudes', *Journal of Service Research*, vol. 5, no.3, pp. 209-224.

Grönroos, C. 2006, 'Adopting a service logic for marketing', *Journal of Travel Research*, vol. 6, no. 3, pp. 317–333.

Holloway, J.C., and R.V. Plant 1988, *Marketing for Tourism*, Pitman, London.

Kotler Philip 1995, *Marketing Management: Analysis, Planning, Implementation and Control*, Prentice Hall of India, New Delhi.

Kotler, Philip 2003, *Marketing Insights from A to Z: 80 Concepts Every Manager Needs to Know*, John Wiley and Sons, New Jersey.

Kotler, Philip et al. 2004, *Marketing for Hospitality and Tourism*, Pearson Education, Delhi.

Lovelock, Christopher and Jochen Wirtz 2004, *Services Marketing: People, Technology, Strategy*, Pearson Education, Delhi.

Middleton, V.T.C. 1988, *Marketing in Travel and Tourism*, Heinemann, Oxford.

Witt, Stephen F. and Luiz Moutinho 1989, *Tourism Marketing and Management Handbook*, Prentice Hall International, Hemel Hempstead, UK.

Website References

www.asi.nic.in, accessed on 14 April 2010
www.hppolice.nic.in, accessed on 14 April 2010
www.makemytrip.com, accessed on 14 April 2010
www.sikkim.nic.in, accessed on 14 April 2010
www.tourism.gov.in, accessed on 14 April 2010

CASE STUDY

NIGHT VIEWING OF TAJ MAHAL

Taj Mahal is a world famous attraction and is very popular among tourists. Previously, viewing it at night was not allowed for security reasons. But now it is allowed and the detailed guidelines for it are provided by the Archeological Survey of India. These are reproduced below.

'Night viewing of Taj Mahal has been allowed from 28th November, 2004 for five nights in a month including the Full Moon night and two days before and two days after, except Fridays and month of Ramzan as per the order of Hon'ble Supreme Court of India. The night viewing of Taj

Mahal is opened from 8:30 p.m. to 12:30 a.m. in eight batches of 50 persons for half an hour. The visitors of the night viewing of Taj Mahal have to report at Shilpagram complex half an hour in advance of the viewing time. Entry is allowed from the Eastern Gate of the Taj Mahal only after security check near the Eastern gate. The visitors have to keep their luggage at the counter free of cost. No video camera is allowed inside the monument during night viewing.

The night viewing tickets can be purchased from the booking counter located in the office of Archaeological Survey of India, Agra Circle, 22 The Mall, Agra, Uttar Pradesh between 10:00 a.m. to 6:00 p.m. one day in advance of the date of night viewing. The night viewing ticket can be cancelled at the booking counter of ASI at 22 The Mall, Agra on the same date of viewing up to 1:00 p.m. with cancellation charge of 25 per cent of the ticket.

Rate of Night Viewing Ticket: Indian (Adult): Rs 510/-, Foreigner (Adult): Rs 750/-, and Children (3 years to 15 years age): Rs. 500/-.

The full moon dates of the years from 2007 to 2010 are given below. The day of full moon may be subject to minor variation.

Visitors are requested to confirm the dates from the office of the Superintending Archaeologist, Archaeological Survey of India, Agra Circle, 22. (*Source:* www.asi.nic.in)

Month	2007	2008	2009	2010
January	3rd	22nd	11th	30th
February	2nd	21st	9th	28th
March	3rd	21st	11th	30th
April	2nd	20th	12th	28th
May	30th	20th	9th	27th
June	30th	18th	7th	26th
July	30th	18th	7th	26th
August	28th	16th	6th	24rd
September	26th	15th	4th	23rd
October	26th	14th	4th	23rd
November	24th	13th	2nd	21st
December	24th	12th	2nd	21st

DISCUSSION QUESTIONS

1. Do you find the above guidelines sufficient for a good tour experience?

2. What other information would you need?

3. Prepare your own guidelines suggesting improvements in the process of delivering night view of the Taj Mahal.

Physical Evidence

LEARNING OBJECTIVES

In this chapter, you will learn about physical evidence as an element of marketing mix. The focus is on understanding its concept, development of physical evidence in services, its components, and the manager's role in designing these evidences. In this chapter, you will learn about the following.

- Concept and importance of physical evidence
- Functions of physical evidence
- Servicescapes and servuction frameworks
- Components of physical evidence
- Managing evidences in tourism

INTRODUCTION

The intangibility of services hinders pre-purchase evaluation and judgement. Consumers approach services with vague notions and develop beliefs during consumption and post consumption. Intangibility makes service consumption experiential and inseparability makes frequent contacts between supplier and buyers an integral part of this experience. The service experience is facilitated by the environment in which service takes place that has both tangible and intangible elements.

Physical evidence provides strategic advantage to overcome the limitations of intangibility, inseparability, and, to some extent, variability.

CONCEPT OF PHYSICAL EVIDENCE

Physical settings or service settings provide cues to buyers about value of services and are considered physical evidences.

Physical evidence is defined as tangible or material part of service that creates environment in which service is experienced. Terms such as environment, servicescape, atmospherics, services settings, physical settings, and physical surroundings are also used for this. Service businesses depend on it to communicate the features of services and provide cues to the consumers. Services are experiential and do not have any evidence. Evidences here are created through the following means.

Evidences in Delivery of Services

The physical aspects of delivery process are used to create evidences. Both automatic systems and people can be part of it. Tourists can use transport systems of hill stations, such as trolleys, to judge the quality of the place. Trolleys are not used as a common means of travel in India but Timber Trail, a resort in Himachal Pradesh, is popular for its connectivity by trolley. Toy trains in Shimla and Darjeeling create a different image of these places. The design of websites plays an important role as evidence in selling tourism attractions. The use of uniforms by employees also acts as evidence.

Evidences in the Environment Where Service is Experienced

A clean destination, good public utilities for tourists, facilitation through information, and booking counters, and so on, are all part of environmental evidences.

Environment decides the total experience of a service. A tourism environment has locals, other tourists, other industries, and infrastructure and industry players as its major components. Good behaviour of hosts will encourage tourists but antagonism will discourage them. All destinations that have seen opposition of tourists by hosts have also noticed tourists moving to newer areas.

Mata Vaishno Devi shrine in Jammu and Kashmir has seen the growth of tourism with the development of physical environment. Building interiors and exteriors also form similar cues (Fig. 13.1). A customer will judge the quality of a hotel and its services from the building and its decor.

Evidences at Every Other Moment of Encounter

Evidences can be created and used at every point of interaction with the tourists. These can be signage, visiting cards, information brochures, tickets, vouchers, letter pads, and complimentaries and takeaways. A tourist using an airport will have good experience if signage and information is in order. Tourists tend to form the image of the tour based on the state of airports and railway platforms.

ROLE OF PHYSICAL EVIDENCE IN TOURISM

Physical setting or the environment influences the mental make-up of consumers and, subsequently, behaviour.

This is more important in tourism where experience occurs outside the periphery and control of serving organizations. The service environment has both controllable and uncontrollable elements. A good vehicle can be provided but quality of roads cannot controlled. Good indoors in a con-

Fig 13.1 Physical Evidence in Surroundings
(*Photo Courtesy:* Sri Krishna Museum, Kurukshetra)

trollable set up can be offered but poor outdoors can be constraints. The role of physical evidences in tourism is marked by the following features.

1. These are elaborate.
2. These are evaluated to judge products and services.
3. These perform many functions.

Elaborate Physical Evidences

Bitner (1992) places hotels, restaurants, and airlines with other service firms that have complex physical setting in servicescape and performers in both customers and employees. All tourism-related organizations use elaborate evidences because tourists expect the same from a place of leisure and recreation. The expectations are entirely different from other places of business such as post office or bank. Physical evidences in tourism are elaborated to appeal to almost every human sense as shown in Table 13.1.

Sight The place of tour experience and all other places of encounter are made attractive. The exteriors and lobby of the hotels, renovated interiors, plush furnishings, and rooms with a view of the swimming pool or beach, impressive highways, employees in uniforms appeal to the eyes (Fig. 13.2). These impressions build the overall opinion of tour.

Table 13.1 Elaborate Physical Evidences in Tourism

	Airlines	Hotels	Restaurants
Sight	Interiors, uniforms	Interiors, uniforms	Interiors, uniforms
Sound	Music	Music	Music
Smell	Perfumed sprays	Perfumed sprays in rooms, lobby, and so on; clean air and avoiding mixing of food smells in food service areas	Perfumed sprays in rooms, lobby, and so on; clean air and avoiding mixing of food smells in food service areas
Taste	Through quality catering	Through quality catering	Through quality catering
Touch	Soft furnishings	Soft furnishings	Soft/metallic/wooden furnishings

Fig 13.2 Physical Evidence to Appeal to Sight (The Leela Beach Resort, Goa)

Sound The sound of a place adds to its charm. A religious place is expected to have sounds of temple bells, mantras, and prayers. A night club goes well with foot tapping music. A sit-down restaurant will have soothing music. This is created not only by playing the music but by making the music instruments visible.

Smell Smells are associated with moods of people. Every place has its smell depending upon its natural features and maintenance, but smells are created artificially too. It is done in airlines, buses, hotels, and so on. The aroma of fresh roasted coffee in coffee bars prepares customers for an experience even before coffee is ordered. In restaurants too, the smell is managed to increase the appetite of visitors.

Taste It can only be built in eatables and food is an important part of tour experience. Availability of local and international cuisines is an example of using foods and associated tastes for promoting tourism, as food is an important factor in the choice of a destination.

Touch Furnishings are used to appeal to touch. Economy and luxury facilities use this extensively to appeal to different segments of tourists.

With increasing competition in the market, evidences are made more and more elaborate.

Physical Evidence and Behaviours of Tourists

Consumers evaluate and judge servicescapes. Their behaviours are based on judgement of different stimuli present in the servicescapes and the total effect created by such stimuli. A hotel may have a grand entrance, big lobby, restaurant with impressive interiors but poor wash rooms. The overall effect may be negative. The poor washrooms may influence evaluation more than other factors. The effect of physical evidence on the behaviour of tourists is shown in Fig. 13.3.

This shows the effect of physical evidences or service settings on behaviours. It begins with perception of stimuli present in the environment. Stimuli use the basic principles of perception, such as threshold level, differential threshold, figure–ground relation, and contrast, to appeal to the senses. These make stimuli stand out and be noticed. Once picked by the senses, these are organized to find place in the buyers' minds. The stimuli liked by buyers create good mood that trigger purchase or related behaviours, such as positive attitude or intention to purchase. A negative mood can trigger opposite behaviours. For example, a good attraction and beautiful locales create servicescape. The hygiene of the place also adds to it but poor sanitation can trigger non-purchase behaviours. A visit to a temple, such as Akshardham in Delhi or Jagannath in Puri, will show

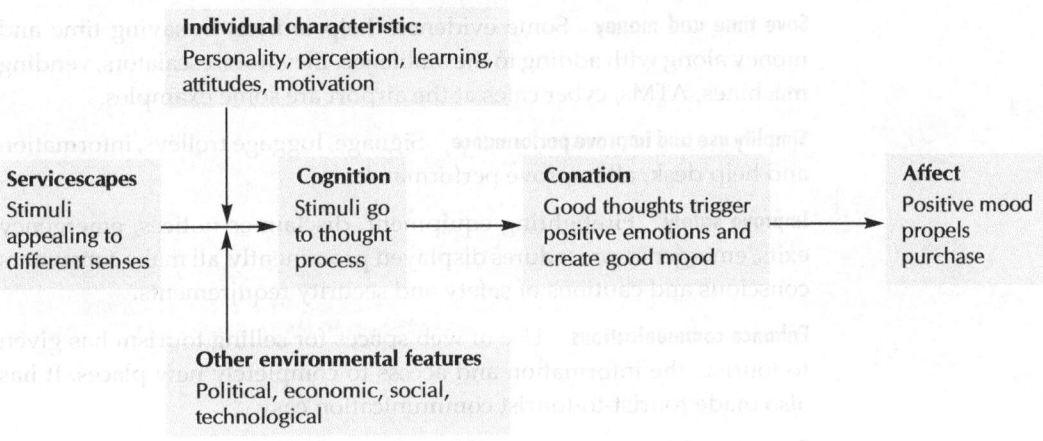

Fig. 13.3 Physical Evidence and Behaviour of Tourists

you how physical evidences are managed differently. When you visit Akshardham Temple, the impressive façade and manicured lawns draw instant attention. The entry to the temple is regulated by visible railings, and the temple has beautiful and intricately carved figurines of Gods on walls. This experience is accentuated by different programmes and shows inside the temple. The whole effect mesmerizes the visitor though it is very different from other temples. Contrary to it the Jagannath Temple has a very different appeal. Its status as a *dham* brings visitors here. The presence of *purohits*, crowd of worshippers praying to deity, distribution of *prasad* creates an entirely different ambience.

> To get the desired behaviours, the physical evidences and stimuli designed should give a coherent and unified message

Functions of Physical Evidence

Physical evidences perform specific functions in tourism and form an integral part of the marketing strategy. The important functions performed by evidences are as follows.

Functional

Airline tickets for information, seats for comfort, interiors for mood creation, good transport for speed and safety, hotel room for relaxation, phones for communication, etc., are cases of evidences that create and enhance the functional value.

Evidences create the following functional utilities for tourists and firms both.

Enhance competitiveness Faster aircrafts, good websites, and modern hotels make business competitive on the basis of performance and costs. Their visibility also attracts tourists.

Save time and money Some evidences help tourists in saving time and money along with adding to the ambience. Elevators, escalators, vending machines, ATMs, cyber cafes at the airport are some examples.

Simplify use and improve performance Signage, luggage trolleys, information and help desk, all improve performance.

Improve safety Firefighting equipment, disclaimer notices, emergency exits, emergency procedures displayed prominently, all make consumers conscious and cautious of safety and security requirements.

Enhance communications Use of web spaces for selling tourism has given to tourists the information and access to completely new places. It has also made tourist-to-tourist communication easy.

Preserve tourist resources Satellite imaging systems are used to map pressure of tourists' movement on natural resources. Pollution levels can also be measured effectively with its help. This information can be used to preserve tourist resources better.

Cultural

Physical evidences are culturally perceived. An evidence may be valued at one place but not at another. The comfort features of a tour are highlighted through evidences for luxury tours and premium markets but not for economy markets. The decor, layout, music, and colour of attraction differ for an economy and luxury hotel or aircraft. Food offered also depends on the culture of tourists and host country.

The attractions too have cultural connotations. For example, giraffe or long-necked women of Padung tribe are displayed as tourist attraction in Thailand, while people in some parts of the world consider it in bad taste and akin to human zoo. The same is applicable to slum and sex tourism. A few may promote it but others may consider it voyeuristic.

It is imperative to use physical evidences in a culturally sensitive manner so that these become much more meaningful.

Personal

Tourists may require certain evidences for purely personal preferences. Location of hotel room, type of decor inside, type of vehicle or seat in train, all fall in this category. Hotels maintain guest history sheet to offer these evidences to guests. They know the type of flowers, wine, or chocolate liked by the guest and offer the same.

Structural

Physical evidences are designed to achieve different objectives of organizations. A heritage property must maintain its look and character to be

Pilgrimage centres cannot allow any evidences such as liquor or meat shops in proximity as they disturb the sanctity of place.

called a heritage attraction. National parks must arrange for the safety of animals and allow restricted access to visitors.

Tourist places should offer sufficient parking. Even the hilly areas that are short of open spaces provide parking on the top of buildings. Star category hotels in India create many evidences, such as swimming pools, to meet the gradation requirements of the Ministry of Tourism. Motels give garage, parking, and fuel station facilities to the motoring public.

Social

Evidences set the social phenomenon. The layout and decor of a restaurant will decide if it will give a quiet or an exciting experience. The joints frequented by families are different from those preferred by couples or for business meets. Providing for joy rides and shopping arcade gives a different character to a hotel. A marketer shall keep in mind its target market and provide the right social ambience.

All the above roles are built in the evidences to make these more valuable for tourists.

SERVICESCAPES AND SERVUCTION

Physical evidences have been discussed as servicescapes, servuction, service framework, and so on by experts in services marketing. A discussion of servicescapes and servuction will help in understanding this better.

Servicescapes

Bitner used the term servicescapes for the environment in which the service is assembled and seller and customer interact, combined with tangible commodities that facilitate the performance or communication of the service. The servicescapes model (Fig. 13.4) investigates the role of physical surroundings in service settings and describes how the built environment affects both consumers and employees in service organizations.

It models the relationship between environmental dimensions and consumer as well as employee behaviour. Environmental dimensions include ambient conditions (temperature, air quality, noise, music, odour), space/function (layout, equipment, furnishing), and signs, symbols and artifacts (signage, personal artifacts, style of decor). Consumer and employee internal response to the perceived servicescape is considered as cognitive, emotional, and physiological response. Consumer and employee response also affect social interaction between and amongst consumers and employees during the consumption process. The servicescape must encourage target customers to enter the service environment in the first place, and to retain them subsequently. Bitner et al. (1990) discuss

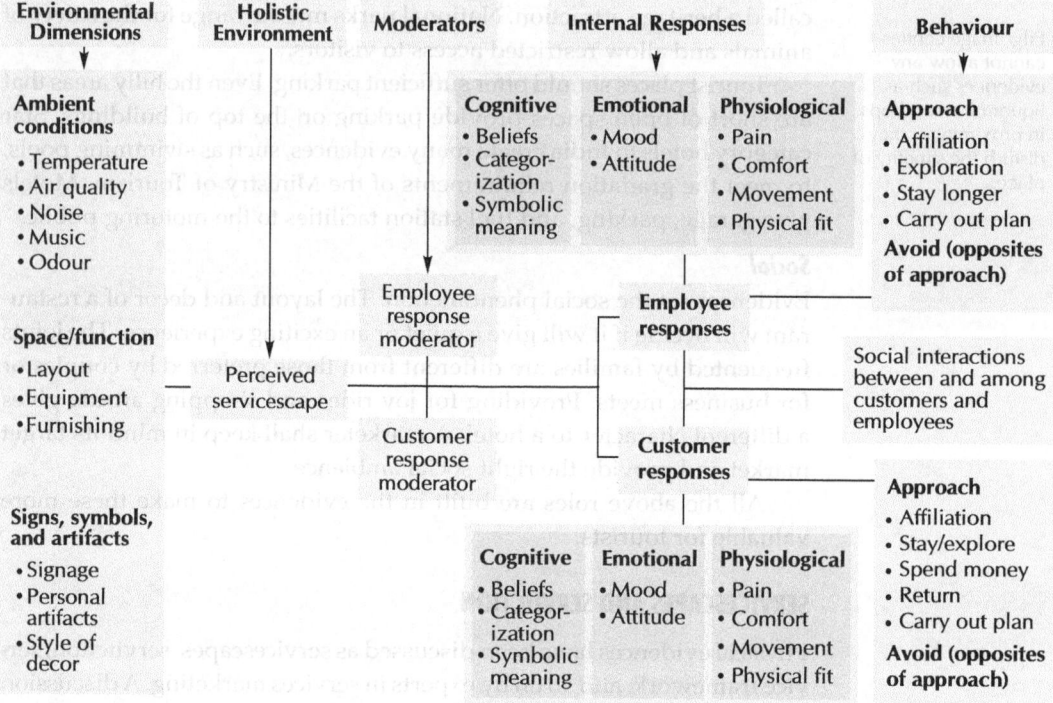

Fig. 13.4 Servicescapes Framework of User–Environment Relationship in Service Organizations (*Source:* Bitner 1992)

'approach behaviour' as involving such responses as physically moving customers towards exploring an unfamiliar environment, affiliating with others in the environment through eye contact, and performing a large number of tasks within the environment. Avoidance behaviour includes an opposite set of responses. The likelihood of approach behaviour is directly linked to the two dimensions of pleasure and arousal, with stimulating and pleasing environment being most likely to attract customers.

Brightly lit window displays, a prominent and open front door, and front-of-house greeting staff are typical actions designed to induce approach. A door which is difficult to find or difficult to open is more likely to achieve the opposite effect. After entering the service production system, the servicescape must be efficient and effective for the service provider in securing the customers' cooperation in the production system. Clearly explained roles for the customer, expressed in a friendly way, will facilitate this process of compliance. The ambience of the environment, such as lighting, floor plan, and signposts, contribute to the servicescape. The physical aspects of the

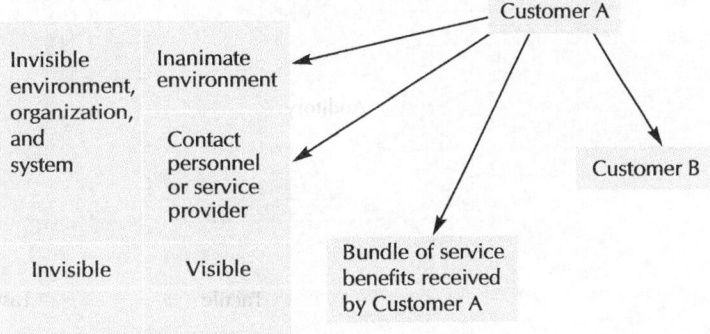

Fig. 13.5 Servuction Model
(*Source:* Langeard and Eiglier 1987)

environment are brought to life by the actions of employees, for example, staff could be at hand to help a customer who gets lost in the service process.

Servuction Model

The servuction model, developed by Eiglier and Langeard (1987), emphasizes experiential aspects of service consumption and is based on the idea of organizations providing consumers with complex bundles of benefits (Fig.13.5).

It is 'used to illustrate the factors that influence the service experience, including those that are visible to the consumer and those that are not'. The servuction model consists of the firm's servicescape, contact personnel/ service providers, other customers, invisible organizations and systems.

The service features provided by an organization providing the service are divided into two parts: visible and invisible. The visible part consists of the physical environment within which the service experience occurs, and the service providers or contact personnel who interact with the consumer during the service experience. The visible part of the organization is supported by the invisible part, comprising the support infrastructure which enables the visible part of the organization to function. The model has other consumers, with whom the original consumer may interact within the system. This is important, because in many service encounters, such as tourism and shopping, the actions of fellow consumers can contribute greatly to the overall encounter.

COMPONENTS OF PHYSICAL EVIDENCE

A servicescape is composed of many elements. These elements translate into specific environmental cues. When an individual perceives these

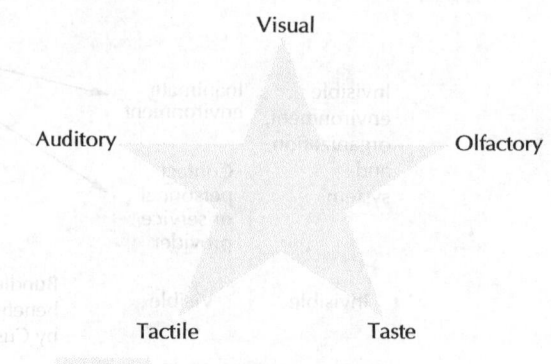

Fig. 13.6 Components of Physical Evidence

specific cues through his or her sensory system, that person is essentially forming a specific mental image. The physical evidences can be created to be picked by the human senses and its components are shown in Fig. 13.6.

Visual component

This appeals to eyes and includes colour, lighting, space and function, personal artifacts and plants, and layout and design. A tourist is able to tell whether a restaurant serves fast food or sit-down meals just by looking at the set-up. Types of walls, height of buildings, furniture arrangement, and lighting create an image. Use of green colour is encouraged in buildings by the Himachal Pradesh government and in national parks in India. This does not make these eco-friendly but the surroundings coordinate well together and is soothing to the eyes.

Auditory component

The sound of the place is very important. Tourists do not expect the noise of a city in a national park. The natural sounds of rainfall, birds, waterfalls, wind, trees create a completely different feel. Religious place must have the sound of *bhajans* and temple bells and these add to the appeal of temples. Discotheques and night clubs need fast paced music.

Olfactory component

The smells of places too create evidences. These are created by natural factors, such as vegetation and climate, but can be artificially created in closed spaces. Aircrafts and train compartments are sprayed with lemon, rose, and lavender fragrances. Each creates a different mood. Cleanliness of a destination also helps in managing smells.

Tactile component

The sense of touch needs evidences. Comfort factor cannot be attached to hard iron or wood furniture. The decor can range from soft and cushy to hard. Curtains, wall textures, furniture, carpets, temperature, etc., help in creating the right evidence as per the needs of target markets.

Taste component
This may not be used everywhere but is an essential part of food. Food festivals use this as an attraction, be it Thai, Chinese, Indian or Continental.

All these evidences can be intelligently combined for a good tour experience.

BUILDING PHYSICAL EVIDENCES
We understand that physical evidences affect behaviour. We also know the components of these evidences and the next stage is to build appropriate evidences. The following process can be used for this.

Recognize the strategic impact of physical evidence
This is one element of marketing mix and its importance depends upon the type of service. It should be understood how important it is in the total marketing plan for the given tourism service.

Blueprint the physical evidence of service
Blueprinting is flowcharting a service operation. Development of complete blueprint to find where and how physical evidences are present clarifies their role better. This also helps in managing each evidence well.

Clarify strategic roles of the servicescape
Servicescape can perform a number of roles. A proper analysis will segregate strategic ones from routine. Focus on these will give edge to the firm. For example, developing countries have understood that modernization of airports is essential to attract tourists. India has already done it at Bangalore and Hyderabad.

Assess and identify physical evidence opportunities
Blueprinting may also bring out areas where no evidences are used at present but an opportunity exists to create new. For example, many hotels create water channels in lobbies to give a natural feel to interiors.

Update and modernize the evidence
This will increase the value of evidences in the eyes of tourists. This is the reason that hotels go for renovation, airlines change interiors of crafts, and uniforms are given a complete makeover.

SUMMARY

Physical evidences are an important part of tourism experience similar to any other service experience. Physical evidence is defined as tangible or material part of service. It may lie in the service itself or in the environment of services. Since the service component of tourism is not physically represented, it is substantiated by external environmental evidences. The importance of evidences can be understood with the help of servicescapes and servuction model. Both highlight that physical elements influence the psyche of the consumers and finally their buying behaviours. These are useful for their functional, cultural, personal, and structural value. In functional role, evidences create utilities of competitiveness, time, money, communication. These are combined with culture to provide the right meaning to tourism experiences and both host and guest cultures play important roles in it. Personal function is performed by meeting personal requirements of tourists such as a preferred welcome drink. Structural function support goals of organizations, such as, the use of solar power in eco-hotels. The importance of physical evidences has been brought out by servicescapes framework and servuction model. Both discuss the effect of physical surroundings on buyers.

The components of physical evidences appeal primarily to human senses of sight, touch, smell and in some cases to sound and taste as well. Evidences can be built by following a systematic process. The identification of role of evidences, blueprinting, identifying additional scope in it is very important.

KEY TERMS

Blueprinting Blueprinting is flowcharting a service operation to find where and how physical evidences are present.

Physical evidence It is defined as tangible or material part of service. It may lie in the service itself or in the environment of services.

Servicescape It is defined as the environment in which the service is assembled and seller and customer interact, combined with tangible commodities that facilitate performance or communication of the service.

Servuction It is production of services and consists of firm's servicescape, contact personnel/service providers, other customers, invisible organizations and systems.

EXERCISES

REVIEW QUESTIONS

1. What are physical evidences? How do these influence evaluation of tourism offers?
2. Explain servicescapes framework and discuss the role of physical evidences with its help.
3. What is the role of physical evidence according to the servuction model?
4. Explain the process of building physical evidences.

PRACTICE EXERCISES

1. Visit a few places and note the details of physical evidences. Prepare a report about similarities and differences in evidences.
2. Conduct a survey of tourists and identify important evidences for them. Are these similar to those discussed in the chapter? What additional evidences do you identify?

1. Compare the physical evidences of luxury and budget hotels and prepare a report.
2. Read the classification guidelines of hotels by the Ministry of Tourism, Government of India. Prepare a table of evidences required for different categories. Explain the reasons for the differences.
3. Ramayana has been declared intangible heritage by UNESCO. What evidences can be created and used to make places associated to it as attractions for tourists?

REFERENCES

Bitner, Mary Jo 1992, 'Servicescapes: The impact of physical surroundings on customers and employees', *Journal of Marketing,* vol.56, no. 2, pp. 57-71.

Bitner, Mary Jo et al. 1994, October, 'Critical service encounters: The employee's viewpoint', *Journal of Marketing,* vol.58, pp. 95-106.

Bitner, Mary Jo, Bernard H. Booms, and Lois A. Mohr 1990, April, 'Evaluating service encounters: The effects of physical surroundings and employee responses', *Journal of Marketing,* vol.54, pp. 69-82.

Kotler, Philip, John Bowen, James Makens 2004, *Marketing for Hospitality and Tourism,* Pearson Education, Delhi, India.

Langeard, Eric. and Pierre Eiglier 1987, *Servuction,* Mc Graw-Hill, Paris.

Lin, Ingrid Y. 2004, 'Evaluating a servicescape: The effect of cognition and emotion', *International Journal of Hospitality Management,* vol.23, pp.163–178.

Lovelock, Christopher and Jochen Wirtz. 2004, *Services Marketing: People, Technology, Strategy,* Pearson Education, Delhi, India.

Mossberg, Lena 2007, 'A marketing approach to the tourist experience', *Scandinavian Journal of Hospitality and Tourism,* vol.7, no.1, pp.59-74.

Parish, Janet Turner , Leonard L. Berry and Shun Yin Lam 2008. 'The effect of the servicescape on service workers', *Journal of Service Research,* vol.10, no. 3, pp.220-238.

Zeithaml, A. Valarie, Mary Jo Bitner 1996, *Services Marketing,* The McGraw Hill Companies Inc., Singapore.

CASE STUDY

MAHABHARATA AND PHYSICAL EVIDENCE

Kurukshetra is a religious town located in Haryana. The place is associated with the Mahabharata war and discourse of Gita. It is mentioned in scriptures for its high religious value and gets a large number of pilgrims during solar eclipses for holy bath in its sacred tanks.

Till the early 1990s it was not getting a regular stream of visitors. Many reasons were cited for this. And the main was absence of any tangible archaeological evidences for Mahabharata and Gita. Tourists who were coming here had nothing to see except hear stories of the intangible heritage. The later development works at this place created three main attractions.

- Shri Krishna Museum in 1991 (Fig 13.7): The theme is Shri Krishna and houses a number of paintings.
- Science Panorama (Fig 13.8): Depicts 18 days of Mahabharata war in 3-D painting
- Light and sound show (Fig 13.9): Hosted daily on Mahabharata war theme

All the above additions created tangible evidences for core attraction. Improvements were also made in the infrastructure and facilities such as roads, lights, accommodation, parks, cleanliness, and so on. Subsequently, the city of Kurukshetra started getting a regular stream of visitors.

Fig 13.7 Shri Krishna Museum, Kurukshetra

(*Photo Courtesy:* Sri Krishna Museum, Kurukshetra)

Fig 13.8 Science Panorama

(*Photo Courtesy:* Sri Krishna Museum, Kurukshetra)

Fig 13.9 Light and Sound Show

(*Photo Courtesy:* Sri Krishna Museum, Kurukshetra)

DISCUSSION QUESTIONS

1. Can intangible heritages be marketed by themselves or is physical evidence an essential prerequisite.

2. What other evidences can you think about Kurukshetra?

3. Was it possible to increase the tourist traffic without such tangibilization?

CHAPTER 14

Market Competition and Competitive Tourism Marketing Strategies

LEARNING OBJECTIVES

Marketing strategies are used to get the best fit with external environment and involve making adjustments with environmental forces. Competition is a major factor in the environment of a firm that leads to choices and good value for buyers. It pushes marketers to rethink and redevelop their goals and offers, often triggering cut-throat competition among them. The heat of competition can be felt in the Indian tourism industry that has seen many developments since 2002, when the tourism policy was declared. It has matured and the scene is filled with a large number of players engaged in marketing warfare. Companies are planning their strategies with focus on competition.

In this chapter, we will explore how firms assess and meet competition. The focus will be on the following.

• Competitive advantages in market places
• Relative competitive positions of firms
• Analysis and understanding of competition
• Competitive marketing strategies

INTRODUCTION

Indian tourism market is getting competitive and is offering a wide choice to tourists, be it selection of a hotel or transport. A tourist can choose among airlines, railways, or road transport for travelling and youth hostels, budget hotels, or star hotels for accomodation. Due to competition the domains of different operators have begun to overlap. Hotels are no longer competing among themselves but are losing market to airlines that fly guests in and out of a city on the same day. Railways are reducing prices to win back the share lost to budget airlines. Travel agents are facing competition from online businesses where principals are directly contacting tourists. Much more is yet to come. These and many other developments require a thorough assessment of market competition and adoption of suitable marketing strategies. This is done by understanding competition, its dynamics, nature of competitors, relative competitive position of a firm, and strategic options available.

UNDERSTAND COMPETITION

Competitive strategies are developed to respond to changes in the market resulting from competition and to counter any advantages that other competitors might get with change in external environment. For example, the online travel companies got an edge in the market after the year 2000 with the laying of fibre optics network in the country, reduced prices of computers, and increased incomes. Prior to that, online companies were not thought of as a challenge. A framework for understanding competition is presented in Fig. 14.1.

> The challenge of competition can be met only after understanding its source, dynamics, nature, goals, competitive strategies, and capabilities.

Source of Competition

Competition for a firm goes beyond similar firms and Michael E. Porter has termed it as extended rivalry. He has listed five forces that drive industry competition and these include buyers and suppliers as well (Fig. 14.2).

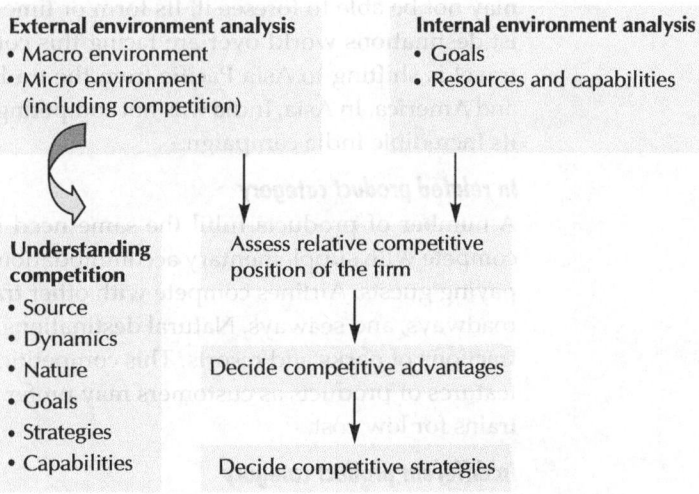

Fig. 14.1 Framework for Understanding Competition

Fig. 14.2 Forces Driving Industry Competition
(*Source:* Porter 1980)

A firm can face competition on many fronts. These are discussed below.

In the same product category

A hotel, travel agent, or other service providers will always face competition where each tries to outdo others in rendering benefits to tourists. It can be a better service, lower prices, or use of advanced technology for improved efficiencies. Every marketer is aware of this competition but may not be able to foresee it. Its form or time may not be known. Tourist destinations world over are facing this competition as international travel is shifting to Asia Pacific from the traditional markets of Europe and America. In Asia, India was not competing effectively till it launched its Incredible India campaign.

In related product category

A number of products fulfil the same need in different forms. Hotels compete with supplementary accommodation such as guest houses and paying guests. Airlines compete with other transports such as railways, roadways, and seaways. Natural destinations compete with artificial attractions of parks and resorts. This competition exists among dissimilar features of products as customers may prefer airlines for fast travel and trains for low cost.

In different product category

A different product may offer a substitute to tourists. Cruise liners offer a complete experience—travel, accommodation, and attraction—thus weaning tourists away from hotels, other modes of transport, and attractions. The growing popularity of fully furnished mobile units, such as roatels and trains, are also examples of substitutes.

In unrelated product categories satisfying similar needs

Completely different products can meet the same basic need. The need for recreation is met by a good movie, sports, or a tour. Weekend travel may be compromised for an Indian Premier League (IPL) match on television. Online participation in puja in temples may lead to deferred religious visits. Virtual tours may pose another threat.

In unrelated product categories satisfying different needs

Marketers compete for the same disposable income of consumers. To an extent their marketing strategies and promotion of their services influence the use of this money. In times of inflation, discretionary purchases such as tours may take a backseat and essentials may take a priority. The intangibility of tourism also influence buyers when they may have to choose between a new car and a trip.

Marketers must constantly analyse the market to judge where competition is coming from.

Dynamics of Competition/Competitors Response Profile

Competition at all levels can follow different patterns. Four patterns can be identified on the basis of speed and aggressiveness of the competitor (Table 14.1).

Aggressive but slow

A competitor enters the market knowing fully that it is snatching the market share from existing operators, but the entry is slow. It gives enough time to the concerned players to devise counter moves. This strategy may be followed when the competitor has an edge that is difficult to counter. For example, the initial growth of budget airlines in

Table 14.1 Dynamics of Competition

| | | Time Taken to Enter Market | |
		More	Less
Aggressiveness	**Aggressive**	Aggressive but slow	Aggressive and fast
	Non-aggressive	Non-aggressive and slow	Non-aggressive and fast

India was slow and regular air operators took a long time to understand its full implications.

Aggressive and fast

A competitor aims at snatching the share of existing players and enters the market quickly, not allowing any time for offsetting moves. For example, new budget hotels are opening very quickly to attract customers from existing ones.

Non-aggressive and slow

A competitor does not target existing players directly but may take away their customers. For example, budget airlines have lured passengers of higher classes of railways.

Non-aggressive and fast

A competitor enters the market quickly, without any intention of directly competing with the existing firms. For example, the railways launched its tour packages through indianrailtourism.com and makemytrip.com. This was done to broaden product portfolio of railways than to compete with tour operators.

Nature of Competitors

Competitors display different behaviours in market. These can be neutral, positive, or negative.

Neutral competitors

These give competition to existing players but do not focus on them. They compete on the basis of unique benefits offered and create pressure on old marketers, who fear customers' shifting choices for novelty and uniqueness. Online travel firms offered completely different choices to tourists without directly confronting offline firms. Though the industry observers declared death of traditional travel agencies, they stayed in business by discovering new functions.

Positive competitors

These enter the market with the premise that enough potential exists for all and more players help in enlarging the market. Each carves a separate place for itself and all coexist. Hotels located together near airport, railway stations, and business centres draw more guests than stand-alone properties.

Negative competitors

These function on the philosophy of win–lose and believe that their survival depends on termination of competitors and vice versa. They adopt all strategies to harm competitors. Their presence in the market can be destructive for other players.

Competitors' Goals

Competitors have different types of goals that decide their strategies and behaviour in the market. These are discussed below.

To become a big player in the market

Competitiors with such a goal pose a threat to the top two and three firms who hold the major share in the market. These face opposition from existing firms.

To exist as one small operator

Some competitors take a small pie in big market and coexist. These do not disturb existing business if the market is big enough for all. But in a saturated market, any small operator will face opposition from existing players.

To focus on one segment and specialize

Some small firms specialize in destinations, channels, or specific type of tourism. These function on a small scale in niche areas where many firms might not be interested.

The goals of competitors decide the challenges to existing firms that design their strategies accordingly.

Competitive Strategies

The competitive strategies in markets fall into broader categories of offensive and defensive. Defensive mode is followed by existing firms which want to hold on to their position. New entrants can be directly offensive or low profiled where entry is made without disturbing the existing players. But such entrants can turn offensive after understanding the market. Existing firms can also adopt offensive strategies to continue their dominance.

> All firms new and old shall watch the strategies of other competitors very closely to be able to devise counter moves.

Competitive Capabilities

Competitive capabilities in tourism can lie at the macro level of the destination/attraction or at the level of firm. For destinations, it is defined in the following main factors (World Economic Forum 2008).

- Cultural and natural resources
- Environment
- Tourism infrastructure
- Focus on travel and tourism

- Safety and security
- Health and hygiene levels
- Availability of trained manpower

A firm operating in a highly-competitive place gets the natural advantage of destination image. At the level of firm, its resource capabilities determine the goals and strategies for competition. A large firm with sound finances is more likely to look for dominant position in market than a small local firm. Acquisitions, tie-ups, mergers, takeovers, franchise agreements, and management contracts change the capabilities. All these moves should be constantly monitored to follow a proactive approach towards strategy.

After analysing competition, a firm must evaluate its position in relation to competitors as both will influence the strategic choices of the firm.

RELATIVE COMPETITIVE POSITION IN THE MARKET

At any given point of time a firm's position is dependent on other operators in the market. Strategies are designed keeping in mind other firms. The relative competitive position of a firm can be analysed with the help of Kotler framework, BCG matrix, and GE grid.

Kotler Framework

Kotler identifies four categories of players in the market on the basis of their market shares (Kotler and Armstrong 1991).

Market leader

The biggest player has the largest market share and leads by setting trends in the market.

Market challenger

The second largest player in the market challenges the leader. It adopts innovation and competitive strategies for this.

Market followers

There are many small players in the market offering products similar to leaders and followers. These corner a small share of the market and do not enter into direct conflict with the leader and challenger.

Nichers

These are small players who specialize in one area and do not directly compete with any of the above.

Table 14.2 BCG Growth Share Matrix

		Relative Market Share	
		High	Low
Market growth rate	High	Stars	Question mark
	Low	Cash cow	Dogs

BCG Matrix

This technique of portfolio analysis helps a firm to evaluate its competitors based on their relative market share and market growth rate. It identifies four positions as shown in Table 14.2.

Stars are best businesses that have a good present and future; cash cows are good in the present; question marks need investment in the present but yield good results in future; and dogs are doubtful businesses. Stars and question marks pose future threat to competitors, cash cows threaten in present, dogs have a short life and are likely to be phased out.

GE Grid

General electric grid, a portfolio analysis technique, assesses a firm's competitive position on business strength and market attractiveness. Relative market share, product quality, sales/promotion effectiveness, and geography are used to judge business strength of a firm. Market attractiveness is taken on the basis of market size, growth rate, profits, competition and intensity (Table 14.3).

All the businesses marked for 'build' are threat to existing businesses. 'Wait and see' need a watch and may evolve strong contenders. 'No growth' firms are unlikely to be a problem.

Table 14.3 GE Grid

Market attractiveness	Business Strengths		
	Strong	Average	Weak
High	Build	Build	Wait and see
Medium	Build	Wait and see	No growth
Low	Wait and see	No growth	No growth

DECIDING COMPETITIVE ADVANTAGES

Marketing strategy aims at getting the competitive advantage and knowledge of competition helps a firm in developing it. Porter (1985) suggested overall cost leadership, differentiation, and focus in markets for competitive advantage.

Overall Cost Leadership

> In tourism, cost leadership is very important where price is used strategically not only for competitive advantage but also for overcoming the supply–demand gap and perishability of offers.

A firm can offer a benefit at a lower cost, which becomes difficult for others to match. It can be because of reasons such as economies of large scale of operations, experience that helps firms to improve efficiencies, control over suppliers and dealers, access to new technology, and so on. Cost leadership gives edge to a firm in the market and acts as a barrier for new firms if existing firms have this advantage. In case new entrants acquire it, old firms feel the competition.

Differentiation

A firm can create a distinct image for itself if it differentiates its offers from others. Differentiation can get a segment of loyal clientele to the firm. Differentiation can lie in patents, expertise, manpower, process improvements, exclusive tie-ups with distribution chains, and so on. In tourism, distribution channels are often used to build differentiation. The choice of CRS or GDS by an agent creates this differentiation. Choice of right websites to sell tickets by airline also creates this differentiation.

Focus

Focus on a particular market or segment helps to achieve a high level of specialization that is difficult to be copied. A firm specializing in business tourism and MICE (meetings, incentives, conferences, events) may have a big share of this market. Take the case of American Express. It has focused on this market and has surveyed corporate travel extensively to convey to its customers benefits accruing from the use of its services over any other option.

DECIDING COMPETITIVE MARKETING STRATEGIES

The use of competitive strategies depends upon the relative competitive position of a firm in the market. These can be used to defend position, attack existing players, follow others and coexist, or to create a niche.

Strategies for Attack

These are used by new entrants in the market who try to destabilize the existing equilibrium to make their way. These can be used by established firms as pre-emptive strike. The common attack strategies are as follow.

Attack the flanks or weekly guarded areas/indirect attack

In flanking strategy, a primary attack is made against competitors' weakness and a secondary attack to divert attention from primary attack. A challenger often enters the market space of other firms who try to resist this.

The approach followed is to initially attack the weakest points rather than the strongholds of competitors and gain competitive advantage. Later, if it is successful, the strongholds are attacked. This increases the chances of success of the attacker as the initial resistance is reduced.

Frontal or direct attack

It is attacking the strengths of competitors by outdoing it. This attack requires heavy resources and is possible only for big firms. Successful entrants do not engage in frontal attacks, because market leaders can react very strongly. Retaliatory measures, such as heavy price cuts or legal actions, may be started.

Budget airlines in Indian skies use direct attack strategy against each other by matching price for price for similar facilities.

Envelopment attack

This strategy envelops the entire market or segments for attack making it difficult for competitors to defend. In trying to defend all areas the resources of competitors get thinly spread and some fronts become weak that can be breached easily. But this attack can be made only if the attacking firm has large resources to launch such a full-fledged attack.

Bypass attack

This approach circumvents competitors and entrants choose new and unrelated products or geographical areas. Selection of niches or small markets is part of this. Enterprises develop offerings with features that do not initially appeal to mainstream customers but attract customers in a fringe segment.

Budget airline Air Deccan made its foray by adopting a new route of low prices and modest facilities for consumers. At that time its impact, that later paved the way for many other firms with similar models, was not foreseen.

Firms with long-term interests in the market do not follow guerilla approach but it can be used by fly by night operators.

Guerilla attack

Small erratic attacks are made to surprise and confuse the market. The attacker uses the confusion to its benefit and goes silent without giving any reaction time to other players. This attack is difficult to counter because of its unpredictability. Sudden price cuts that others find difficult to match or heavy promotion are such instances.

Strategies for Defence

Defence is used as a protective measure by the existing players, either from new entrants or from each other. It sustains competitive advantage, lowers probability of attacks, and diverts attacks to less threatening areas. These are counter moves against attack as frontal defence for frontal attack and flank defence for flank attack. The specific strategies used are as follows.

Frontal defence

A firm guards its strengths to ensure that no competitor stakes a parallel claim. For example, the main attraction of budget hotels is low price. They increase their efficiencies to a high level to give services at lowest possible price. New competitors may find it difficult to match this mix of low price and good service.

Flanks defence

The peripheral parts of business are kept under watch to see if any competition comes in those parts. Any competition is checked as soon as it is noticed. For example, big hotel groups in India are strengthening their presence in both budget and luxury segments, not allowing new firms of luxury or budget hotels to fill the gaps in the product line.

Encirclement defence

All businesses of a firm are defended strongly as the attack comes. It is like fortification to stop competitors' moves. It requires large amount of resources to build defences. It can be difficult for a firm if it has spread its business too wide.

Mobile defence

To counter guerrilla attack, a firm keeps on strengthening different areas continuously. It is similar to patrolling in military science.

The following tactics are used in defence strategies.

Make entry less attractive

It can be done by raising structural barriers such as lowering prices or controlling channels.

Increase retaliation

Increased and aggressive retaliation can also fend off new players. Increasing promotional budgets, making improvements in offers, and tie-up agreements to control markets are some steps.

Strategies for Followers

A large number of small operators can not use strategies of attack or defence because of limited resources. They corner a small market share and follow the strategies of dominant firms. These do not enter into any direct conflict with big players and adopt the following strategies.

Copying or me-too

These copy the popular brands in the market to the extent of names and logos and operate in smaller towns where customers cannot distinguish between original and fake. Small hotels, *dhabas*, and restaurants often use brand names of big players. It is quite common to find a Taj restaurant or *dhaba* in small Indian towns.

Imitation

Product features are copied but a different identity is provided to the seller. A tour package similar to that of big travel agent may be provided by smaller agents under their own name.

Modification

The original product may be improved or modified to meet the market needs. Tour packages may be altered and modified to be sold as completely new packages.

Niche Strategies

A few firms may operate in niches by going for high level of specialization. A travel agent may only handle outbound business tours for information technology (IT) firms from India to the UK. These do not enter into direct conflict with others and fetch good margins for their high-end services.

PREPARING DETAILED STRETEGIES

Once a firm has finalized its strategic choices, the next decision is to prepare details of strategies through a marketing mix. If a firm wants to go for frontal attack it should be specific about the combination of product, price, promotion, etc., used for the same. A detailed strategic plan can be prepared as per Table 14.4.

This worksheet can be used to develop specific competitive strategies.

The complete framework of understanding competition and developing competitive marketing strategies is given in Fig. 14.3.

The implementation of strategies needs continuous monitoring to see the impact in the market. The change in environment or a firm's capabilities may change the choice of strategies by a firm.

Table 14.4 Preparing Competitive Marketing Strategy

Strategic Approach	Product	Place	Price	Promotion	People	Process	Physical Evidence
Frontal attack							
Envelopment attack							
Flanks attack							
Guerilla attack							
Bypass attack							
Frontal defence							
Encirclement defence							
Flanks defence							
Mobile defence							
Copying							
Imitation							
Modification							
Destination niche							
Channel niche							
Functional niche							

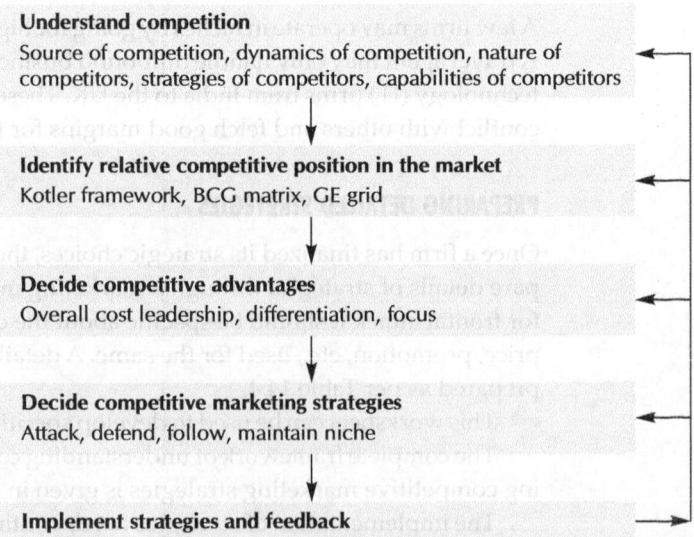

Understand competition
Source of competition, dynamics of competition, nature of competitors, strategies of competitors, capabilities of competitors

Identify relative competitive position in the market
Kotler framework, BCG matrix, GE grid

Decide competitive advantages
Overall cost leadership, differentiation, focus

Decide competitive marketing strategies
Attack, defend, follow, maintain niche

Implement strategies and feedback

Fig. 14.3 Framework for Developing Competitive Marketing Strategies

SUMMARY

Meeting competition effectively is an important determinant for the success of a firm. This is possible after a thorough analysis of marketplace competition. The intensity and source of competition, response profile, nature, strategies, and capabilities of competitors give insight into the behaviour of competition. Competition can come from within the industry or from outside in the form of substitutes and unrelated products. The competitors may be aggressive or docile, slow or fast movers, good or bad. Their strategies and capabilities decide the future of competition. After understanding competition, a firm shall find its relative position. It may be a leader, challenger, follower, or nicher. The Kotler framework, BCG matrix, and GE matrix tell about relative position. With this understanding appropriate competitive strategies can be devised. These strategies use competitive advantages to provide edge. Advantages can be created through overall cost leadership, differentiation, and focus. These advantages are strategically used with the help of attack, defence, follow, and niche strategies. A market leader defends its existing position and uses attack to hold on to its position. New entrants use attack to gain entry in market and can use frontal, flanking, encirclement, bypass, and guerilla strategies. Defence strategies counter the attacks through frontal, flanks, encirclement, and mobile defences. Small players in the market can follow the leader and followers by using strategies of copy, imitation, and modification. Few may opt for markets that are very small and called niches. These offer no competition but provide space for specialization. The high level of specialization deters any new firm from entering in the niche.

Competitive strategies need continuous monitoring and are adjusted to meet the changes in competition.

KEY TERMS

Attack strategies These try to destabilize the existing equilibrium in the market to make inroads.

Competitive advantage The strengths of an organization that provide relative advantage in the market.

Competitive marketing strategies These are the strategies developed to respond to changes in the market resulting from competition and to counter any advantages that other competitors might get with change in external environment.

Defence strategies These are used as a protective measure by the existing players, either from new entrants or from each other.

Follow strategies These strategies are used to follow leaders and challengers in the market.

Market challengers These are small firms in the market that corner little share in the market and survive by the following leader and challenger.

Market follower The firm with the second largest market share is called the market follower.

Market leader The firm with the largest market share is called the market leader. It is characterized by innovative strategies to maintain lead.

Niche strategies These are the strategies used to focus on very small areas by developing high level of expertise.

Nichers Firms that develop highly specialized offers and operate in a very small segment are called nichers.

EXERCISES

REVIEW QUESTIONS

1. What is marketing strategy? How is it prepared?
2. How can BCG matrix be used to assess the relative competitive position of a firm in the market?
3. What are attack strategies? How are these used?
4. Why should dynamics of competition and competitors' response profile be studied?

PRACTICE EXERCISES

1. Prepare BCG matrix of domestic airlines in India and find its stars. Where do you place Indian

Airlines in comparison to private airlines?
2. Select a comparative advertisement of tour packages and find the attack strategies used by advertiser. Also watch and note reaction of those attacked.

PROJECTS

1. Visit a new smart business hotel and survey its strategies.
2. Compare the competitive strategies of old and established travel agents and new ones. Report the differences and their causes.

REFERENCES

Bryce, David J. and Jeffrey H. Dyer 2007, May, 'Strategies to crack well-guarded markets', *Harvard Business Review*, pp. 84-92.

Gatignon, Hubert, Erin Anderson, and Kristiaan Helsen 1989, 'Competitive reactions to market entry: Explaining interfirm differences', *Journal of Marketing Research*, vol. 26, no. 1, pp. 44-55.

Kotler, Philip and Gary Armstrong 1991, *Principles of Marketing*, Prentice Hall of India, New Delhi.

Paley, Norton 2006, *The Manager's Guide to Competitive Marketing Strategies*, Thorogood, London.

Porter, Michael E. 1980, *Competitive Strategy: Techniques for Analyzing Industries and Competitors*, The Free Press, New York.

Porter, Michael E. 1985, *Competitive Advantage: Creating and Sustaining Superior Performance*, The Free Press, New York.

World Economic Forum 2008, *Highlights of the Travel and Tourism Competitiveness Report*.

CASE STUDY

BEATING THE COMPETITION—PARAMOUNT AIRWAYS

The Indian air travel market in 2008 was under tremendous pressures with decreasing demand and increasing prices. Airlines had seen fall of up to 33 per cent in passengers. The main issues were as follows.

(a) The cost of operations was increasing because of hike in fuel prices. Aviation turbine fuel had become dearer by 77 per cent in 2008 compared to 2007.

(b) Low cost or budget airlines were not able to set reasonable prices for fear of loosing market and were loosing Rs 1,500 to Rs 2,000 per person flown.

(c) Domestic passenger growth rate had decreased from 28 per cent in January to March, 2007 to 11 per cent in 2008.

Planes were flying at 80 per cent capacity.

As a result, almost all airlines were loosing revenues. These were adopting measures to cut cost such as getting strict on excess baggage, delaying deliveries of new aircrafts, using sale–leaseback, cancelling flights, and so on. The market shares of different operators in June 2008 were Jet–Jetlite 29.3, Kingfisher–Deccan 27.1, Air India domestic 16.4, Indigo 12, Spice Jet 10.4, Go Air 3.1, and Paramount 1.7. The smallest paramount airways had adopted an entirely different model and earned profits even in such difficult situations. It differentiated itself from other operators and ran as premium service regional airline with a small fleet of five planes. It used smaller Embraer 170 aircraft with 70–75 seat capacity that weighed less than 40,000 tonnes. These provided savings in lower 4 per cent tax on ATF compared to 34 per cent on bigger crafts, higher fuel efficiency, lower break even levels, exemption from parking and landing charges. The impact of increased fuel prices was much lower on this airline, thus enabling it to earn profits. It had also temporarily suspended flights to Bangalore anticipating lower capacities.

(*Source: Business Today*, June 29, 2008 and *The Times of India*, July 14, 2008.

DISCUSSION QUESTIONS

1. What was the competitive position of Paramount airways?
2. Compare the measures adopted by it with the strategies suggested in chapter.
3. What could have been done to increase the profitability by other airlines?

CHAPTER 15

Technology In Tourism Marketing

LEARNING OBJECTIVES

Technology is changing tour experiences and is evolving from the stage of only information search to purchases and exploration of destinations. It is expected to reshape the industry.

In this chapter, you will learn about the role of technology in tourism with focus on the following.

• Technology used in tourism marketing
• Impact of technology on marketing
• Networks and virtual travel
• E-travel or online travel

INTRODUCTION

Tour information, tour advice, planning, and purchase are just a click away because of penetration of technology in the markets. Today a tourist searches for information on the Internet, gets independent opinions through blogs and social networking sites, such as Orkut and Facebook, take familiarization tours virtually, makes online purchases through credit cards, uses the latest options of transport and hotel technology, and posts his/her feedback on the Internet for others to see. This was unthinkable earlier but newer technologies have made it possible. Marketers too are adopting and using technology in all spheres, which is closely linked to its use in tourism. Stipanuk (1993) suggested multiple roles played by technology in tourism.

Technology as contributor to tourism growth

Transportation technology has given faster and better vehicles to facilitate movement of tourists to remote places. Even the space and deep seas are not beyond the reach of tourists. Transport technology decides the nature of tours to be offered to markets.

Technology as creator of tourism experience

Parasailing, hang-gliding, jet-skiing, and amusement parks are instances where technology creates the tourism experience. More advancement in such areas changes the complete tour experience.

Technology as protector of tourism experience

Technology is used to protect the environment in which the tourism experiences take place. Use of satellite mapping to track tourists' movements and subsequent impacts on green cover is one example where technology protects the tourism experience.

Technology as enhancer of tourism experience

Phones, videos, and wireless fidelity (Wi-Fi) connectivity in hotels and at airports enhance tourism experience.

Technology as focal point of tourism

Exhibitions based on technology, such as auto expos and computer fairs, use technology as a theme that attracts tourists.

Technology as destroyer of tourism

Snags in aircrafts, lifts, and networks destroy the tourism experience.

TECHNOLOGY IN TOURISM MARKETING

In all of the above roles technology becomes integral to a tourism product, its delivery, and consumption by tourists. Tourism marketing applies information technology (IT) to manage information and carry out transactions. System of information technologies (SIT) in tourism comprises computers, centralized reservation system (CRS), digital telephone networks, videos, videotext, teleconferencing, electronic locking systems, e-commerce, and so on. The diffusion of SIT in tourism increases the efficiency, quality, and flexibility with which travel services are supplied. Multimedia, CRS/global distribution system (GDS), and the Internet have changed tourism marketing completely.

> Tourism is an information-intensive industry and its intelligent manipulation helps in understanding and profitably satisfying tourism markets, and this had led to adoption of information systems in tourism marketing.

Multimedia

Developments in media technology have immensely enhanced the quality of interface with users. These appeal to human senses in a much better way. It is possible through a travel programme on television (TV) to show a destination completely. Interactive compact discs (CDs) with hyperlinks offer tourists the choice of navigating freely. Electronic brochures give interfaces to net by listing links that give large amount of information with assistance from different quarters as advice. Interactive TV and touch screen kiosks are very useful in disseminating tourism information. The options are many and a marketer shall choose a suitable mix to target its market to convey the message.

Virtual Reality and Virtual Tours

These advancements in technology are seen as breakthroughs for tourism marketing. Virtual reality is a computer mediated multi-sensory experience that attempts to replace the physical world with the artificial world. It is similar to sampling, in which tourists undertake different experiences and then choose one for final purchase. It enhances the tourism experience by giving an almost real feel prior to the tour and overcomes the intangibility part. It provides for complete exploration of a destination or tour, unlike brochures that give limited information. There are apprehensions that in future it may emerge a substitute of actual travel to some extent. There is a risk that consumers may get addicted to these tours in place of real tours.

> A tourist can experience trekking by using artificially simulated computerized trekking and then decide whether or not to go for the real experience.

Networks

The perishability and packaged nature of tourism products makes it difficult to balance demand and supply; more so when information is not available. Earlier it was not possible to know stocks available for sale at different places and times. But with the development of computers and networks, the instant access to accurate inventory position and consumer requirements is very easy. Centralized reservation system and GDS have played a very important role in it.

Centralized reservation systems

Centralized reservation systems were developed by airlines for their operations to increase efficiency and American Airlines was the first to develop it in 1962. Its CRS Sabre was used by travel agents to make direct reservations through terminals in their offices. A CRS maintains complete databases of products (airline seats) that can be accessed through terminals located at different places. Airlines put these in travel agents' offices who could see the stock position and book seats. Centralized reservation systems connect airlines and agents in a better way. Later CRS were developed by hotels and railways.

Global distribution systems

Global distribution systems distribute more than one CRS to users who are usually travel agents, unlike the CRS used solely by an airline or hotel chain. Global distribution systems distribute reservation and information services through sales outlets. They were formed from airlines' CRS that included other products such as hotels, car rentals, and so on in its data base. Over time, four main GDS, namely Amadeus, Galileo, Sabre, and Worldspan emerged.

Amadeus was started by Air France and Lufthansa in 1987 and is presently owned by Amadeus IT Group. Galileo from United Airlines came into existence in 1971 and is now owned by Travelport. Travelport acquired Worldspan that was started by Delta and North-West Airlines in 1990. Sabre from American Airlines is with Sabre Holdings.

> Indian railways used PRS (passenger reservation systems) effectively to sell a stock of 6.5 million tickets daily in 2009-2010.

Implications of CRS and GDS in tourism

These systems connect many suppliers with a large number of buyers and have the following important implications.

1. A CRS/GDS gives access to a large market and is very useful for small or stand-alone hotels or other facility providers who cannot establish direct contact with buyers on a big scale. Just by affiliating to CRS/GDS, their products are made accessible for sales through the CRS/GDS network.
2. It connects a large base of products to a large number of buyers. This helps in creating a better balance between supply and demand.
3. It helps in yield management. The revenues can be enhanced by analysing the behaviour of CRS/GDS users to predict the prices at which sales will take place at different times. The price buckets can be very effectively used with CRS/GDS.
4. It provides instant confirmation at fast speed to its users.
5. It offers a large choice of products.

CRS and GDS have certain downsides too.

1. Costs of reservation through CRS and GDS can be high. All the outside stocks that are listed with CRS pay a fee for it and that increases the price of products.
2. It may not lead to sales. Presence of products on CRS/GDS gives access to its market but does not guarantee sales.
3. CRS/GDS lists stocks but cannot ensure the correctness of information. Quality control of facilities listed is a concern.
4. CRS/GDS may give different priorities to affiliates attached to it. Its own products will get priority over others in sales.
5. CRS and GDS are big firms and control others attached to them for listing their products. Small firms loose control over marketing when using CRS/GDS.

Internet

Internet arrived on the scene in the 1980s and has developed very fast since then. It was developed as an open network and not for business. But its commercial applications soon surpassed the intranets and extranets. Internet connects everybody, be it marketer, dealers, or consumers. Its biggest advantage is networking the buyers directly to suppliers. Each supplier could be independently present on the Net without being dependent on others like CRS or GDS. It gives equal power to both big and small businesses. The changing forms of tourism marketing before CRS, after CRS, and post Internet are shown in Table 15.1.

Internet provides a platform in the form of World Wide Web where all can be present and can interact. Its penetration has increased rapidly and is given in Table 15.2. This is important as familiarity with the Internet is a necessary condition for the use of the Web for search and reservation of tourist services.

Internet offers the following advantages for marketers and customers.

1. Presence on it costs less than CRS or GDS.
2. Tourists can configure tours by collecting all information.

Table 15.1 Tourism Distribution prior to CRS, pre Internet and post Internet

Producers	Intermediaries		Consumers
Pre CRS/GDS			
Hotels	Tour operators		
Restaurants	Travel agents		
Airlines	National tourism		Tourists
Attractions	organizations		
Pre Internet			
Hotels	Tour operators		
Restaurants	Travel agents		
Airlines	CRS/GDS		Tourists
Attractions	National tourism		
	organizations		
Post Internet			
Hotels	Tour operators	Web-based travel and tour	
Restaurants	Travel agents	companies	
Airlines	CRS/GDS	Middlemen on the Web	Tourists
Attraction	National tourism		
	organizations		

Table 15.2 Internet Penetration in 2009 (in per cent)

World	26.6
Asia	20.1
India	7.0

(*Source*: internetworldstats.com, accessed on 20 April 2010)

3. It is more transparent where information from all suppliers is open and other tourists also post the opinions.
4. CRS and GDS provide access to their networks and inventory through it.
5. It can be accessed from anywhere using broadband or 3 G networks.
6. It enables a company to individually 'address' consumers in its marketing communication, because each time a user visits its website, its server has a record of the user's electronic address. The company can send customized message to a smaller target audience or an individual consumer. The addressability of the Web provides the opportunity for marketing to create individual relationships, managing markets, and addressing each in terms of its stage of development.
7. It is a very interactive medium and is capable of giving feedback in response to the actions users perform on the computer. Various interactions—company-to-consumer, consumer-to-company, consumer-to-consumer, and company-to-company—are possible. Tourist groups on the Net are used by potential tourists to get information similar to offline word of mouth.
8. In the travel business, the Web's flexibility and instantaneousness in information transmission is invaluable, where the brochure is the main means for marketing package tours. The electronic brochure can be indexed in many ways and the user can be provided with search facilities to locate items quickly.
9. Improved access to information covering all aspects of tourist activities has provided marketers the opportunity to offer personalized services at price levels comparable to those of standard packages.
10. It facilitates tourism industry transactions through search and reservation, payment, and delivery (Hultkrantz L. 2002).

Search and reservation

Customers can search from any access point on their own for up-to-date information on supply, for example, information on places and events, timetables, open hours, prices, real time (or close to real time) availability, etc. and make reservations.

Payment

Payments cannot be directly made over the Web. However, several forms of payment methods can be linked to a reservation through the Web, such as authorization for withdrawal of a credit card account, sending of an invoice, and so on.

Delivery

Information services, such as guidebooks, can be conveyed electronically. Also, simple access to tickets, lodging, etc. can be provided with reservation codes transmitted over the Web.

The example of Indian Railways can be taken to gauge the contribution of technology to travel and tourism. It accounts for more than 63 per cent online transactions in the country and is the largest revenue generator in business-to-consumer (B2C) e-commerce category. With a stock of 8,500 trains and 2,50,000 daily real-time bookings and e-payments, it is a star business.

ONLINE TRAVEL OR ELECTRONIC TOURISM

Electronic tourism (e-tourism) or online travel and electronic marketing (e-marketing) are parts of electronic (e-commerce) commerce that is defined as digitally carrying out business or transactions. Buhalis (2006) defines e-tourism as the digitization of all processes and value chains in the tourism, travel, hospitality, and catering industry. It uses e-marketing and distribution, where all functions are digitally performed. Digitization is the key to such marketing. Information can be digitized and, therefore, can be accessed through the Internet. Similarly, products such as music and books can be digitized and are transferable to buyers as soft copy. In tourism, attractions are not digitized but proof of purchase, such as vouchers and tickets, can be e-mailed to tourists.

The amount of information used for tourism marketing is extensive and that propels the extensive application of online business models.

It is called online travel because real-time information exchange takes place between buyers and sellers. A marketing, sale, delivery, payment (MSDP) model applied to tourism is shown in Fig 15.1.

The model considers sequential approach of e-commerce functions with the sequence marketing, sales, delivery, and payment. All functions are performed on electronic space or website. The function of marketing research and sales can be performed offline in the initial stages to popularize the website.

If you want to book an air or train ticket, the choice of seat can be given to the marketer on the Net. The payment can be made through credit cards and instantly the proof of ticket can be taken as printout.

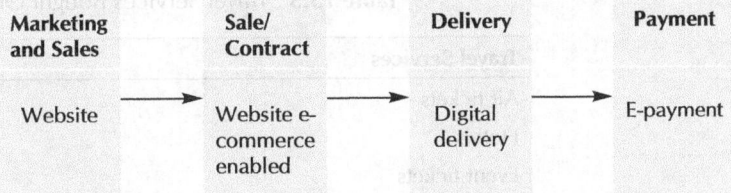

Fig. 15.1 MSDP model of Electronic Travel

Important features of this marketing are as follows.

1. Availability of information: Intangible, interactive, rich and topical information is accessible anytime. The cost of search is very low.
2. Interactive: Sellers and buyers can find the type of information searched.
3. Easy transactions: Transactions can be easily performed.
4. Customer satisfaction: It is high as buyers play an active role. Purchase is made after evaluating complete information.
5. High quality sites: It is possible to design websites of very high quality that act as sales point for the marketers.
6. Volume of business on the net is large: All Internet users are potential customers.
7. Time is important for buyers: Real-time transactions can be performed here on $24 \times 7 \times 365$ basis.
8. Personalization of services: This helps in giving individualized treatment to customers.
9. Direct contact with customers: All members of a distribution chain can establish direct contact with customers.

> The size of online travel in India stood at USD 4209 million in 2009 and Phocus Wright has predicted it to touch USD 6028 million by 2010.

All the above features are making online travel popular and according to the e-marketer survey 2007, India accounted for 4.4 per cent of Asia Pacific online travel booking and it is expected to reach 10.7 per cent by 2011. Online travel industry is the largest contributor to business to consumer e-commerce in the country.

A Microsoft Network (MSN)/Windows Live online travel survey conducted by Synovate* also pointed towards the increasing role of Internet in tour planning in 2007 (Table 15.3 and 15.4).

The size of the Indian market is small compared to developed nations. Europe had a market size of 58.4 billion euros with 22.5 per cent of total travel market in 2008.

---

* Synovate is a market research firm.

Table 15.3 Travel Services Bought Online (2006-07)

Travel Services	Per cent of Respondents
Air tickets	48
Hotels	21
Event tickets	10
Travel packages	15
Travel insurance	5

(*Source:* MSN online survey 2007)

Table15.4 Sources used for Planning Researching Travel (2007)

Source	Per cent of Respondents
Internet	81
Printed travel brochures	65
Guidebooks	29
Newspapers	40
Travel agents	40
Friends/relatives/colleagues	40
Magazines	40

(*Source*: MSN online survey 2007)

Online bookings have a few drawbacks as well. Forrester* Research points out three main irritants of credit card security, inability to make specific requests, and frustration with websites.

Players in Online Travel Market

Four categories of main players are identifiable: the traditional travel agents and tour operators, hotels with new online models, railways, and the new-age infomediaries or tour aggregators.

Travel agents and tour operators

These traditional service providers have added one more channel for marketing and distribution of their products. This is helping to compete with pure online firms, as well as to be in tune with changing buying patterns of

---

* Forrester is an independent technology and market research company.

tourists. Many big operators in India have launched separate brands such as ezeego from Cox and Kings and thomascook.in from Thomas Cook.

Hotels

Many hotels have also opened an additional distribution channel and are offering their stocks through websites.

Railways

Online ticketing of railways has emerged as the single largest e-commerce site in the country. The transaction value has increased from Rs 3,000 crore in 2008-09 to Rs 6,000 crore in 2009-10.

Tour aggregators

They provide packages, hotels, air tickets, rail tickets, car rentals, and so on through their websites and function in collaboration with other service providers. They offer most economical deals and generate a large volume of traffic on their websites. These operate online with 24-hour services. Their revenues come through commission on sales.

USING WEBSITES FOR TOURISM MARKETING

Online business is conducted in cyberspace and marketers use websites as shops to display their products. A good site is very important for marketing. A consumer will not wait for information and will navigate to other sites if access is not smooth. Tourism websites need graphics to show products and these pages may take a long time if bandwidth is less. Therefore, a balance is required between graphic content required and speed of loading. The contents on the site are also planned judiciously to avoid supplying unnecessary information and not miss any relevant information. Customers want all the information in an easy format, rather than following the hierarchy of information. If sales are conducted electronically, the privacy of buyers and security in payment are other important considerations.

A good website attracts tourists and also builds business. The home page of online travel company yatra.com is shown in Fig. 15.2. The following criteria are used to design a good tourism website.

Contents

A tourism website should include the following.

About organization

Tourists will be interested in knowing about the organization before entering into any deals with it.

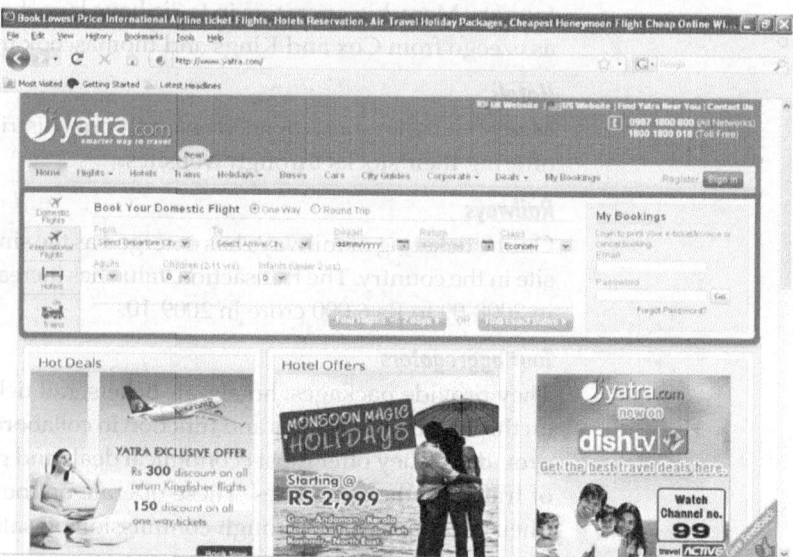

Fig 15.2   Home Page of yatra.com

About products and services

A brief description will help tourists in knowing if their requirements can be met. It will save time.

Frequently asked questions

Tourists evaluate products from a different perspective and may need additional information. A large number of queries may be repetitive in nature such as what preparations are required for the tour. Provision for such questions and their answers under a separate head helps tourists in getting most of the answers. Frequently asked questions (FAQs) also save time for marketers who need not answer these questions repeatedly.

Online ordering

Websites can be used for both information and transactions. Provision of online ordering makes a site more interactive.

Interactive guest book/survey

Opinions and feedback of tourists are very important to improve services as well as the website. A mechanism for accepting their suggestions is very helpful.

Giveaways

Tourists need to be rewarded for visiting sites and giveaways, such as wallpapers, postcards, screensavers, can be offered.

Navigation

Navigation through a site should be smooth and interesting. Inclusion of the following features makes navigation easy.

Menu

A drop down menu avoids unnecessary congestion on the page and tourists can move to the desired information.

Image maps/buttons

These are very important in tourism where pictures are used to show an attraction. Buttons help in moving to details of the images instantly.

Search engines

Websites should be powered by search engines. This helps tourists in moving to the desired location quickly, rather than following the complete hierarchy for search.

Hyperlinks

These links with other pages and related sites can be very useful for tourists who can easily get the relevant details.

Irritants

Certain irritants on websites can dissatisfy tourists.

Slow download times

Tourists want sites to be fast. Information should be stored in formats that increase speed. Simple rules, such as keeping the size of graphics small, can help.

Outdated information

Information should be regularly updated.

Privacy

The search behaviour and purchases of tourists should not be shared anywhere.

Security

Tourists want secure transactions regarding payments. Their credit card information is not to be divulged by marketers.

Quality control

Tourists cannot check quality of offers on the Net. They want promises to be met. This is an important issue for online companies that stock offers of many suppliers.

Impact of Online Business on Existing Intermediaries

Internet connects sellers, middlemen, and customers with each other. Principals use this network to bypass middlemen and link with buyers directly. Customers too see the savings in cutting middlemen's share.

Fears and doubts were expressed about the extinction of travel agents. But only a part of the total tour business became direct and the rest continued through agents. There were many services that could not be digitized such as personal consultation and advice, and these continue to be performed through middlemen. Moreover, virtual shopping places on the Net came into being to link potential tourists with sellers. These became the new middlemen. These are used to get information and actual business can be transacted offline, and therefore the term infomediaries was coined. The web space is marked by the presence of the following tourism firms.

> The online business practices led to concern about longevity of existence of middlemen and a debate over disintermediation began.

Principals

Airlines and hotels are present and sell through sites directly.

Intermediaries

Travel agents and tour operators have joined the net to gain access to online buyers. For example, Cox and Kings started ezeego.com.

Online-tourism-only intermediaries

These do not own any product but provide a meeting point for both buyers and sellers such as yatra.com and cleartrip.com. Their expertise lies in the use of online technology.

Online firms

These are big firms that sell a large number of products online and tourism is a part of their portfolio such as indiatimes.com.

Infomediaries

These do not sell anything but provide information.

TECHNOLOGY AND MARKETING MIX

Marketing mix strategies and decisions are influenced by technology as it bears on all components of the mix.

Product Decisions

Tourism products can be natural and man made. Both are enhanced by technology. Marketers can decide the inputs of technology in its products.

A tour package can include travel to Amarnath by road or air. The difference here is created by technology.

Place

The CRS, the GDS, and the Internet have changed the old distribution systems in tourism and the marketers are placing themselves on the Internet. Train/flight timings and waiting tickets can be confirmed on phones or SMS. Tickets can be purchased online and printouts taken immediately.

Price

Reverse auction for hotel prices, where buyers quote the prices and hotel decides to sell rooms at a particular price, is possible only through the Internet. E-mails and SMS to buyers about prices is the result of technology. Centralized reservation systems help in revenue management. Price buckets can be used only with online systems.

Promotion

Multimedia has changed the way promotion is carried out. The print guide books have been replaced by interactive electronic versions. Messages can be customized. Call centres can answer queries immediately. Information can be checked from websites. Tourists can take virtual tours before finalizing purchases.

People

Better services can be offered with the help of technology. Close circuit cameras can be installed at points of encounters to watch employee and customer behaviour. Computerized data minimizes the chances of mixed up bookings and gives greater confidence to employees in dealing with customers.

Process

Automated processes make operations efficient and effective. Digital displays of order numbers in restaurants make waiting less anxious. Vending machines free employees' time and also offer uniform supplies. Palm tops to take orders in hotels make food delivery almost error free.

Physical Evidence

Virtual reality replicates physical experiences and gives a good experience of the real thing. Three-dimensional tours also give a near-real experience.

Infrastructure created with the help of technology boosts tourism. It also helps in restoring and maintaining tourism attractions such as monuments.

The above discussion indicates that technology finds application in all areas of the marketing mix and it is up to a marketer to decide the right combination. It is commonly said that high technology and high touch or technology with human face is the best option.

SUMMARY

Technology plays a very important role in tourism and tourism marketing. It can contribute to tourism growth, enhance tourism experiences, create tourism experiences, protect tourism, destroy tourism, and can be the focal point of tourism experiences. Its contribution in marketing is equally important. It is used for almost all managerial functions of marketing and for developing the marketing mix. Of all technologies, information and communication technology (ICT) plays an important role in tourism marketing because of its information-intensive nature. It helps in digitizing the information and some products that are distributed online. The important technologies for tourism marketing are multimedia, virtual tours, CRS, GDS, and the

Internet. These have changed decision making in tourism. All activities are performed in cyberspace except the actual travel. Websites are emerging as new shops and attracting tourists to web spaces. Their designing has become a challenge. Encouraging online purchase needs a good website. Good content, navigation, and security develops an effective site.

Direct link between marketers and tourists has initiated change in established traditional distribution channels. Old middlemen are finding competition in new online firms. Traditional firms are going online to face this challenge. Good technology and good management can deliver very effective results for tourism businesses.

KEY TERMS

Centralized reservation systems These are reservation systems with centralized databases and decentralized distributions.

Disintermediation It is the elimination of intermediaries from the distribution chain as a result of online direct contact between sellers and buyers.

E-tourism It is digitization of all processes and value chains in the tourism, travel, hospitality, and catering industry.

Global distribution systems These are computerized reservation systems that distribute reservation and information services of many CRSs through their sales outlets.

Model of electronic travel (MDSD) The model considers sequential approach of e-commerce

functions with the sequence marketing, sales, delivery, and payment.

Reintermediation It is replacement of old intermediaries such as travel agents with new ones such as online agents.

System of Information Technologies (SIT) In tourism it comprises computers, CRS, digital telephone networks, videos, videotext, teleconferencing, electronic locking systems, e-commerce, and so on.

Virtual reality It is a computer mediated multisensory experience that attempts to replace physical world with artificial world.

Virtual tours These are computer mediated multisensory experiences of tours.

EXERCISES

REVIEW QUESTIONS

1. What is the role of technology in tourism?
2. How does ICT help in tourism marketing?
3. What is disintermediation? Is the threat real? Discuss.
4. What role is played by CRS and GDS in tourism marketing?
5. Discuss the role of Internet in tourism.

PRACTICE EXERCISES

1. Visit websites of different tourism firms. Write your experiences and relate good experiences with the features of sites. What do you learn about the websites?

2. Book a tour online and record the steps. How is it different from offline purchase?

PROJECTS

1. Visit a travel agency and explore the GDS used by it. What categories of facilities are distributed through it? Ask the agent about its benefits and drawbacks and report.
2. Conduct a small survey in your city to find the use of online travel. What encourages or discourages people to go or not to go for it? What improvements should be made in online systems to increase the acceptance?

REFERENCES

Bennett, Marion M. 1995, 'The consumer marketing revolution: The impact of IT on tourism', *Journal of Vacation Marketing*, vol.1, pp. 376-382.

Buhalis, Dimitrios 2003, *E-tourism: Information Technology for Strategic Management*, FT Prentice Hall, London.

Cheong, Roger 1995, 'The virtual threat to travel and tourism', Tourism Management, vol. 16, no.6, pp. 417-422.

E-marketer report 2007, 'Asia-Pacific Online Travel: Focus on China and India.'

Forrester Research 2006, Asia Pacific Consumer Technographics.

Go, Frank M. 1992, March, 'The role of computerized reservation system in the hospitality industry', *Tourism Management*, vol. 13, no. 1, pp. 22-26.

Hultkrantz, Lars 2002, 'Will there be a unified wireless marketplace for tourism?' *Current Issues in Tourism*, vol. 5, no. 2, pp.149-161.

IAMAI 2007, September, 'Consumer E-commerce Market in India 2006-2007.'

Lindsay, Patricia 1992, March, *Tourism Management*, 'CRS supply and Demand', vol. 13, no. 1, pp. 11.

Marcussen, Carl H. 2009, March, 'Trends in European Internet distribution of travel and tourism services', Centre for Regional and Tourism Research, Denmark, accessed on 20 April, 2010.

PhoCusWright 2008 Indian Online Travel Overview, PhoCus Wright Inc.

Poon, A. 1989, 'Competitive strategies in new tourism', in Cooper, C. P (ed), *Progress in Tourism, Recreation and Hospitality Management*, CBS Publishers, New Delhi.

Leticia, S.A., Ana M. D. Marttin, and V. C. Rodolfo 2007, 'Relationship marketing and information and communication technologies: Analysis of retail travel agencies', *Journal of Travel Research*, vol. 45, no. 4, pp. 453-463.

Stipanuk, David M. 1993, 'Tourism and technology-interactions and implications', *Tourism Management*, vol. 14, pp. 269-278.

The Hindu 2007, June 13, 'Now make your trips online'.

UNCTAD 2000, 'Electronic commerce and tourism-New perspectives and challenges for developing countries', UNCTAD TD/B/COM.3/EM.9/2 July 27, 2000.

UNCTAD 2005, 'Report of the expert meeting on ICT and tourism for development', TD/B/COM.3/EM.25/3 December 20, 2005.

Werthner, Hannes and Stefan Klein 1999, 'ICT and the changing landscape of global tourism distribution', *Electronic Markets*, vol. 9, no. 4, pp. 256 -262.

Website References

Zhenhua, Liu(nd), 'Internet tourism marketing: Potential and constraints', hotelonline.com, accessed on 9 July, 2008.

CASE STUDY

YATRA ONLINE

The online travel market in India has a number of players trying to ride the new wave of technology. These compete on the platform of information highway by giving instant access to quality service. One of the big players in this league is yatra.com, with 35 per cent market share of online travel business in the country. A recipient of awards and recognitions of 'Best Online Travel Agency' of the year 2008 at the Galileo Express TravelWorld Awards, the only Indian travel company among the 'Top 100 Startups in Asia' by Red Herring and the 'most used travel website' by Juxt Consult in their India Online Survey 2008.

Its portfolio includes services for travel-related information, pricing, availability and reservations for airlines, hotels, holiday packages, buses and car rentals across 5,000 large cities and small rural areas throughout India. It uses multi-language customer service centre and offers its travel services on mobile and through its exclusive holiday lounges and other distribution outlets.

It was founded in December 2005 and since then it has grown fast and expanded to 10 Indian cities, the USA, and the UK and received revenues of $ 9.4 million, $ 112 million, and $ 240 million in 2006, 2007, and 2008 respectively. It posted profits only in the quarter ending March, 2009. Its real-time inventory in May 2009 gave access to 10 domestic and 72 international airlines and provided instant reach to over 3,500 hotels in India and over 90,000 hotels across the globe.

The journey of Yatra has been phenomenal from a 2 people company to a 700 people strong company in 2 years. Gross Revenue for Yatra grew from $200k per month to $20 million per month in just 2 years time. It has been supported by the name itself, entry in market at the right time, and its marketing initiatives. It has its fair share of competition from makemytrip.co.in, cleartrip.com, and travelocity.co.in. All of these provide the same online flight and hotel booking facilities. But it differentiates itself by the prices offered, the availability of seats/rooms, website usability, after sales service, and smart product innovations (such as its wap portal and holiday lounges).

It plans to migrate from a predominantly flight business to a hotel and holiday-led business and maintain the market leadership position in sight of competition from existing and new foreign players. It believes in its endeavour to instil attention to detail in all aspects to provide flawless and excellent travel services.

(*Source:* www.yatra.com)

DISCUSSION QUESTIONS

1. What makes online company Yatra distinct from offline suppliers?
2. Can other firms entering the market now repeat the same story?
3. What makes offers of Yatra innovative?

CHAPTER 16

Tourism Marketing and Development

LEARNING OBJECTIVES

Marketing identifies needs and wants and builds demand by suggesting means to potential buyers. This creates a cycle of development in the economy. But it can also have negative effects when it fuels demand of luxuries in poor economies or adds to the social costs. A judicious application of marketing can ensure overall benefits to the society.

The focus of this chapter is a synergistic link between tourism marketing and inclusive development. In this chapter, the following areas are explored.

- Tourism marketing and development
- Socially responsible marketing
- Social marketing
- Participants in tourism marketing and their role in development
- Public or government organizations
- Private organizations
- Non-governmental organizations

INTRODUCTION

Tourism marketing builds image of an attraction, draws tourists, and triggers forces that affect both the hosts and the guests. A destination may not be able to attract a good number of tourists without marketing. Marketing can influence behaviours of tourists during tours and also those of host communities with tourists. It can initiate both positive and negative changes in the host and guest societies.

The impacts of tourism marketing can be negative when it begins with short-term objectives such as increasing tourist flows or revenues. It can attract mass of tourists who are not concerned with the sustainability of the place, thus shortening its life cycle. It also has the power to promote responsible tourism, thus initiating developmental forces.

A systematic promotional and informational campaign can help in regulating the behaviour of both guests and hosts, thus bringing greater benefits through longer stays and higher satisfaction.

For instance, take the case of developing countries that want to develop tourism quickly because of late entry on world tourism scene. They open their destinations for tourists and market aggressively. Tourists come for novelty and low prices and might believe in unlimited opportunities for pleasure, as promised through promotional campaigns. This often contradicts with the expectations of hosts and shocks them as they might have not thought of it. As a result, anti tourists sentiments are developed. A well planned marketing can achieve better results in such cases.

Volunteer tourism is another example where tourists are marketed the idea of higher level of involvement in host communities. Tourists stay for longer periods and participate in community activities and contribute through their expertise, be it in hygiene, education, or energy. They do not stay as passive outsiders who pay and get services. Without marketing it would be difficult to sell the idea of working for social and moral reasons.

Tourism marketing contributes to the development of society by triggering positive forces in its environment. It has been able to increase the tourist flow at many destinations that in turn has led to the economic, social, and cultural development of host societies.

A properly regulated marketing can persuade concerned parties to adopt sustainable approach. It can suggest ways of transferring benefits of tourism to different stakeholders and can also generate many benefits by itself.

TOURISM MARKETING AND DEVELOPMENT

Tourism marketing helps in the economic, social, and cultural development of both host and guest communities. A discussion on the role of tourism marketing on development will help you in understanding it better.

Tourism Marketing and Economic Development

Tourism is an economic activity and a business. It brings investment, jobs, incomes, foreign exchange, and other benefits. But if all these benefits go to the outsiders who invest capital and establish business and the locals receive the burden of inflation and shortage of goods, then tourism fails in its responsibilities.

The nature of tourism industry is such that the employment and revenue generation happens in both the host and the home countries because the travel is arranged through a chain of agents working in both the countries.

Tourism marketing is done through a chain of tour operators and travel agents who assemble packages for further selling. The activities of buying components of packages, bundling, costing, and selling require large amount of manpower, thus creating employment. A good number of job opportunities are added by principals or suppliers of package components. Manpower is also needed in call centres and knowledge centres of travel companies. The high employment generated in tourism marketing soon cascades to other sectors of the economy.

Tourism marketing is a big revenue generator. If tourism marketers are able to promote inbound tourism then it brings foreign exchange too.

Tourism Marketing and Social Development

The presence of tourists from different places infuses diverse cultural values among hosts. It becomes visible in adopted mannerisms, commercial staged festivals, new social relationships, and so on. Crimes such as sex tourism and drug peddling may also begin. An aware host society can help in controlling it but they need to be informed about its various dimensions and marketing steps in here. Tourism marketing can put the behaviours of host and guest societies in proper perspective for each other to understand and appreciate. The cultural diversities can be promoted for learning from each other, rather than closing the doors for anything foreign or blindly accepting novelty .

Tourists from individualistic societies of the West can learn about collectivism of the East and vice versa. An exposure to a developed country helps to begin a process of thinking in visitors from developing world to have similar levels in their nations.

The *Atithi Devo Bhava* campaign of the Ministry of Tourism is an example of developing sensitivity towards the country's resources and visitors, thus leading to positive social changes in the long term.

Tourism Marketing and Development of Ecology

The popularity of a destination often brings large number of tourists to a place, much beyond its carrying capacity. As a result, its attraction and beauty diminishes, be it a beach, hill, or forest. Along with it, the essential resources, such as water and power, fall short of requirements. These are then transported from other places, thus further increasing the pressure of vehicles.

Marketing can go a long way in mitigating such effects. It can persuade tour operators to adopt sustainable practices. Rather than government putting a cap on the number of tourists, a responsible tourism industry can itself devise regulations for its members. It might be difficult in the short run considering the loss in business, but will sustain the destination and business in the long run. The problems of litter, waste, and garbage can be solved in a similar manner.

Tourism marketing can contribute to development only if socially responsible approach is adopted, otherwise it will benefit only the tourism sellers and tourists.

Socially responsible marketing balances the interests of society with those of customers/tourists. The other objectives such as tourist satisfaction, profitability, market share, etc. still remain intact.

SOCIALLY RESPONSIBLE MARKETING

Modern marketing management considers interests of society as an integral part of marketing process and its welfare is weighed in the process of identification and satisfaction of consumers' needs. Marketing of sustainable and responsible tourism, and ecotourism takes into account the long-term impacts of promoting tourism. It emphasizes preservation of tourism attractions and associated environments for future and involves responsible behaviour by the participants. It might even increase the cost of tour to generate revenues needed to invest back into maintenance of destinations. Persuading tourists to pay more is not an easy task and that is done through socially responsible marketing.

Socially responsible approach to marketing considers impacts of all marketing activities on the society and follows a proactive approach to ensure that it is not harmed. In tourism marketing, it takes the cause of either sustainable forms of tourism or promotes sustainable practices in the form of do's and don'ts. For example, tourists can enjoy their vacation but may be asked to respect local traditions and follow dress codes acceptable in host destinations. It means putting little restrictions on behaviours of tourists in the interests of healthy interaction with hosts.

SOCIAL MARKETING

Social marketing is a step up on socially responsible marketing where marketing principles are used for the promotion of social causes such as keeping the city clean, safe driving, do not smoke, and so on. Kotler and Andreasen (1991) define social marketing as 'differing from other areas of marketing only with respect to the objectives of the marketer and his or her organization. Social marketing seeks to influence social behaviours not to benefit the marketer, but to benefit the target audience and the general society.' Here, the objective is betterment of society. It uses the marketing principles used to sell products to 'sell' ideas, attitudes, and behaviours. Social marketing is very relevant for tourism as it builds those values and practices in the environment that portray friendly image. Nobody would like to visit a place that is full of touts, beggars, potholes, filth and garbage, graffiti on monuments, and so on. Social marketing works on such issues and has the potential to address many similar causes. This marketing does not bring revenues immediately, but rather in long term and can be undertaken both by the government or the associations/federations of private operators. Some business can engage in such marketing as part of their programmes of business ethics.

Thus, social marketing can contribute enormously to the overall betterment of the society.

PARTICIPANTS IN SOCIALLY RESPONSIBLE MARKETING AND THEIR ROLES

The marketers, tourists, society, host populations, and government are active participants in socially responsible marketing as shown in Fig. 16.1.

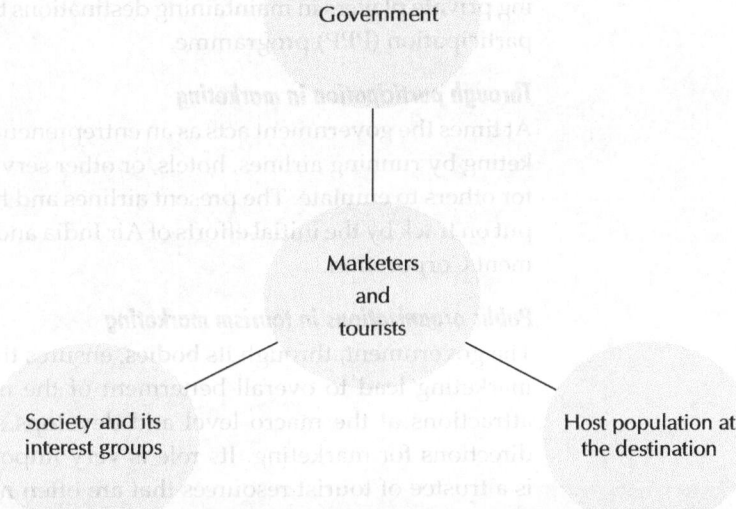

Fig. 16.1 Players in Socially Responsible Marketing

A discussion on their roles explains how each performs its part.

Government

The government controls marketing of tourism resources and pressure of man-made tourism on nature through regulatory and participative mechanisms. It uses the following methods.

Through laws and rules

The government frames legislation to ensure ethical and responsible practices. The general business legislation applies to tourism marketing in India in the absence of tourism specific legislation. Consumer Protection Act, 1986 protects tourists and so does Competition Act 2000. The increase in airfare by private airlines in the first week of February 2009 and its investigation by the government to see if it is a case of cartelization is an example of such regulation. Medical visa procedure has been streamlined to promote medical tourism in the country.

Through policies and procedures

Government can control marketing through its policies that are guiding in nature and marketers are encouraged to follow these voluntarily. The

Incredible India and *Atithi Devo Bhava* campaigns are such cases where private sector is encouraged to participate. The government is also involving private players in maintaining destinations through its public-private participation (PPP) programme.

Through participation in marketing
At times the government acts as an entrepreneur and participates in marketing by running airlines, hotels, or other services. It sets the standards for others to emulate. The present airlines and hotel market in India was put on track by the initial efforts of Air India and India Tourism Development Corporation.

Public organizations in tourism marketing
The government, through its bodies, ensures that benefits from tourism marketing lead to overall betterment of the nation. It markets tourist attractions at the macro level and develops strategies to give future directions for marketing. Its role is very important as the government is a trustee of tourist resources that are often national assets. These can be national parks, beaches, or mountains that can be fully exploited but without any damage. The Himalayas, the Ganges, the *Char Dhams*, and the Taj Mahal all are marketed to potential visitors. Private operators do not market at the macro level. They all market their own services at the micro level. It is the government that makes a destination popular and then benefits are reaped by private players by organizing tours to such destinations. For example, the government of India through its bodies, the Archaeological Survey of India and the Ministry of Forests, makes all the initial efforts to get its properties listed under UNESCO's World Heritage Sites. Once a site gets inscribed in the list, marketers promote tours to these sites.

For the marketing of tourism attractions, the government tries to establish a balance in the following important areas.

1. Nature and types of attractions: A balance is required in order to attract visitors throughout the year for different reasons and in different seasons (seasonal distribution).
2. Geographic distribution of attractions (regional distribution): These may be spread throughout the country to cascade benefits to maximum possible area or may be confined to few areas if it feels that host populations and resources are not yet ready to be opened.
3. Extent of exploitation allowed: It may give guidelines to be followed by private players for sustainable use of resources

4. Develop and market new destinations and maintain old ones: This will help in maintaining its product basket as per the market requirements.

5. Maintain a balance between old and new markets: The government wants to ensure sustenance in flow of tourists by constantly monitoring changes in preferences and finding new markets for its attractions.

GOVERNMENT BODIES—NATIONAL TOURISM OFFICES, STATE TOURISM OFFICES, AND LOCAL BODIES

Tourism product is a combination of large number of inputs derived from different businesses. The tourism-related activities and functions find place in different government bodies related to tourism. As per the Constitution of India, pilgrimages outside India, railways, national highways, waterways, airways, foreign exchange, archaeological sites, and monuments of national importance all find place in the union list. The state list covers domestic pilgrimages, inns, sites, monuments not declared of national importance, state roads and the concurrent list has forests, adulteration of foodstuffs, protection of wild animals, and so on.

Tourism in India is managed through a hierarchy that generally corresponds with the administrative levels of the country. It uses the National Tourism Office (NTO) at the national level, followed by the State Tourism Office (STO) at the state level and the local bodies at lower levels of cities and destinations.

> Tourism as a separate subject is not listed in the seventh schedule of the Constitution of India that defines distribution of powers among different levels of government bodies.

National Tourism Offices

A central coordinating body is essential to direct tourism development and in most of the countries a National Tourism Organization or Corporation regulates tourism at the top level. The Ministry of Tourism, Government of India acts as NTO and is responsible for the advancement of tourism in the country. Its interest lies in increasing the revenues through tourism by adopting strategies such as increasing the number of visitors, their length of stay and spending.

It functions through its various divisions to focus on different dimensions of tourism such as hospitality, education, marketing, and so on. The organization chart (Fig. 16.2) of the Ministry of Tourism along with a description of its functions presents a view of its role in the country.

> The tourism development and its marketing are regulated at different levels and for this a hierarchy of public bodies works.

Ministry of Tourism

An independent minister heads the Ministry of Tourism. The administrative head of the Ministry is the Secretary (Tourism) who also acts as

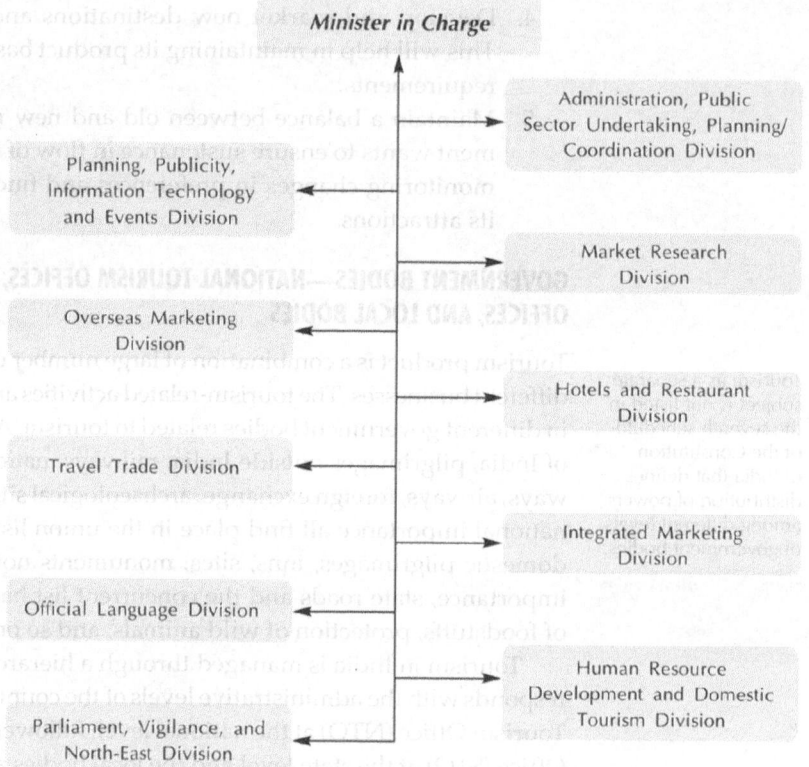

Fig. 16.2 Organization Chart of Ministry of Tourism

the Director General (DG), Tourism. The Directorate General of Tourism has 20 offices within the country, 13 offices abroad, and one subordinate office/project, that is, the Indian Institute of Skiing and Mountaineering (IISM)/Gulmarg Winter Sports Project (GWSP). The Ministry of Tourism has the following important institutions under its charge.

1. India Tourism Development Corporation (ITDC)
2. Indian Institute of Tourism and Travel Management (IITTM)
3. National Council for Hotel Management and Catering Technology (NCHMCT) and the Institutes of Hotel Management

The Ministry of Tourism functions through 10 divisions, each headed by a director. The divisions are as follows.

1. Administration, Public Sector Undertaking, Planning/Coordination Division

2. Planning, Publicity, Information Technology and Events Division
3. Market Research Division
4. Overseas Marketing Division
5. Hotels and Restaurant Division
6. Travel Trade Division
7. Integrated Marketing Division
8. Official Language Division
9. Human Resource Development and Domestic Tourism Division
10. Parliament, Vigilance, and North-East Division

These divisions assist in performing the following functions of the ministry.

1. All policy matters, including:
   a. Development policies
   b. Incentives
   c. External assistance
   d. Manpower development
   e. Promotion and marketing
   f. Investment facilitation
2. Planning
3. Coordination with other Ministries, Department, State/UT Governments
4. Regulations through standards and guidelines
5. Infrastructure and product development
6. Human resource development
7. Publicity and marketing
8. Research, analysis, monitoring, and evaluation
9. International cooperation and external assistance
   a. International bodies
   b. Bilateral agreements
   c. External assistance
   d. Foreign technical collaboration
10. Legislation and Parliamentary work
11. Establishment matters
12. Overall review of the functioning of the field offices
13. Vigilance matters
14. Official language and implementation of official language policy
15. VIP references
16. Budget coordination and related matters
17. Plan coordination and monitoring
18. Integrated finance division

19. Organization and management work
20. Welfare, grievances, and protocol
21. Assistance in the formulation of policies by providing feedback from the field offices
22. Monitoring of plan projects and assisting in the plan formulation
23. Coordinating the activities of field offices and their supervision
24. Regulation of hotels and tour operators
    a. Approval and classification of hotels and restaurants
    b. Approval of travel agents, tour operators, and tourist transport operators, and so on.
25. Inspection and quality control
26. a. Guide service
    b. Complaints and redressal
27. Infrastructure development
    a. Release of incentives
    b. Tourist facilitation and information
    c. Field publicity, promotion, and marketing
    d. Hospitality programmes
    e. Conventions and conferences

Thus, it is seen that the work of the ministry is comprehensive and covers almost every aspect of tourism.

But the transport sector is not covered by the Ministry of Tourism. The government regulates airlines and railways through its Ministry of Civil aviation and Ministry of Railways. The dominant presence of Air India is used to offer connectivity to tourist places. Railways actively market tours through the Indian Railway Catering and Tourism Corporation Limited (IRCTC). Similarly, roadways are controlled by the State Roadways corporations.

State Tourism Departments/Councils/Corporations/Offices

These function at the province or state level. In India, the Ministry of Tourism of the state with the State Tourism Corporation performs functions similar to national bodies. These run hotels and motels to promote tourism, develop destinations and attractions, frame policies, and also act as controlling authority. The bodies at this level promote tourism with a better understanding of local conditions. The organization structure here differs from state to state. Tourism-centric states maintain a relatively elaborate set up.

These have been very successful in promoting state attractions. For example, Haryana state pioneered the development of highway tourism in the country through its chain of motels that was later adopted by many other states. Similarly, Rajasthan worked on its heritage, Goa on beaches, Himachal on nature, Uttarakhand on nature and pilgrimage, and Kerala on ayurveda.

All these bodies work closely with the central government. These bodies prepare tourism policies and plans at the state level and make efforts regarding land availability for tourism projects, putting single window system, and encouraging public-private partnership.

Local Bodies

The functions of local bodies cover many areas important for tourism such as the maintenance of area. These also control rest houses, museums, and so on.

In the Indian political set-up, the panchayats at the village level and the municipal bodies in the city are involved in developing tourism. The government may also constitute boards for the management of places of tourist attractions or temples, and so on. These bodies have local citizens as representatives that make sure that local interests are not sacrificed for the interests of tourists or tourism marketers. Kerala has effectively used these local bodies for tourism promotion and its three Ps model involves public-private partnership and panchayats (local governments). Its District Tourism Promotion Councils with District Collector as Chairman and selected people's representatives and official members coordinate the development of lesser known tourist centres within the districts. This has led to enhanced focus on tourism in the districts.

The powers given to these bodies are in accordance to Panchayati Raj Acts, Municipality rules, and Land Development Acts of respective states. The Ministry of Tourism of Government of India, in its guidelines on development of camp sites in remote areas, specifically mentions the role of local administration and local participation.

> Local bodies are involved in the development of tourism so that local requirements are appreciated and residents can participate in the decision-making.

PRIVATE ORGANIZATIONS

The role of private sector in tourism varies from country to country. In India, its role was secondary and became prominent after the opening of economy in the 1990s. Being a controlled economy, the government took all the responsibility till the market was mature enough to yield benefits for the private sector. After that, the government confined itself to the job of regulator and allowed market to go competitive, be it through open sky policy or allowing foreign direct investment. Even the Ministry of Tourism is promoting public-private partnership in areas of heritage conservation, promotion, infrastructure development, and so on, hitherto considered an exclusive domain of the government. However, till date the share of private sector for funding of national tourism promotion is nil and the government provides the entire amount of the funds. While in other countries, the private sector pitches to the extent of 50 per cent.

The private sector needs to undertake greater social responsibility by investing in tourism at the macro level, where gains flow over a long period and benefit industry in general than a particular marketer. With this view, the government has signed a memorandum of understanding (MoU) with the private sector where private operators will give a bank guarantee for 100 per cent repayment of allowance within 2-4 years given to them for developing Indian market abroad.

In the National Tourism Policy, 2002 the following roles are specified for the private sector.

1. Build and manage the required tourist facilities in all places of tourist interest.
2. Assume collective responsibility for laying down industry standards, ethics, and fair practices.
3. Ensure preservation and protection of tourist attractions and give lead in green practices.
4. Sponsor maintenance of monuments, museums and parks, and provision of public conveniences and facilities.
5. Involve the local community in tourism projects and ensure that the benefits of tourism accrue to them in right measure.
6. Undertake industry training and manpower development to achieve excellence in quality of services.
7. Participate in the preparation of investment guidelines and marketing strategies and assist in database creation and research.
8. Facilitate safety and security of tourists
9. Endeavour to promote tourism on a sustained and long-term perspective.
10. Collaborate with the government in the promotion and marketing of destinations.

Private organizations have contributed to the image of India through their professionalism and quality of service in all the above areas.

NON-GOVERNMENTAL ORGANIZATIONS

These fulfil social causes. A number of these work in areas of education, wildlife, rural development, and are concerned with tourism when tourism impacts these areas. These work for protection from impacts of tourism or development of responsible forms of tourism. These may focus on preservation of environment and adoption of good practices, education of hosts and guests, community participation, preservation of heritage, and so on. The Indian National Trust on Art and Cultural Heritage (INTACH) is one such organization working for protection of heritage in the country and also promotes tourism to popularize the heritage. Aga Khan Trust is another organization that focuses on preserving heritage. The rural tourism scheme of the government of India involves these actively for the execution of projects. All United Nations Development Programme (UNDP) supported rural tourism projects also take these as active partners.

Thus, the government and non-government bodies play their part and proactively use tourism marketing to ensure that tourism benefits the society at large.

SUMMARY

Tourism as an industry has both advantages and disadvantages. Tourism is self-destructive. But tourism marketing can make all the players in tourism more conscious and involved, thus minimizing the negativity and maximizing benefits. Tourism marketing itself can unleash many developmental forces in the sociocultural and economic environment. But it needs a little regulation, otherwise the short-term motives of profit tend to override other concerns. This regulatory role is performed by the government through its bodies at national, state, and local levels. Through

policies and controls these regulatory bodies ensure that tourism is marketed with development in mind. Even the government becomes a marketer by direct participation in tourism business. Lately government has been preparing to involve private sector in tourism and its marketing through its private-public participation (PPP) scheme. The NGOs are involved in rural tourism and community based tourism.

Tourism marketing is not all about unabashed selling and use of natural resources; it is equally concerned with development of host societies.

KEY TERMS

Development It is the betterment of environment and quality of life of humans.

Economic development It is the development of economic wealth of countries/regions for the well being of their inhabitants. It is usually measured in terms of gross national product (GNP) and per capita income.

National Tourism Organization/Office It is a central coordinating body that directs tourism development in a country.

Regional tourism organizations These are the coordinating bodies that look after development of tourism at the regional level.

Social marketing It is the type of marketing that seeks to influence social behaviours to benefit the society and uses the general principles of marketing.

Socially responsible marketing A modern marketing concept that considers interests of society as an integral part of marketing process and its welfare is weighed in the process of identification and satisfaction of consumers' needs.

State tourism organizations These are the coordinating bodies that regulate and direct development of tourism at the state level.

EXERCISES

REVIEW QUESTIONS

1. What is the role of tourism marketing in development? Discuss social development of a destination.
2. 'The economic benefits of tourism marketing do not reach the masses.' Discuss.
3. Discuss the role of government bodies in tourism marketing.

PRACTICE EXERCISES

1. Write the advantages and disadvantages of tourism to the host societies. Then suggest marketing strategies to maximize each advantage and minimize each disadvantage.
2. Study the National Tourism Policy, 2002 thoroughly and find the developmental goals included in it. How does it relate tourism and development?
3. Visit a site of rural tourism and try to understand the developmental role of tourism in a village.

PROJECTS

1. Survey the tourism projects in the nearby areas and prepare a worksheet explaining the role played by government bodies in its execution and marketing.
2. Read the guidelines for inclusion of a site in world heritage list from the website, www.unesco.org. Find out how much work is to be done by the government and the conditions of development included in the project.

REFERENCES

Directorate of Science, Technology and Industry 2003, July, 'Organization of economic co-operation and development', National tourism Policy of Australia.

Hall, C.M. 1999, 'Rethinking collaboration and partnership: A public policy perspective', *Journal of Sustainable Tourism*, vol. 7, Nos. 3&4, pp.274.

Kotler, Philip and A. Andreasen 1991, Strategic Marketing for Non-profit Organizations, Prentice Hall, Engleswood, Cliffs, New Jersey.

National Tourism Policy 2002, Ministry of Tourism, Government of India.

SRI International 1999, October, 'Tourism promotion agencies: International experience and best practices', Strategy Report for Lebanon National Council for Tourism Promotion.

UNEP 2002, 'Sustainable tourism', Tourism Briefing towards Earth Summit 2002.

WTO 2004, April, Survey of Destination Management Organisations Report.

WTTC 2003, Blueprint for New Tourism.

Website References

www.tourism.gov.in, accessed on 14 April 2010
www.unwto.org, accessed on 14 April 2010
www.unesco.org, accessed on 14 April 2010

CASE STUDY

TOURISM FOR WHOM?

Tourism development at a destination is closely linked to all dimensions of development. It brings economic, social, and cultural changes in the host society. The notable ones are as follows.

Multiplier Effect

Tourism is inevitably linked to all other industries and every rupee spent on tourism finds its place as an input in other industries, either directly through purchases in tourism or indirectly through increased incomes of people engaged in tourism industry.

Foreign Exchange

Most countries focus on inbound tourism to earn foreign exchange. It improves the balance of payments position of a nation.

Employment

Tourism is labour-intensive industry and generates large employment for both skilled and unskilled categories and is particularly important for a populous India.

Cultural Development

Tourism brings an exchange of different cultures and a process of learning from each other is initiated. The foreign travels of Indians have made them learn about the work culture and punctuality of the societies in the West.

Social Development

The cultural exchanges broaden the outlook of people and make them look critically at their own systems. Many changes in Indian society, such as women empowerment, are the results of such interactions.

But tourism has its downsides too. Foreign exchange gains may not be enough if outbound expense exceeds inbound revenues. Further, there can be leakages when the goods consumed by tourists are imported and this leakage can be as high as 90 per cent.

The sheen is taken out of employment benefits when only low-paying jobs are offered to locals in the absence of suitable skill sets. Moreover, the tourism places get expensive with increased demand from tourists. As a result, the increased incomes from tourism are not sufficient to sustain.

Cultural and social development too experience a cultural shock when hosts and guests with completely different values come together. Sex tourism, and slum tourism are some of the voyeuristic forms resulting from such exchanges. Sometimes the visible aspects of a culture may be absorbed by another for its attraction than goodness. It is often seen at tourist places where the host society copies the guests.

When the negative aspects overpower the positive effects the opposition to tourists starts breeding. This is further compounded by control of tourism facilities by outside businessmen who can afford to finance ventures and employ locals as labour. The increased tourism often creates pollution, degradation of environment, shortage of resources such as water and power, inflation, and so on. What host population gets is a new form of employment, which may be marginally better than traditional occupations in terms of money but places them at a low level in the social ladder.

DISCUSSION QUESTIONS

1. Tourism is for whom? Is it for guests who have transitory interest in a place and will shift to a new one soon, or the hosts who get a new economy?

2. How can the impacts of tourism be balanced with the help of marketing?

Case Studies

1. AIR TRAVEL IN INDIA—THE TURBULENT SKIES

Air Transport in India has undergone tremendous changes in the past decade. It started with the limited opening of Indian skies in 1994 with the scrapping of Air Corporation Act, when scheduled flights were allowed to private operators. Beginning with Jet Airlines, it soon saw the tables turning with the entry of Deccan Airways in the budget segment. And suddenly a large segment of people could afford to fly. This was followed by the entry of large number of operators in airlines business. It increased the traffic in air, leading to congestion at airports that were found to be small and unprepared for the rush. But the gold rush was given a break by rising fuel costs that started bleeding the airlines' profits. Airlines adopted all strategies to cut costs such as reducing in-flight services and facilities. Efforts were even made to reduce the weight of the crafts to cut fuel consumption through strategies such as substitution of metal cutlery by plastic. At the same time, the global economy started feeling the recessional effects in 2008 that led to reduced business in many sectors and affected the load factor of airlines. The higher costs and lowering revenues put airlines in a downward spiral, resulting in job cuts. One such large-scale attempt by Jet Airways in 2008 got nationwide exposure on mass media and the government intervened to fulfil its social responsibility. It impressed upon the Jet management not to fire employees and also reduced the charges on fuel price to help airlines tide over losses.

While all these developments were happening, the government was also working on modernization and expansion of airports through private participation. The developers of airports were allowed to levy airport development fee (ADF) that further added to the cost of flying, as this charge is passed to buyers. The airlines in India also face the challenge of operating from airports that are among the costliest in the world with charges such as landing, passenger, security, infrastructure, navigation, and parking.

The airlines are caught in a difficult situation with markets under recession and costs going up, and a business that seemed promising in 2006-07 seems to be losing its sheen.

1. What marketing strategies can be adopted by airlines to increase revenues?
2. Suggest the changes in the product and services mix that can help in controlling costs.
3. How can strategies such as price hedging be used to counter fuel price increases?

2. GOD'S OWN COUNTRY—A MODEL OF INTEGRATED TOURISM DEVELOPMENT

'God's Own Country' Kerela has captured the attention of the international tourism market and is listed among the top 100 brands of India and has been accorded the highly coveted 'Super Brand' status. Kerala is cited as 'one of the 50 destinations of a lifetime' by *National Geographic Traveller and* 'one of the 10 paradises found'. It is also a 'partner state' to the World Tourism and Travel Council. Kerala as a destination is mentioned in international travel magazines such as the *National Geographic, Conde Nast Traveller, Geo Saison,* and *Newsweek.*

While the state initiatives in tourism date back to the late 1980s, the agenda for systematic tourism planning and development was set in 1995.

Its inclusive approach for tourism development rests on the following pillars.

Policy

Its policy focuses on supporting a transparent and inclusive policy process, promoting fair and open competition, strengthening institutional capacity to implement and enforce policies, and drawing international support to augment expertise.

Holy Spirit
(*Courtesy:* Poras Chaudhary)

Product Development

The approach adopted followed leveraging core strengths, creating new products, building unique selling point (USP), focusing on sustainable development to offer products of international quality, creating an enabling investment

Backwaters
(*Courtesy:* Poras Chaudhary)

environment, stimulating demand, and promoting partnerships to ensure the flow of funds into the tourism sector.

The state has created tourism products purely out of its natural and traditional strengths that successfully meet international quality expectations and compete with international destinations in marketing. Today, Kerala's 'backwaters' and 'ayurveda' are globally identified and uniquely positioned.

Marketing

Hallmarks of its marketing have been building a brand, emphasizing quality assurances, providing demand-driven information, competing at a global level, and collaborating on international and regional platforms to create a highly visible platform for the state.

Infrastructure

Focusing on the core and linkage infrastructure and investing in strategically focused capacity to support development priorities are the main points of infrastructure development.

Tourism Services

It focuses on building a critical mass of tourism workers, increasing technical skills, strengthening community entrepreneurial skills, and augmenting managerial capacity to build a service sector sensitive to tourists and tourism.

Active Role of District-level Institutions

Through decentralization, Kerala has fully involved its district level institutions in tourism development. The District Tourism Promotion Councils (DTPCs), with the District Collector as Chairman, are actively involved in the tourism activity of their region, especially in matters related to sustainable tourism development, environment control and visitor management, local-level infrastructure, and promotional projects. The amendment in its local bodies act proposes for tourism conservation and preservation and envisages the presence of the district-level officers in the environment committee with responsibility for the preparation of sustainable tourism development plans for their regions. It is also envisaged that these councils will have the freedom to launch their own development schemes by mobilizing funds with local support.

Certifications for Tourism Products and Services

Kerala tourism has put in place certifications for its key tourism products—houseboats, ayurveda, and hotels—to ensure that the tourist receives products that are acceptable, uniform, and adhering to certain basic standards.

'Gold star' and 'silver star' certifications for houseboats

Considering the sustainability of this unique tourism product and the fragile backwater environment, Kerala Tourism has an approval scheme. This covers the quality of the houseboats—materials used for their construction, facilities offered by them, the quality of furniture, services, and safety and security measures.

'Green palm' certifications for eco-friendly measures

Houseboats that adopt environment-friendly practices in their operation are awarded the 'Green Palm Certification'. Specifications for obtaining this certification include mainly non-discharge of solid wastes and sewage directly to the water, alternative arrangements for disposal of solid wastes and sewage by providing scientifically designed septic tanks or bio-chemical toilets, and use of environmentally-friendly materials and local employment.

'Green leaf' and 'olive leaf' certifications for ayurveda centres

To sustain ayurveda in its original form and ensure the survival of the unique tourism product, Kerala Tourism has a classification scheme for ayurveda centres. Standards of the ayurvedic centres are evaluated in terms of the authenticity of the treatment provided, the training of the staff, the conveniences and amenities, and the quality of furniture.

'STEP' certification for safe-to-eat places

Kerala certifies eating places with the STEP (safe-to-eat places) certification to build confidence, especially among foreign tourists. Such certifications rigorously take into account the hygiene and quality standards of restaurants in the preparation and serving of cuisine.

The above measures have positioned Kerala as a brand on international tourism scene.

(*Source:* Kerala's Approach to Tourism Development: A Case Study, Ministry of Tourism and Culture, Government of India*)*

DISCUSSION QUESTIONS

1. How have various types of certification systems helped Kerala in developing its tourism?
2. Discuss the measures taken by Kerala under the six S framework of six key result areas of *swagat* (hospitality), *soochna* (information), *suvidha* (facilitation), *suraksha* (security/protection), *sahyog* (cooperation) and *sanrachna* (infrastructure development).
3. What has made Kerala emerge as a role model in tourism development?
4. How has marketing of Kerala tourism been integrated with the product development and building of support services?

3. SURAJKUND—CREATING A TOURISM PRODUCT

Surajkund is a place located on Delhi-Agra national highway and is around 8 kms from South Delhi. It has become popular for its annual 15-day craft fair organized every year from 1 Febuary to 15 Febuary. It showcases crafts from all over the country and mixes it with fun, fair, and music.

But a look at its uneven ravine terrain is enough to indicate its uselessness for purposes such as agriculture and inhabitation. The same inhospitable land mass has been used to create tourism attraction. It began in 1987 and since then has grown in stance.

Growth of Surajkund as an Attraction

Year	Theme State	Number of Craftsmen	Number of Visitors (in lakhs)
1989	Rajasthan	204	1.75
1990	West Bengal	171	2.00
1991	Kerala	224	2.00
1992	Madhya Pradesh	231	2.79
1993	Orissa	244	4.66
1994	Karnataka	242	7.10
1995	Punjab	274	8.51
1996	Himachal Pradesh	278	2.33
1997	Gujarat	249	2.96
1998	North-Eastern States	244	3.46
1999	Andhra Pradesh	312	4.51
2000	Jammu and Kashmir	357	5.05
2001	Goa	348	3.93
2002	Sikim	413	4.74
2003	Uttaranchal	378	5.00
2004	Tamil Nadu	317	2.77
2005	Chattisgarh	347	3.56
2006	Maharashtra	269	5.70
2007	Andhra Pradesh	304	6.00
2008	West Bengal	325	7.00
2009	Madhya Pradesh	595	More than 7.5
2010	Rajasthan	563	More than 7.5

(*Source:* www.haryanatourism.gov.in and www.festivalsofindia.in, accessed on 31 July 2010)

Though there have been variations in the number of visitors over different years, still the numbers speak of its popularity. Consistent efforts in infrastructure building, selection of theme and creation of right ambience coupled with promotion have yielded results. A tourism product has been created out of nothing and the closeness to the national capital region has given it a natural access to a big market.

DISCUSSION QUESTIONS

1. What has gone into making of Surajkund a tourism product?
2. What factors have supported its growth?
3. Where do you see competition for Surajkund?
4. Can any inferences be made about its life cycle stage with the help of number of visitors and number of craftsmen?
5. What other value additions do you suggest for further enhancing its appeal?

4. RURAL AND COMMUNITY-BASED TOURISM—SUSTAINABLE APPROACH

The tourism sector can address development issues such as poverty reduction, developing local economy, revival and regeneration of arts and crafts, preservation of culture and most important, gender equity. Tourism also encourages preservation of monuments and heritage properties and helps the survival of art forms. The Indian government is trying to reap these gains through schemes of rural and community based tourism which also help in distributing the gains of tourism to all segments of society.

The government felt the need for involving community in tourism and rural tourism project with UNDP support. It identified 31 villages to be developed as tourist spots. It helps develop necessary infrastructure and UNDP helps in capacity building, involvement of NGOs, local communities and artisans, and so on.

Hill states Uttarakhand and Sikkim have launched community-based tourism in which certain number of villages/clusters are developed for attracting foreign tourists. Development of environment-friendly policies such as cooperative societies of rag pickers to maintain clean environment and self-employment ventures for locals are its important parts. Similarly, to promote tribal life and tribal products, the Tribal Cooperative Marketing Development Federation of India (TRIFED), the national level organization of tribal cooperatives in the country, has identified certain regions for promoting tourism. TRIFED is planning to start tribal shops in all the major international airports so that all the traditional and ethnic tribal products are showcased for foreign tourists.

The inclusion of development with local participation is central to these tourism approaches.

DISCUSSION QUESTIONS

1. What are the benefits of promoting tourism in a larger geographic area through schemes such as rural and tribal tourism?
2. What are the areas in which communities can participate in tourism development?
3. What can be the effects of changing forms of livelihood on local communities through programmes such as rural tourism?

5. UNFAIR FARES

The Indian traveller has seen airfares going up and down so frequently that doubts have cropped up about ethics in airline pricing. The level of prices and the method of quoting the prices raise a few questions.

The air prices started coming down with Deccan Airways offering budgeted fares. Travellers were paying as low as Rs 500 from the no-frills flexi pricing. But soon an upward spiral began and aviation turbine fuel (ATF) cost was cited as the prime reason for enhanced fares.

The ATF cost, passenger traffic, and number of aircrafts in India in 2003 and 2008 are shown below.

Year	Number of Aircraft	Aviation Turbine Fuel Cost (in Rs per km)	Passenger Count (in million)
March 2003	138	22,380	14
March 2008	350	47,048	44

The structure of airlines market has witnessed some very important changes in 2007-08. Air Sahara was acquired by Jet Airways. Kingfisher and Jet Airways entered into an alliance cornering 60 per cent of the total market. Kingfisher acquired Air Deccan in 2007, thus reducing the competition in the market. Though the presence of new players, such as Indigo, was important yet a cartel-like situation was created in the absence of many players. Its impact was clearly seen on prices that turned upwards. Moreover, when the government reduced charges on ATF, these were not passed on to the buyers (ATF prices came down to approximately Rs 32,000 in January 2009).

The buyers felt burdened with the increased fares. The promotion of low airfares that were not really low, added to the woes of buyers and also created doubts about the fairness of pricing. Airfares are advertised as low at Rs 0 (Go Air) or Rs 500. But what the buyer pays is Rs 5,500 for a long distance return fare if the basic fare is 0. The buyer pays many additional charges that are not advertised and are known only at the time of buying the ticket. Charges include fuel surcharge (to compensate for rising fuel prices), congestion charges (to take care of hovering time), and development costs (of airports that are being renovated by private parties or under joint ventures). The quoting of low base price for promotion is cheating of customer.

In the long run, such practices in pricing may deter buyers who might appreciate a more transparent policy.

(Source: Business Today, June 2008 and November 2008)

DISCUSSION QUESTIONS

1. What problems do you see in the pricing of airlines?
2. What is no-frills pricing?
3. What should be done to give more objective price information to buyers?
4. Do the above pricing strategies result from external environmental factors only?

Index